34th EDITION

OXFORD SCHOOL ATLAS

OXFORD

UNIVERSITY PRESS

OXFORD
UNIVERSITY PRESS

Oxford University Press is a department of the University of Oxford.
It furthers the University's objective of excellence in research, scholarship,
and education by publishing worldwide. Oxford is a registered trade mark of
Oxford University Press in the UK and in certain other countries.

Published in India by
Oxford University Press
YMCA Library Building, 1 Jai Singh Road, New Delhi 110001, India

© Oxford University Press 1915, 2014

The moral rights of the author/s have been asserted.

First Edition published in 1915
Thirtieth Edition published in 2000
Thirtieth revised Edition published in 2002
Thirty-first Edition published in 2006
Thirty-second Edition published in 2009
Thirty-third Edition published in 2012
Thirty-fourth Edition published in 2014
Third impression 2014

ISBN-13: 978-0-19-809246-9
ISBN-10: 0-19-809246-6

Printed in India by Multivista Global Ltd., Chennai

Cartographed by Oxford University Press, India

Acknowledgements

The following are applicable to all the maps in this atlas wherever India-
International boundaries and coastlines appear:
* © Government of India, Copyright, 2013
* Based upon Survey of India maps with the permission of the Surveyor General
  of India.
* The responsibility for the correctness of internal details rests with the publisher.
* The territorial waters of India extend into the sea to a distance of twelve nautical
  miles measured from the appropriate base line.
* The administrative headquarters of Chandigarh, Haryana and Punjab are at
  Chandigarh.
* The interstate boundaries amongst Arunachal Pradesh, Assam and Meghalaya
  shown on this map are as interpreted from the "North-Eastern Areas
  (Reorganization) Act' 1971", but has yet to be verified.
* The external boundaries and coastlines of India on the maps agree with the
  Record/Master Copy certified by the Survey of India, Dehra Dun vide their letter
  no. TB-330/62-A-3/29 dated 17.06.2013.
* The state boundaries between Uttarakhand & Uttar Pradesh, Bihar & Jharkhand
  and Chhattisgarh & Madhya Pradesh have not been verified by the Governments
  concerned.
* The spellings of names in this map, have been taken from various sources.

The publisher would also like to thank the following for permission to use
photographs and other copyright material:

Getty Images:

P4: World by Gerardus Mercator: Historic Map Works LLC and Osher Map
Library; World by Claudius Ptolemy: Historic Map Works LLC and Osher
Map Library; Satellite Image: Planet Observer; **P6**: Lunar Surface: NASA/
Science Source; Sun's Corona: Stephen & Donna O'Meara; **P60**: Kumbal-
garh Fort: Richard I'Anson; Manas: Manoj Shah; Sundarbans: Kim Sullivan;
P61: Jewellery making, Nagaland: Danita Delimont; Bamboo & Cane Craft,
Arunachal Pradesh: Annabelle Breakey; Christmas, NE States: AFP/Getty
Images; Dree Festival, Arunachal Pradesh: AFP/Getty Images; Embroidery
and weaving, Rajasthan: UIG via Getty Images; Ganesh Utsav, Maharashtra:
India Today Group/Getty Images; Garba, Gujarat: AFP/Getty Images; Goa
Carnival: UIG via Getty Images; Gudi Parva, Maharashtra: AFP/Getty Images;
Japi, Assam: AFP/Getty Images; Kangra Painting, Himachal Pradesh: UIG via
Getty Images; Kullu Dusshera: UIG via Getty Images; Lohri, Chandigarh:
AFP/Getty Images; Masi Magam, Puducherry: Win Initiative; Nicobari Tribal
Art: SSPL via Getty Images; Onam, Kerala: AFP/Getty Images; Pongal, Tamil
Nadu: Religious Images/UIG; Puri Rath Yatra: AFP/Getty Images; Saga Dawa,
Sikkim: M. Gebicki; Shivratri: Hindustan Times via Getty Images; Chapchar
Kut Festival, Mizoram: Danita Delimont; Tribal Handicraft, Tripura: UIG via
Getty Images; Ugadi, Karnataka: UIG via Getty Images; Yakshagana, Karna-
taka: UIG via Getty Images; **P63**: Asian Elephant: Mint Images - Frans Lant-
ing; Black Necked Crane: Keren Su; Ganga Dolphin: Encyclopaedia Britan-
nica/UIG; Himalayan Musk Deer: Stanley Kaisa Breeden; Indian Desert Cat:
Mike Powles; Indian Python: Ajay Desai; Lion: Robin Smith; Nicobar Pigeon:
Juergen und Christine Sohns; Nilgiri Tahr: Koshy Johnson; Red Panda: Jerry
Redfern/Contributor; Rhinoceros: Nicholas Reuss; Siberian Crane: Christer
Fredriksson; Snow Leopard: Steve Winter: Swamp Deer: Nicholas Reuss;
P74 Oasis: Pankaj & Insy Shah; **P76l** Fjord: Olivier Cirendini

Shutterstock:

P6br: Globe; **P6cl**: Phases of the Moon; **P7bl**: Granite; **P7bm**: Limestone;
P7br: Marble; **P7cr**: Inside the Earth; **P8cr**: Biosphere; **P60**: Agra Fort;
Ajanta Cave; Basilica of Bom Jesus; Bhimbetka; Champaner; Chhatrapati
Shivaji Terminus; Darjeeling Himalayan Railway; Elephanta Cave; Ellora
Cave; Fatehpur Sikri; Hampi; Jantar Mantar, Jaipur; Qutb Minar; Kaziranga;
Keoladeo National Park; Khajuraho; Mahabodhi Temple; Nanda Devi; Nilgiri
Railway; Pattadakal; Red Fort Delhi; Sanchi; Shore Temple; Sun Temple;
Sundarbans; Taj Mahal; Tomb of Humayun; Valley of Flowers; Western
Ghats; **P61**: Bhangra; Bharatnatyam; Bihu; Diwali; Durga Puja; Kartik
Purnima; Kathak; Kathakali; Khajuraho Dance Festival; Kolkali Dance;
Kuchipudi; Kumbh; Madhubani Painting; Manipuri Dance; Monastic Festi-
val, Ladakh; Odissi; Pushkar Fair; Folk Dance, Rajasthan; Surajkund Crafts
Mela; **P63**: Royal Bengal Tiger; **P76r**: Mount Elbrus; **P120t**: Earth from
Moon; **P120cr**: Sahara Desert; **P120cl**: Angel Falls; **P120b**: Mount Everest;
P114-117: Flags of the world

Dinodia Photo LLP:

P4 Babylonian clay tablet: IAM-017795©IMAGE ASSET/AGE/DIN; **P61**:
Dhokra Art, Chhattisgarh: DPA-PKD-68617–P K DE/Dinodia; Dussehra,
Mysore: SSB-1340-193©SuperStock/Dinodia; Handicraft, Mizoram: ESY-
005392496-Debashish Banerjee/Dinodia; Kumbh, Nashik: DPA-NMK-34066–
Nitin Kelvalkar/Dinodia; Andaman Bulbul: BWI-BS236939©K Wothe/AGE/
Dinodia; Bengal Florican: FHR-07047-00002-865©FLPA/Martin Hale/AGE/
Dinodia; Great Indian Bustard: T96-668012©Dhritiman Mukherjee/AGE/Di-
nodia; White Winged Wood Duck: FHR-02073-00004-855©FLPA/Bill Coster/
AGE/Dinodia

Other Images:

P6t Solar System: NASA/JPL-Caltech; **P7t** Earth's Crust: EnchantedLearning.
com, used by permission; **P61** Bastar Triibal Art: HandCraft; **P61** Chhath,
Bihar: Rekha Sinha; **P61** Embroidery, J & K: Crafts and Artisans

CONTENTS

4-5 Maps and Map Making
6 The Universe
7 The Earth
8 Realms of the Earth
9 Contours and Landforms

THE INDIAN SUBCONTINENT—PHYSICAL
10-11 The Indian Subcontinent - Physical
12-13 The Indian Subcontinent - Political
14-15 Northern India and Nepal
16-17 North-Central and Eastern India
18 North-Eastern India, Bhutan and Bangladesh
19 Western India and Pakistan
20-21 Southern India and Sri Lanka

THE INDIAN SUBCONTINENT—POLITICAL
22 Jammu and Kashmir, Himachal Pradesh, Punjab, Haryana, Delhi and Chandigarh
23 Rajasthan, Gujarat, Daman & Diu and Dadra & Nagar Haveli
24 Uttarakhand, Uttar Pradesh, Bihar and Jharkhand
25 Sikkim, West Bengal and the North-Eastern States
26 Madhya Pradesh, Chhattisgarh and Odisha
27 Maharashtra, Andhra Pradesh and Goa
28 Karnataka, Tamil Nadu, Kerala and Puducherry
29 The Islands

INDIA—THEMATIC
30 India – Temperature and Pressure
31 India – Rainfall and Winds
32 India – Relative Humidity, Annual Rainfall & Monsoon and Climatic Regions
33 India – Geology, Geological Formations, Structure and Physiographic Divisions
34 India – Natural Vegetation and Forest Cover
35 India – Biogeographic Zones, Wildlife and Wetlands
36 India – Drainage Basins
37 India – Soil and Land Use
38 India – Irrigation
39 India – Food grain Production, Livestock Population, Milk Production and Fish Production
40-41 India – Food Crops
42-43 India – Cash Crops
44 India – Metallic Minerals
45 India – Non-Metallic Minerals
46 India – Mineral Deposits and Mineral Fuels
47 India – Mining Industry and Levels of Industrial Development
48-49 India – Industries
50 India – Mass Media and Power & Energy
51 India – Roads and Inland Waterways
52 India – Railways
53 India – Air and Sea Routes
54-55 India – Population
56-57 India – Human Development
58 India – Religions and Languages
59 India – Tourism and Foreign Tourist Arrivals
60 India – World Heritage Sites
61 India – Cultural Heritage
62-63 India – Environmental Concerns
64-65 India – Natural Hazards

CONTINENTS AND REGIONS
ASIA
66 Asia – Physical
67 Asia – Political
68 Asia – Climate, Natural Vegetation, Population and Economy
69 SAARC Countries
70 China, Mongolia and Taiwan
71 Japan, North Korea and South Korea
72 South-Eastern Asia
73 Myanmar, Thailand, Laos, Cambodia and Vietnam
74 West Asia
75 Afghanistan and Pakistan

EUROPE
76 Europe – Physical
77 Europe – Political
78 Europe – Climate, Natural Vegetation, Population and Economy
79 United Kingdom
80 France and Central Europe
81 Russia and Neighbouring Countries

AFRICA
82 Africa – Physical
83 Africa – Political
84 Africa – Climate, Natural Vegetation, Population and Economy
85 Southern Africa and Madagascar

NORTH AMERICA
86 North America – Physical
87 North America – Political
88 North America – Climate, Natural Vegetation, Population and Economy
89 United States of America and Alaska

SOUTH AMERICA
90 South America – Physical
91 South America – Political
92 South America – Climate, Natural Vegetation, Population and Economy
93 Brazil

OCEANIA
94 Oceania – Physical
95 Oceania – Political
96 Oceania – Climate, Natural Vegetation, Population and Economy

OCEANS AND ANTARCTICA
97 Pacific Ocean and Central Pacific Islands
98 Indian Ocean and Atlantic Ocean
99 The Arctic Ocean and Antarctica

WORLD
100-101 World – Physical
102-103 World – Political
104 World – Climate
105 World – Climatic Regions and Water Resources
106 World – Soil and Natural Vegetation
107 World – Agriculture and Industrial Regions
108 World – Minerals, Mineral Fuels, Trade and Economic Development
109 World – World – Air Routes and Sea Routes
110 World – Population Density, Urbanization, Religions and Languages
111 World – Human Development
112 World – Environmental Concerns
113 World – Natural Hazards and Biomes at Risk

WORLD – FACTS AND FIGURES
114-117 Countries of the World – Flag, Area, Population, Capital, Language, Currency and GDP
118-119 World Statistics – Human Development and Economy
120-121 World – Geographic Comparisons
122 World – Time Zones

123-132 Index

History of Cartography

The history of cartography is not older than 5,000 years. The earliest maps of which we have knowledge were made by the Babylonians on clay tablets, dating around 2300 BC (Fig.1). Early attempts at maps were severely limited by lack of knowledge of anything other than very local features. Of course what constitutes a map is hard to say, especially when one goes back to the very earliest times. In around 6200 BC in **Catal Hyük** in Anatolia a wall painting was made depicting the positions of the streets and houses of the town together with surrounding features such as the volcano close to the town. Whether it is a map or a stylised painting is a matter of debate. Early world maps also reflect the religious beliefs of the form of the world.

Fig. 1: A clay tablet showing land holdings of Babylon

The earliest ancient Greek who is said to have constructed a map of the world is **Anaximander**, who was born in 610 BC in Miletus (now in Turkey) and died in 546 BC. Sadly, no details of his map have survived. Notable Greek philosophers and mathematicians such as Pythagoras, Aristotle, Eratosthenes and Hipparchus made notable contributions to the study of ancient cartography.

The final ancient Greek contribution to cartography, considered the most important, was written by a noted mathematician. In about AD 140 **Ptolemy** wrote his major work, *Guide to Geography*, in eight books, which attempted to map the known world giving coordinates of the major places in terms of what are essentially latitude and longitude (Fig. 2). Given the way that he gathered the data it is not surprising that the maps were inaccurate but they did represent a considerable advance on all previous maps and it would be many centuries before more accurate world maps would be drawn.

Fig. 2: Compilation of a world map by Claudius Ptolemy

In 1569, **Gerardus Mercator** of Flanders, Belgium, the leading cartographer of the 16th century developed a map projection and drew a world map (Fig.3). Mercator made many new maps and globes, but his greatest contribution to cartography was what is now known as the Mercator projection.

Since then, several leading cartographers from Europe and Asia developed cartographic techniques, giving a boost to map production and the invention of different scientific surveying techniques, instruments and projections. In addition to these developments, the

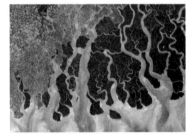

Fig. 3: The first map of the entire world by Gerardus Mercator

broadening of knowledge with the introduction of new fields of studies such as astronomy, geology, meteorology, biology, and the social sciences gave rise to thematic cartography.

As the world advances, as the unknown is revealed and surveyed, as humans alter the face of the earth with their new settlements, new states, railways, canals, land reclamation and cultivation, these changes are reflected in the maps of the times.

The Age of Modern Cartography: Remote Sensing and GIS

In the 20th century, the invention of the airplane followed by satellite remote sensing technology added a new dimension to mapping and widened its scope through the method of remote sensing. This provided a bird's-eye view of the earth and saved time and money required for conventional surveying of ground realities.

In the broadest sense, remote sensing is the measurement or acquisition of information of an object or phenomenon, by a recording device that is not in physical or intimate contact with the object. It is the utilization at a distance (as from aircraft, spacecraft, satellite, or ship) of any device for gathering information about the environment. The technique can make use of devices such as a camera, laser, radar, sonar, seismograph or a gravimeter. Modern remote sensing normally includes digital processes but can be done as well with non-digital methods.

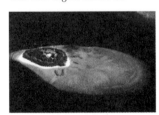

Fig. 4: An aerial photograph of islands and Atolls of Maldives

Aerial photography is the original form of remote sensing. An aerial photograph can be defined as a photograph taken from an aircraft with a camera specially designed for aircraft use (Fig.4). The occurrence of the two world wars led to a demand for aerial photography for military purposes. In India, aerial photographs have been in use since 1920 for aerial surveys and for interpretation of specific fields such as topographical mapping, geology, engineering, environmental studies, and exploration of oil and minerals.

With the development of satellite technology between 1970 and 1980, remote sensing through satellites received more attention from researchers, cartographers and general users. An image taken from space using a spacecraft as the platform and scanners or specially designed cameras as sensors to detect the given area of the earth's surface is termed **satellite imagery** (Fig. 5).

Fig. 5: A satellite image showing Ganges delta, India and Bangladesh

The remote sensor system makes use of the emitted or reflected electromagnetic radiation of the examined object and measures a larger area of the earth. Satellite imagery can be widely applied and is extensively used by scientists, researchers, and planners in map-making, urban and regional planning, agriculture, forestry, ecology and environment, soil survey, natural resource mapping, oil and mineral exploration, and so on.

In traditional cartography, the map represented both the database and the display of geographic information whereas in **GIS** (Geographical Information Systems), the database, analysis, and display are physically and conceptually separate aspects. Geographic information systems include several elements such as computer hardware, software, digital data, people, and institutions for collecting, storing, retrieving, analysing, and displaying georeferenced data or information about the Earth. Modern map-making relies much more on GIS, which provides flexible computer-aided database and maps.

Scale

A scale is essential for reading a map accurately. It is defined as the ratio between two points on the ground and their corresponding distance on a piece of paper (the map). A scale can be expressed as:

1. Representative Fraction (R.F.)

The units of measurement of distances are the same both on the ground and on paper. It is always expressed as a ratio, e.g. 1:100,000, where 1 cm on the map represents 100,000 cm or 1 inch =100,000 inches.

2. Written statement

The system of measurement is clearly stated, e.g.
1 cm = 1 km
or 1 inch = 1 mile.

3. Graphical method

A diagram of a ruler is drawn to show the given scale, e.g. 1 cm = 1 km or 1:100,000. A segment of a ruler measuring 15 cm will represent 15 km.

km 1   0   1   2 km

Maps and Globes

A map is a graphic representation of the round earth or the real world on a flat piece of paper. Maps show us what the earth would look like if we could see it from above. The main purpose of preparing a map is to show the things as they appear in their true location, in terms of latitudes and longitudes, either in isolation or in relation to some other feature. On the other hand, a globe represents the whole surface in the form of a sphere on which all its continents and features are shown at the same scale and with their correct shapes and areas.

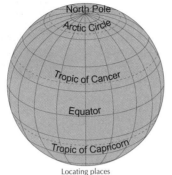

Locating places

Map Projections

A map projection is a systematic and orderly drawing of a grid of parallels of latitude and meridians of longitude used to represent the spherical surface of the earth, or a part of it, on a reduced scale on a flat piece of paper. It is not possible to make a map (of the world or of any part of it) that is accurate in area, shape, distance and direction. Every map is distorted in at least one of these aspects.

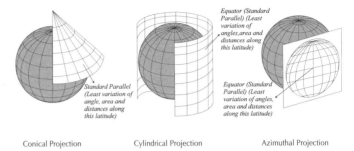

Conical Projection   Cylindrical Projection   Azimuthal Projection

---

Types of Maps

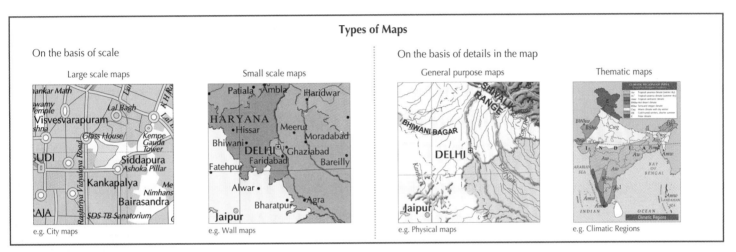

On the basis of scale

Large scale maps — e.g. City maps

Small scale maps — e.g. Wall maps

On the basis of details in the map

General purpose maps — e.g. Physical maps

Thematic maps — e.g. Climatic Regions

Physical Relief: Representation of the Earth's Surface

One of the challenges of map-making is to adequately represent the physical relief of any region i.e., the delineation of hills and plains, the distinguishing of high ground and low ground. The two methods generally used to represent physical relief are *hill-shading and contour lines*, each of which may be treated in a variety of ways and are sometimes combined.

Figure A shows a mountainous island with the hill slopes indicated by a method of hill–shading called `hachures' (lines indicating the direction of the slope). Figure B shows the same island with the hills indicated by contour lines. The principle of showing elevation by contour lines can be seen by comparing Figure C with the profile section in Figure B.

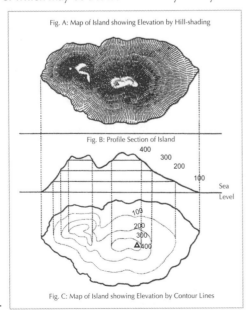

Fig. A: Map of Island showing Elevation by Hill-shading

Fig. B: Profile Section of Island

Fig. C: Map of Island showing Elevation by Contour Lines

Symbols and Shades

Maps cannot show everything nor can the features of the landscape be contained in a limited area. Therefore, symbols, often termed as conventional symbols, have been developed to represent the features on a map. Some symbols are like pictures while others are initial letters such as `PO´ for post office. Colours are also used as symbols such as green for forests or woodlands and blue for water. Shades ranging from deepest to lightest can represent the range of occurrences of any phenomenon, such as altitude.

Conventional symbols can be found on a topographical sheet, a weather chart, or on physical or thematic maps. It is always important to refer to the key or legend of a map to find out what the symbols mean. Symbols are designed to be easy to remember.

The Solar System

The Solar System

The solar system was formed about 4,600 million years ago. It is located in the Orion arm of the Milky Way galaxy, around two-thirds away from the central bulge, about 27,000 light-years from the centre of the galaxy. It takes the solar system about 220 million years to orbit the galaxy once.

The solar planets can be divided into an inner system of four small, solid planets made up of materials similar to that of the Earth. The outer system of four larger planets, known as the `gas giants´, has rings and lots of moons. The gas giants are made up mostly of hydrogen, helium, frozen water, ammonia, methane, and carbon monoxide. Pluto does not belong to any group but is a tiny rocky body at the edge of the solar system. Some people think it is a giant comet rather than a planet. Its composition is similar to a comet (ice and rock) but its orbit is different from the other comets and planets. Between these two planetary systems is a belt of asteroids containing pieces of rock of varying size.

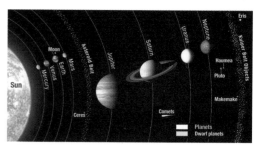

Planet Profile

Planet	Mean distance from Sun (million km)	Orbital period	Diameter (km)	No. of known satellites
Mercury	57.9	88.0 days	4,879	0
Venus	108.2	224.7 days	12,104	0
Earth	149.6	365.3 days	12,756	1
Mars	227.9	687.0 days	6,787	2
Jupiter	778.4	11.86 years	142,800	67
Saturn	1426.7	29.46 years	120,660	62
Uranus	2871.0	84.01 years	51,118	27
Neptune	4498.73	164.8 years	49,528	14

Dwarf Planets and Plutoids

Pluto, which was considered to be a planet since its discovery in 1930, was reclassified as a `dwarf planet´ on 24 August 2006 by the International Astronomical Union.

According to the IAU, a dwarf planet fulfils the following criteria:
• It is in orbit around the Sun.
• It has sufficient mass for its self-gravity to overcome rigid body forces so that it assumes a hydrostatic equilibrium (nearly round) shape.
• It has not `cleared the neighbourhood´ around its orbit.
• It is not a satellite of a planet, or other non-stellar body.

Two years after coining the term `dwarf planets´, the IAU has decided to call trans-neptunian dwarf planets similar to Pluto, `plutoids´. While all plutoids are dwarf planets, all dwarf planets are not plutoids. Currently, there are five celestial bodies that have been redefined by the IAU as dwarf planets, of which four belong to the subset plutoids. Eris, Pluto, and most recently, MakeMake and Haumea have been classified as plutoids and dwarf planets, while Ceres remains in the category dwarf planet.

Sun

The Sun is a giant ball of hot gas, 150 million kilometers from the Earth. The surface of this burning ball of gas is 5500°C, with the core reaching an unimaginable 15.6 million°C. The Sun is so large that you could fit over one million Earths inside it. The Sun's internal structure includes the core, radiation zone, convection zone, and photosphere.

The turbulence in the photosphere is visible from the earth in the form of sunspots, solar flares, prominences and small patches of gas called granules. The Sun consumes four million tonnes of hydrogen every second. Even so, it is so vast that our star has enough fuel to keep it shining for another five billion years.

The corona is the outermost part of the Sun's atmosphere, visible during a solar eclipse only.

Phases of the Moon

The moon seems to have different shapes at different times of the month because of its changing position in relation to the Earth. These different shapes are known as the phases of the Moon. The interval between one full Moon and the next is 29.5 days.

NEW MOON   FIRST QUARTER   FULL MOON   THIRD QUARTER

WAXING CRESCENT   WAXING GIBBOUS   WANING GIBBOUS   WANING CRESCENT

Facts about the Moon

The lunar surface

• The only natural satellite of the planet Earth
• Distance from Earth– 384,400 km
• Diameter– 3,476 km
• Mass– 0.0123 of the Earth's
• Surface gravity– 0.165 of the Earth's
• Time taken to orbit Earth (interval between one full moon and the next) – 29.53 days or 709 hours
• Surface temperature– 120 °C maximum to –163 °C at night

Tides

At new Moon and full Moon, when the Moon and the Sun are in line with the Earth, tides are at their highest and are called **spring tides.**

At quarter and three-quarter Moon, the Sun and Moon are at right angles, so that the gravitational pull of the Moon is partly cancelled out by the gravitational pull of the Sun, the tides are at their lowest and are called **neap tides**.

Sun

New Moon

Full Moon

Fig. 2: Spring tides

Sun

First Quarter

Last Quarter

Fig. 1: Neap tides

The Seasons, Equinoxes and Solstices (in the Northern Hemisphere)

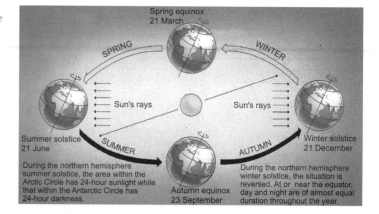

Spring equinox 21 March

SPRING   WINTER

Sun's rays   Sun's rays

Summer solstice 21 June

SUMMER   AUTUMN

Winter solstice 21 December

Autumn equinox 23 September

During the northern hemisphere summer solstice, the area within the Arctic Circle has 24-hour sunlight while that within the Antarctic Circle has 24-hour darkness.

During the northern hemisphere winter solstice, the situation is reversed. At or near the equator, day and night are of almost equal duration throughout the year.

Continental Drift

The Earth's crust is not a single continuous layer. It is made up of a number of gigantic pieces like a huge jigsaw puzzle. Each piece is called a crustal plate. Currents of molten rock rise up through the mantle like boiling water in a saucepan. These form convection cells that drive the movement of the plates so that they are continuously moving away or towards each other. Geologically, the most important things happen at the plate boundaries, including most of the earthquakes, volcanoes, igneous rocks, major metamorphism, and mountain building processes. There are 10 crustal plates:

250 million years ago

175 million years ago

Present day

1. Pacific
2. Antarctic
3. Indian
4. African
5. South American
6. Nazca
7. North American
8. Eurasian
9. Cocos
10. Australian

The Giant Jigsaw Puzzle

Alfred Wegener (1880-1930), a German meteorologist and geologist, was the first person to propose the theory of continental drift. In his book, **Origin of Continents and Oceans**, he calculated that 200 million years ago the continents were originally joined together, forming a large supercontinent. He named this supercontinent Pangaea, meaning `All-earth´. Pangaea split into plates to form Eurasia in the north and Gondwanaland in the south. Further splitting over millions of years formed the continents as we know them today. Wegener's concept was originally based on the apparent `jigsaw´ fit. The continents look as if they were pieces of a giant jigsaw puzzle that could fit together to make one giant super-continent. The bulge of Africa fits the shape of the coast of North America while Brazil fits along the coast of Africa beneath the bulge. There are three kinds of plate boundaries:

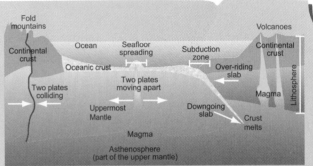

Movement in the Earth's crust

Divergent boundaries are where plates separate from each other, and magma oozes up from the mantle into the crack (a fissure volcano) making the ocean basin wider. This is known as sea floor spreading.

Convergent boundaries are where plates come together, but to do so one of the plates must dive below the surface into the mantle along a subduction zone. These often result in deep-sea trenches. Convergent boundaries also produce mountain chains and very large, explosive volcanoes.

Plates slide past each other where transform boundaries occur, ideally with little or no vertical movement. Most transform boundaries are below sea level and therefore not easy to see. The San Andreas fault in California is a transform boundary. It has been estimated that these plates are moving at a speed of 1 to 10 cm per year.

Inside the Earth

The Earth is made up of four main layers—the **inner core**, **outer core**, the **mantle**, and the **crust** (Fig.23). We live on the outer part of the Earth, which is called the crust. This layer consists of the upper 30-100 km. The crust mostly consists of igneous rocks; the rest consists of sedimentary and metamorphic rocks. The layer from 0-20 km is called the **sial** as the two main constituents are **silicon** and **aluminium**. It is 2.7 times denser than water. The next layer is known as **sima** as a large quantity of **silicon** and **magnesium** is found in this layer. The average density of this layer is 3.4 times that of water.

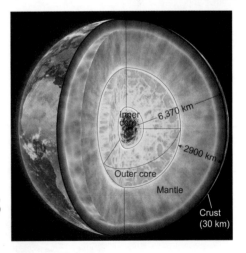

The next layer called the **mantle** is 100-2,900 km thick. The upper part of the mantle is a plastic layer over which the crust floats. The mantle is composed of silicate material, but it is chemically distinct from the crust.

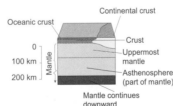

The Earth's **outer core** (2,900-5,100 km) is composed of liquid metallic material (primarily iron and nickel). The solid **inner core** (5,100-6,370 km) of the Earth is made up of iron. It has been discovered that the inner core is rotating and is the cause of Earth's magnetic field.

Rocks and Minerals

Rocks are the substances that make up the Earth. They include loose and unconsolidated deposits, as well as the hard, solid parts that make up the Earth's lithosphere. Rocks can be classified into three main groups on the basis of their origin—igneous, sedimentary and metamorphic. Minerals are the building materials of rocks. Rocks may be composed of only one mineral, while others contain many of them.

Granite

Igneous (or primary) rocks are the first rocks to be formed from magma or molten rock beneath the earth's crust, e.g. granite and basalt.

Limestone

Sedimentary (stratified or layered) rocks are formed by the collection of sediments over a long span of time, e.g. sandstone and shale.

Marble

Metamorphic rocks are formed when the nature of any rock is altered by subjecting it to intense heat and/or pressure, e.g. graphite (from coal) and quartzite (from sandstone).

The lithosphere (geosphere), atmosphere and hydrosphere comprise the three realms of the Earth. We can define the biosphere (the fourth realm of the Earth) as the parts of the Earth's lithosphere (land), hydrosphere (water) and atmosphere (air) occupied by living organisms.

Lithosphere or Geosphere

The lithosphere or geosphere is the solid, rocky crust covering the entire planet. This crust is inorganic and is composed of rocks, minerals and elements. It covers the entire surface of the Earth from the top of Mount Everest to the bottom of the Mariana Trench. On the surface of the Earth, the lithosphere is composed of three main types of rocks—igneous, sedimentary and metamorphic. The land area constitutes about 29 per cent of the total surface area of the Earth.

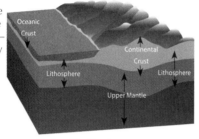

Structure of the lithosphere

Hydrosphere

The hydrosphere is the combined mass of water found on, under and over the surface of the Earth. About 71 per cent of the Earth's surface is covered by water in the form of oceans, seas, bays, gulfs, lakes, rivers, etc. The oceans contain most of the Earth's surface water. Most fresh water is frozen into glaciers. Most available fresh water is stored underground as groundwater.

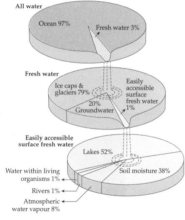

Atmosphere

The atmosphere is made up of gases such as nitrogen (78 per cent), oxygen (21 per cent) and small amounts of carbon dioxide, argon, ammonia and a few others. Water vapour (1 per cent approximately) is also present in the atmosphere. The atmosphere has several different layers. Higher up, the air gets thinner and colder, and there is less oxygen to breathe. In the very highest layers there is hardly any air at all.

Structure of the Atmosphere

The layers of the atmosphere are not of uniform thickness or density. They also vary in other aspects.

Troposphere

It is the lowest layer of the atmosphere. It contains 75 per cent of the gases in the atmosphere. All weather phenomena that we experience on the Earth occur in this sphere.

Stratosphere

The stratosphere has a layer of ozone which protects life on Earth from the harmful ultraviolet light of the Sun.

Mesosphere

The temperature in the mesosphere decreases with height, reaching about –100°C in the upper mesosphere. This is the coldest region of the atmosphere.

Thermosphere

The temperature in the thermosphere increases with height. The thermosphere is also known as the heat sphere of the atmosphere.

Exosphere

It is the outermost layer of the atmosphere. This layer has the lightest gases like hydrogen and helium in extremely low densities. Most of the Earth's satellites orbit here.

Biosphere

The biosphere is made up of all living organisms of the Earth, as well as the physical environment in which they live and with which they interact. Most living organisms actually live within a small area in the biosphere, from about 500 m below the ocean's surface to about 6 km above sea level.

Structure of the atmosphere

Atmospheric Clouds

High-level clouds such as cirrus, cirrostratus and cirrocumulus are usually thin and white in appearance.

Mid-level clouds are the altocumulus and altostratus clouds.

While altocumulus may appear as parallel bands or rounded masses of clouds, altostratus clouds are generally uniform grey sheet or layered clouds.

Low clouds are the cumulus, stratus, nimbostratus and stratocumulus clouds. Cumulus clouds are 'puffy' clouds; stratus clouds are flat, featureless clouds; and nimbostratus and stratocumulus clouds are large, dark clouds.

Types of cloud

Heat Budget of the Earth

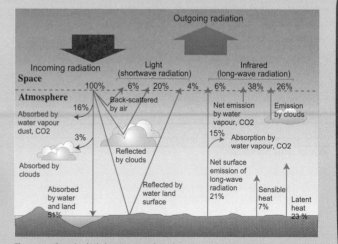

The process through which the incoming solar radiation on Earth is balanced by its outgoing terrestrial radiation is called heat balance. It is essential for the maintenance of the correct temperature of the planet to prevent it from getting hotter or cooler.

Contours and Landforms—One of the challenges of map-making is to adequately represent the physical relief of any region, i.e., the delineation of high ground and low ground. The main method of showing relief features on a flat sheet of paper is by using contours. A contour is a line on a map joining all points which are of the same height above sea level. Contour lines are used to show the height and shapes of landforms in lowland and highland areas. Some of the relief features or landforms are shown below using certain contour patterns.

CONICAL HILL

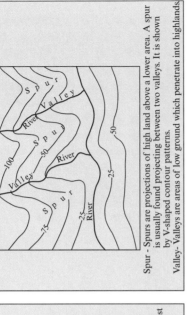

A hill has fairly regular slopes like a cone. It is shown by closed contours almost circular in shape.

PLATEAU

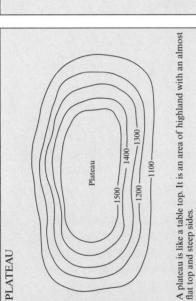

A plateau is like a table top. It is an area of highland with an almost flat top and steep sides.

SPUR AND VALLEY

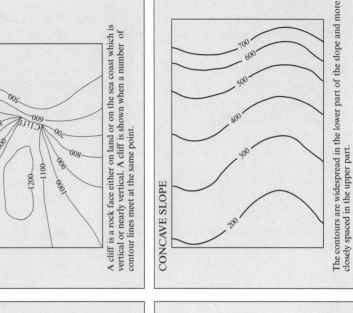

Spur - Spurs are projections of high land above a lower area. A spur is usually found projecting between two valleys. A spur is shown by V-shaped contour patterns.
Valley - Valleys are areas of low ground which penetrate into highlands.

COL AND PASS

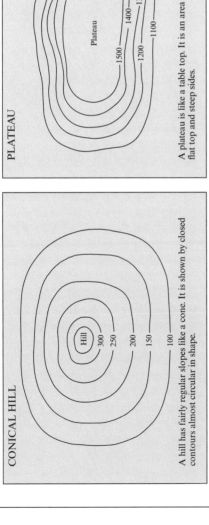

Col or Saddle - A col or saddle is a shallow depression between two hills or peaks.
Pass or Gap - A pass or gap is a deep depression in a mountain range. It is generally used as a route for roads and railways.

GORGE

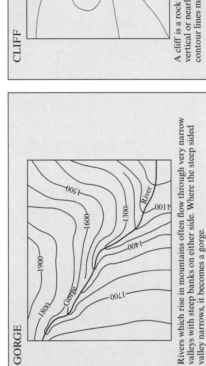

Rivers which rise in mountains often flow through very narrow valleys with steep banks on either side. Where the steep sided valley narrows, it becomes a gorge.

CLIFF

A cliff is a rock face either on land or on the sea coast which is vertical or nearly vertical. A cliff is shown when a number of contour lines meet at the same point.

KNOLL

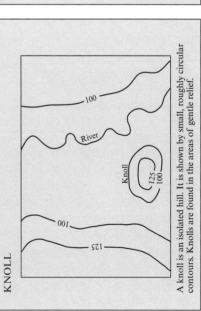

A knoll is an isolated hill. It is shown by small, roughly circular contours. Knolls are found in the areas of gentle relief.

CONVEX SLOPE

The contours are closely spaced in the lower part of the slope and more widely spaced in the upper part.

CONCAVE SLOPE

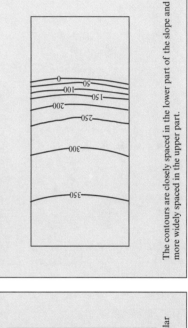

The contours are widespread in the lower part of the slope and more closely spaced in the upper part.

Heights given are in metres

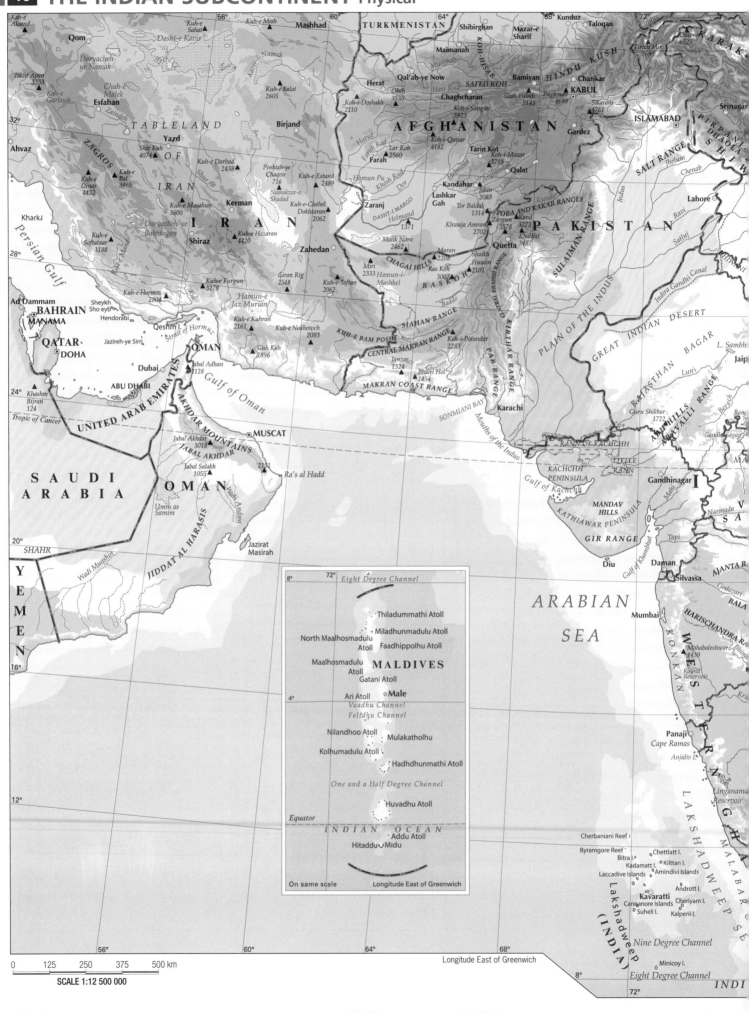

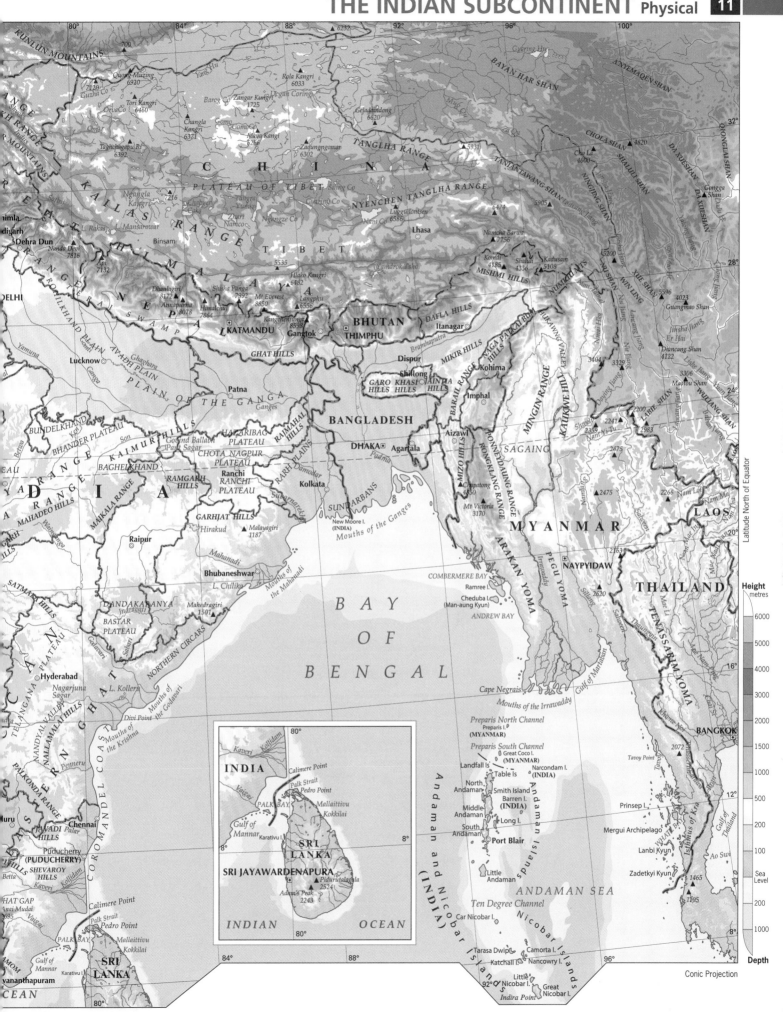

KUNLUN MOUNTAINS
7120 Guzha Co
Tori Kangri 6920
OrbaCo 6460
Quong Muzing 6920
Yang Hu
6232
Rola Kangri 6033
Zingar Kangri 1725
Pogan Coring

Changla Kangri 6321
Gomo Gomba
Nluva Kangri 6266
Zaqungngomar 6302
Geladandong 6620

BAYAN HAR SHAN

CHINA

Taghchagpu Ri 6392

PLATEAU OF TIBET
Biling Co
NYENCHEN TANGLHA RANGE

TANGLHA RANGE
5931

A·NYEMAQEN SHAN
CHOLA SHAN 4820
Chu La 4600
DA XUE SHAN
Gongga Shan

KAILAS RANGE
Ngangla Ringco
Chutygin
Yangtri Yumco
Ngangze Co
Gyaring Co
Nam Co
Luggudontsen 6586
6474
6905
XUE SHAN
WIN LING
5200
5596 4023
Guangmao Shan

Binsam
L. Rakas
L. Mansarowar
TIBET
Lhasa

Dehra Dun
Nanda Devi 7816
Apî 7132

Jinsha Jiang
Diancang Shan 4122
3306
Maofou Shan

HIMALAYA
NEPAL
SWAMP
5535
Hlako Kangri 6482
MISHMI HILLS
Komdi 4385
Shahli 4336
Kadusam 5108
Namcha Barwa 7756

DELHI
Dhaulagiri 8172
Annapurna 8078
Himalchuli 7864
Shisha Panga 7992
Mt Everest 8850
Langtha 6556
Langphu
Kangchenjunga 8598
KATMANDU
Gangtok
BHUTAN
THIMPHU
DAFLA HILLS
Itanagar
NUMTI HILLS
NAGA PAKAI BUM
LUKAWNG VALLEY
3404
3329
LABIE SHAN
2200
2983
WULIANG SHAN

GHAT HILLS
Dispur
Brahmaputra
MIKIR HILLS
Kohima
2359 2241
2875

Lucknow
Yamuna
ROHILKHAND PLAIN
AVADH PLAIN
Ghaghara
PLAIN OF THE GANGA
Ganges
Patna
Shillong
GARO KHASI AINTIA HILLS HILLS HILLS
BARAIL RANGE
Imphal
MINGIN RANGE
PONNEYDAUNG RANGE
KATUKWE HILL
2475
2266 Nam Lot

BUNDELKHAND
Ken
BHANDER PLATEAU
Betwa
Son
KAIMUR HILLS
Govind Ballabh Pant Sagar
HAZARIBAG PLATEAU
RAIMAHAL HILLS
BANGLADESH
DHAKA Agartala
MIZO HILLS
Aizawl
SAGAING
LAOS

INDIA RANGE
BAGHELKHAND
CHOTA NAGPUR PLATEAU
RAMGARH HILLS
RANCHI PLATEAU
Ranchi
RARH PLAINS
Damodar
Padma
Chapatong 4850
RONGKLANG RANGE

MAHADEO HILLS
MAIKALA RANGE
Kolkata
Subarnarekha
Mt Victoria 3170

Raipur
Hirakud
GARHJAT HILLS
Malayagiri 1187
SUNDARBANS
New Moore I. (INDIA)
Mouths of the Ganges
MYANMAR

Mahanadi
Mouths of the Mahanadi
2163
NAYPYIDAW
THAILAND

SATMAI HILLS
DANDAKARANYA
Indravati
BASTAR PLATEAU
Mahedragiri 1501
NORTHERN CIRCARS
COMBERMERE BAY
Ramree I.
ARAKAN YOMA
PEGU YOMA
2620
Height
metres

Godavari
Sabari
L. Chilika
Bhubaneshwar
Cheduba I. (Man-aung Kyun)
ANDREW BAY
Irrawaddy
6000

DECCAN PLATEAU
Hyderabad
Nagarjuna Sagar
EASTERN GHAT
L. Kolleru
BAY
OF
BENGAL
Cape Negrais
Mouths of the Irrawaddy
Gulf of Martaban
5000
4000

TELANGANA
NANDYAL VALLEY
NALLAMALAI HILLS
Pennaru
Divi Point
Mouths of the Krishna
Mouths of the Godavari
Preparis North Channel
Preparis I. (MYANMAR)
BANGKOK
3000
2000

PALKONDA RANGE
COROMANDEL COAST
Preparis South Channel
Great Coco I. (MYANMAR)
2072
Tavoy Point
1500
1000

Chennai
Tavadi Palar
SHEVAROY HILLS
Betta
Kaveri
INDIA
80°
Kaveri Kollidam
Calimere Point
Palk Strait
Pedro Point
PALK BAY
Mallaittivu
Kokkilai
Landfall Is.
Table Is.
North Andaman
Narcondam I. (INDIA)
Smith Island
Barren I. (INDIA)
Andaman Islands
Prinsep I.
Mergui Archipelago
Lanbi Kyun
Isthmus of Kra
Gulf of Thailand
Ao Swi
500
200
100

Puducherry (PUDUCHERRY)
GHAT GAP
Anai Mudai 695
Calimere Point
Vaigai
Gulf of Mannar
Karativu I.
SRI LANKA
SRI JAYAWARDENAPURA
Pidurutalagala 2524
Adam's Peak 2243
INDIAN OCEAN
80°
Middle Andaman
South Andaman
Long I.
Port Blair
Little Andaman
Andaman and Nicobar Islands (INDIA)
Zadetkyi Kyun
1465
1195
ANDAMAN SEA
Ten Degree Channel
Car Nicobar I.
Nicobar Islands
Sea Level
200
1000

PALK BAY
Palk Strait
Pedro Point
Mallaittivu
Kokkilai
SRI LANKA
vananthapuram
Karativu I.
Gulf of Mannar
OCEAN
80°
84°
88°
92°
96°
Tarasa Dwip
Katchall I.
Camorta I.
Nancowry I.
Little Nicobar I.
Great Nicobar I.
Indira Point
Depth

Conic Projection

Latitude North of Equator
32°
28°
24°
20°
16°
12°
8°

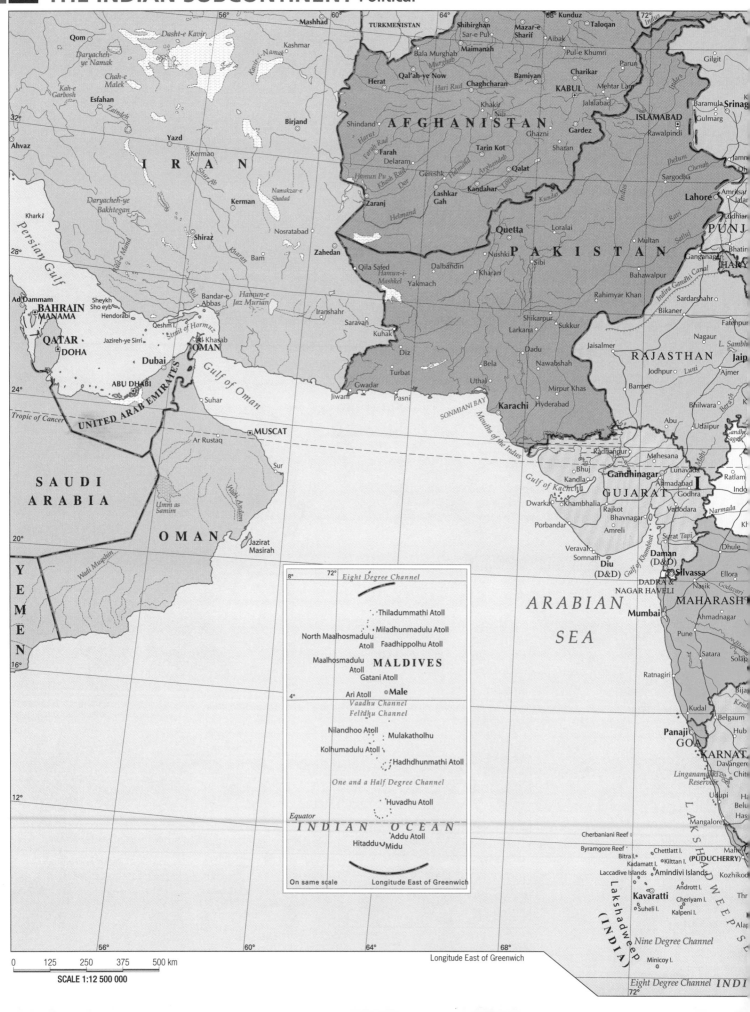

Qom
Dasht-e Kavir
Kashmar
Mashhad
TURKMENISTAN
Shibirghan
Sar-e Pul
Mazar-e Sharif
Aibak
Kunduz
Taloqan
Pul-e Khumri
Gilgit

Daryacheh-ye Namak
Chah-e Malek
Kah-e Garbosh
Esfahan
Zaindeh

Birjand
Herat
Qal'ah-ye Now
Bala Murghab
Maimanah
Murghab
Chaghcharan
Bamiyan
Charikar
Mehtar Lam
Parun
Baramula Srinagar
Gulmarg

I R A N

Yazd
Kerman

Shindand
Hari Rud
Farah Rud
AFGHANISTAN
Khakir
Nili
KABUL
Jalalabad
ISLAMABAD
Rawalpindi
Amritsar
Jalan

Ahvaz
Shur Ab
Namakzar-e Shadad
Farah
Delaram
Gereshk
Arghandab
Ghazni
Gardez
Sharan
PUNJ

Khark
Kharan
Bam
Nosratabad
Zaranj
Lashkar Gah
Kandahar
Qalat
Lahore
Ludhiar

Shiraz
Zahedan
Qila Safed
Hamun-i-Mashkel
Dalbandin
Nushki
Quetta
Loralai
Sibi
Multan
Sargodha
Bhatin
Ganganagar
HARY

Persian Gulf
Ad Dammam
BAHRAIN
MANAMA
Sheykh Sho'eyb
Hendorabi
Bandar-e Abbas
Qeshm I.
Hamun-e Jaz Murian
Iranshahr
Saravan
Kuhak
Yakmach
Kharan
Bahawalpur
Rahimyar Khan
Bikaner
Nagaur
L. Sambh

QATAR
DOHA
Jazireh-ye Sirri
Al Khasab
Strait of Hormuz
OMAN
Diz
Bela
Larkana
Shikarpur
Sukkur
Jaisalmer
Jodhpur
Luni
Sardarshahr
Fatehpur
Ajmer
RAJASTHAN
Jaip

Dubai
ABU DHABI
Suhar
Gulf of Oman
Kuhak
Turbat
Gwadar
Jiwani
Pasni
Uthal
Dadu
Nawabshah
Mirpur Khas
Barmer
Abu
Bhilwara
Udaipur

UNITED ARAB EMIRATES
Tropic of Cancer
Ar Rustaq
MUSCAT
Karachi
Hyderabad
SONMIANI BAY
Mouths of the Indus
Radhanpur
Mahesana

SAUDI ARABIA
Sur
Umm as Samin
Wadi Andam
Bhuj
Kandla
Gandhinagar
Lunavada
Ratlam
Indo

OMAN
Jazirat Masirah
Wadi Muqshin
Gulf of Kachchh
GUJARAT
Ahmadabad
Godhra
Dwarka
Khambhalia
Rajkot
Vadodara
Narmada
Bhavnagar
Amreli
Surat
Tapi
Dhule
Kh

Y E M E N
Porbandar
Veraval
Somnath
Diu (D&D)
Daman (D&D)
Silvassa
Ellora
DADRA & NAGAR HAVELI
Nasik
Godavari
MAHARASH
Gulf of Khambhat

ARABIAN SEA
Mumbai
Ahmadnagar
Pune
Satara
Solap

Ratnagiri

Kudal
Bijar
Krish

Panaji
GOA
KARNAT
Belgaum
Hub
Davangere
Chit

Linganamakki Reservoir

Ula pi
Ha
Belu
Has
Mangalore

Cherbaniani Reef
Byramgore Reef
Bitra I.
Chettlatt I.
Kadamatt I.
Kilttan I.
Mahe
(PUDUCHERRY)
LAKSHADWEEP
Laccadive Islands
Amindivi Islands
Kozhikod

Andrott I.
Kavaratti
Cheriyam I.
Thr
Suheli I.
Kalpeni I.

Lakshadweep (INDIA)
Nine Degree Channel
Minicoy I.
Alap

Maldives inset

8° 72° Eight Degree Channel

Thiladummathi Atoll
Miladhunmadulu Atoll
North Maalhosmadulu Atoll
Faadhippolhu Atoll

Maalhosmadulu Atoll
MALDIVES
Gatani Atoll

4° Ari Atoll Male
Vaadhu Channel
Felidhu Channel

Nilandhoo Atoll
Mulakatholhu
Kolhumadulu Atoll
Hadhdhunmathi Atoll

One and a Half Degree Channel

Huvadhu Atoll

Equator
INDIAN OCEAN
Addu Atoll
Hitaddu Midu

On same scale   Longitude East of Greenwich

12°

ARABIAN SEA

Conic Projection

Latitude North of Equator

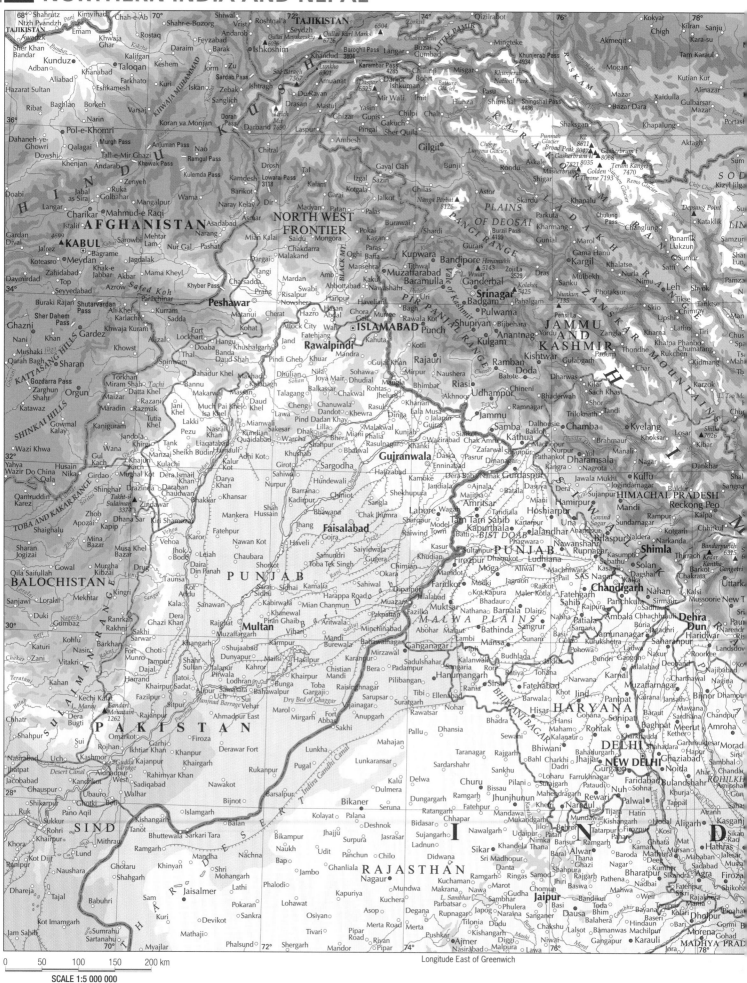

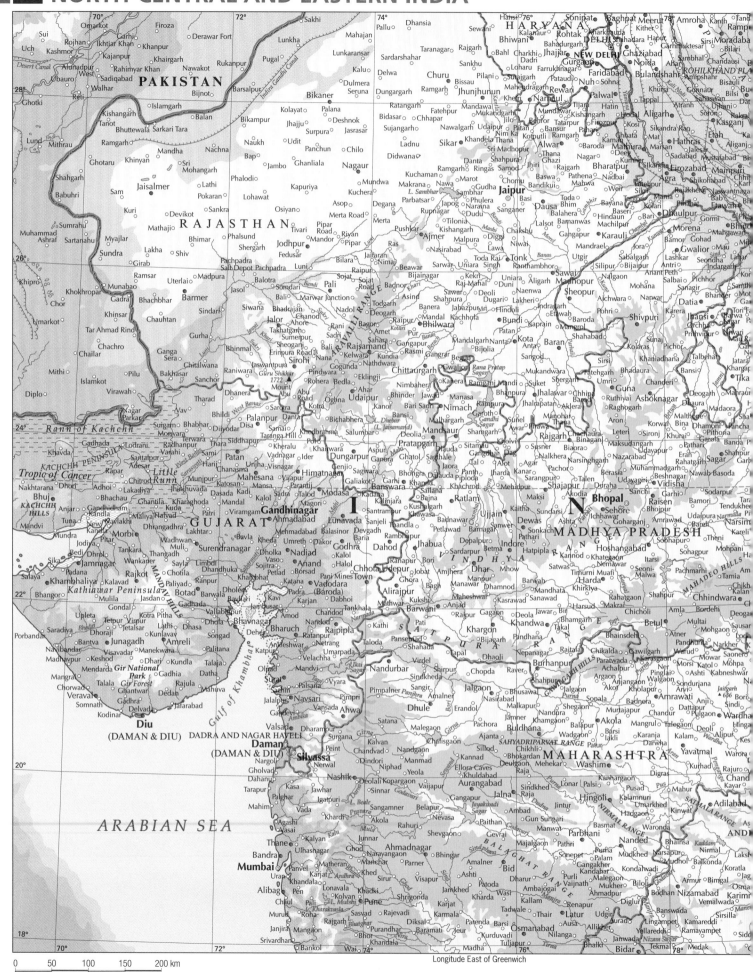

0   50   100   150   200 km

SCALE 1:5 000 000

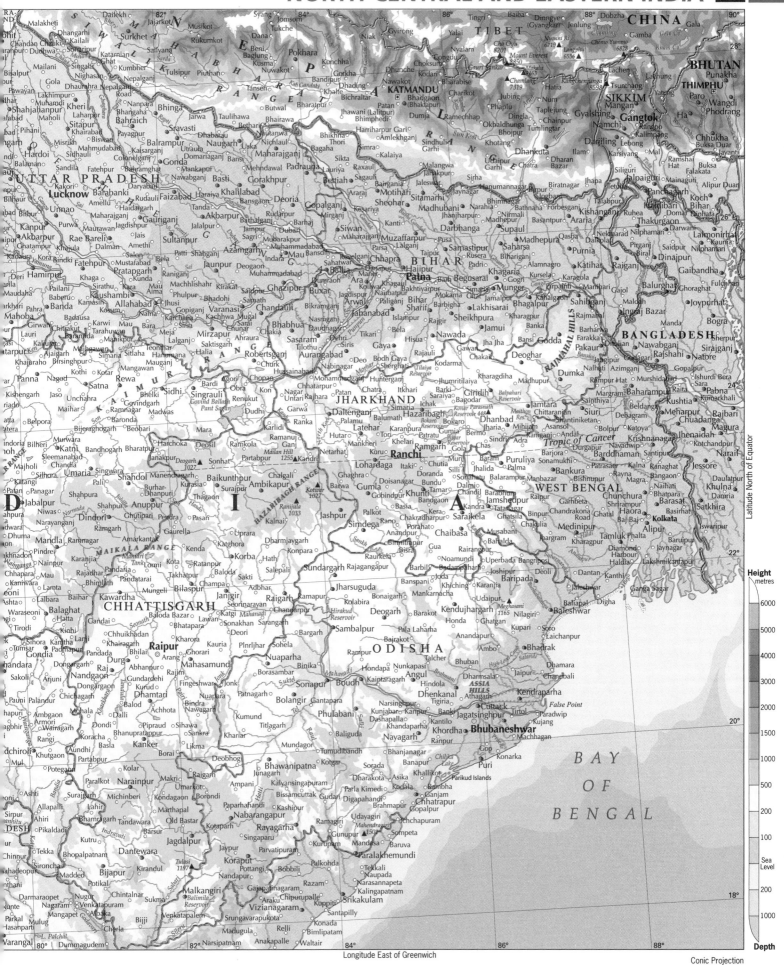

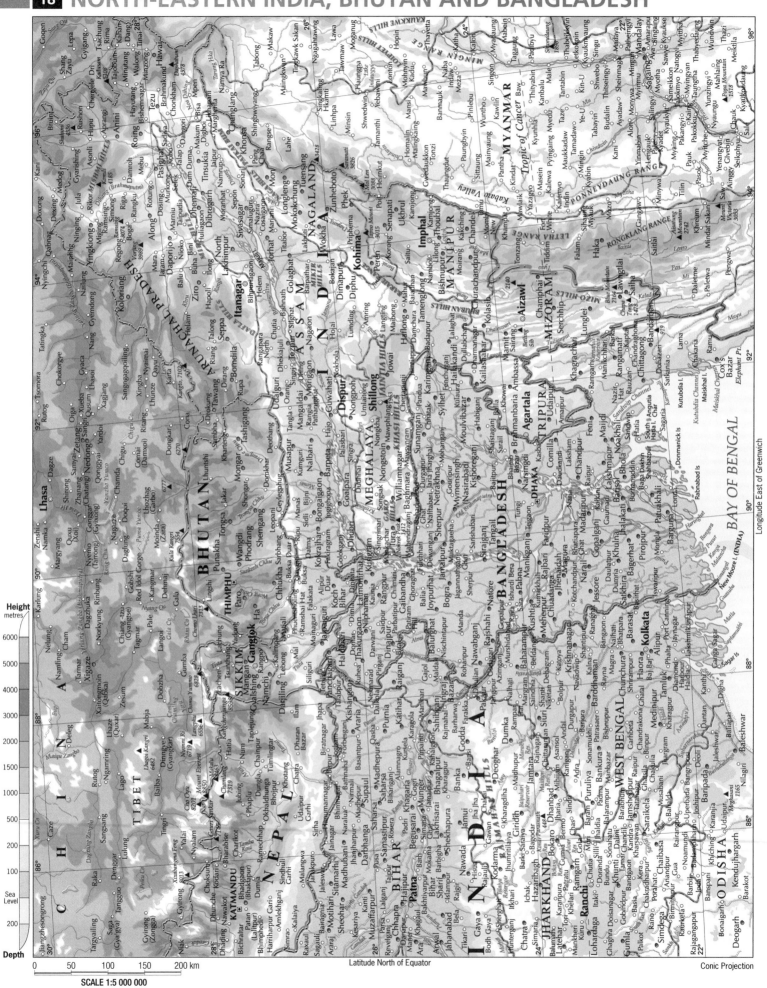

Height
metres

6000
5000
4000
3000
2000
1500
1000
500
200
100
Sea Level
200

Depth

0   50   100   150   200 km

SCALE 1:5 000 000

Latitude North of Equator

Longitude East of Greenwich

BAY OF BENGAL

Conic Projection

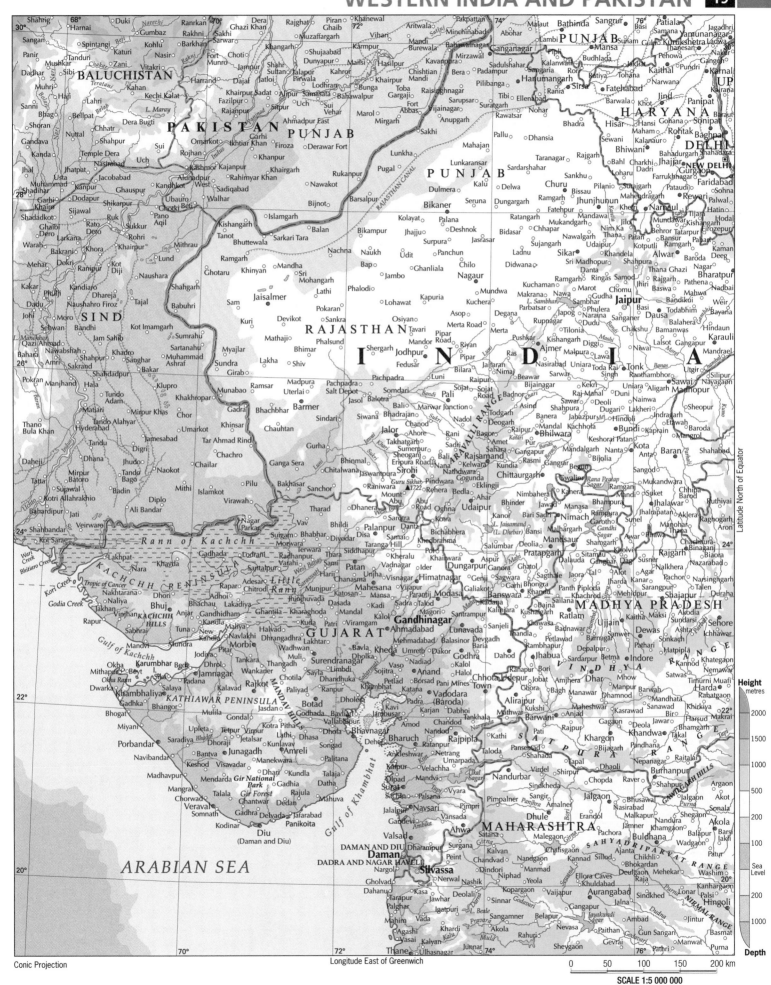

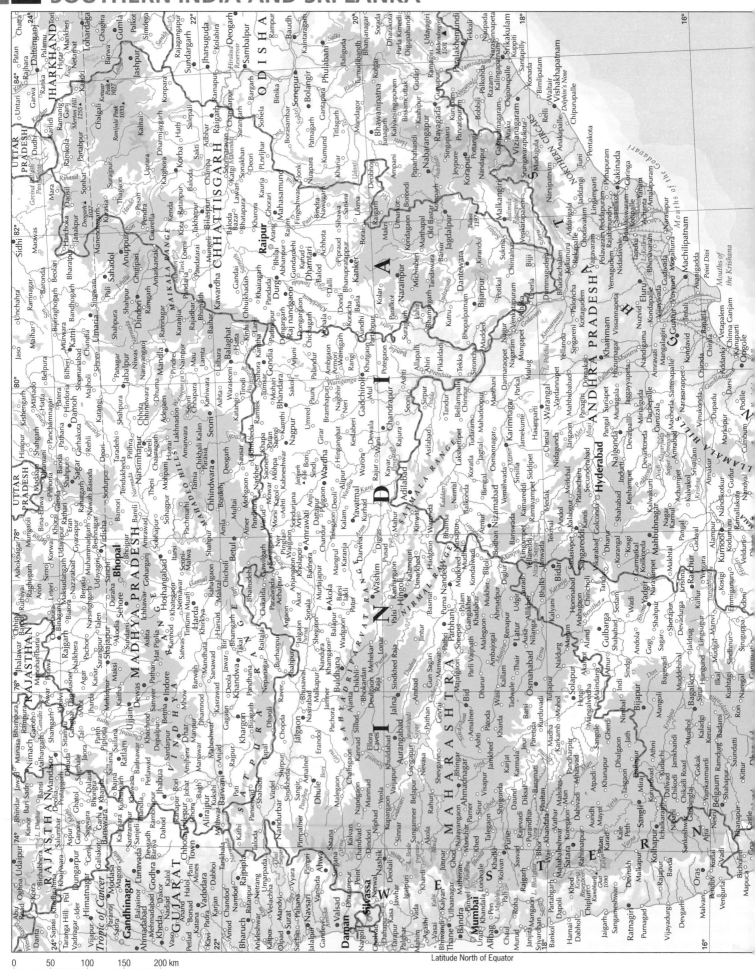

SCALE 1:5 000 000

0   50   100   150   200 km

Latitude North of Equator

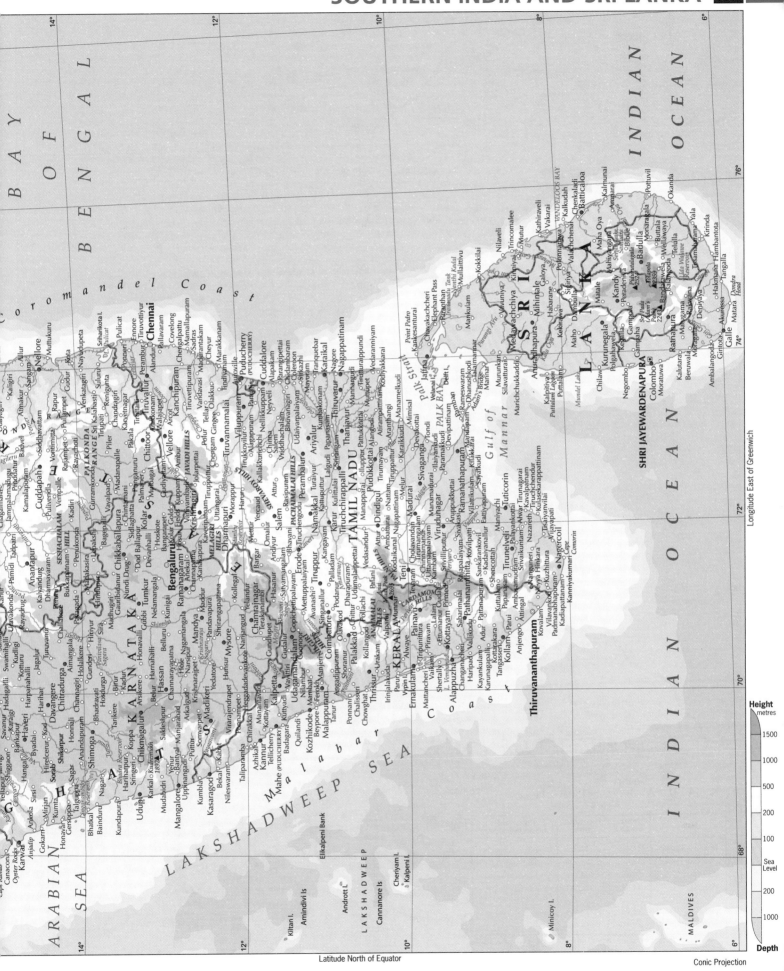

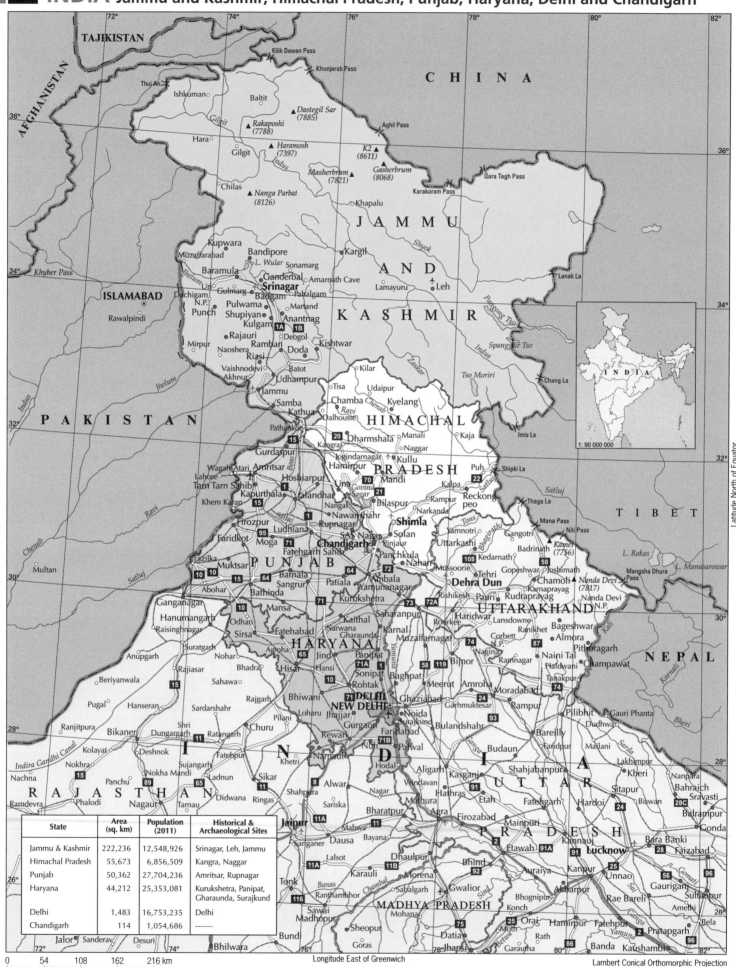

State	Area (sq. km)	Population (2011)	Historical & Archaeological Sites
Jammu & Kashmir	222,236	12,548,926	Srinagar, Leh, Jammu
Himachal Pradesh	55,673	6,856,509	Kangra, Naggar
Punjab	50,362	27,704,236	Amritsar, Rupnagar
Haryana	44,212	25,353,081	Kurukshetra, Panipat, Gharaunda, Surajkund
Delhi	1,483	16,753,235	Delhi
Chandigarh	114	1,054,686	-------

SCALE 1:5 400 000

0   54   108   162   216 km

Longitude East of Greenwich

Lambert Conical Orthomorphic Projection

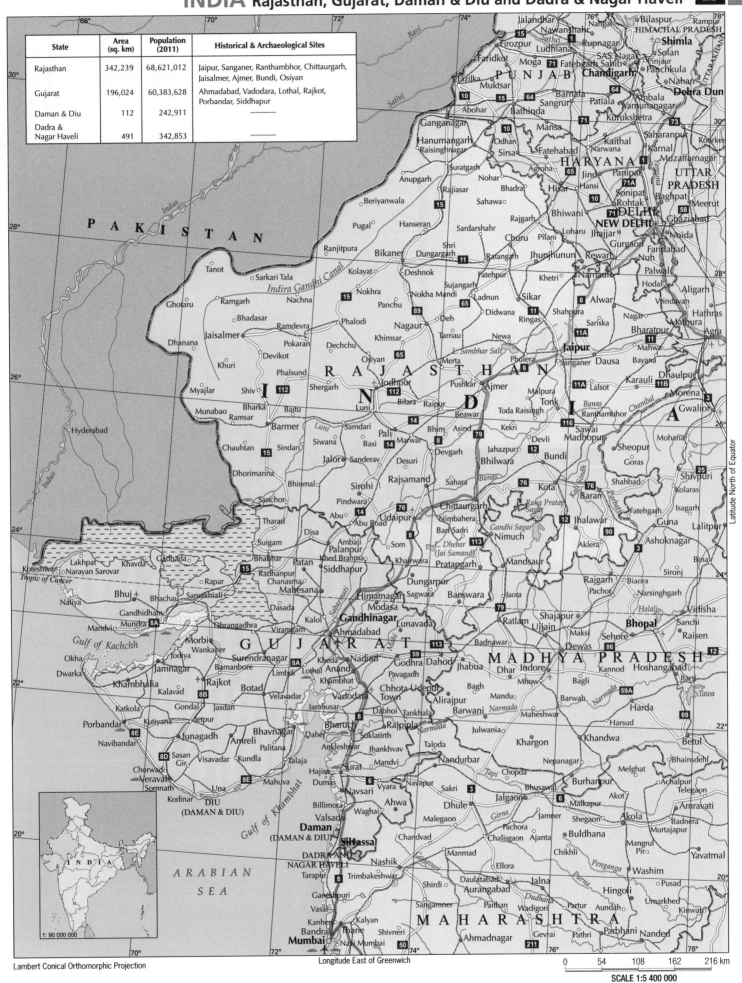

State	Area (sq. km)	Population (2011)	Historical & Archaeological Sites
Rajasthan	342,239	68,621,012	Jaipur, Sanganer, Ranthambhor, Chittaurgarh, Jaisalmer, Ajmer, Bundi, Osiyan
Gujarat	196,024	60,383,628	Ahmadabad, Vadodara, Lothal, Rajkot, Porbandar, Siddhapur
Daman & Diu	112	242,911	----------
Dadra & Nagar Haveli	491	342,853	----------

Lambert Conical Orthomorphic Projection

Longitude East of Greenwich

Latitude North of Equator

0   54   108   162   216 km

SCALE 1:5 400 000

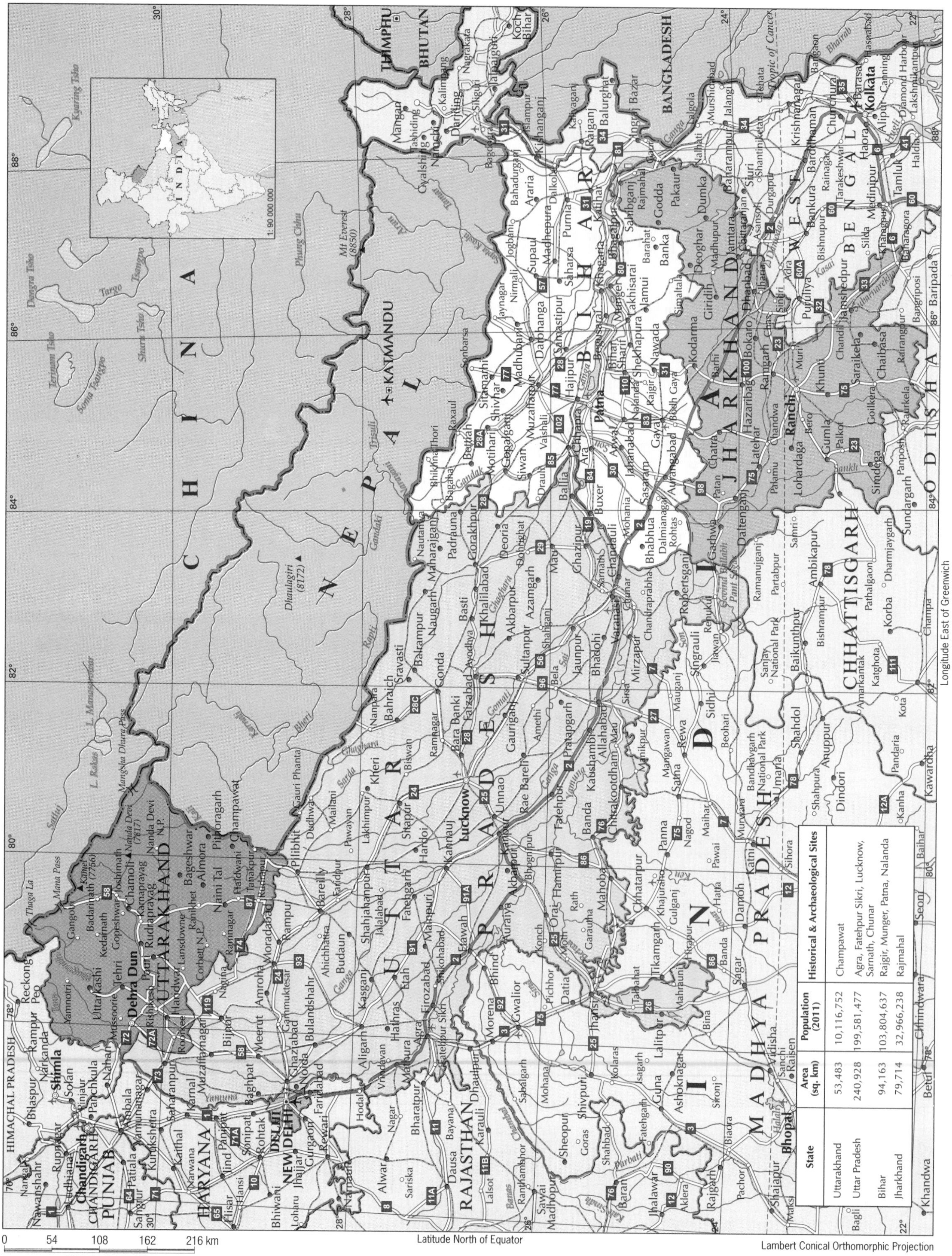

State	Area (sq. km)	Population (2011)	Historical & Archaeological Sites
Uttarakhand	53,483	10,116,752	Champawat
Uttar Pradesh	240,928	199,581,477	Agra, Fatehpur Sikri, Lucknow, Sarnath, Chunar
Bihar	94,163	103,804,637	Rajgir, Munger, Patna, Nalanda
Jharkhand	79,714	32,966,238	Rajmahal

SCALE 1:5 400 000

0   54   108   162   216 km

Latitude North of Equator

Longitude East of Greenwich

Lambert Conical Orthomorphic Projection

1:90 000 000

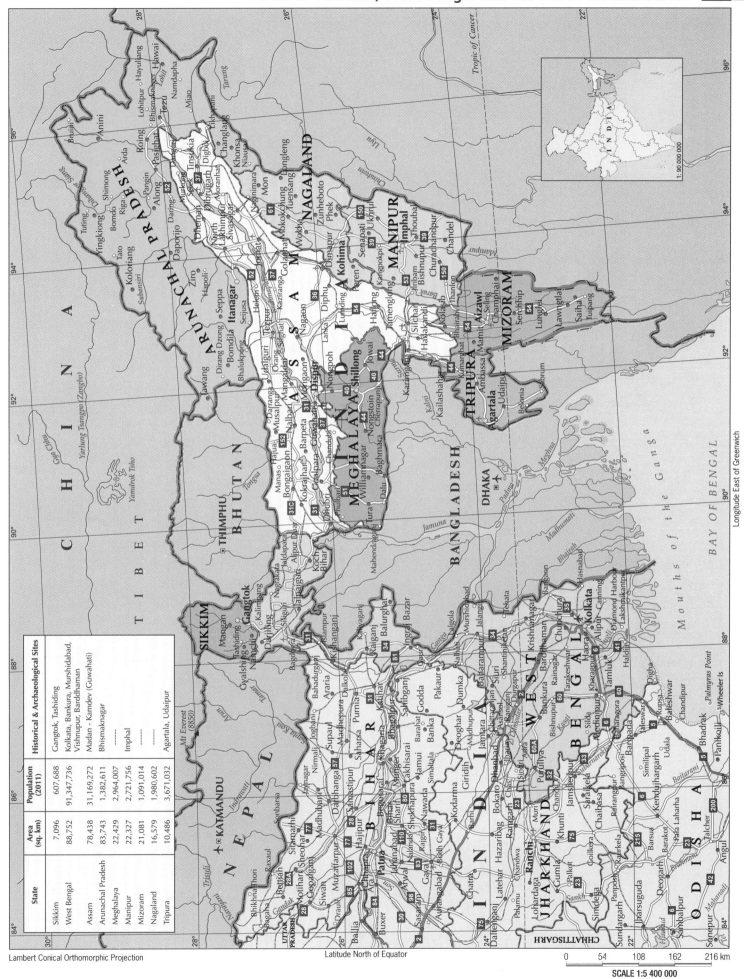

State	Area (sq. km)	Population (2011)	Historical & Archaeological Sites
Sikkim	7,096	607,688	Gangtok, Tashiding
West Bengal	88,752	91,347,736	Kolkata, Bankura, Murshidabad, Vishnupur, Barddhaman
Assam	78,438	31,169,272	Madan - Kamdev (Guwahati)
Arunachal Pradesh	83,743	1,382,611	Bhismaknagar
Meghalaya	22,429	2,964,007	-----
Manipur	22,327	2,721,756	Imphal
Mizoram	21,081	1,091,014	-----
Nagaland	16,579	1,980,602	-----
Tripura	10,486	3,671,032	Agartala, Udaipur

Lambert Conical Orthomorphic Projection

Latitude North of Equator

SCALE 1:5 400 000

0   54   108   162   216 km

1:90 000 000

State	Area (sq. km)	Population (2011)
Madhya Pradesh	308,245	72,597,565
Chhattisgarh	135,191	25,540,196
Odisha	155,707	41,947,358

Historical & Archaeological Sites
Gwalior, Khajuraho, Jabalpur, Mandu, Sanchi, Bhopal, Chanderi, Indore
Jagdalpur
Hirapur, Udaygiri, Lalitgiri, Ratnagiri

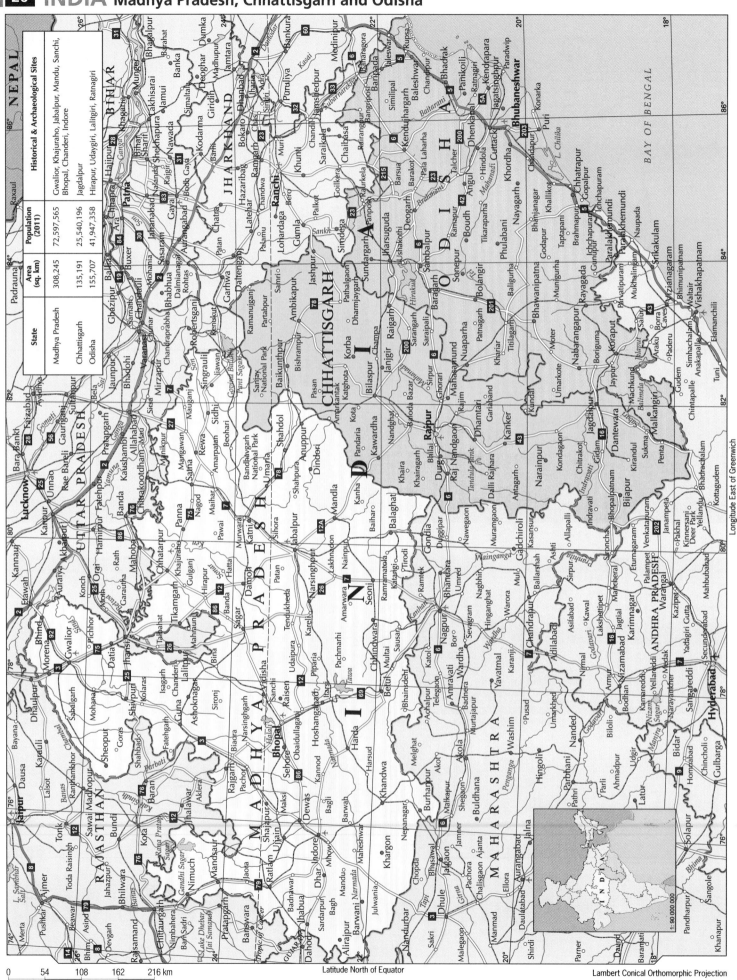

SCALE 1:5 400 000

0   54   108   162   216 km

Latitude North of Equator

Longitude East of Greenwich

Lambert Conical Orthomorphic Projection

1:90 000 000

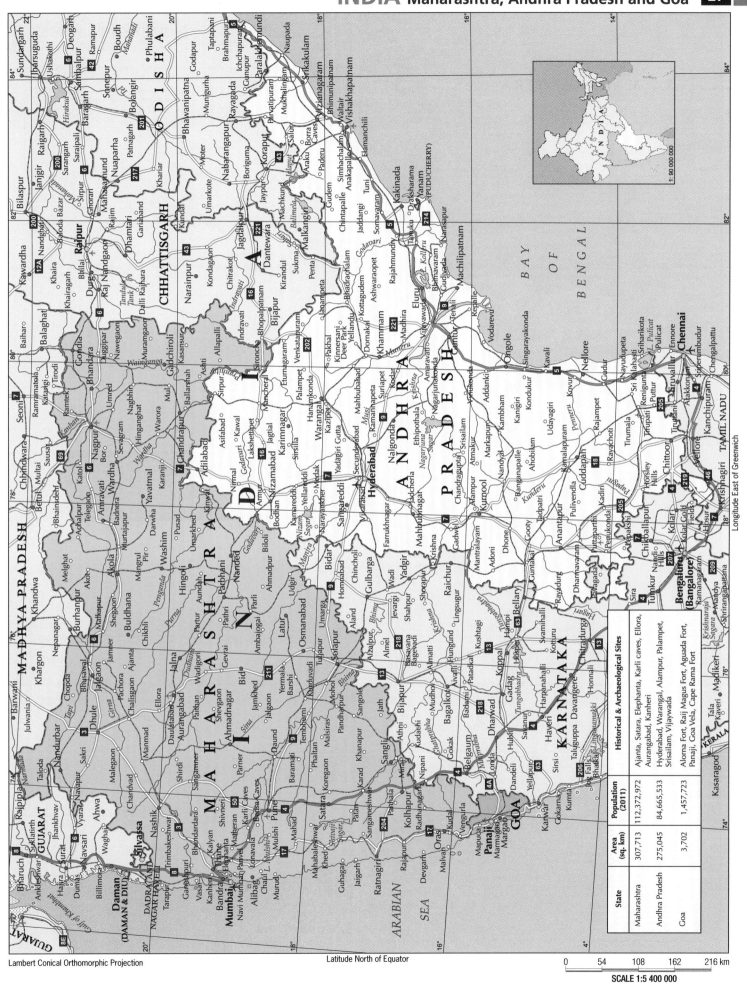

State	Area (sq. km)	Population (2011)	Historical & Archaeological Sites
Maharashtra	307,713	112,372,972	Ajanta, Satara, Elephanta, Karli caves, Ellora, Aurangabad, Kanheri
Andhra Pradesh	275,045	84,665,533	Hyderabad, Warangal, Alampur, Palampet, Srisailam, Vijaywada
Goa	3,702	1,457,723	Aloma Fort, Raji Magus Fort, Aguada Fort, Panaji, Goa Vela, Cape Rama Fort

Lambert Conical Orthomorphic Projection

Latitude North of Equator

0   54   108   162   216 km

SCALE 1:5 400 000

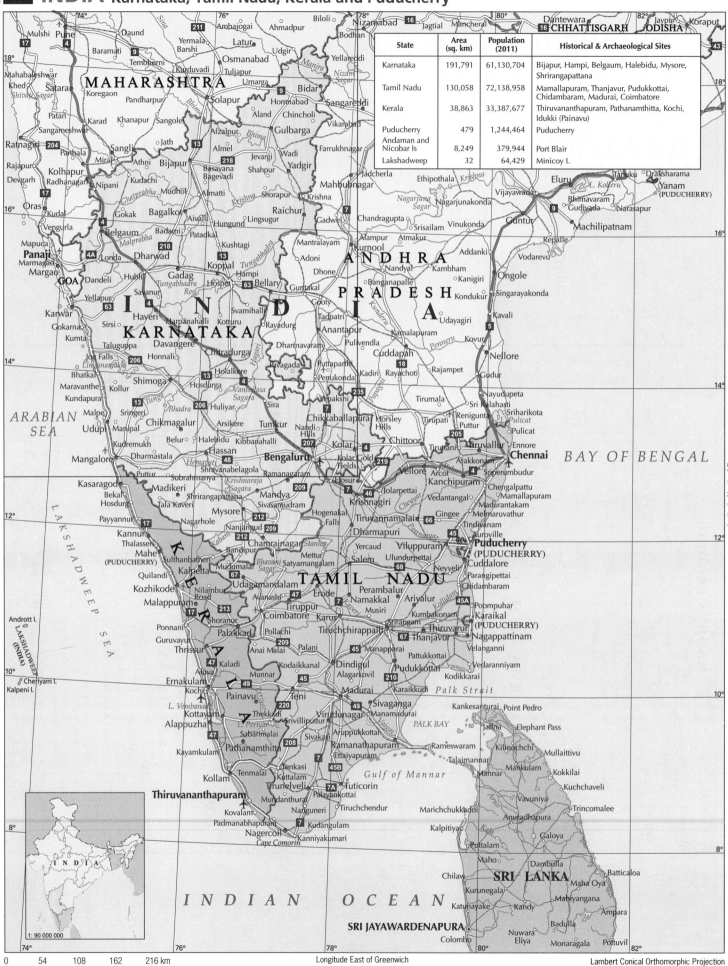

State	Area (sq. km)	Population (2011)	Historical & Archaeological Sites
Karnataka	191,791	61,130,704	Bijapur, Hampi, Belgaum, Halebidu, Mysore, Shrirangapattana
Tamil Nadu	130,058	72,138,958	Mamallapuram, Thanjavur, Pudukkottai, Chidambaram, Madurai, Coimbatore
Kerala	38,863	33,387,677	Thiruvananthapuram, Pathanamthitta, Kochi, Idukki (Painavu)
Puducherry	479	1,244,464	Puducherry
Andaman and Nicobar Is	8,249	379,944	Port Blair
Lakshadweep	32	64,429	Minicoy I.

Longitude East of Greenwich

Latitude North of Equator

Lambert Conical Orthomorphic Projection

0   54   108   162   216 km

SCALE 1:5 400 000

1 : 90 000 000

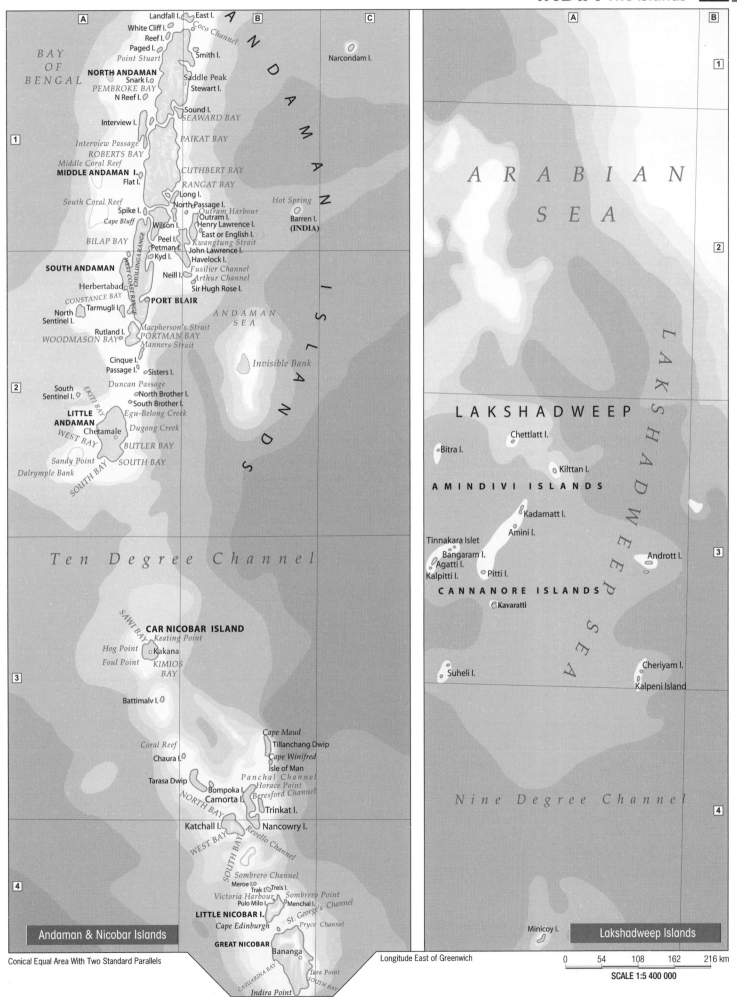

Landfall I.
East I.
White Cliff I.
Coco Channel
Reef I.
Paged I.
Smith I.
Point Stuart
Narcondam I.

BAY
OF
BENGAL

NORTH ANDAMAN
Snark I.
Saddle Peak
PEMBROKE BAY
Stewart I.
N Reef I.

Interview I.
Sound I.
SEAWARD BAY

Interview Passage
PAIKAT BAY
ROBERTS BAY
Middle Coral Reef
MIDDLE ANDAMAN I.
CUTHBERT BAY
Flat I.
RANGAT BAY
Long I.
South Coral Reef
North Passage I.
Hot Spring
Spike I.
Outram Harbour
Cape Bluff
Outram I.
Barren I.
Wilson I.
Henry Lawrence I.
(INDIA)
BILAP BAY
East or English I.
Peel I.
Kwangtung Strait
Petman I.
John Lawrence I.
Kyd I.
Havelock I.
SOUTH ANDAMAN
Neill I.
Fusilier Channel
Arthur Channel
Herbertabad
Sir Hugh Rose I.
CONSTANCE BAY
PORT BLAIR
North
Tarmugli I.
ANDAMAN
Sentinel I.
SEA
Rutland I.
Macpherson's Strait
WOODMASON BAY
PORTMAN BAY
Manners Strait

ANDAMAN ISLANDS

Cinque I.
Passage I.
Sisters I.
Invisible Bank
Duncan Passage
South
North Brother I.
Sentinel I.
South Brother I.
Egu-Belong Creek
LITTLE ANDAMAN
Chetamale
Dugong Creek
WEST BAY
BUTLER BAY
Sandy Point
SOUTH BAY
Dalrymple Bank
SOUTH BAY

WEST COAST RANGE
LONGITUDINAL RANGE
EKITI BAY

T e n   D e g r e e   C h a n n e l

SAWI BAY
CAR NICOBAR ISLAND
Keating Point
Hog Point
Kakana
Foul Point
KIMIOS BAY

Battimalv I.

Cape Maud
Tillanchang Dwip
Coral Reef
Cape Winifred
Chaura I.
Isle of Man
Panchal Channel
Tarasa Dwip
Horace Point
Bompoka I.
Beresford Channel
Camorta I.
NORTH BAY
Trinkat I.
Katchall I.
Nancowry I.
WEST BAY
Revello Channel
SOUTH BAY
Sombrero Channel
Meroe I.
Trak I.
Treis I.
Sombrero Point
Victoria Harbour
Pulo Milo I.
Menchal I.
LITTLE NICOBAR I.
St. George's Channel
Cape Edinburgh
Pryce Channel
GREAT NICOBAR
Bananga
CASUARINA BAY
Tara Point
SOUTH BAY
Indira Point

Conical Equal Area With Two Standard Parallels

Andaman & Nicobar Islands

A R A B I A N
S E A

LAKSHADWEEP
Chettlatt I.
Bitra I.
Kilttan I.
A M I N D I V I   I S L A N D S
Kadamatt I.
Amini I.
Tinnakara Islet
Bangaram I.
Andrott I.
Agatti I.
Kalpitti I.
Pitti I.
C A N N A N O R E   I S L A N D S
Kavaratti

L A K S H A D W E E P   S E A

Suheli I.
Cheriyam I.
Kalpeni Island

N i n e   D e g r e e   C h a n n e l

Minicoy I.
Lakshadweep Islands

Longitude East of Greenwich

0   54   108   162   216 km

SCALE 1:5 400 000

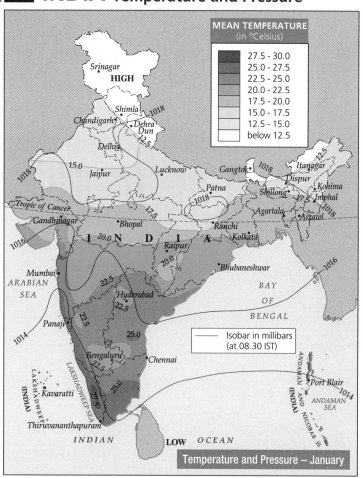

Temperature and Pressure – January

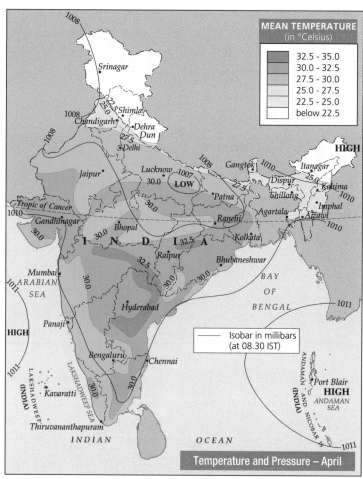

Temperature and Pressure – April

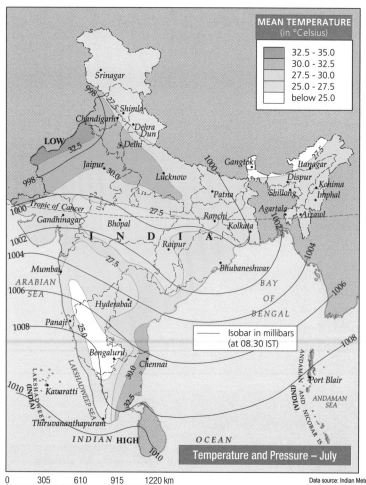

Temperature and Pressure – July

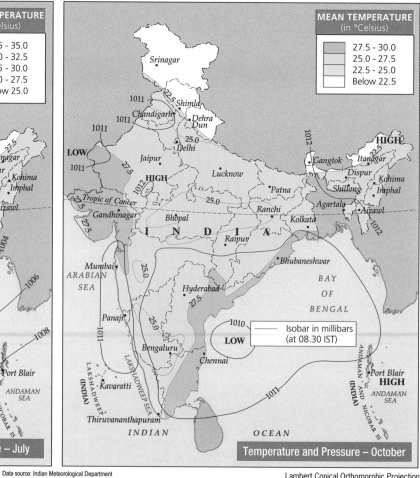

Temperature and Pressure – October

SCALE 1:30 500 000

0   305   610   915   1220 km

Data source: Indian Meteorological Department

Lambert Conical Orthomorphic Projection

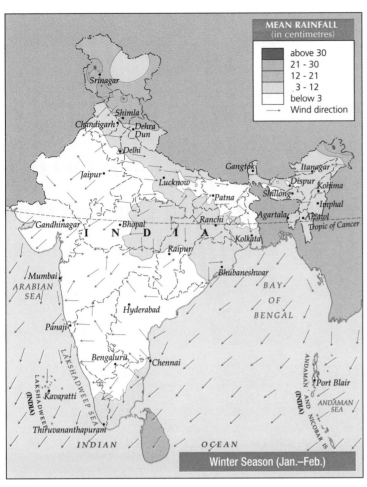

MEAN RAINFALL (in centimetres)
- above 30
- 21 - 30
- 12 - 21
- 3 - 12
- below 3
- → Wind direction

Winter Season (Jan.–Feb.)

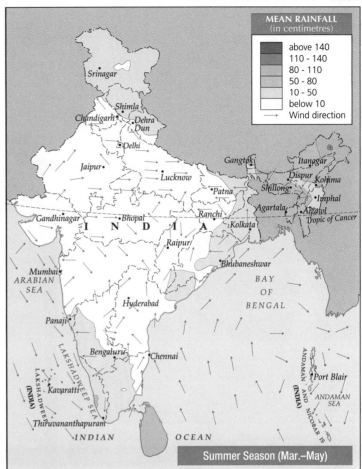

MEAN RAINFALL (in centimetres)
- above 140
- 110 - 140
- 80 - 110
- 50 - 80
- 10 - 50
- below 10
- → Wind direction

Summer Season (Mar.–May)

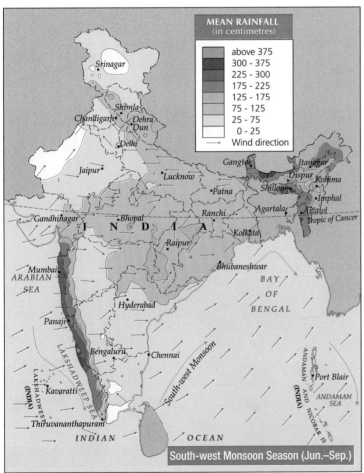

MEAN RAINFALL (in centimetres)
- above 375
- 300 - 375
- 225 - 300
- 175 - 225
- 125 - 175
- 75 - 125
- 25 - 75
- 0 - 25
- → Wind direction

South-west Monsoon Season (Jun.–Sep.)

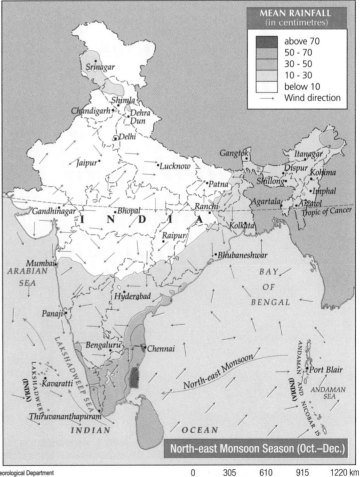

MEAN RAINFALL (in centimetres)
- above 70
- 50 - 70
- 30 - 50
- 10 - 30
- below 10
- → Wind direction

North-east Monsoon Season (Oct.–Dec.)

Lambert Conical Orthomorphic Projection

Data source: Indian Meteorological Department

0   305   610   915   1220 km

SCALE 1:30 500 000

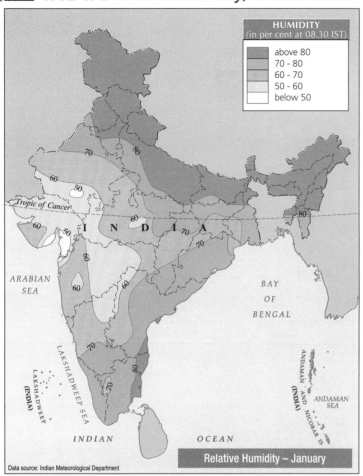

Relative Humidity – January

HUMIDITY
(in per cent at 08.30 IST)
- above 80
- 70 - 80
- 60 - 70
- 50 - 60
- below 50

Data source: Indian Meteorological Department

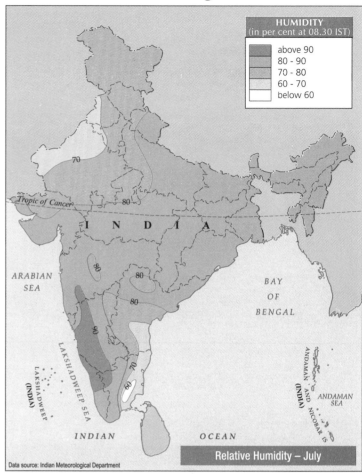

Relative Humidity – July

HUMIDITY
(in per cent at 08.30 IST)
- above 90
- 80 - 90
- 70 - 80
- 60 - 70
- below 60

Data source: Indian Meteorological Department

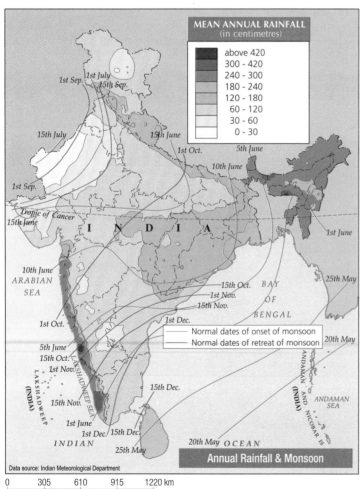

Annual Rainfall & Monsoon

MEAN ANNUAL RAINFALL
(in centimetres)
- above 420
- 300 - 420
- 240 - 300
- 180 - 240
- 120 - 180
- 60 - 120
- 30 - 60
- 0 - 30

—— Normal dates of onset of monsoon
—— Normal dates of retreat of monsoon

Data source: Indian Meteorological Department

0   305   610   915   1220 km

SCALE 1:30 500 000

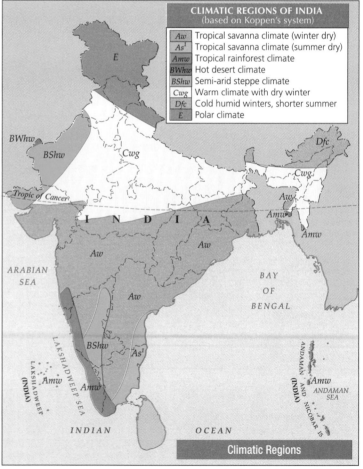

Climatic Regions

CLIMATIC REGIONS OF INDIA
(based on Koppen's system)

Aw	Tropical savanna climate (winter dry)
As¹	Tropical savanna climate (summer dry)
Amw	Tropical rainforest climate
BWhw	Hot desert climate
BShw	Semi-arid steppe climate
Cwg	Warm climate with dry winter
Dfc	Cold humid winters, shorter summer
E	Polar climate

Lambert Conical Orthomorphic Projection

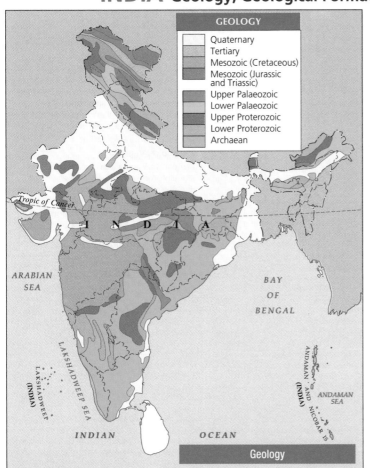

GEOLOGY

- Quaternary
- Tertiary
- Mesozoic (Cretaceous)
- Mesozoic (Jurassic and Triassic)
- Upper Palaeozoic
- Lower Palaeozoic
- Upper Proterozoic
- Lower Proterozoic
- Archaean

Geology

MAJOR GEOLOGICAL FORMATIONS OF INDIA

	Era / Group	Period / System		Major Formations
Phanerozoic	Quaternary	Recent		Recent Alluvia, Coral reef, Sand dunes, Soils
		Pleistocene		Older Alluvia, Karewas of Kashmir, and Pleistocene river terraces
	Tertiary or Kainozoic	Mio-Pliocene		Shiwalik, Irrawaddy and Manchhar Systems, Cuddalore, Warkilli and Rajamahendri sandstones
		Oligo-Miocene		Murree and Pegu Systems, Nari and Gaj series, Kasauli and Dagshai beds
		Eocene		Ranikot-Laki-Kirthar-Chharat series, Eocene of Burma, Jaintia and Disang series, Subathu beds
	Secondary or Mesozoic	Cretaceous		Deccan Traps and Inter-trappeans, Giumal and Chikkim Series, Umia beds
		Jurassic		Kioto limestone and Spiti shales, Kota-Rajmahal and Jabalpur series
		Triassic		Lilang system including Kioto limestone, Mahadeva and Panchet series
	Primary or Palaeozoic	Upper	Permian	Kulling system, Damuda system
			Carboniferous	Lipak and Po series, Talchir series
			Devonian	Muth Quartzite
		Lower	Silurian	Silurian of Burma and Himalayas
			Ordovician	Ordovician of Burma and Himalayas
			Cambrian	Haimanta series, Garbyang series
Pre-Cambrian	Pre-Cambrian or Proterozoic	Upper		Vindhyan systems, Darjiling series, Daling series, Dogra and Simla slates,
		Lower		Cuddapah systems, Delhi systems, Shillong series, Martoli series
	Archaean or Azoic	Archaean		Dharwar and Aravalli systems, Salkhala, Jutogh and Chail series, Gniesses etc.

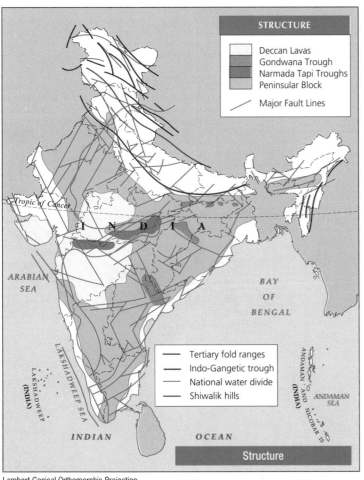

STRUCTURE

- Deccan Lavas
- Gondwana Trough
- Narmada Tapi Troughs
- Peninsular Block
- Major Fault Lines

—— Tertiary fold ranges
—— Indo-Gangetic trough
—— National water divide
—— Shiwalik hills

Structure

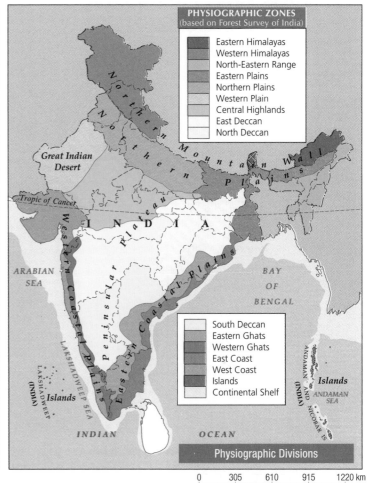

PHYSIOGRAPHIC ZONES
(based on Forest Survey of India)

- Eastern Himalayas
- Western Himalayas
- North-Eastern Range
- Eastern Plains
- Northern Plains
- Western Plain
- Central Highlands
- East Deccan
- North Deccan

- South Deccan
- Eastern Ghats
- Western Ghats
- East Coast
- West Coast
- Islands
- Continental Shelf

Physiographic Divisions

Lambert Conical Orthomorphic Projection

0   305   610   915   1220 km

SCALE 1:30 500 000

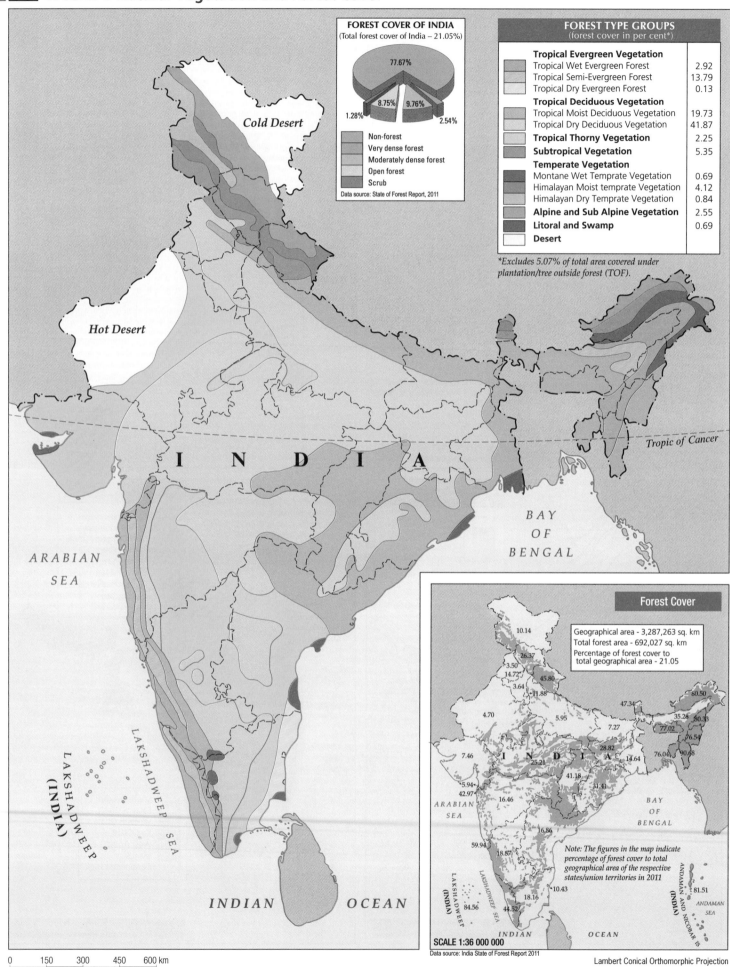

FOREST COVER OF INDIA
(Total forest cover of India – 21.05%)

77.67%

8.75%   9.76%

1.28%   2.54%

Non-forest
Very dense forest
Moderately dense forest
Open forest
Scrub

Data source: State of Forest Report, 2011

FOREST TYPE GROUPS (forest cover in per cent*)	
Tropical Evergreen Vegetation	
Tropical Wet Evergreen Forest	2.92
Tropical Semi-Evergreen Forest	13.79
Tropical Dry Evergreen Forest	0.13
Tropical Deciduous Vegetation	
Tropical Moist Deciduous Vegetation	19.73
Tropical Dry Deciduous Vegetation	41.87
Tropical Thorny Vegetation	2.25
Subtropical Vegetation	5.35
Temperate Vegetation	
Montane Wet Temprate Vegetation	0.69
Himalayan Moist temprate Vegetation	4.12
Himalayan Dry Temprate Vegetation	0.84
Alpine and Sub Alpine Vegetation	2.55
Litoral and Swamp	0.69
Desert	

*Excludes 5.07% of total area covered under plantation/tree outside forest (TOF).

Cold Desert

Hot Desert

Tropic of Cancer

I N D I A

ARABIAN
SEA

BAY
OF
BENGAL

LAKSHADWEEP
(INDIA)

LAKSHADWEEP
SEA

INDIAN   OCEAN

Forest Cover

Geographical area - 3,287,263 sq. km
Total forest area - 692,027 sq. km
Percentage of forest cover to
 total geographical area - 21.05

10.14
26.37
3.50
14.72
3.64   45.80
11.88
4.70   47.34   80.50
5.95   35.28 80.33
7.27   77.02   76.54
7.46   28.82   76.04 90.68
25.21   14.64
41.18
5.94 31.41
42.97   16.46
16.86
59.94
18.87
10.43
18.16
84.56   44.52   81.51

I N D I A

ARABIAN
SEA

BAY
OF
BENGAL

ANDAMAN
SEA

LAKSHADWEEP
(INDIA)

ANDAMAN AND NICOBAR IS
(INDIA)

Note: The figures in the map indicate
percentage of forest cover to total
geographical area of the respective
states/union territories in 2011

SCALE 1:36 000 000
Data source: India State of Forest Report 2011

Lambert Conical Orthomorphic Projection

0   150   300   450   600 km

SCALE 1:15 000 000

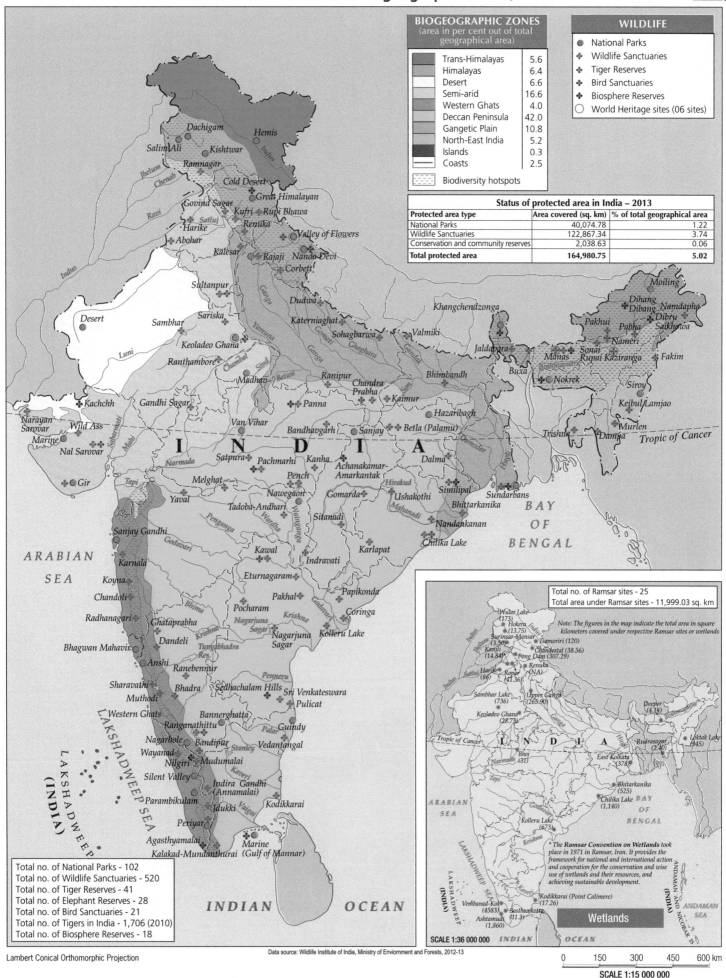

BIOGEOGRAPHIC ZONES
(area in per cent out of total geographical area)

Zone	%
Trans-Himalayas	5.6
Himalayas	6.4
Desert	6.6
Semi-arid	16.6
Western Ghats	4.0
Deccan Peninsula	42.0
Gangetic Plain	10.8
North-East India	5.2
Islands	0.3
Coasts	2.5

Biodiversity hotspots

WILDLIFE

- National Parks
- Wildlife Sanctuaries
- Tiger Reserves
- Bird Sanctuaries
- Biosphere Reserves
- World Heritage sites (06 sites)

Status of protected area in India – 2013

Protected area type	Area covered (sq. km)	% of total geographical area
National Parks	40,074.78	1.22
Wildlife Sanctuaries	122,867.34	3.74
Conservation and community reserves	2,038.63	0.06
Total protected area	**164,980.75**	**5.02**

Total no. of Ramsar sites - 25
Total area under Ramsar sites - 11,999.03 sq. km

Note: The figures in the map indicate the total area in square kilometers covered under respective Ramsar sites or wetlands

* The Ramsar Convention on Wetlands took place in 1971 in Ramsar, Iran. It provides the framework for national and international action and cooperation for the conservation and wise use of wetlands and their resources, and achieving sustainable development.

Wetlands

Wular Lake (173)
Hokera (13.75)
Surinsar-Mansar (3.50)
Tsomoriri (120)
Kanjli (14.84)
Chandertal (38.56)
Pong Dam (307.29)
Harike (86)
Renuka (NA)
Ropar (41.36)
Sambhar Lake (736)
Upper Ganga (265.90)
Keoladeo Ghana (28.73)
Deepor (4.14)
Rudrasagar (2.40)
Loktak Lake (945)
Bhoj (31)
East Kolkata (378)
Bhitarkanika (525)
Chilka Lake (1,140)
Kolleru Lake (673)
Kodikkarai (Point Calimere) (17.26)
Vembanad-Kol (4583)
Sasthamkotta (1,860)
Ashtamudi (61.31)

Total no. of National Parks - 102
Total no. of Wildlife Sanctuaries - 520
Total no. of Tiger Reserves - 41
Total no. of Elephant Reserves - 28
Total no. of Bird Sanctuaries - 21
Total no. of Tigers in India - 1,706 (2010)
Total no. of Biosphere Reserves - 18

Lambert Conical Orthomorphic Projection

Data source: Wildlife Institute of India, Ministry of Enviornment and Forests, 2012-13

SCALE 1:36 000 000

0 150 300 450 600 km

SCALE 1:15 000 000

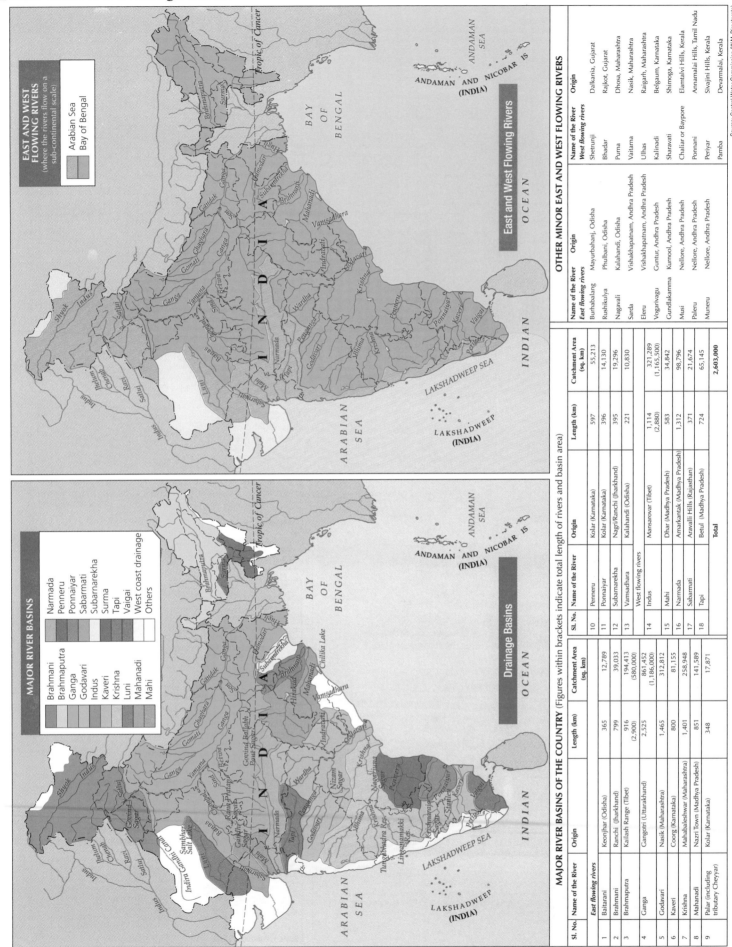

MAJOR RIVER BASINS

- Brahmani
- Brahmaputra
- Ganga
- Godavari
- Indus
- Kaveri
- Krishna
- Luni
- Mahanadi
- Mahi
- Narmada
- Penneru
- Ponnaiyar
- Sabarmati
- Subarnarekha
- Surma
- Tapi
- Vaigai
- West coast drainage
- Others

Drainage Basins

EAST AND WEST FLOWING RIVERS (where the rivers flow on a sub-continental scale)

- Arabian Sea
- Bay of Bengal

East and West Flowing Rivers

MAJOR RIVER BASINS OF THE COUNTRY (Figures within brackets indicate total length of rivers and basin area)

Sl. No.	Name of the River	Origin	Length (km)	Catchment Area (sq. km)
	East flowing rivers			
1	Baitarani	Keonjhar (Odisha)	365	12,789
2	Brahmani	Ranchi (Jharkhand)	799	39,033
3	Brahmaputra	Kailash Range (Tibet)	916 (2,900)	194,413 (580,000)
4	Ganga	Gangotri (Uttarakhand)	2,525	861,452 (1,186,000)
5	Godavari	Nasik (Maharashtra)	1,465	312,812
6	Kaveri	Coorg (Karnataka)	800	81,155
7	Krishna	Mahabaleshwar (Maharashtra)	1,401	258,948
8	Mahanadi	Nazri Town (Madhya Pradesh)	851	141,589
9	Palar (including tributary Cheyyar)	Kolar (Karnataka)	348	17,871
10	Penneru	Kolar (Karnataka)	597	55,213
11	Ponnaiyar	Kolar (Karnataka)	396	14,130
12	Subarnarekha	Nagri/Ranchi (Jharkhand)	395	19,296
13	Vamsadhara	Kalahandi (Odisha)	221	10,830
	West flowing rivers			
14	Indus	Mansarovar (Tibet)	1,114 (2,880)	321,289 (1,165,500)
15	Mahi	Dhar (Madhya Pradesh)	583	34,842
16	Narmada	Amarkantak (Madhya Pradesh)	1,312	98,796
17	Sabarmati	Aravalli Hills (Rajasthan)	371	21,674
18	Tapi	Betul (Madhya Pradesh)	724	65,145
		Total		**2,603,000**

OTHER MINOR EAST AND WEST FLOWING RIVERS

Name of the River *East flowing rivers*	Origin	Name of the River *West flowing rivers*	Origin
Burhabalang	Mayurbhanj, Odisha	Shetrunji	Dalkania, Gujarat
Rushikulya	Phulbani, Odisha	Bhadar	Rajkot, Gujarat
Nagavali	Kalahandi, Odisha	Purna	Dhosa, Maharashtra
Sarda	Vishakhapatnam, Andhra Pradesh	Vaitarna	Nasik, Maharashtra
Eleru	Vishakhapatnam, Andhra Pradesh	Ulhas	Raigarh, Maharashtra
Vogarivagu	Guntur, Andhra Pradesh	Kalinadi	Belgaum, Karnataka
Gundlakamma	Kurnool, Andhra Pradesh	Sharavati	Shimoga, Karnataka
Musi	Nellore, Andhra Pradesh	Chaliar or Baypore	Elantalvi Hills, Kerala
Paleru	Nellore, Andhra Pradesh	Ponmani	Annamalai Hills, Tamil Nadu
Muneru	Nellore, Andhra Pradesh	Periyar	Sivajini Hills, Kerala
		Pamba	Devarmalai, Kerala

Source: Central Water Commission (W.M. Directorate)

SCALE 1:24 000 000

0 240 280 720 960 km

Lambert Conical Orthomorphic Projection

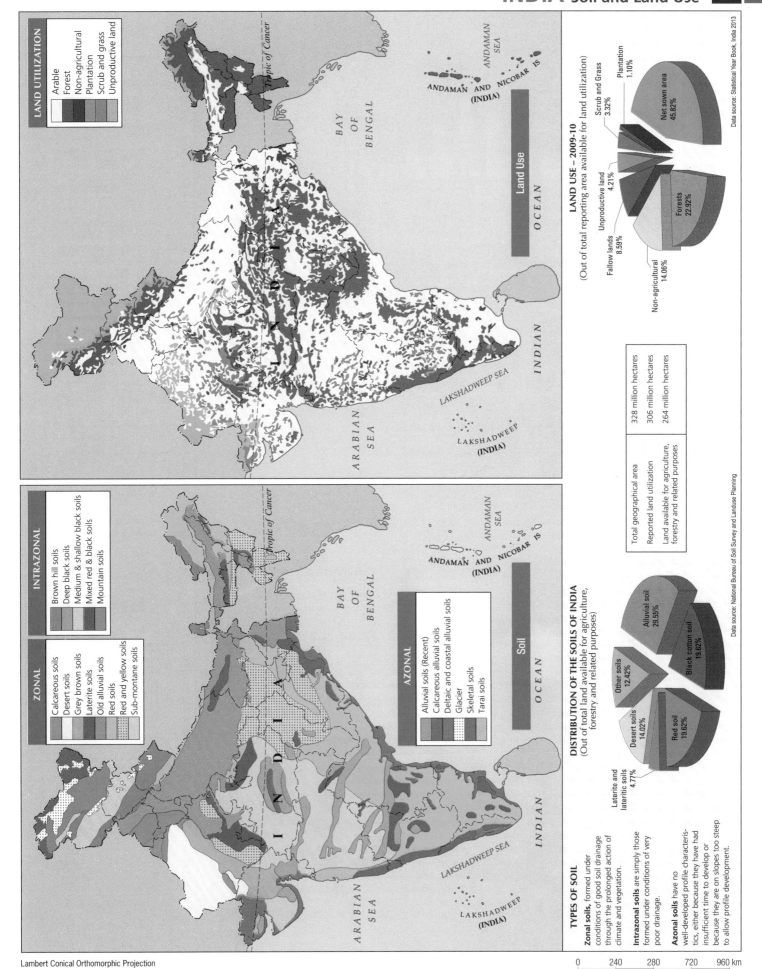

LAND UTILIZATION
- Arable
- Forest
- Non-agricultural
- Plantation
- Scrub and grass
- Unproductive land

Land Use

ZONAL
- Calcareous soils
- Desert soils
- Grey brown soils
- Laterite soils
- Old alluvial soils
- Red soils
- Red and yellow soils
- Sub-montane soils

INTRAZONAL
- Brown hill soils
- Deep black soils
- Medium & shallow black soils
- Mixed red & black soils
- Mountain soils

AZONAL
- Alluvial soils (Recent)
- Calcareous alluvial soils
- Deltaic and coastal alluvial soils
- Glacier
- Skeletal soils
- Tarai soils

Soil

LAND USE – 2009-10
(Out of total reporting area available for land utilization)

- Net sown area 45.82%
- Forests 22.92%
- Plantation 1.10%
- Scrub and Grass 3.32%
- Unproductive land 4.21%
- Fallow lands 8.59%
- Non-agricultural 14.06%

Data source: Statistical Year Book, India 2013

Total geographical area	328 million hectares
Reported land utilization	306 million hectares
Land available for agriculture, forestry and related purposes	264 million hectares

DISTRIBUTION OF THE SOILS OF INDIA
(Out of total land available for agriculture, forestry and related purposes)

- Alluvial soil 29.55%
- Black cotton soil 19.62%
- Red soil 19.62%
- Desert soils 14.02%
- Laterite and lateritic soils 4.77%
- Other soils 12.42%

Data source: National Bureau of Soil Survey and Landuse Planning

TYPES OF SOIL

Zonal soils, formed under conditions of good soil drainage through the prolonged action of climate and vegetation.

Intrazonal soils are simply those formed under conditions of very poor drainage.

Azonal soils have no well-developed profile characteristics, either because they have had insufficient time to develop or because they are on slopes too steep to allow profile development.

Lambert Conical Orthomorphic Projection

0   240   280   720   960 km

SCALE 1:24 000 000

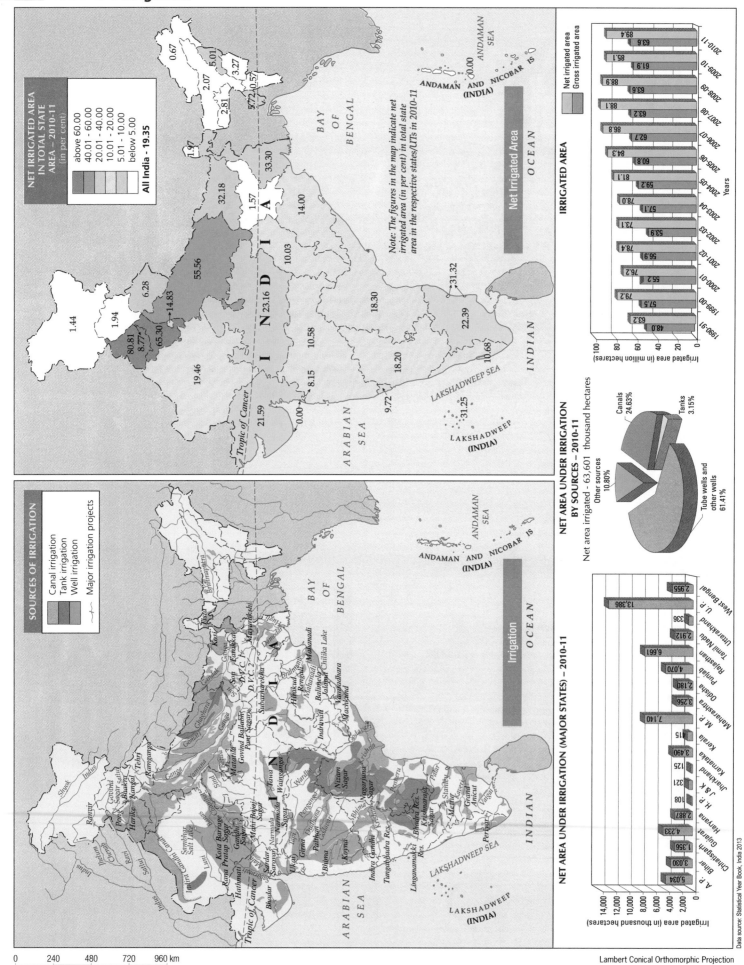

NET IRRIGATED AREA IN TOTAL STATE AREA – 2010-11 (in per cent)

- above 60.00
- 40.01 - 60.00
- 20.01 - 40.00
- 10.01 - 20.00
- 5.01 - 10.00
- below 5.00

All India - 19.35

Note: The figures in the map indicate net irrigated area (in per cent) in total state area in the respective states/UTs in 2010-11

Net Irrigated Area

SOURCES OF IRRIGATION

- Canal irrigation
- Tank irrigation
- Well irrigation
- Major irrigation projects

Irrigation

IRRIGATED AREA

Net irrigated area
Gross irrigated area

NET AREA UNDER IRRIGATION BY SOURCES – 2010-11
Net area irrigated - 63,601 thousand hectares

- Canals 24.63%
- Tanks 3.15%
- Tube wells and other wells 61.41%
- Other sources 10.80%

NET AREA UNDER IRRIGATION (MAJOR STATES) – 2010-11

Lambert Conical Orthomorphic Projection

SCALE 1:24 000 000

0   240   480   720   960 km

Data source: Statistical Year Book, India 2013

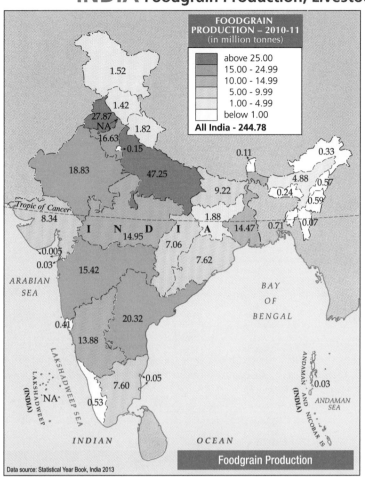

FOODGRAIN PRODUCTION – 2010-11
(in million tonnes)

above 25.00
15.00 - 24.99
10.00 - 14.99
5.00 - 9.99
1.00 - 4.99
below 1.00

All India - 244.78

1.52
1.42
27.87
NA
16.63
1.82
0.15
18.83
47.25
0.11
0.33
9.22
4.88
0.57
0.24
0.59
Tropic of Cancer
8.34
1.88
INDIA
14.95
14.47
0.71
0.07
7.06
0.005
7.62
0.03
ARABIAN SEA
15.42
BAY OF BENGAL
0.41
20.32
13.88
LAKSHADWEEP (INDIA)
7.60
0.05
ANDAMAN AND NICOBAR IS (INDIA)
0.03
NA
0.53
ANDAMAN SEA
INDIAN
OCEAN

Data source: Statistical Year Book, India 2013

Foodgrain Production

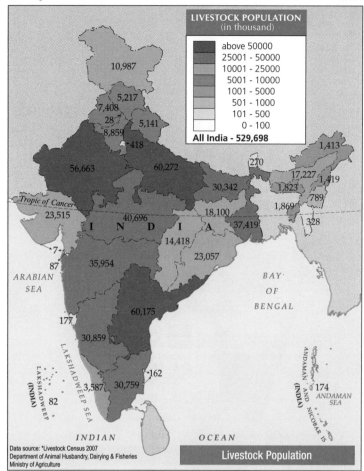

LIVESTOCK POPULATION
(in thousand)

above 50000
25001 - 50000
10001 - 25000
5001 - 10000
1001 - 5000
501 - 1000
101 - 500
0 - 100

All India - 529,698

10,987
5,217
7,408
28
5,141
8,859
418
1,413
56,663
60,272
270
17,227
1,419
30,342
1,823
789
Tropic of Cancer
23,515
18,100
37,419
1,869
328
INDIA
40,696
7
14,418
23,057
87
35,954
BAY OF BENGAL
60,175
177
30,859
ARABIAN SEA
LAKSHADWEEP (INDIA)
3,587
30,759
162
174
82
ANDAMAN AND NICOBAR IS
ANDAMAN SEA
INDIAN
OCEAN

Data source: *Livestock Census 2007
Department of Animal Husbandry, Dairying & Fisheries
Ministry of Agriculture

Livestock Population

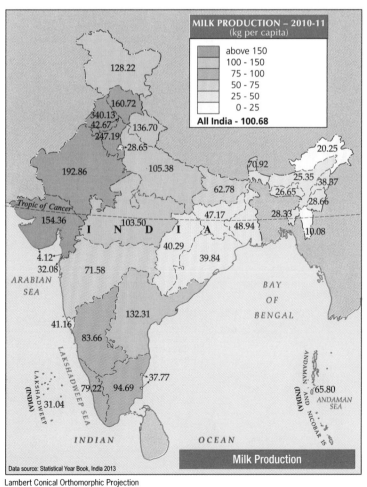

MILK PRODUCTION – 2010-11
(kg per capita)

above 150
100 - 150
75 - 100
50 - 75
25 - 50
0 - 25

All India - 100.68

128.22
160.72
340.13
42.67
136.70
247.19
28.65
192.86
20.25
105.38
70.92
25.35
38.87
62.78
26.65
28.66
47.17
28.33
Tropic of Cancer
154.36
48.94
INDIA
103.50
10.08
40.29
4.12
39.84
32.08
71.58
ARABIAN SEA
BAY OF BENGAL
132.31
41.16
83.66
LAKSHADWEEP (INDIA)
37.77
79.22
94.69
65.80
31.04
ANDAMAN AND NICOBAR IS
ANDAMAN SEA
INDIAN
OCEAN

Data source: Statistical Year Book, India 2013

Milk Production

Lambert Conical Orthomorphic Projection

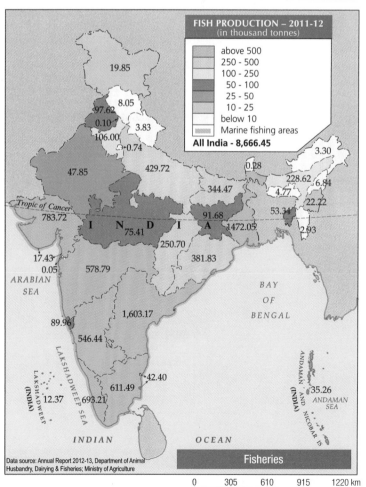

FISH PRODUCTION – 2011-12
(in thousand tonnes)

above 500
250 - 500
100 - 250
50 - 100
25 - 50
10 - 25
below 10
Marine fishing areas

All India - 8,666.45

19.85
97.62
8.05
0.10
3.83
106.00
0.74
3.30
47.85
429.72
228.62
6.84
344.47
4.77
22.22
91.68
53.34
Tropic of Cancer
783.72
INDIA
1472.05
2.93
75.41
250.70
381.83
17.43
0.05
578.79
ARABIAN SEA
BAY OF BENGAL
1,603.17
89.96
546.44
LAKSHADWEEP (INDIA)
42.40
611.49
35.26
12.37
693.21
ANDAMAN AND NICOBAR IS
ANDAMAN SEA
INDIAN
OCEAN

Data source: Annual Report 2012-13, Department of Animal
Husbandry, Dairying & Fisheries; Ministry of Agriculture

Fisheries

0   305   610   915   1220 km

SCALE 1:30 500 000

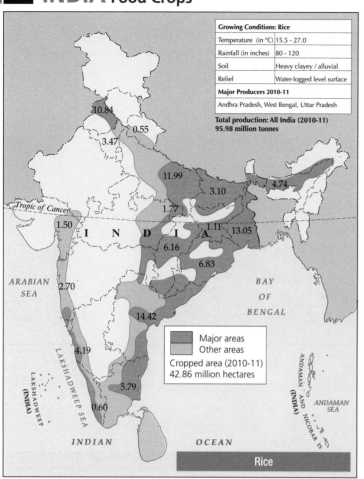

Growing Conditions: Rice

Temperature (in °C)	15.5 - 27.0
Rainfall (in inches)	80 - 120
Soil	Heavy clayey / alluvial
Relief	Water-logged level surface

Major Producers 2010-11

Andhra Pradesh, West Bengal, Uttar Pradesh

Total production: All India (2010-11)
95.98 million tonnes

Major areas
Other areas
Cropped area (2010-11)
42.86 million hectares

Rice

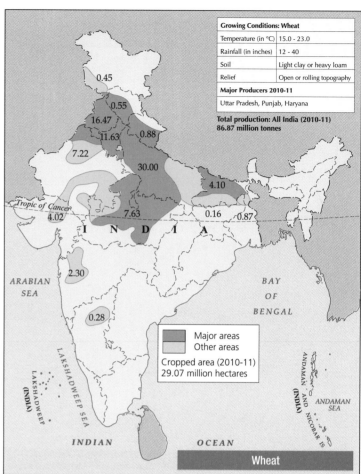

Growing Conditions: Wheat

Temperature (in °C)	15.0 - 23.0
Rainfall (in inches)	12 - 40
Soil	Light clay or heavy loam
Relief	Open or rolling topography

Major Producers 2010-11

Uttar Pradesh, Punjab, Haryana

Total production: All India (2010-11)
86.87 million tonnes

Major areas
Other areas
Cropped area (2010-11)
29.07 million hectares

Wheat

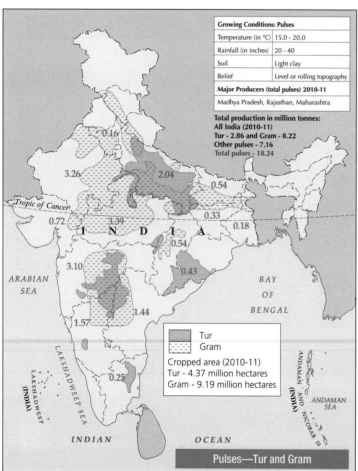

Growing Conditions: Pulses

Temperature (in °C)	15.0 - 20.0
Rainfall (in inches)	20 - 40
Soil	Light clay
Relief	Level or rolling topography

Major Producers (total pulses) 2010-11

Madhya Pradesh, Rajasthan, Maharashtra

Total production in million tonnes:
All India (2010-11)
Tur - 2.86 and Gram - 8.22
Other pulses - 7.16
Total pulses - 18.24

Tur
Gram
Cropped area (2010-11)
Tur - 4.37 million hectares
Gram - 9.19 million hectares

Pulses—Tur and Gram

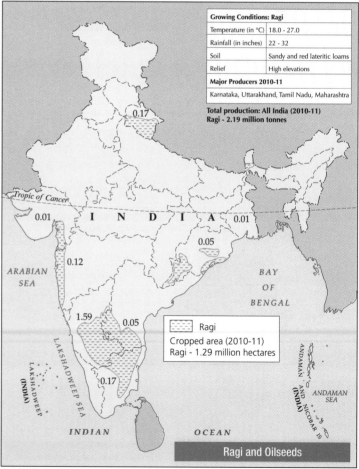

Growing Conditions: Ragi

Temperature (in °C)	18.0 - 27.0
Rainfall (in inches)	22 - 32
Soil	Sandy and red lateritic loams
Relief	High elevations

Major Producers 2010-11

Karnataka, Uttarakhand, Tamil Nadu, Maharashtra

Total production: All India (2010-11)
Ragi - 2.19 million tonnes

Ragi
Cropped area (2010-11)
Ragi - 1.29 million hectares

Ragi and Oilseeds

0	305	610	915	1220 km

SCALE 1:30 500 000

Note: The figures in the map indicate total production in million tonnes
in the respective state/union territory in 2010-11.
Data source: Statistical Year Book, India 2013

Lambert Conical Orthomorphic Projection

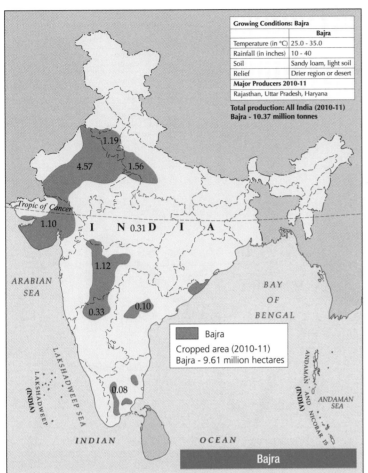

Growing Conditions: Bajra	
	Bajra
Temperature (in °C)	25.0 - 35.0
Rainfall (in inches)	10 - 40
Soil	Sandy loam, light soil
Relief	Drier region or desert
Major Producers 2010-11	
Rajasthan, Uttar Pradesh, Haryana	

Total production: All India (2010-11)
Bajra - 10.37 million tonnes

■ Bajra
Cropped area (2010-11)
Bajra - 9.61 million hectares

Bajra

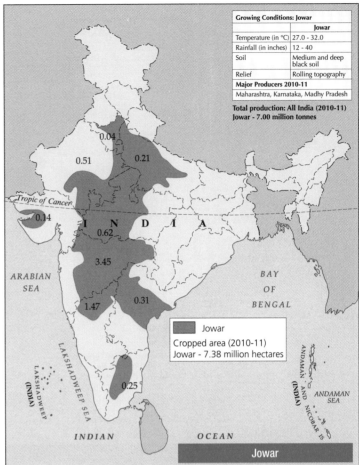

Growing Conditions: Jowar	
	Jowar
Temperature (in °C)	27.0 - 32.0
Rainfall (in inches)	12 - 40
Soil	Medium and deep black soil
Relief	Rolling topography
Major Producers 2010-11	
Maharashtra, Karnataka, Madhy Pradesh	

Total production: All India (2010-11)
Jowar - 7.00 million tonnes

■ Jowar
Cropped area (2010-11)
Jowar - 7.38 million hectares

Jowar

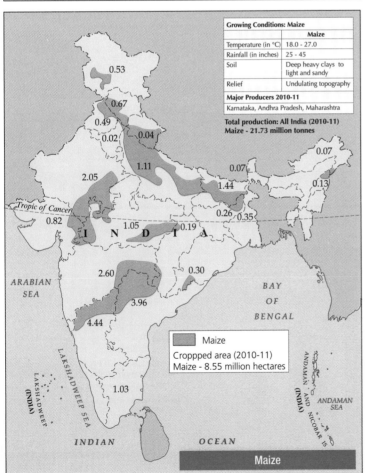

Growing Conditions: Maize	
	Maize
Temperature (in °C)	18.0 - 27.0
Rainfall (in inches)	25 - 45
Soil	Deep heavy clays to light and sandy
Relief	Undulating topography
Major Producers 2010-11	
Karnataka, Andhra Pradesh, Maharashtra	

Total production: All India (2010-11)
Maize - 21.73 million tonnes

■ Maize
Croppped area (2010-11)
Maize - 8.55 million hectares

Maize

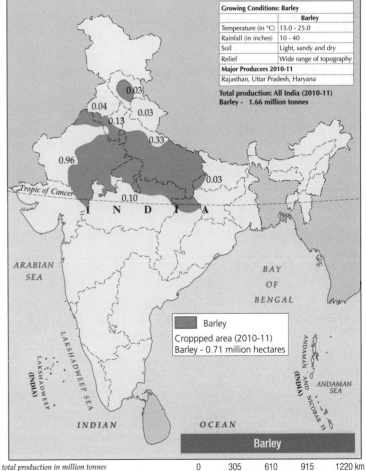

Growing Conditions: Barley	
	Barley
Temperature (in °C)	15.0 - 25.0
Rainfall (in inches)	10 - 40
Soil	Light, sandy and dry
Relief	Wide range of topography
Major Producers 2010-11	
Rajasthan, Uttar Pradesh, Haryana	

Total production: All India (2010-11)
Barley - 1.66 million tonnes

■ Barley
Croppped area (2010-11)
Barley - 0.71 million hectares

Barley

Lambert Conical Orthomorphic Projection

Note: The figures in the map indicate total production in million tonnes
in the respective state/union territory in 2010-11.
Data source: Statistical Year Book, India 2013

0   305   610   915   1220 km

SCALE 1:30 500 000

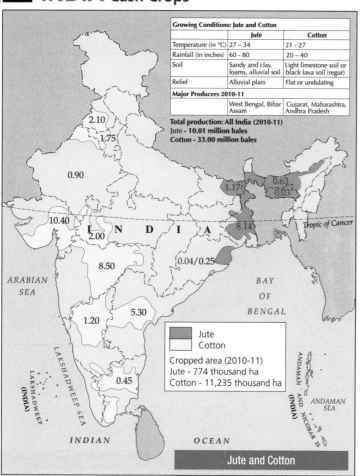

Growing Conditions: Jute and Cotton

	Jute	Cotton
Temperature (in °C)	27 – 34	21 – 27
Rainfall (in inches)	60 – 80	20 – 40
Soil	Sandy and clay, loams, alluvial soil	Light limestone soil or black lava soil (regur)
Relief	Alluvial plain	Flat or undulating
Major Producers 2010-11		
	West Bengal, Bihar, Assam	Gujarat, Maharashtra, Andhra Pradesh

Total production: All India (2010-11)
Jute - 10.01 million bales
Cotton - 33.00 million bales

Legend:
- Jute
- Cotton

Cropped area (2010-11)
Jute - 774 thousand ha
Cotton - 11,235 thousand ha

Jute and Cotton

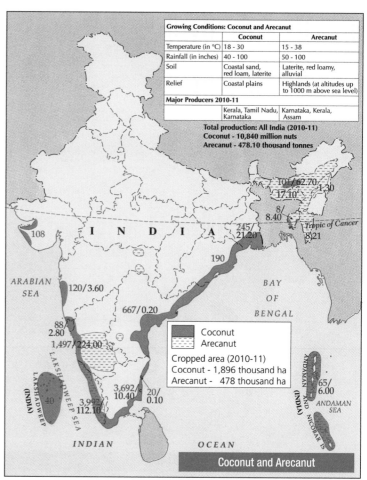

Growing Conditions: Coconut and Arecanut

	Coconut	Arecanut
Temperature (in °C)	18 - 30	15 - 38
Rainfall (in inches)	40 - 100	50 - 100
Soil	Coastal sand, red loam, laterite	Laterite, red loamy, alluvial
Relief	Coastal plains	Highlands (at altitudes up to 1000 m above sea level)
Major Producers 2010-11		
	Kerala, Tamil Nadu, Karnataka	Karnataka, Kerala, Assam

Total production: All India (2010-11)
Coconut - 10,840 million nuts
Arecanut - 478.10 thousand tonnes

Legend:
- Coconut
- Arecanut

Cropped area (2010-11)
Coconut - 1,896 thousand ha
Arecanut -   478 thousand ha

Coconut and Arecanut

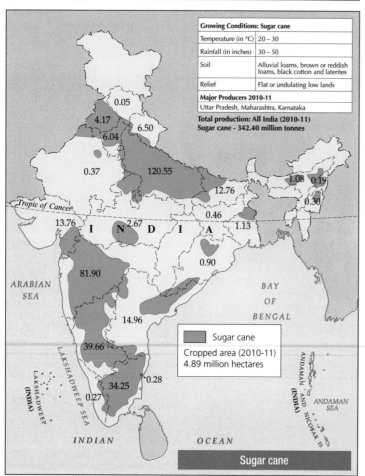

Growing Conditions: Sugar cane

Temperature (in °C)	20 – 30
Rainfall (in inches)	30 – 50
Soil	Alluvial loams, brown or reddish loams, black cotton and laterites
Relief	Flat or undulating low lands

Major Producers 2010-11
Uttar Pradesh, Maharashtra, Karnataka

Total production: All India (2010-11)
Sugar cane - 342.40 million tonnes

Legend:
- Sugar cane

Cropped area (2010-11)
4.89 million hectares

Sugar cane

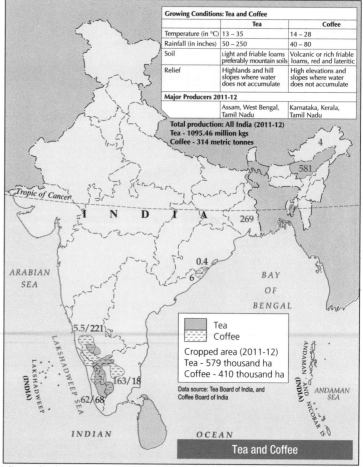

Growing Conditions: Tea and Coffee

	Tea	Coffee
Temperature (in °C)	13 – 35	14 – 28
Rainfall (in inches)	50 – 250	40 – 80
Soil	light and friable loams preferably mountain soils	Volcanic or rich friable loams, red and lateritic
Relief	Highlands and hill slopes where water does not accumulate	High elevations and slopes where water does not accumulate
Major Producers 2011-12		
	Assam, West Bengal, Tamil Nadu	Karnataka, Kerala, Tamil Nadu

Total production: All India (2011-12)
Tea - 1095.46 million kgs
Coffee - 314 metric tonnes

Legend:
- Tea
- Coffee

Cropped area (2011-12)
Tea - 579 thousand ha
Coffee - 410 thousand ha

Data source: Tea Board of India, and Coffee Board of India

Tea and Coffee

0   305   610   915   1220 km

SCALE 1:30 500 000

Note: The figures in the map indicate total production in the respective state/union territory in 2010-11.
Data source: Statistical Year Book, India 2013

Lambert Conical Orthomorphic Projection

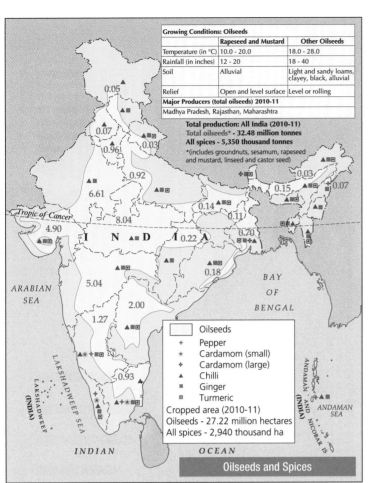

Growing Conditions: Oilseeds		
	Rapeseed and Mustard	**Other Oilseeds**
Temperature (in °C)	10.0 - 20.0	18.0 - 28.0
Rainfall (in inches)	12 - 20	18 - 40
Soil	Alluvial	Light and sandy loams, clayey, black, alluvial
Relief	Open and level surface	Level or rolling
Major Producers (total oilseeds) 2010-11		
Madhya Pradesh, Rajasthan, Maharashtra		

Total production: All India (2010-11)
Total oilseeds* - 32.48 million tonnes
All spices - 5,350 thousand tonnes

*(includes groundnuts, sesamum, rapeseed and mustard, linseed and castor seed)

	Oilseeds
+	Pepper
✳	Cardamom (small)
✤	Cardamom (large)
▲	Chilli
■	Ginger
⊡	Turmeric

Cropped area (2010-11)
Oilseeds - 27.22 million hectares
All spices - 2,940 thousand ha

Oilseeds and Spices

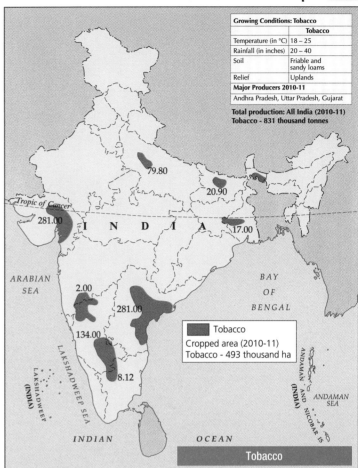

Growing Conditions: Tobacco	
	Tobacco
Temperature (in °C)	18 – 25
Rainfall (in inches)	20 – 40
Soil	Friable and sandy loams
Relief	Uplands
Major Producers 2010-11	
Andhra Pradesh, Uttar Pradesh, Gujarat	

Total production: All India (2010-11)
Tobacco - 831 thousand tonnes

	Tobacco

Cropped area (2010-11)
Tobacco - 493 thousand ha

Tobacco

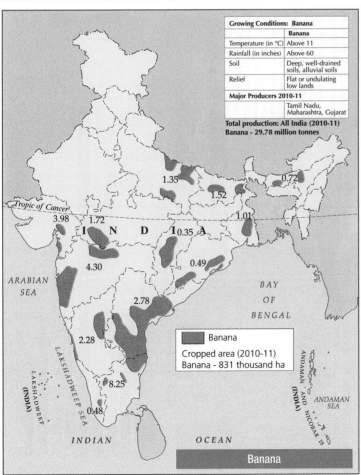

Growing Conditions: Banana	
	Banana
Temperature (in °C)	Above 11
Rainfall (in inches)	Above 60
Soil	Deep, well-drained soils, alluvial soils
Relief	Flat or undulating low lands
Major Producers 2010-11	
	Tamil Nadu, Maharashtra, Gujarat

Total production: All India (2010-11)
Banana - 29.78 million tonnes

	Banana

Cropped area (2010-11)
Banana - 831 thousand ha

Banana

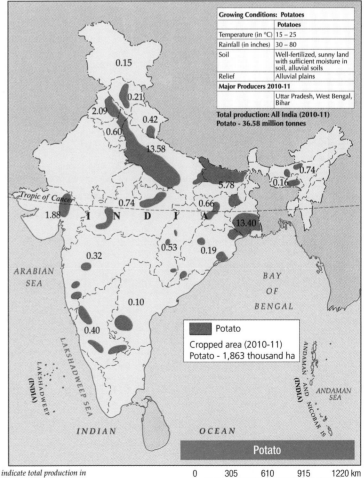

Growing Conditions: Potatoes	
	Potatoes
Temperature (in °C)	15 – 25
Rainfall (in inches)	30 – 80
Soil	Well-fertilized, sunny land with sufficient moisture in soil, alluvial soils
Relief	Alluvial plains
Major Producers 2010-11	
	Uttar Pradesh, West Bengal, Bihar

Total production: All India (2010-11)
Potato - 36.58 million tonnes

	Potato

Cropped area (2010-11)
Potato - 1,863 thousand ha

Potato

Lambert Conical Orthomorphic Projection

Note: The figures in the map indicate total production in the respective state/union territory in 2010-11.
Data source: Statistical Year Book, India 2013

0   305   610   915   1220 km

SCALE 1:30 500 000

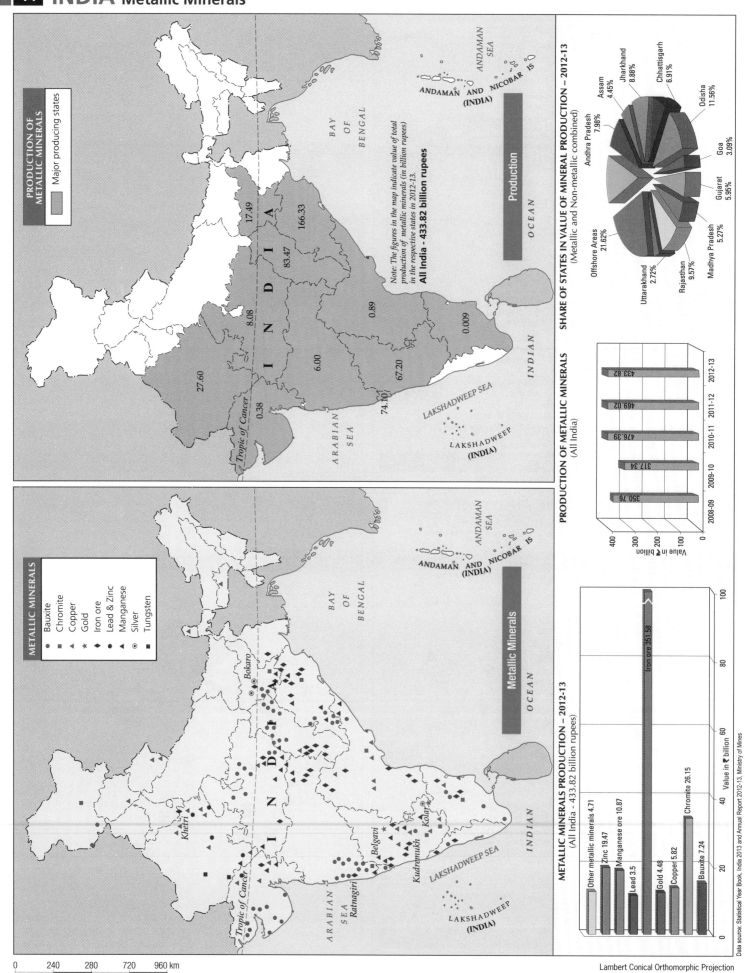

PRODUCTION OF METALLIC MINERALS

Major producing states

Note: The figures in the map indicate value of total production of metallic minerals (in billion rupees) in the respective states in 2012-13.
All India - 433.82 billion rupees

17.49

166.33

83.47

8.08

0.89

27.60

6.00

0.009

0.38

74.10

67.20

Production

METALLIC MINERALS

Bauxite
Chromite
Copper
Gold
Iron ore
Lead & Zinc
Manganese
Silver
Tungsten

Bokaro

Khetri

Belgavi

Kolar

Kudremukh

Ratnagiri

Metallic Minerals

SHARE OF STATES IN VALUE OF MINERAL PRODUCTION – 2012-13
(Metallic and Non-metallic combined)

Jharkhand 8.88%

Assam 4.45%

Chhattisgarh 6.91%

Andhra Pradesh 7.98%

Odisha 11.56%

Offshore Areas 21.62%

Goa 3.09%

Gujarat 5.95%

Uttarakhand 2.72%

Madhya Pradesh 5.27%

Rajasthan 9.57%

PRODUCTION OF METALLIC MINERALS
(All India)

433.82	469.02	476.39	317.34	350.76	
2012-13	2011-12	2010-11	2009-10	2008-09	

Value in ₹ billion

METALLIC MINERALS PRODUCTION – 2012-13
(All India - 433.82 billion rupees)

Other metallic minerals 4.71
Zinc 19.47
Manganese ore 10.87
Lead 3.5
Iron ore 351.58
Gold 4.48
Copper 5.82
Chromite 26.15
Bauxite 7.24

Value in ₹ billion

0   20   40   60   80   100

Data source: Statistical Year Book, India 2013 and Annual Report 2012-13, Ministry of Mines

0   240   280   720   960 km

SCALE 1:24 000 000

Lambert Conical Orthomorphic Projection

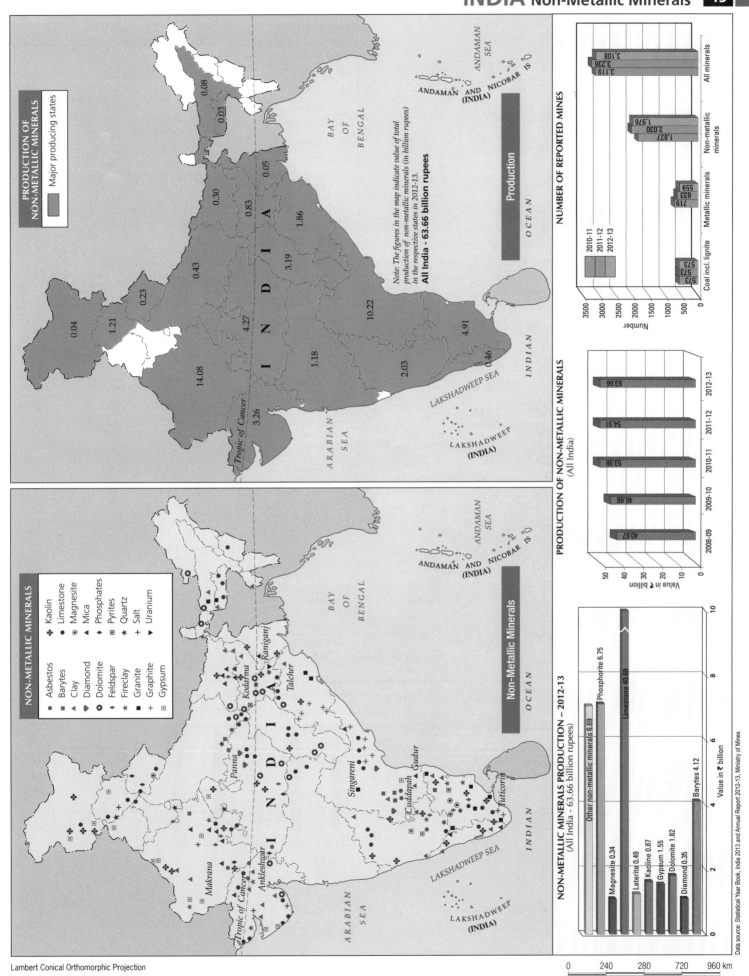

PRODUCTION OF NON-METALLIC MINERALS

Major producing states

Note: The figures in the map indicate value of total production of non-metallic minerals (in billion rupees) in the respective states in 2012-13. **All India - 63.66 billion rupees**

Production

NON-METALLIC MINERALS

● Asbestos	♣ Kaolin		
■ Barytes	⬣ Limestone		
▲ Clay	● Magnesite		
▼ Diamond	◄ Mica		
◉ Dolomite	◆ Phosphates		
◆ Feldspar	▣ Pyrites		
★ Fireclay	★ Quartz		
■ Granite	+ Salt		
+ Graphite	▼ Uranium		
▣ Gypsum			

Non-Metallic Minerals

NUMBER OF REPORTED MINES

- 2010-11
- 2011-12
- 2012-13

All minerals: 3,108 / 3,236 / 3,119
Non-metallic minerals: 1,976 / 2,030 / 1,827
Metallic minerals: 559 / 633 / 719
Coal incl. lignite: 573 / 573 / 573

PRODUCTION OF NON-METALLIC MINERALS (All India)

Value in ₹ billion

2008-09: 40.67
2009-10: 46.66
2010-11: 53.98
2011-12: 54.91
2012-13: 63.66

NON-METALLIC MINERALS PRODUCTION – 2012-13 (All India - 63.66 billion rupees)

Value in ₹ billion

- Other non-metallic minerals 6.69
- Phosphorite 6.75
- Limestone 40.68
- Magnesite 0.34
- Laterite 0.49
- Kaolin 0.87
- Gypsum 1.55
- Dolomite 1.82
- Diamond 0.35
- Barytes 4.12

Lambert Conical Orthomorphic Projection

SCALE 1:24 000 000
0   240   280   720   960 km

Data source: Statistical Year Book, India 2013 and Annual Report 2012-13, Ministry of Mines

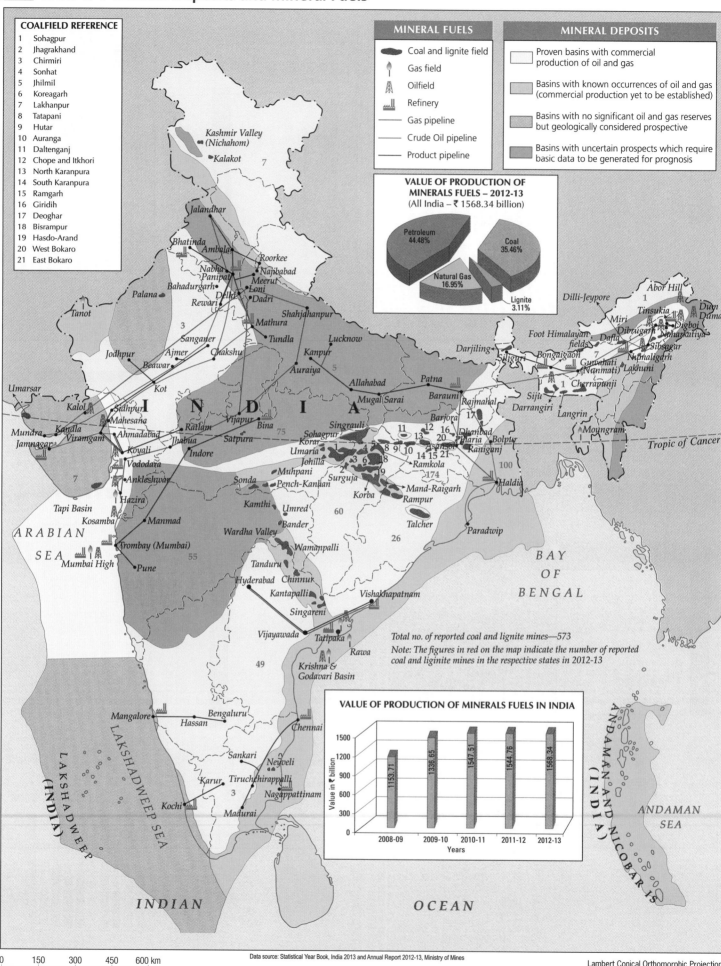

COALFIELD REFERENCE

1 Sohagpur
2 Jhagrakhand
3 Chirmiri
4 Sonhat
5 Jhilmil
6 Koreagarh
7 Lakhanpur
8 Tatapani
9 Hutar
10 Auranga
11 Daltenganj
12 Chope and Itkhori
13 North Karanpura
14 South Karanpura
15 Ramgarh
16 Giridih
17 Deoghar
18 Bisrampur
19 Hasdo-Arand
20 West Bokaro
21 East Bokaro

MINERAL FUELS

- Coal and lignite field
- Gas field
- Oilfield
- Refinery
- Gas pipeline
- Crude Oil pipeline
- Product pipeline

MINERAL DEPOSITS

- Proven basins with commercial production of oil and gas
- Basins with known occurrences of oil and gas (commercial production yet to be established)
- Basins with no significant oil and gas reserves but geologically considered prospective
- Basins with uncertain prospects which require basic data to be generated for prognosis

VALUE OF PRODUCTION OF MINERALS FUELS – 2012-13
(All India – ₹ 1568.34 billion)

- Petroleum 44.48%
- Coal 35.46%
- Natural Gas 16.95%
- Lignite 3.11%

Total no. of reported coal and lignite mines—573

Note: The figures in red on the map indicate the number of reported coal and liginite mines in the respective states in 2012-13

VALUE OF PRODUCTION OF MINERALS FUELS IN INDIA

Years	Value in ₹ billion
2008-09	1153.71
2009-10	1336.65
2010-11	1547.51
2011-12	1544.76
2012-13	1568.34

Data source: Statistical Year Book, India 2013 and Annual Report 2012-13, Ministry of Mines

SCALE 1:15 000 000
0 150 300 450 600 km

Lambert Conical Orthomorphic Projection

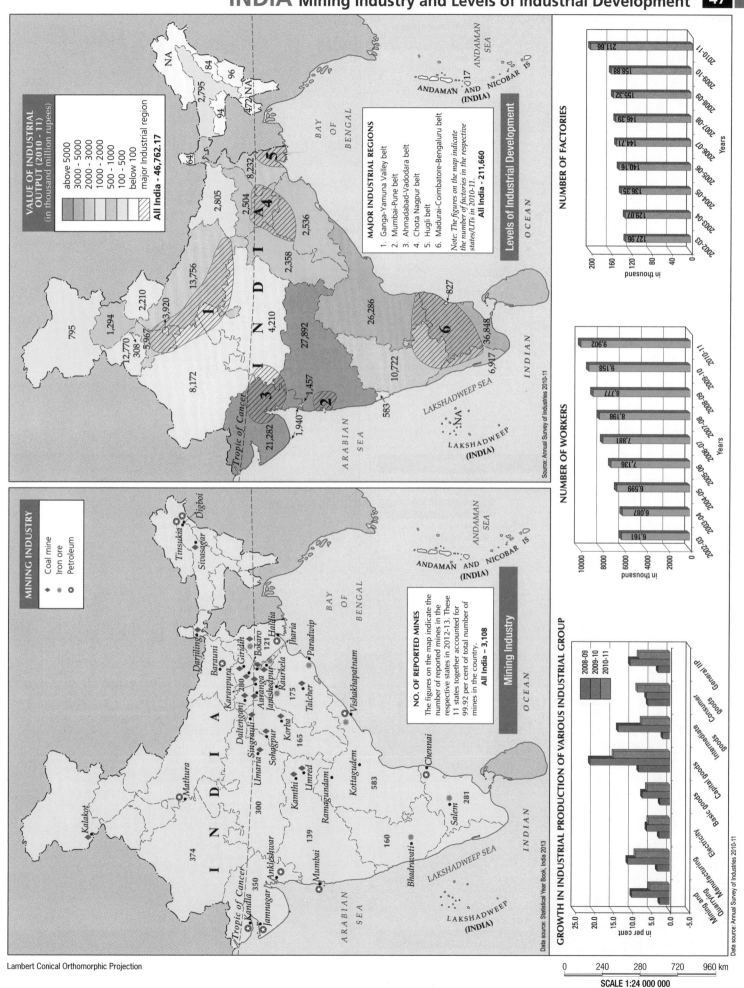

VALUE OF INDUSTRIAL OUTPUT (2010-11) (in thousand million rupees)

- above 5000
- 3000 - 5000
- 2000 - 3000
- 1000 - 2000
- 500 - 1000
- 100 - 500
- below 100
- major Industrial region

All India - 46,762.17

MAJOR INDUSTRIAL REGIONS

1. Ganga-Yamuna Valley belt
2. Mumbai-Pune belt
3. Ahmadabad-Vadodara belt
4. Chota Nagpur belt
5. Hugli belt
6. Madurai-Coimbatore-Bengaluru belt

Note: The figures on the map indicate the number of factories in the respective states/UTs in 2010-11.

All India - 211,660

Levels of Industrial Development

Source: Annual Survey of Industries 2010-11

NUMBER OF FACTORIES

NUMBER OF WORKERS

GROWTH IN INDUSTRIAL PRODUCTION OF VARIOUS INDUSTRIAL GROUP

- 2008-09
- 2009-10
- 2010-11

Data source: Annual Survey of Industries 2010-11

MINING INDUSTRY

- Coal mine
- Iron ore
- Petroleum

NO. OF REPORTED MINES

The figures on the map indicate the number of reported mines in the respective states in 2012-13. These 11 states together accounted for 99.92 per cent of total number of mines in the country.

All India – 3,108

Mining Industry

Data source: Statistical Year Book, India 2013

Lambert Conical Orthomorphic Projection

0   240   280   720   960 km

SCALE 1:24 000 000

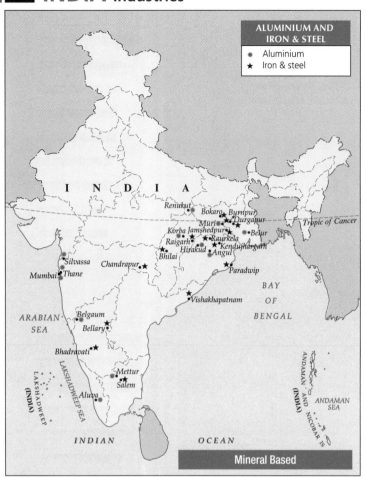

ALUMINIUM AND IRON & STEEL
- Aluminium
- ★ Iron & steel

Mineral Based

Srinagar, Renukut, Bokaro, Burnpur, Durgapur, Muri, Korba, Jamshedpur, Belur, Raigarh, Raurkela, Hirakud, Kendujhargarh, Bhilai, Angul, Silvassa, Chandrapur, Paradwip, Mumbai, Thane, Vishakhapatnam, Belgaum, Bellary, ARABIAN SEA, Bhadravati, Mettur, Salem, Aluva, LAKSHADWEEP (INDIA), LAKSHADWEEP SEA, BAY OF BENGAL, ANDAMAN AND NICOBAR IS, ANDAMAN SEA, INDIAN OCEAN, Tropic of Cancer, I N D I A

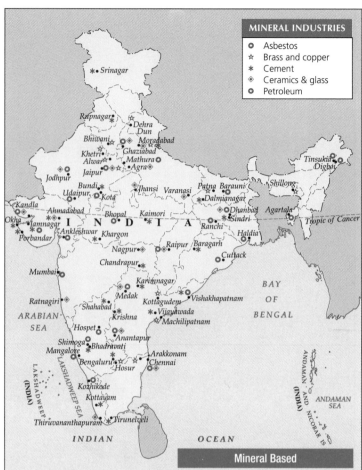

MINERAL INDUSTRIES
- ⊙ Asbestos
- ☆ Brass and copper
- ✳ Cement
- ◈ Ceramics & glass
- ◉ Petroleum

Mineral Based

Srinagar, Rupnagar, Dehra Dun, Bhiwani, Moradabad, Khetri, Ghaziabad, Alwar, Mathura, Agra, Jodhpur, Jaipur, Tinsukia, Digboi, Bundi, Jhansi, Varanasi, Patna, Barauni, Shillong, Udaipur, Kota, Dalmianagar, Kandla, Ahmadabad, Bhopal, Kaimori, Dhanbad, Agartala, Okha, Jamnagar, Sindri, Ranchi, Porbandar, Ankleshwar, Khargon, Haldia, Nagpur, Raipur, Baragarh, Mumbai, Chandrapur, Cuttack, Karimnagar, Ratnagiri, Medak, Kottagudem, Vishakhapatnam, Shahabad, Krishna, Vijayawada, Machilipatnam, Hospet, Anantpur, Shimoga, Bhadravati, Arakkonam, Mangalore, Bengaluru, Chennai, Hosur, Kozhikode, Kottayam, Thiruvananthapuram, Tirunelveli, ARABIAN SEA, BAY OF BENGAL, LAKSHADWEEP (INDIA), LAKSHADWEEP SEA, ANDAMAN AND NICOBAR IS, ANDAMAN SEA, INDIAN OCEAN, Tropic of Cancer, I N D I A

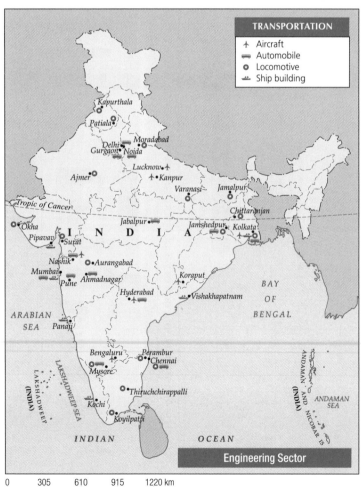

TRANSPORTATION
- ✈ Aircraft
- 🚌 Automobile
- ⊙ Locomotive
- ⛴ Ship building

Engineering Sector

Kapurthala, Patiala, Delhi, Moradabad, Gurgaon, Noida, Ajmer, Lucknow, Kanpur, Varanasi, Jamalpur, Chittaranjan, Jabalpur, Jamshedpur, Kolkata, Okha, Pipavav, Surat, Nashik, Aurangabad, Mumbai, Ahmadnagar, Pune, Koraput, Hyderabad, Vishakhapatnam, Panaji, Bengaluru, Perambur, Chennai, Mysore, Thiruchchirappalli, Kochi, Koyilpatti, ARABIAN SEA, BAY OF BENGAL, LAKSHADWEEP SEA, LAKSHADWEEP (INDIA), ANDAMAN AND NICOBAR IS, ANDAMAN SEA, INDIAN OCEAN, Tropic of Cancer, I N D I A

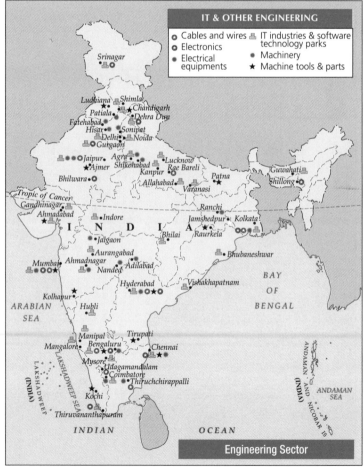

IT & OTHER ENGINEERING
- ⊙ Cables and wires
- ◉ Electronics
- ● Electrical equipments
- 🖳 IT industries & software technology parks
- ● Machinery
- ★ Machine tools & parts

Engineering Sector

Srinagar, Ludhiana, Shimla, Chandigarh, Patiala, Dehra Dun, Fatehabad, Sonipat, Hisar, Delhi, Noida, Gurgaon, Jaipur, Agra, Lucknow, Ajmer, Shikohabad, Rae Bareli, Kanpur, Patna, Guwahati, Bhilwara, Allahabad, Varanasi, Shillong, Gandhinagar, Ranchi, Ahmadabad, Indore, Jamshedpur, Kolkata, Jalgaon, Bhilai, Raurkela, Aurangabad, Bhubaneshwar, Mumbai, Ahmadnagar, Nanded, Adilabad, Hyderabad, Vishakhapatnam, Kolhapur, Hubli, Manipal, Tirupati, Mangalore, Bengaluru, Chennai, Mysore, Udagamandalam, Coimbatore, Thiruchchirappalli, Kochi, Thiruvananthapuram, ARABIAN SEA, BAY OF BENGAL, LAKSHADWEEP SEA, LAKSHADWEEP (INDIA), ANDAMAN AND NICOBAR IS, ANDAMAN SEA, INDIAN OCEAN, Tropic of Cancer, I N D I A

0   305   610   915   1220 km

SCALE 1:30 500 000

Lambert Conical Orthomorphic Projection

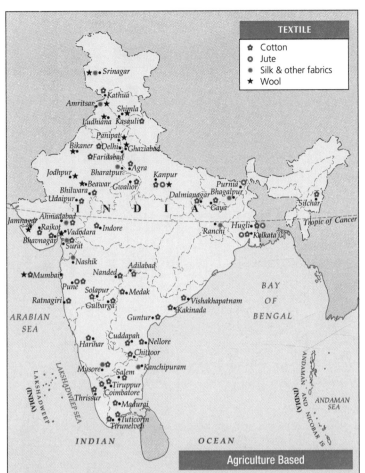

TEXTILE

- ✿ Cotton
- ◉ Jute
- ✳ Silk & other fabrics
- ★ Wool

Agriculture Based

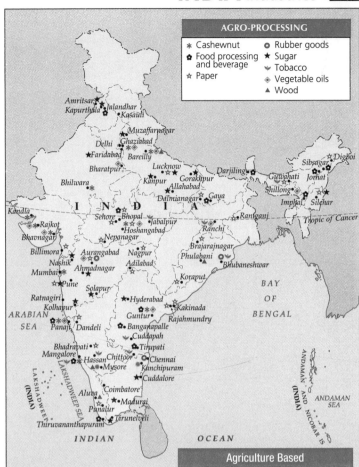

AGRO-PROCESSING

- ✳ Cashewnut
- ✿ Food processing and beverage
- ✪ Paper
- ◉ Rubber goods
- ★ Sugar
- ⚘ Tobacco
- ◈ Vegetable oils
- ▲ Wood

Agriculture Based

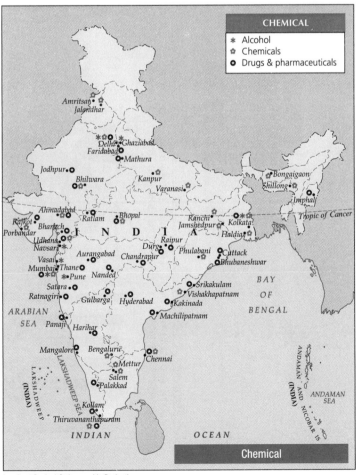

CHEMICAL

- ✳ Alcohol
- ✿ Chemicals
- ◉ Drugs & pharmaceuticals

Chemical

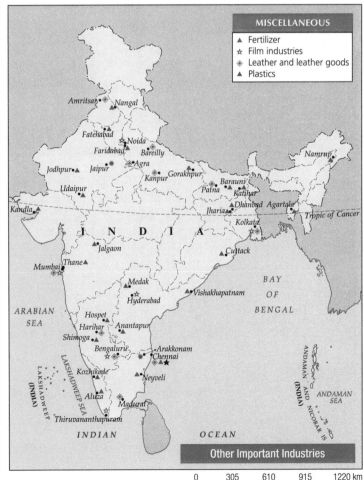

MISCELLANEOUS

- ▲ Fertilizer
- ★ Film industries
- ◈ Leather and leather goods
- ▲ Plastics

Other Important Industries

Lambert Conical Orthomorphic Projection

0   305   610   915   1220 km

SCALE 1:30 500 000

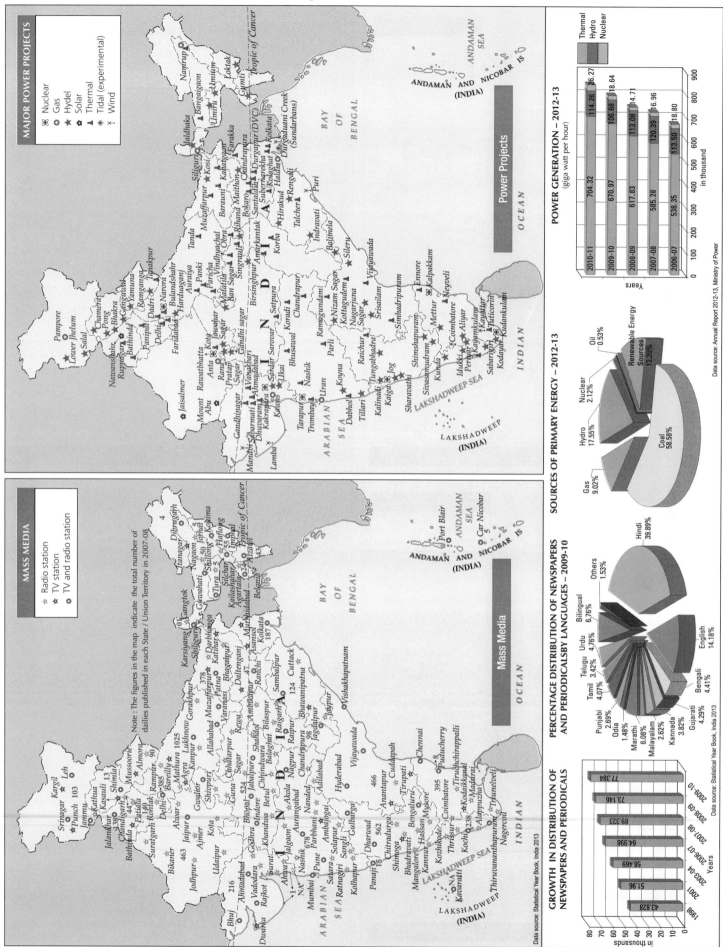

MAJOR POWER PROJECTS

- ⊗ Nuclear
- ⊗ Gas
- ★ Hydel
- ❀ Solar
- ▲ Thermal
- ◢ Tidal (experimental)
- ⅄ Wind

Power Projects

MASS MEDIA

- ★ Radio station
- ★ TV station
- ◉ TV and radio station

Note : The figures in the map indicate the total number of dailies published in each State / Union Territory in 2007-08

Data source: Statistical Year Book, India 2013

Mass Media

SCALE 1:24 000 000

0   240   480   720   960 km

POWER GENERATION – 2012-13
(giga watt per hour)

Years	Thermal	Hydro	Nuclear
2010-11	704.32	114.26	26.27
2009-10	670.97	106.68	18.64
2008-09	617.83	113.08	14.71
2007-08	585.28	120.39	16.96
2006-07	538.35	113.50	18.80

in thousand

Data source: Annual Report 2012-13, Ministry of Power

SOURCES OF PRIMARY ENERGY – 2012-13

- Coal 58.58%
- Hydro 17.55%
- Renewable Energy Sources 12.20%
- Gas 9.02%
- Nuclear 2.12%
- Oil 0.53%

Data source: Statistical Year Book, India 2013

PERCENTAGE DISTRIBUTION OF NEWSPAPERS AND PERIODICALS BY LANGUAGES – 2009-10

- Hindi 39.89%
- English 14.18%
- Bilingual 6.76%
- Marathi 6.08%
- Urdu 4.76%
- Bengali 4.41%
- Gujarati 4.29%
- Tamil 4.07%
- Kannada 3.82%
- Telugu 3.42%
- Punjabi 2.69%
- Malayalam 2.62%
- Others 1.53%
- Odia 1.48%

GROWTH IN DISTRIBUTION OF NEWSPAPERS AND PERIODICALS

Years	in thousands
1998	43.828
2001	51.96
2003-04	58.469
2006-07	64.998
2007-08	69.323
2008-09	73.146
2009-10	77.384

Lambert Conical Orthomorphic Projection

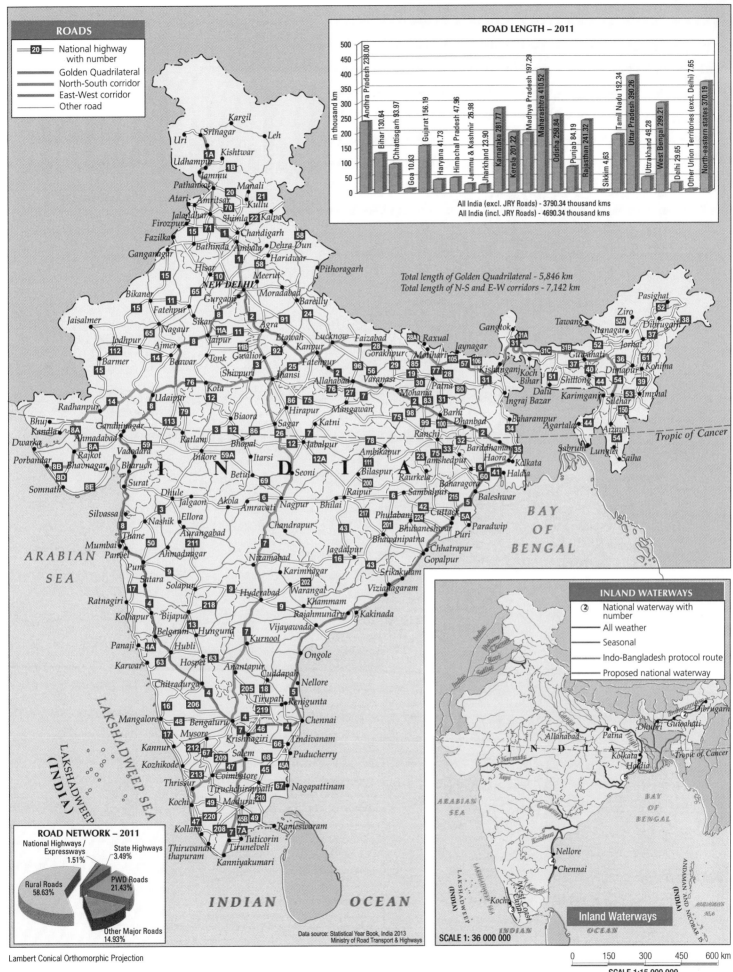

ROADS

- 20 National highway with number
- Golden Quadrilateral
- North-South corridor
- East-West corridor
- Other road

ROAD LENGTH – 2011

in thousand km

- Andhra Pradesh 238.00
- Bihar 130.64
- Chhattisgarh 93.97
- Goa 10.63
- Gujarat 156.19
- Haryana 41.73
- Himachal Pradesh 47.96
- Jammu & Kashmir 26.98
- Jharkhand 23.90
- Karnataka 281.77
- Kerala 201.22
- Madhya Pradesh 197.29
- Maharashtra 410.52
- Odisha 258.84
- Punjab 84.19
- Rajasthan 241.32
- Sikkim 4.63
- Tamil Nadu 192.34
- Uttar Pradesh 390.26
- Uttrakhand 49.28
- West Bengal 299.21
- Delhi 29.65
- Other Union Territories (excl. Delhi) 7.65
- North-eastern states 370.19

All India (excl. JRY Roads) - 3790.34 thousand kms
All India (incl. JRY Roads) - 4690.34 thousand kms

Total length of Golden Quadrilateral - 5,846 km
Total length of N-S and E-W corridors - 7,142 km

INLAND WATERWAYS

- 2 National waterway with number
- All weather
- Seasonal
- Indo-Bangladesh protocol route
- Proposed national waterway

ROAD NETWORK – 2011

- National Highways / Expressways 1.51%
- State Highways 3.49%
- PWD Roads 21.43%
- Rural Roads 58.63%
- Other Major Roads 14.93%

Data source: Statistical Year Book, India 2013
Ministry of Road Transport & Highways

Inland Waterways

SCALE 1: 36 000 000

Lambert Conical Orthomorphic Projection

ARABIAN SEA

BAY OF BENGAL

INDIAN OCEAN

LAKSHADWEEP (INDIA)

LAKSHADWEEP SEA

Tropic of Cancer

0   150   300   450   600 km
SCALE 1:15 000 000

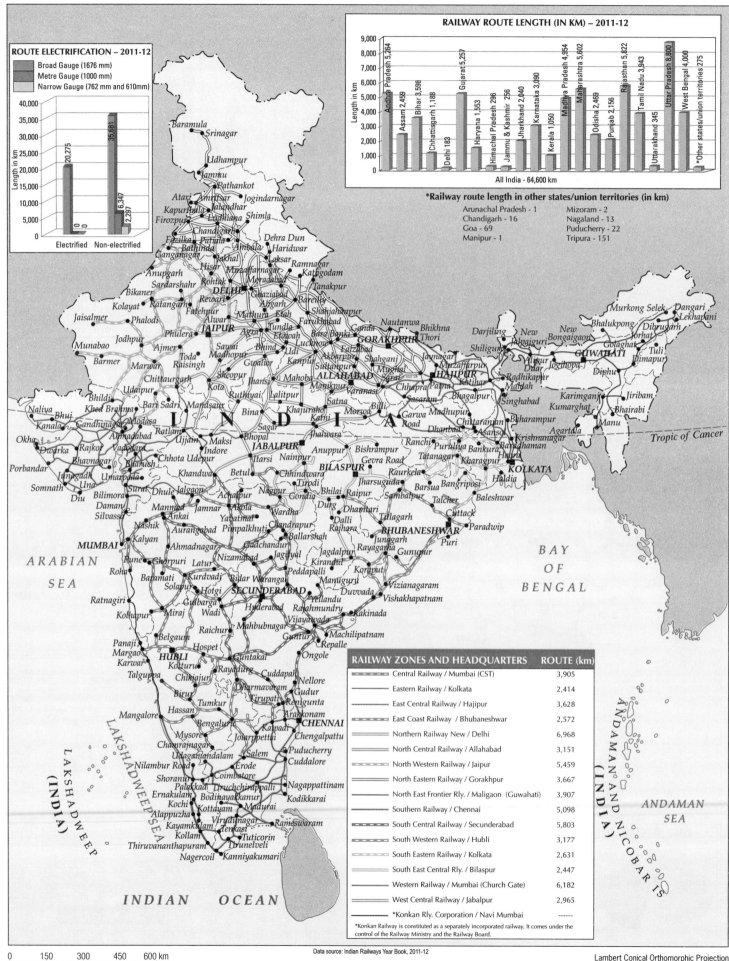

ROUTE ELECTRIFICATION – 2011-12
- Broad Gauge (1676 mm)
- Metre Gauge (1000 mm)
- Narrow Gauge (762 mm and 610mm)

RAILWAY ROUTE LENGTH (IN KM) – 2011-12

Andhra Pradesh 5,264; Assam 2,459; Bihar 3,598; Chhattisgarh 1,188; Delhi 183; Gujarat 5,257; Haryana 1,553; Himachal Pradesh 296; Jammu & Kashmir 256; Jharkhand 2,040; Karnataka 3,090; Kerala 1,050; Madhya Pradesh 4,954; Maharashtra 5,602; Odisha 2,469; Punjab 2,156; Rajasthan 5,822; Tamil Nadu 3,943; Uttarakhand 345; Uttar Pradesh 8,800; West Bengal 4,000; *Other states/union territories 275

All India - 64,600 km

*Railway route length in other states/union territories (in km)

Arunachal Pradesh - 1	Mizoram - 2
Chandigarh - 16	Nagaland - 13
Goa - 69	Puducherry - 22
Manipur - 1	Tripura - 151

RAILWAY ZONES AND HEADQUARTERS — ROUTE (km)

Railway Zone / Headquarters	ROUTE (km)
Central Railway / Mumbai (CST)	3,905
Eastern Railway / Kolkata	2,414
East Central Railway / Hajipur	3,628
East Coast Railway / Bhubaneshwar	2,572
Northern Railway New / Delhi	6,968
North Central Railway / Allahabad	3,151
North Western Railway / Jaipur	5,459
North Eastern Railway / Gorakhpur	3,667
North East Frontier Rly. / Maligaon (Guwahati)	3,907
Southern Railway / Chennai	5,098
South Central Railway / Secunderabad	5,803
South Western Railway / Hubli	3,177
South Eastern Railway / Kolkata	2,631
South East Central Rly. / Bilaspur	2,447
Western Railway / Mumbai (Church Gate)	6,182
West Central Railway / Jabalpur	2,965
*Konkan Rly. Corporation / Navi Mumbai	------

*Konkan Railway is constituted as a separately incorporated railway. It comes under the control of the Railway Ministry and the Railway Board.

ARABIAN SEA

BAY OF BENGAL

LAKSHADWEEP (INDIA)

LAKSHADWEEP SEA

ANDAMAN AND NICOBAR IS (INDIA)

ANDAMAN SEA

INDIAN OCEAN

Tropic of Cancer

Data source: Indian Railways Year Book, 2011-12

Lambert Conical Orthomorphic Projection

0   150   300   450   600 km

SCALE 1:15 000 000

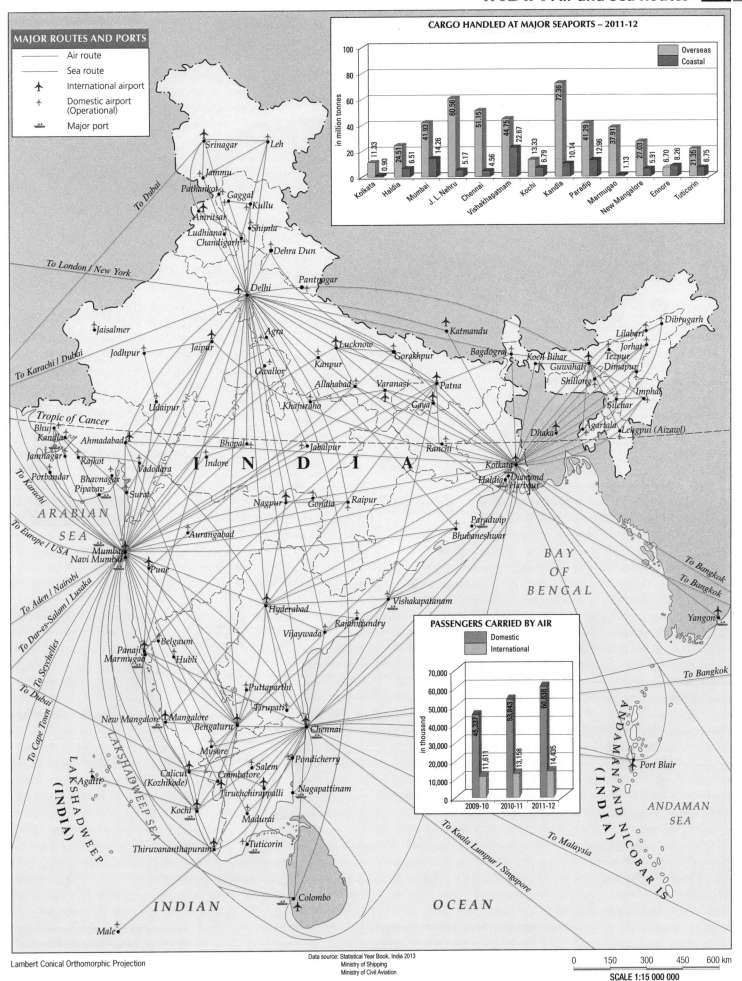

MAJOR ROUTES AND PORTS

- Air route
- Sea route
- ✈ International airport
- ✈ Domestic airport (Operational)
- ⚓ Major port

CARGO HANDLED AT MAJOR SEAPORTS – 2011-12

in million tonnes

- Overseas
- Coastal

Port	Overseas	Coastal
Kolkata	11.33	0.90
Haldia	24.51	6.51
Mumbai	41.93	14.26
J. L. Nehru	60.56	5.17
Chennai	51.15	4.56
Vishakhapatnam	44.75	22.67
Kochi	13.33	6.79
Kandla	72.36	10.14
Paradip	41.29	12.96
Marmugao	37.91	1.13
New Mangalore	27.03	5.91
Ennore	6.70	8.26
Tuticorin	21.35	6.75

PASSENGERS CARRIED BY AIR

- Domestic
- International

in thousand

Year	Domestic	International
2009-10	45,337	11,611
2010-11	53,843	13,158
2011-12	60,838	14,435

ARABIAN SEA

LAKSHADWEEP SEA

LAKSHADWEEP (INDIA)

INDIAN OCEAN

I N D I A

BAY OF BENGAL

ANDAMAN AND NICOBAR IS. (INDIA)

ANDAMAN SEA

Tropic of Cancer

To Dubai
To London / New York
To Karachi / Dubai
To Karachi
To Europe / USA
To Aden / Nairobi
To Dar-es-Salam / Lusaka
To Seychelles
To Dubai
To Cape Town
To Bangkok
To Bangkok
To Bangkok
To Kuala Lumpur / Singapore
To Malaysia

Lambert Conical Orthomorphic Projection

Data source: Statistical Year Book, India 2013
Ministry of Shipping
Ministry of Civil Aviation

0 150 300 450 600 km

SCALE 1:15 000 000

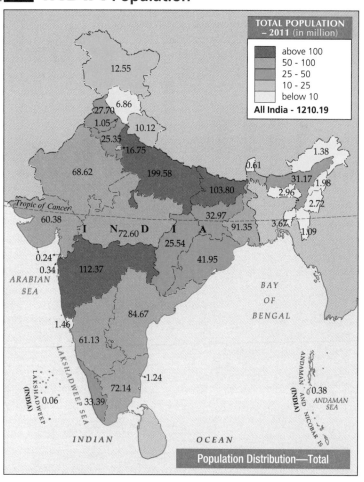

TOTAL POPULATION
– 2011 (in million)

above 100
50 - 100
25 - 50
10 - 25
below 10

All India - 1210.19

12.55

27.70 6.86
1.05 10.12
25.35
16.75
68.62 199.58
103.80
0.61 31.17 1.38
2.96 1.98
32.97 2.72
60.38 I N 72.60 D I A 91.35 3.67 1.09
25.54
0.24 41.95
0.34 112.37
ARABIAN
SEA
84.67 BAY OF BENGAL
1.46
61.13
1.24
72.14 0.38
33.39
0.06
INDIAN OCEAN

Population Distribution—Total

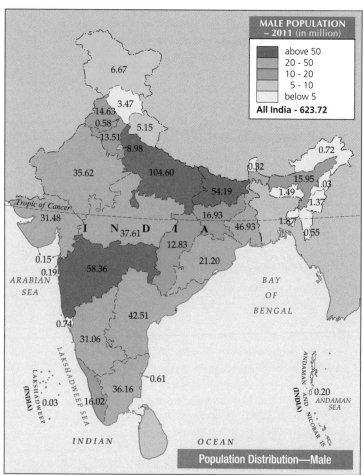

MALE POPULATION
– 2011 (in million)

above 50
20 - 50
10 - 20
5 - 10
below 5

All India - 623.72

6.67

14.63 3.47
0.58 5.15
13.51
8.98
35.62 104.60
54.19
0.32 15.95 0.72
1.49 1.03
16.93 1.37
31.48 I N 37.61 D I A 46.93 1.87 0.55
12.83
0.15 21.20
0.19 58.36
ARABIAN
SEA
42.51 BAY OF BENGAL
0.74
31.06
0.61
36.16 0.20
16.02
0.03
INDIAN OCEAN

Population Distribution—Male

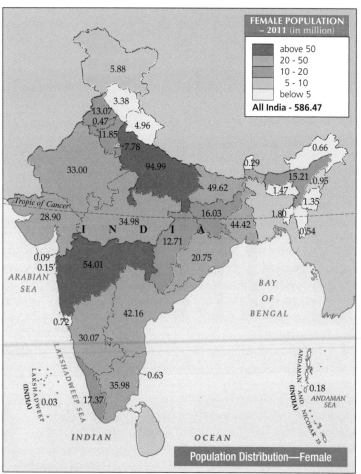

FEMALE POPULATION
– 2011 (in million)

above 50
20 - 50
10 - 20
5 - 10
below 5

All India - 586.47

5.88

13.07 3.38
0.47 4.96
11.85
7.78
33.00 94.99
49.62
0.29 15.21 0.66
1.47 0.95
16.03 1.35
28.90 I N D 34.98 I A 44.42 1.80 0.54
12.71
0.09 20.75
0.15 54.01
ARABIAN
SEA
42.16 BAY OF BENGAL
0.72
30.07
0.63
35.98 0.18
17.37
0.03
INDIAN OCEAN

Population Distribution—Female

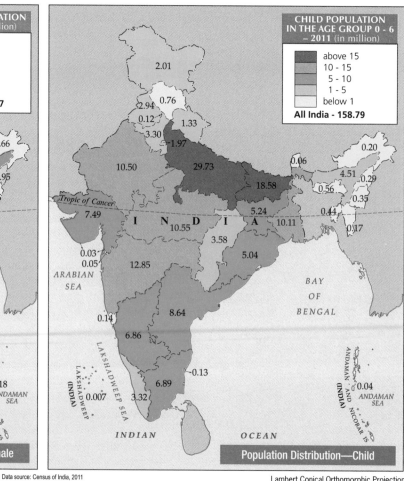

CHILD POPULATION
IN THE AGE GROUP 0 - 6
– 2011 (in million)

above 15
10 - 15
5 - 10
1 - 5
below 1

All India - 158.79

2.01

2.94 0.76
0.12 1.33
3.30
1.97
10.50 29.73
18.58
0.06 4.51 0.20
0.56 0.29
5.24 0.35
7.49 I N 10.55 D I A 10.11 0.44 0.17
3.58
0.03 5.04
0.05 12.85
ARABIAN
SEA
8.64 BAY OF BENGAL
0.14
6.86
0.13
6.89 0.04
3.32
0.007
INDIAN OCEAN

Population Distribution—Child

0   305   610   915   1220 km

SCALE 1:30 500 000

Data source: Census of India, 2011

Lambert Conical Orthomorphic Projection

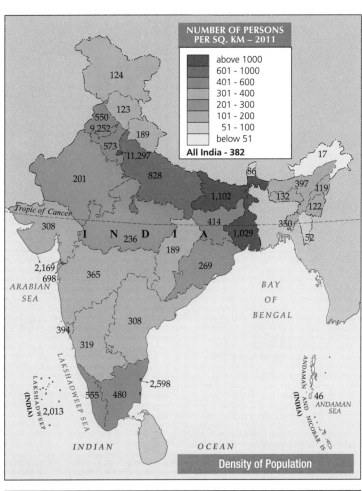

NUMBER OF PERSONS PER SQ. KM – 2011

above 1000
601 – 1000
401 – 600
301 – 400
201 – 300
101 – 200
51 – 100
below 51

All India – 382

124
123
550
9,252
189
573
11,297
201
828
17
86
397
119
132
122
1,102
350
414
236
1,029
52
189
308
269
2,169
698
365
ARABIAN SEA
BAY OF BENGAL
308
394
319
555
480
2,598
LAKSHADWEEP (INDIA)
2,013
ANDAMAN AND NICOBAR IS (INDIA)
46
ANDAMAN SEA
INDIAN OCEAN

Tropic of Cancer

Density of Population

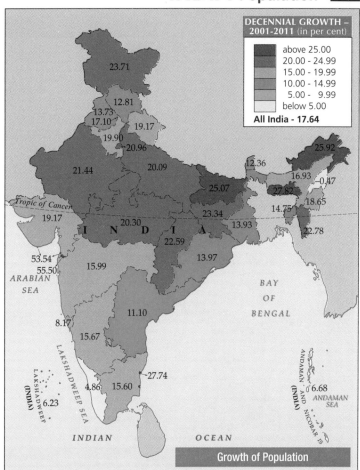

DECENNIAL GROWTH – 2001-2011 (in per cent)

above 25.00
20.00 – 24.99
15.00 – 19.99
10.00 – 14.99
5.00 – 9.99
below 5.00

All India – 17.64

23.71
12.81
13.73
17.10
19.17
19.90
20.96
20.09
25.92
21.44
12.36
16.93
25.07
27.82
23.34
14.75
18.65
13.93
22.78
19.17
20.30
22.59
13.97
53.54
55.50
ARABIAN SEA
15.99
8.17
11.10
15.67
BAY OF BENGAL
27.74
4.86
15.60
LAKSHADWEEP (INDIA)
6.23
ANDAMAN AND NICOBAR IS (INDIA)
6.68
ANDAMAN SEA
INDIAN OCEAN

Tropic of Cancer

Growth of Population

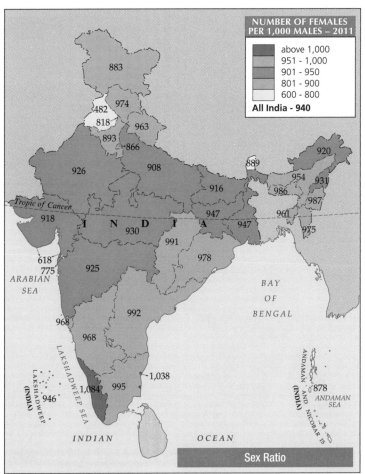

NUMBER OF FEMALES PER 1,000 MALES – 2011

above 1,000
951 – 1,000
901 – 950
801 – 900
600 – 800

All India – 940

883
974
482
818
963
893
866
920
926
908
889
954
931
916
986
987
947
961
930
947
975
991
918
978
618
775
925
BAY OF BENGAL
ARABIAN SEA
992
968
968
1,038
LAKSHADWEEP (INDIA)
1,084
995
878
946
ANDAMAN AND NICOBAR IS (INDIA)
ANDAMAN SEA
INDIAN OCEAN

Tropic of Cancer

Sex Ratio

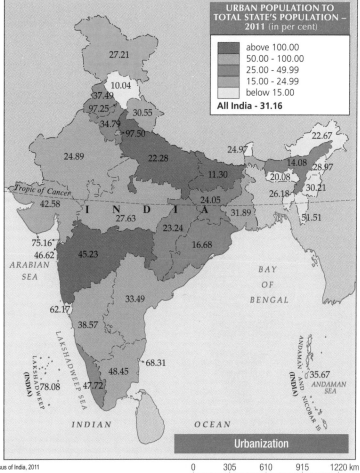

URBAN POPULATION TO TOTAL STATE'S POPULATION – 2011 (in per cent)

above 100.00
50.00 – 100.00
25.00 – 49.99
15.00 – 24.99
below 15.00

All India – 31.16

27.21
10.04
37.49
97.25
30.55
34.79
97.50
22.67
24.89
24.97
14.08
28.97
22.28
20.08
11.30
30.21
26.18
42.58
24.05
31.89
27.63
51.51
23.24
75.16
46.62
16.68
45.23
62.17
33.49
38.57
68.31
48.45
47.72
78.08
35.67
LAKSHADWEEP (INDIA)
ANDAMAN AND NICOBAR IS (INDIA)
ANDAMAN SEA
ARABIAN SEA
BAY OF BENGAL
INDIAN OCEAN

Tropic of Cancer

Urbanization

Lambert Conical Orthomorphic Projection

Data source: Census of India, 2011

0   305   610   915   1220 km

SCALE 1:30 500 000

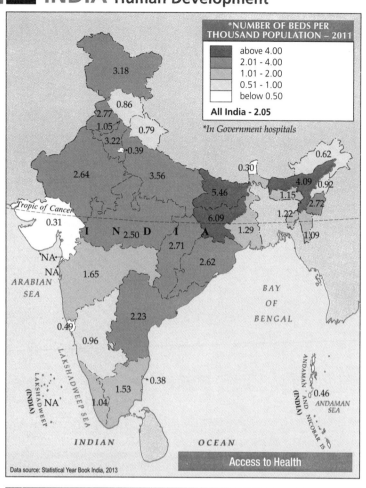

*NUMBER OF BEDS PER THOUSAND POPULATION – 2011

- above 4.00
- 2.01 - 4.00
- 1.01 - 2.00
- 0.51 - 1.00
- below 0.50

All India - 2.05

In Government hospitals

3.18
0.86
2.77
1.05
0.79
3.22
0.39
2.64
3.56
0.62
0.30
4.09
0.92
5.46
1.15
2.72
6.09
1.22
0.31
2.50
1.29
1.09
2.71
2.62
1.65
2.23
0.49
0.96
0.38
1.53
1.04
NA
NA
NA
0.46

Tropic of Cancer

I N D I A

ARABIAN SEA
BAY OF BENGAL
LAKSHADWEEP (INDIA)
LAKSHADWEEP SEA
ANDAMAN AND NICOBAR IS (INDIA)
ANDAMAN SEA
INDIAN OCEAN

Data source: Statistical Year Book India, 2013

Access to Health

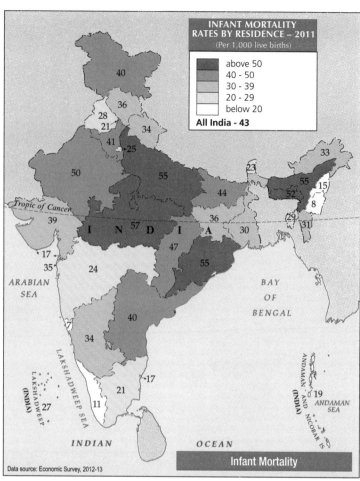

INFANT MORTALITY RATES BY RESIDENCE – 2011
(Per 1,000 live births)

- above 50
- 40 - 50
- 30 - 39
- 20 - 29
- below 20

All India - 43

40
36
28
21
34
41
25
50
55
23
33
44
55
52
15
36
8
39
57
30
29
31
17
47
35
24
55
40
7
34
21
17
11
27
19

Tropic of Cancer

I N D I A

ARABIAN SEA
BAY OF BENGAL
LAKSHADWEEP (INDIA)
LAKSHADWEEP SEA
ANDAMAN AND NICOBAR IS (INDIA)
ANDAMAN SEA
INDIAN OCEAN

Data source: Economic Survey, 2012-13

Infant Mortality

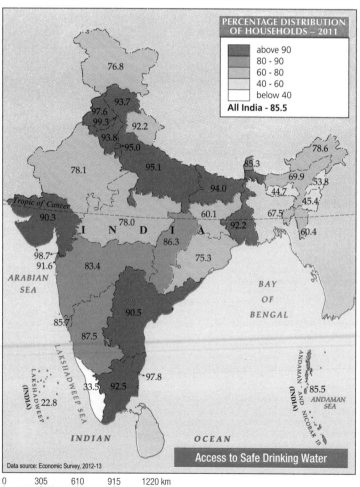

PERCENTAGE DISTRIBUTION OF HOUSEHOLDS – 2011

- above 90
- 80 - 90
- 60 - 80
- 40 - 60
- below 40

All India - 85.5

76.8
93.7
97.6
99.3
92.2
93.8
95.0
78.1
95.1
78.6
85.3
69.9
53.8
44.7
94.0
45.4
60.1
67.5
90.3
78.0
92.2
60.4
86.3
98.7
91.6
83.4
75.3
85.7
90.5
87.5
97.8
33.5
92.5
22.8
85.5

Tropic of Cancer

I N D I A

ARABIAN SEA
BAY OF BENGAL
LAKSHADWEEP (INDIA)
LAKSHADWEEP SEA
ANDAMAN AND NICOBAR IS (INDIA)
ANDAMAN SEA
INDIAN OCEAN

Data source: Economic Survey, 2012-13

Access to Safe Drinking Water

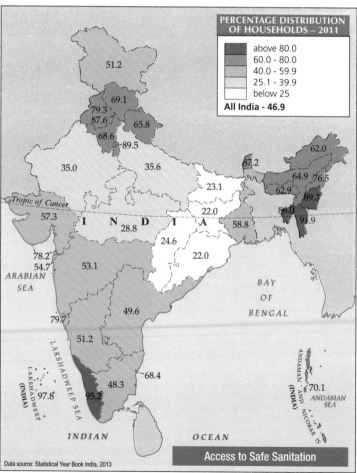

PERCENTAGE DISTRIBUTION OF HOUSEHOLDS – 2011

- above 80.0
- 60.0 - 80.0
- 40.0 - 59.9
- 25.1 - 39.9
- below 25

All India - 46.9

51.2
69.1
79.3
87.6
65.8
68.6
89.5
87.2
62.0
35.0
35.6
64.9
76.5
23.1
62.9
89.3
22.0
86.0
57.3
28.8
58.8
91.9
78.2
24.6
54.7
22.0
53.1
79.7
49.6
51.2
48.3
68.4
97.8
95.2
70.1

Tropic of Cancer

I N D I A

ARABIAN SEA
BAY OF BENGAL
LAKSHADWEEP (INDIA)
LAKSHADWEEP SEA
ANDAMAN AND NICOBAR IS (INDIA)
ANDAMAN SEA
INDIAN OCEAN

Data source: Statistical Year Book India, 2013

Access to Safe Sanitation

0   305   610   915   1220 km

SCALE 1:30 500 000

Lambert Conical Orthomorphic Projection

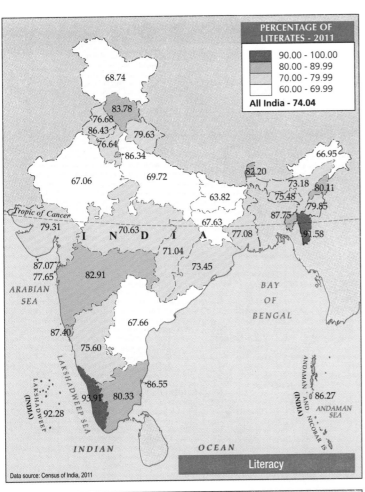

PERCENTAGE OF LITERATES - 2011

	90.00 - 100.00
	80.00 - 89.99
	70.00 - 79.99
	60.00 - 69.99

All India - 74.04

68.74
83.78
76.68
86.43
79.63
76.64
86.34
66.95
67.06
69.72
82.20
73.18
80.11
75.48
79.85
63.82
87.75
Tropic of Cancer
67.63
91.58
79.31
70.63
77.08
71.04
73.45
87.07
82.91
77.65
ARABIAN SEA
BAY OF BENGAL
67.66
87.40
75.60
86.55
LAKSHADWEEP SEA
93.91
80.33
LAKSHADWEEP (INDIA)
92.28
86.27
ANDAMAN AND NICOBAR IS
ANDAMAN SEA
INDIAN
OCEAN

Literacy

Data source: Census of India, 2011

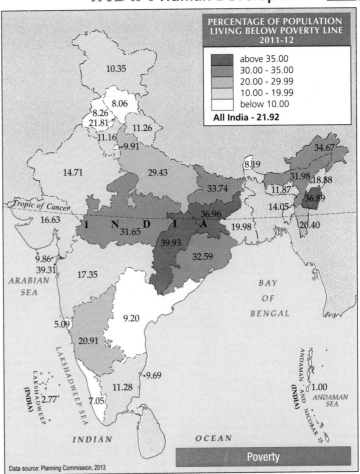

PERCENTAGE OF POPULATION LIVING BELOW POVERTY LINE 2011-12

	above 35.00
	30.00 - 35.00
	20.00 - 29.99
	10.00 - 19.99
	below 10.00

All India - 21.92

10.35
8.06
8.26
21.81
11.26
11.16
9.91
34.67
14.71
29.43
33.74
31.98
18.88
8.19
11.87
36.89
14.05
Tropic of Cancer
36.96
31.65
19.98
20.40
16.63
39.93
32.59
9.86
39.31
17.35
ARABIAN SEA
BAY OF BENGAL
5.09
9.20
20.91
11.28
9.69
LAKSHADWEEP SEA
2.77
7.05
LAKSHADWEEP (INDIA)
1.00
ANDAMAN AND NICOBAR IS
ANDAMAN SEA
INDIAN
OCEAN

Poverty

Data source: Planning Commission, 2013

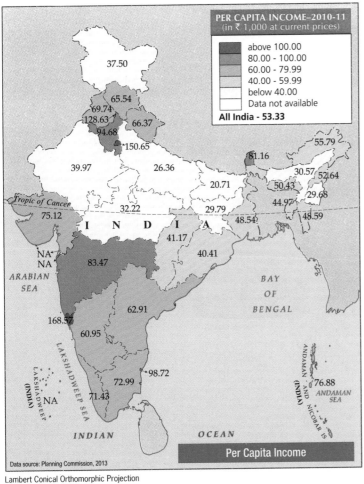

PER CAPITA INCOME–2010-11
(in ₹ 1,000 at current prices)

	above 100.00
	80.00 - 100.00
	60.00 - 79.99
	40.00 - 59.99
	below 40.00
	Data not available

All India - 53.33

37.50
65.54
69.74
128.63
66.37
94.68
150.65
55.79
81.16
39.97
26.36
30.57
52.64
20.71
50.43
29.68
44.97
Tropic of Cancer
32.22
29.79
48.54
48.59
75.12
41.17
NA
NA
40.41
83.47
ARABIAN SEA
BAY OF BENGAL
168.57
62.91
60.95
LAKSHADWEEP SEA
98.72
LAKSHADWEEP (INDIA)
72.99
NA
71.43
76.88
ANDAMAN AND NICOBAR IS
ANDAMAN SEA
INDIAN
OCEAN

Per Capita Income

Data source: Planning Commission, 2013

Lambert Conical Orthomorphic Projection

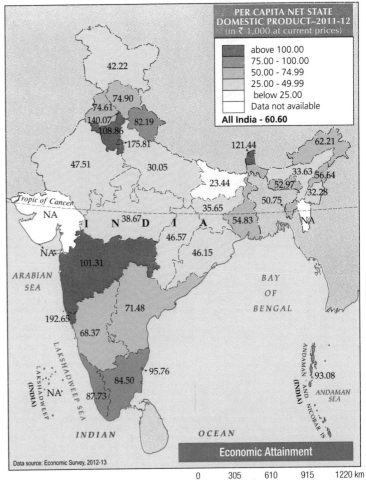

PER CAPITA NET STATE DOMESTIC PRODUCT–2011-12
(in ₹ 1,000 at current prices)

	above 100.00
	75.00 - 100.00
	50.00 - 74.99
	25.00 - 49.99
	below 25.00
	Data not available

All India - 60.60

42.22
74.90
74.61
82.19
140.07
108.86
175.81
121.44
62.21
47.51
30.05
33.63
56.64
23.44
52.97
32.28
50.75
Tropic of Cancer
NA
38.67
54.83
NA
35.65
NA
46.57
46.15
101.31
ARABIAN SEA
BAY OF BENGAL
192.65
71.48
68.37
LAKSHADWEEP SEA
95.76
LAKSHADWEEP (INDIA)
NA
84.50
93.08
ANDAMAN AND NICOBAR IS
ANDAMAN SEA
87.73
INDIAN
OCEAN

Economic Attainment

Data source: Economic Survey, 2012-13

0	305	610	915	1220 km

SCALE 1:30 500 000

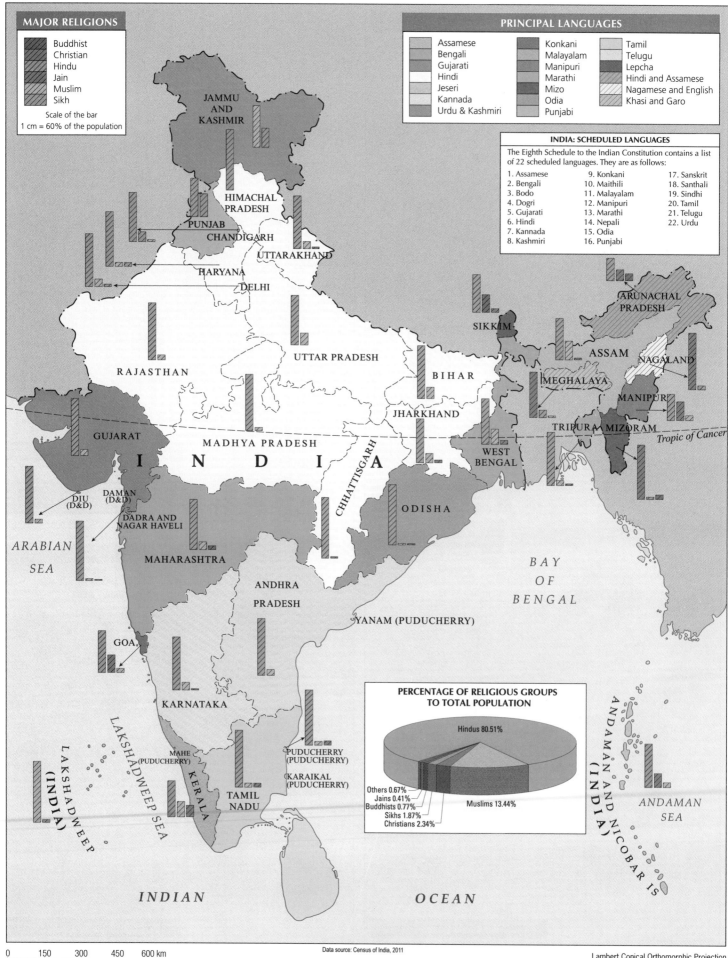

MAJOR RELIGIONS

Buddhist
Christian
Hindu
Jain
Muslim
Sikh

Scale of the bar
1 cm = 60% of the population

PRINCIPAL LANGUAGES

Assamese
Bengali
Gujarati
Hindi
Jeseri
Kannada
Urdu & Kashmiri

Konkani
Malayalam
Manipuri
Marathi
Mizo
Odia
Punjabi

Tamil
Telugu
Lepcha
Hindi and Assamese
Nagamese and English
Khasi and Garo

INDIA: SCHEDULED LANGUAGES

The Eighth Schedule to the Indian Constitution contains a list of 22 scheduled languages. They are as follows:

1. Assamese
2. Bengali
3. Bodo
4. Dogri
5. Gujarati
6. Hindi
7. Kannada
8. Kashmiri

9. Konkani
10. Maithili
11. Malayalam
12. Manipuri
13. Marathi
14. Nepali
15. Odia
16. Punjabi

17. Sanskrit
18. Santhali
19. Sindhi
20. Tamil
21. Telugu
22. Urdu

JAMMU AND KASHMIR

HIMACHAL PRADESH

PUNJAB
CHANDIGARH

HARYANA

DELHI

UTTARAKHAND

UTTAR PRADESH

RAJASTHAN

SIKKIM

ARUNACHAL PRADESH

ASSAM

NAGALAND

MEGHALAYA

MANIPUR

BIHAR

JHARKHAND

TRIPURA MIZORAM

Tropic of Cancer

GUJARAT

DIU (D&D)

DAMAN (D&D)

DADRA AND NAGAR HAVELI

MADHYA PRADESH

I N D I A

CHHATTISGARH

WEST BENGAL

ODISHA

ARABIAN SEA

MAHARASHTRA

ANDHRA PRADESH

YANAM (PUDUCHERRY)

B A Y O F B E N G A L

GOA

KARNATAKA

LAKSHADWEEP SEA

MAHE (PUDUCHERRY)

LAKSHADWEEP (INDIA)

KERALA

TAMIL NADU

PUDUCHERRY (PUDUCHERRY)

KARAIKAL (PUDUCHERRY)

ANDAMAN SEA

ANDAMAN AND NICOBAR IS (INDIA)

PERCENTAGE OF RELIGIOUS GROUPS TO TOTAL POPULATION

Hindus 80.51%

Others 0.67%
Jains 0.41%
Buddhists 0.77%
Sikhs 1.87%
Christians 2.34%

Muslims 13.44%

I N D I A N   O C E A N

0   150   300   450   600 km

SCALE 1:15 000 000

Data source: Census of India, 2011

Lambert Conical Orthomorphic Projection

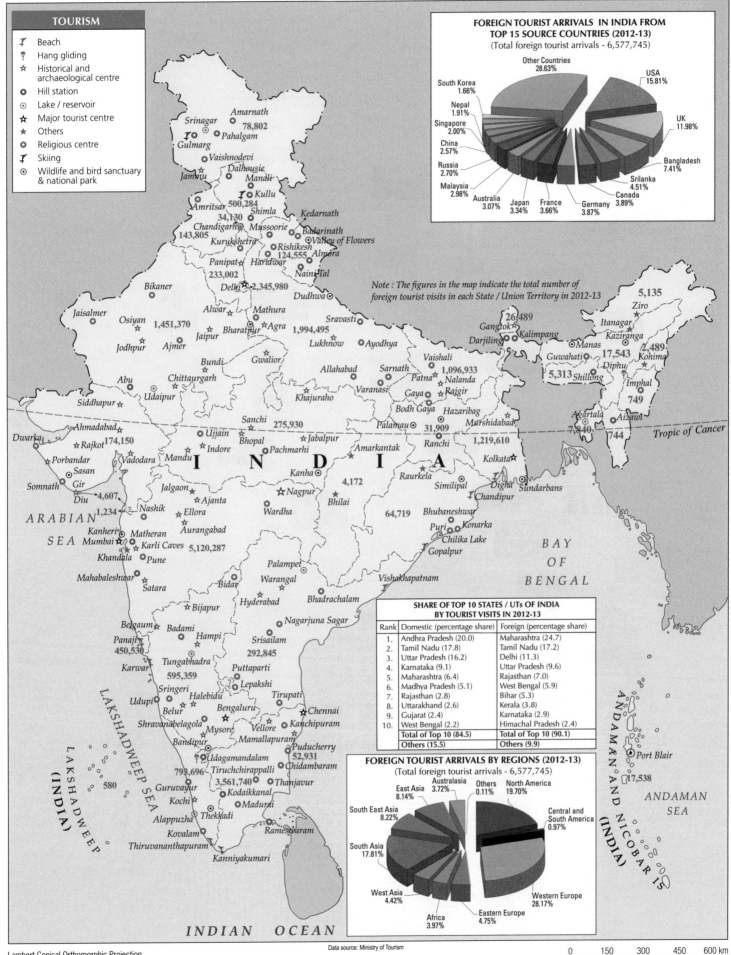

TOURISM

- ⊥ Beach
- ⚲ Hang gliding
- ★ Historical and archaeological centre
- ⊙ Hill station
- ⊙ Lake / reservoir
- ★ Major tourist centre
- ★ Others
- ⊙ Religious centre
- ⊥ Skiing
- ⊙ Wildlife and bird sanctuary & national park

FOREIGN TOURIST ARRIVALS IN INDIA FROM TOP 15 SOURCE COUNTRIES (2012-13)
(Total foreign tourist arrivals - 6,577,745)

Other Countries 28.63%, USA 15.81%, UK 11.98%, Bangladesh 7.41%, Srilanka 4.51%, Canada 3.89%, Germany 3.87%, France 3.66%, Japan 3.34%, Australia 3.07%, Malaysia 2.98%, Russia 2.70%, China 2.57%, Singapore 2.00%, Nepal 1.91%, South Korea 1.66%

Note : The figures in the map indicate the total number of foreign tourist visits in each State / Union Territory in 2012-13

SHARE OF TOP 10 STATES / UTs OF INDIA BY TOURIST VISITS IN 2012-13

Rank	Domestic (percentage share)	Foreign (percentage share)
1.	Andhra Pradesh (20.0)	Maharashtra (24.7)
2.	Tamil Nadu (17.8)	Tamil Nadu (17.2)
3.	Uttar Pradesh (16.2)	Delhi (11.3)
4.	Karnataka (9.1)	Uttar Pradesh (9.6)
5.	Maharashtra (6.4)	Rajasthan (7.0)
6.	Madhya Pradesh (5.1)	West Bengal (5.9)
7.	Rajasthan (2.8)	Bihar (5.3)
8.	Uttarakhand (2.6)	Kerala (3.8)
9.	Gujarat (2.4)	Karnataka (2.9)
10.	West Bengal (2.2)	Himachal Pradesh (2.4)
	Total of Top 10 (84.5)	Total of Top 10 (90.1)
	Others (15.5)	Others (9.9)

FOREIGN TOURIST ARRIVALS BY REGIONS (2012-13)
(Total foreign tourist arrivals - 6,577,745)

East Asia 8.14%, Australasia 3.72%, Others 0.11%, North America 19.70%, Central and South America 0.97%, South East Asia 8.22%, South Asia 17.81%, West Asia 4.42%, Africa 3.97%, Eastern Europe 4.75%, Western Europe 28.17%

Lambert Conical Orthomorphic Projection

Data source: Ministry of Tourism

SCALE 1:15 000 000

NAME OF THE WORLD HERITAGE SITES (CULTURAL)	STATE	YEAR OF INSCRIPTION ON THE WORLD HERITAGE LIST
Agra Fort	Uttar Pradesh	1983
Ajanta Caves	Maharashtra	1983
Ellora Caves	Maharashtra	1983
Taj Mahal	Uttar Pradesh	1983
Group of monuments at Mamallapuram (Mahabalipuram)	Tamil Nadu	1984
Sun Temple	Konarak, Odisha	1984
Churches and convents of Goa	Goa	1986
Fatehpur Sikri	Uttar Pradesh	1986
Group of monuments at Hampi	Karnataka	1986
Khajuraho group of monuments	Madhya Pradesh	1986
Elephanta Caves	Maharashtra	1987
Great Living Chola Temples	Tamil Nadu	1987
Group of monuments at Pattadakal	Karnataka	1987
Buddhist monuments at Sanchi	Madhya Pradesh	1989
Humayun's Tomb	Delhi	1993
Qutb Minar and its monuments	Delhi	1993
Mountain Railways of India	West Bengal and Tamil Nadu	1999, 2005
Mahabodhi Temple Complex	Bodh Gaya, Bihar	2002
Rock Shelters of Bhimbetka	Madhya Pradesh	2003

Red Fort *(Delhi)*

Humayun's Tomb *(Delhi)*

Agra Fort *(Agra)*

Fatehpur Sikri *(Agra)*

Valley of Flowers *(Uttarakhand)*

Valley of Flowers
Nanda Devi

Qutb Minar *(Delhi)*

Delhi

Nanda Devi *(Uttarakhand)*

Keoladeo Ghana *(Bharatpur)*

Keoladeo Ghana

Jaipur

Agra

Taj Mahal *(Agra)*

Darjiling Himalayan Railway

Darjiling

Manas

Manas

Kaziranga

Kaziranga

Hill Forts of Rajasthan *(Chittorgarh, Kumbhalgarh, Sawai Madhopur, Jhalawar, Jaipur and Jaisalmer)*

Jantar Mantar *(Jaipur)*

Khajuraho

Khajuraho Temple

Sanchi

Bhimbetka

I N D I A

Gaya

Mahabodhi Temple *(Bodh Gaya)*

Tropic of Cancer

Champaner-Pavagadh Archaeological Park

Pavagarh

Bhimbetka

Sanchi Stupa

Sunderbans

Sunderbans

New Moore I. (India)

B A Y
O F
B E N G A L

Ajanta

Ajanta Cave

Ellora

Ellora Cave

A R A B I A N
S E A

Elephanta Cave

Mumbai

Elephanta

Sun Temple *(Konark)*

Konark

Chhatrapati Shivaji Terminus

Pattadakal

Pattadakal

Hampi

Goa

Hampi

Basilica of Bom Jesus *(Goa)*

Western Ghats

Shore Temple *(Mamallapuram)*

Mamallapuram (Mahabalipuram)

Udagamandalam

Nilgiri Railway

Preparis I. (MYANMAR)

Coco Is (MYANMAR)

Narcondam I. (INDIA)

Barren I. (INDIA)

ANDAMAN AND NICOBAR IS (INDIA)

ANDAMAN SEA

L A K S H A D W E E P (INDIA)

LAKSHADWEEP SEA

NAME OF THE WORLD HERITAGE SITES (CULTURAL)	STATE	YEAR OF INSCRIPTION ON THE WORLD HERITAGE LIST
Champaner-Pavagadh Archaeological Park	Gujarat	2004
Chhatrapati Shivaji Terminus	Maharashtra	2004
Red Fort Complex	Delhi	2007
The Jantar Mantar	Jaipur, Rajasthan	2010
Hill Forts of Rajasthan	Rajasthan	2013

NAME OF THE WORLD HERITAGE SITES (NATURAL)	STATE	YEAR OF INSCRIPTION ON THE WORLD HERITAGE LIST
Kaziranga National Park	Assam	1985
Keoladeo National Park	Rajasthan	1985
Manas Wildlife Sanctuary	Assam	1985
Sundarbans National Park	West Bengal	1987
Nanda Devi National Park and Valley of Flowers	Uttarakhand	1988, 2005
Western Ghats	Kerala, Karnataka, Maharashtra and Tamil Nadu	2012

I N D I A N   O C E A N

Lambert Conical Orthomorphic Projection

0   150   300   450   600 km

SCALE 1:15 000 000

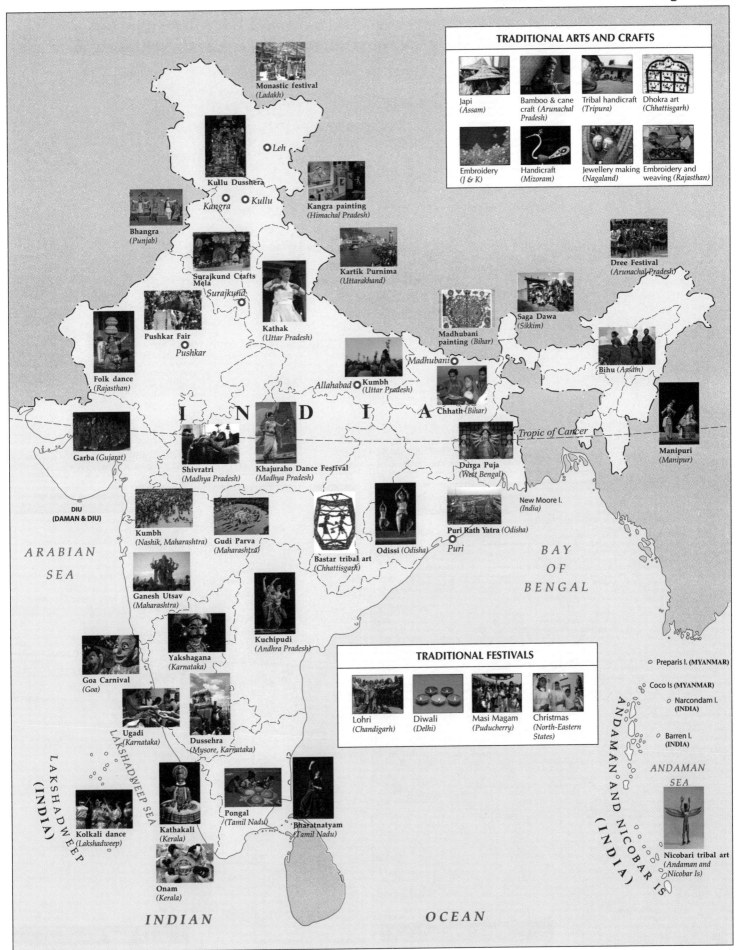

TRADITIONAL ARTS AND CRAFTS

Japi (Assam)

Bamboo & cane craft (Arunachal Pradesh)

Tribal handicraft (Tripura)

Dhokra art (Chhattisgarh)

Embroidery (J & K)

Handicraft (Mizoram)

Jewellery making (Nagaland)

Embroidery and weaving (Rajasthan)

Monastic festival (Ladakh)

Kullu Dusshera

Leh

Kangra painting (Himachal Pradesh)

Bhangra (Punjab)

Kangra

Kullu

Dree Festival (Arunachal Pradesh)

Surajkund Crafts Mela

Surajkund

Kartik Purnima (Uttarakhand)

Saga Dawa (Sikkim)

Kathak (Uttar Pradesh)

Madhubani painting (Bihar)

Bihu (Assam)

Pushkar Fair

Pushkar

Madhubani

Folk dance (Rajasthan)

Allahabad

Kumbh (Uttar Pradesh)

Chhath (Bihar)

Manipuri (Manipur)

I N D I A

Garba (Gujarat)

Shivratri (Madhya Pradesh)

Khajuraho Dance Festival (Madhya Pradesh)

Tropic of Cancer

Durga Puja (West Bengal)

DIU (DAMAN & DIU)

New Moore I. (India)

Kumbh (Nashik, Maharashtra)

Gudi Parva (Maharashtra)

Bastar tribal art (Chhattisgarh)

Odissi (Odisha)

Puri Rath Yatra (Odisha)

Puri

A R A B I A N S E A

B A Y O F B E N G A L

Ganesh Utsav (Maharashtra)

Kuchipudi (Andhra Pradesh)

Yakshagana (Karnataka)

Preparis I. (MYANMAR)

Coco Is (MYANMAR)

TRADITIONAL FESTIVALS

Lohri (Chandigarh)

Diwali (Delhi)

Masi Magam (Puducherry)

Christmas (North-Eastern States)

Narcondam I. (INDIA)

Goa Carnival (Goa)

Barren I. (INDIA)

Ugadi (Karnataka)

Dussehra (Mysore, Karnataka)

ANDAMAN AND NICOBAR IS (INDIA)

ANDAMAN SEA

L A K S H A D W E E P   S E A

LAKSHADWEEP (INDIA)

Kolkali dance (Lakshadweep)

Kathakali (Kerala)

Pongal (Tamil Nadu)

Bharatnatyam (Tamil Nadu)

Nicobari tribal art (Andaman and Nicobar Is)

Onam (Kerala)

I N D I A N   O C E A N

Lambert Conical Orthomorphic Projection

0   150   300   450   600 km

SCALE 1:15 000 000

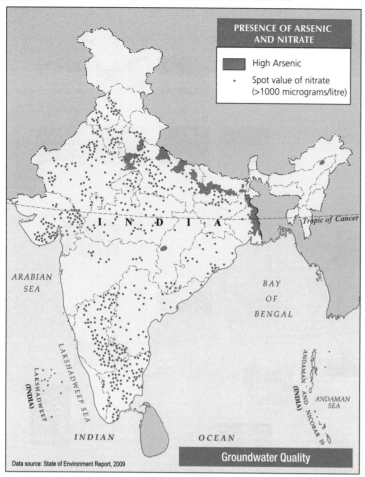

Groundwater Quality

Data source: State of Environment Report, 2009

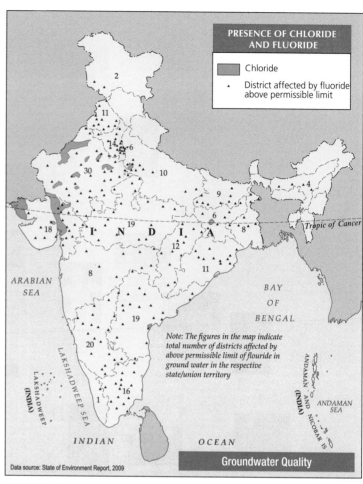

Groundwater Quality

Data source: State of Environment Report, 2009

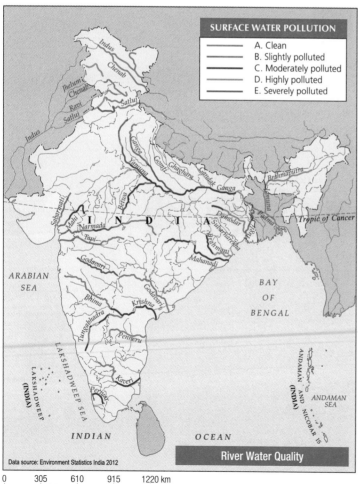

River Water Quality

Data source: Environment Statistics India 2012

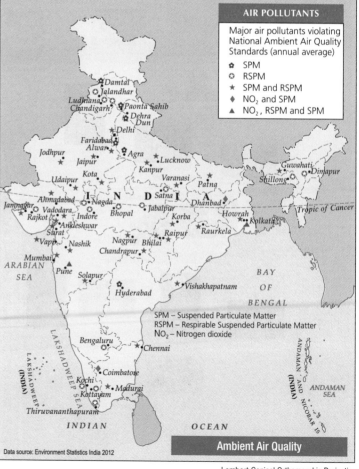

Ambient Air Quality

Data source: Environment Statistics India 2012

Lambert Conical Orthomorphic Projection

SCALE 1:30 500 000

0   305   610   915   1220 km

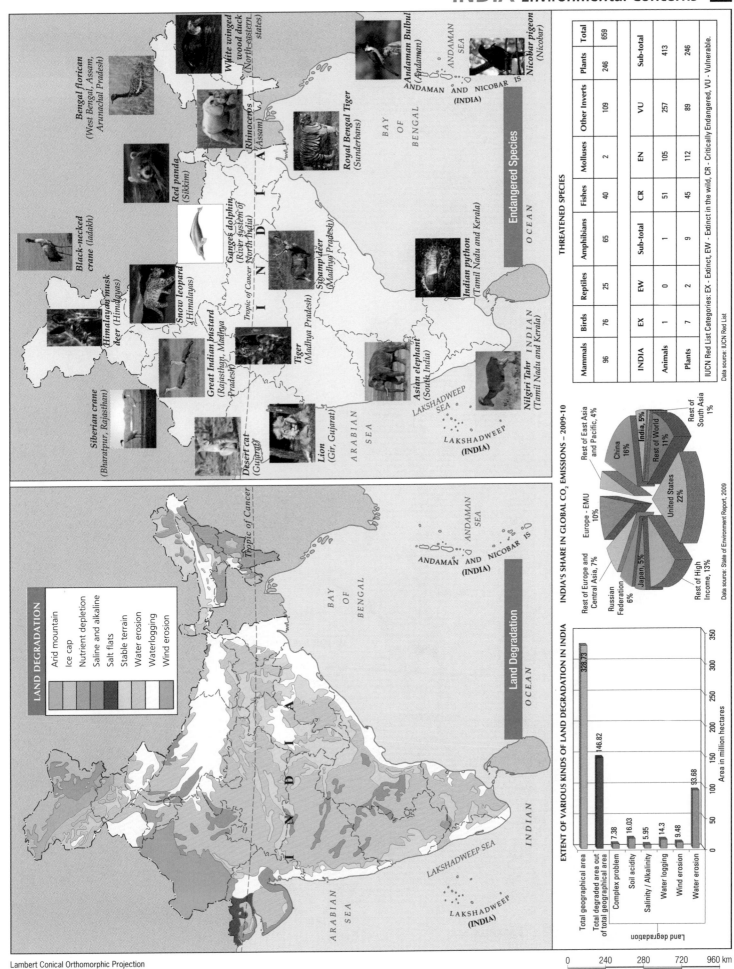

Endangered Species

Bengal florican (West Bengal, Assam, Arunachal Pradesh)
White winged wood duck (North-eastern states)
Andaman Bulbul (Andaman)
Nicobar pigeon (Nicobar)
Rhinoceros (Assam)
Royal Bengal Tiger (Sunderbans)
Red panda (Sikkim)
Himalayan musk deer (Himalayas)
Black-necked crane (Ladakh)
Snow leopard (Himalayas)
Ganges dolphin (River system of North India)
Swamp deer (Madhya Pradesh)
Great Indian bustard (Rajasthan, Madhya Pradesh)
Tiger (Madhya Pradesh)
Indian python (Tamil Nadu and Kerala)
Asian elephant (South India)
Nilgiri Tahr (Tamil Nadu and Kerala)
Siberian crane (Bharatpur, Rajasthan)
Desert cat (Gujarat)
Lion (Gir, Gujarat)

THREATENED SPECIES

Mammals	Birds	Reptiles	Amphibians	Fishes	Molluscs	Other Inverts	Plants	Total
96	76	25	65	40	2	109	246	659

INDIA	Sub-total	EX	EW	CR	EN	VU	Sub-total
Animals	1	1	0	51	105	257	413
Plants	9	7	2	45	112	89	246

IUCN Red List Categories: EX - Extinct; EW - Extinct in the wild; CR - Critically Endangered; VU - Vulnerable.

Data source: IUCN Red List

INDIA'S SHARE IN GLOBAL CO$_2$ EMISSIONS – 2009-10

Rest of East Asia and Pacific, 4%
India, 5%
Rest of South Asia 1%
Rest of World 11%
China 16%
United States 22%
Europe - EMU 10%
Japan, 5%
Rest of High Income, 13%
Russian Federation 6%
Rest of Europe and Central Asia, 7%

Data source: State of Environment Report, 2009

LAND DEGRADATION

- Arid mountain
- Ice cap
- Nutrient depletion
- Saline and alkaline
- Salt flats
- Stable terrain
- Water erosion
- Waterlogging
- Wind erosion

Land Degradation

EXTENT OF VARIOUS KINDS OF LAND DEGRADATION IN INDIA

Land degradation	Area in million hectares
Total geographical area	328.73
Total degraded area out of total geographical area	146.82
Complex problem	7.38
Soil acidity	16.03
Salinity / Alkalinity	5.95
Water logging	14.3
Wind erosion	9.48
Water erosion	93.68

Lambert Conical Orthomorphic Projection

0   240   280   720   960 km

SCALE 1:24 000 000

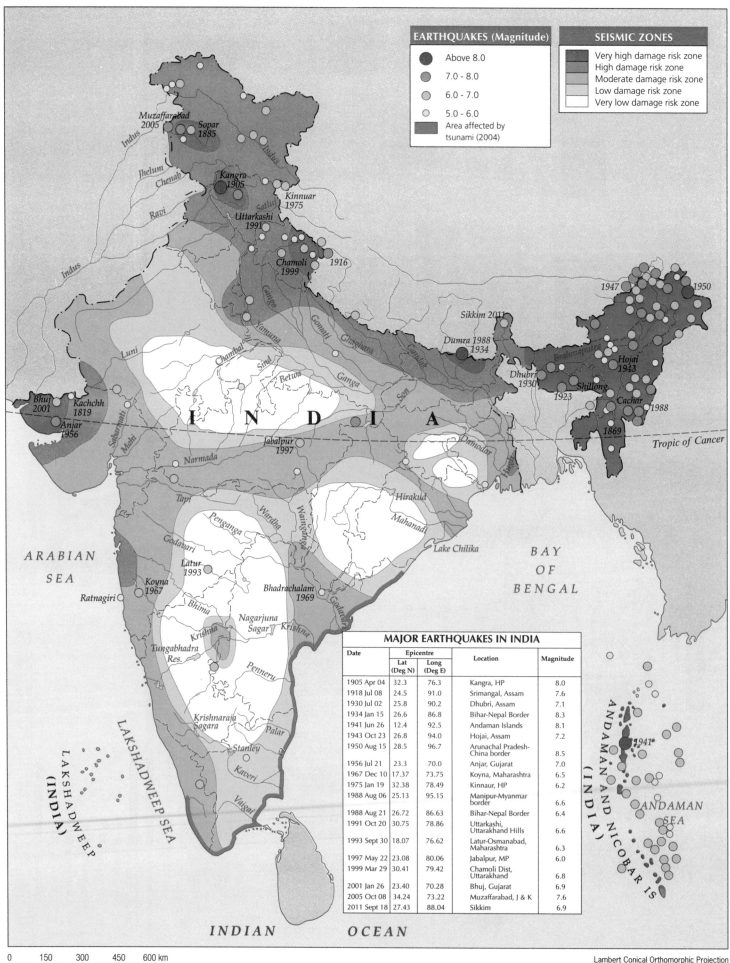

EARTHQUAKES (Magnitude)

- Above 8.0
- 7.0 - 8.0
- 6.0 - 7.0
- 5.0 - 6.0
- Area affected by tsunami (2004)

SEISMIC ZONES

- Very high damage risk zone
- High damage risk zone
- Moderate damage risk zone
- Low damage risk zone
- Very low damage risk zone

MAJOR EARTHQUAKES IN INDIA

Date	Epicentre		Location	Magnitude
	Lat (Deg N)	Long (Deg E)		
1905 Apr 04	32.3	76.3	Kangra, HP	8.0
1918 Jul 08	24.5	91.0	Srimangal, Assam	7.6
1930 Jul 02	25.8	90.2	Dhubri, Assam	7.1
1934 Jan 15	26.6	86.8	Bihar-Nepal Border	8.3
1941 Jun 26	12.4	92.5	Andaman Islands	8.1
1943 Oct 23	26.8	94.0	Hojai, Assam	7.2
1950 Aug 15	28.5	96.7	Arunachal Pradesh-China border	8.5
1956 Jul 21	23.3	70.0	Anjar, Gujarat	7.0
1967 Dec 10	17.37	73.75	Koyna, Maharashtra	6.5
1975 Jan 19	32.38	78.49	Kinnaur, HP	6.2
1988 Aug 06	25.13	95.15	Manipur-Myanmar border	6.6
1988 Aug 21	26.72	86.63	Bihar-Nepal Border	6.4
1991 Oct 20	30.75	78.86	Uttarkashi, Uttarakhand Hills	6.6
1993 Sept 30	18.07	76.62	Latur-Osmanabad, Maharashtra	6.3
1997 May 22	23.08	80.06	Jabalpur, MP	6.0
1999 Mar 29	30.41	79.42	Chamoli Dist, Uttarakhand	6.8
2001 Jan 26	23.40	70.28	Bhuj, Gujarat	6.9
2005 Oct 08	34.24	73.22	Muzaffarabad, J & K	7.6
2011 Sept 18	27.43	88.04	Sikkim	6.9

SCALE 1:15 000 000

0   150   300   450   600 km

Lambert Conical Orthomorphic Projection

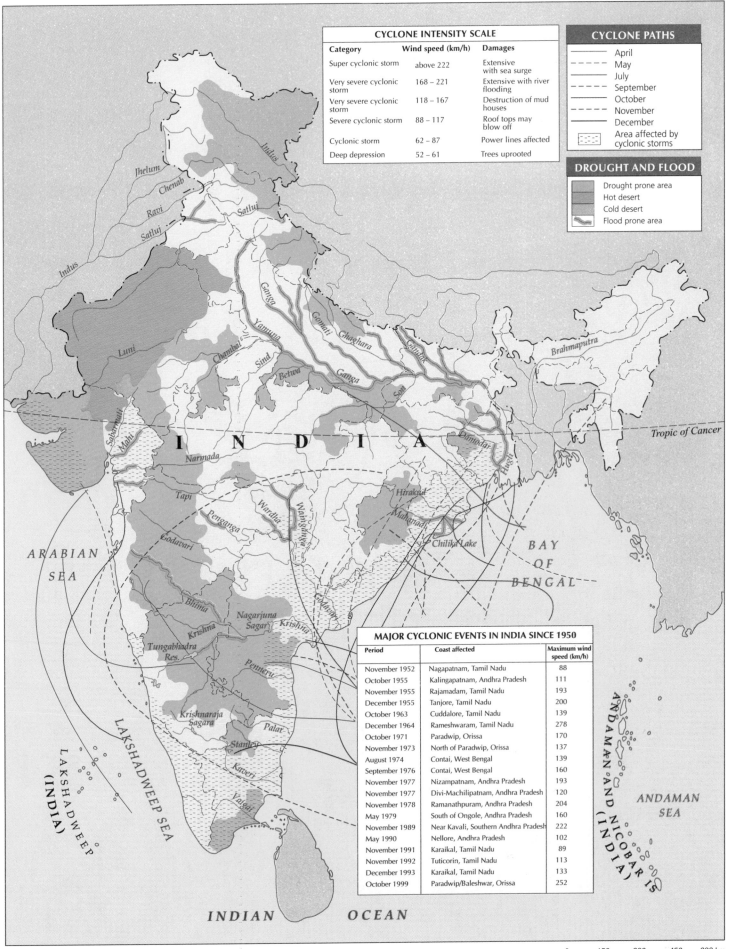

CYCLONE INTENSITY SCALE

Category	Wind speed (km/h)	Damages
Super cyclonic storm	above 222	Extensive with sea surge
Very severe cyclonic storm	168 – 221	Extensive with river flooding
Very severe cyclonic storm	118 – 167	Destruction of mud houses
Severe cyclonic storm	88 – 117	Roof tops may blow off
Cyclonic storm	62 – 87	Power lines affected
Deep depression	52 – 61	Trees uprooted

CYCLONE PATHS

——	April
– – –	May
——	July
– – –	September
——	October
– – –	November
——	December
[- - -]	Area affected by cyclonic storms

DROUGHT AND FLOOD

- Drought prone area
- Hot desert
- Cold desert
- Flood prone area

MAJOR CYCLONIC EVENTS IN INDIA SINCE 1950

Period	Coast affected	Maximum wind speed (km/h)
November 1952	Nagapatnam, Tamil Nadu	88
October 1955	Kalingapatnam, Andhra Pradesh	111
November 1955	Rajamadam, Tamil Nadu	193
December 1955	Tanjore, Tamil Nadu	200
October 1963	Cuddalore, Tamil Nadu	139
December 1964	Rameshwaram, Tamil Nadu	278
October 1971	Paradwip, Orissa	170
November 1973	North of Paradwip, Orissa	137
August 1974	Contai, West Bengal	139
September 1976	Contai, West Bengal	160
November 1977	Nizampatnam, Andhra Pradesh	193
November 1977	Divi-Machilipatnam, Andhra Pradesh	120
November 1978	Ramanathpuram, Andhra Pradesh	204
May 1979	South of Ongole, Andhra Pradesh	160
November 1989	Near Kavali, Southern Andhra Pradesh	222
May 1990	Nellore, Andhra Pradesh	102
November 1991	Karaikal, Tamil Nadu	89
November 1992	Tuticorin, Tamil Nadu	113
December 1993	Karaikal, Tamil Nadu	133
October 1999	Paradwip/Baleshwar, Orissa	252

Tropic of Cancer

ARABIAN SEA

BAY OF BENGAL

LAKSHADWEEP SEA

LAKSHADWEEP (INDIA)

ANDAMAN AND NICOBAR IS (INDIA)

ANDAMAN SEA

INDIAN OCEAN

Lambert Conical Orthomorphic Projection

0 150 300 450 600 km

SCALE 1:15 000 000

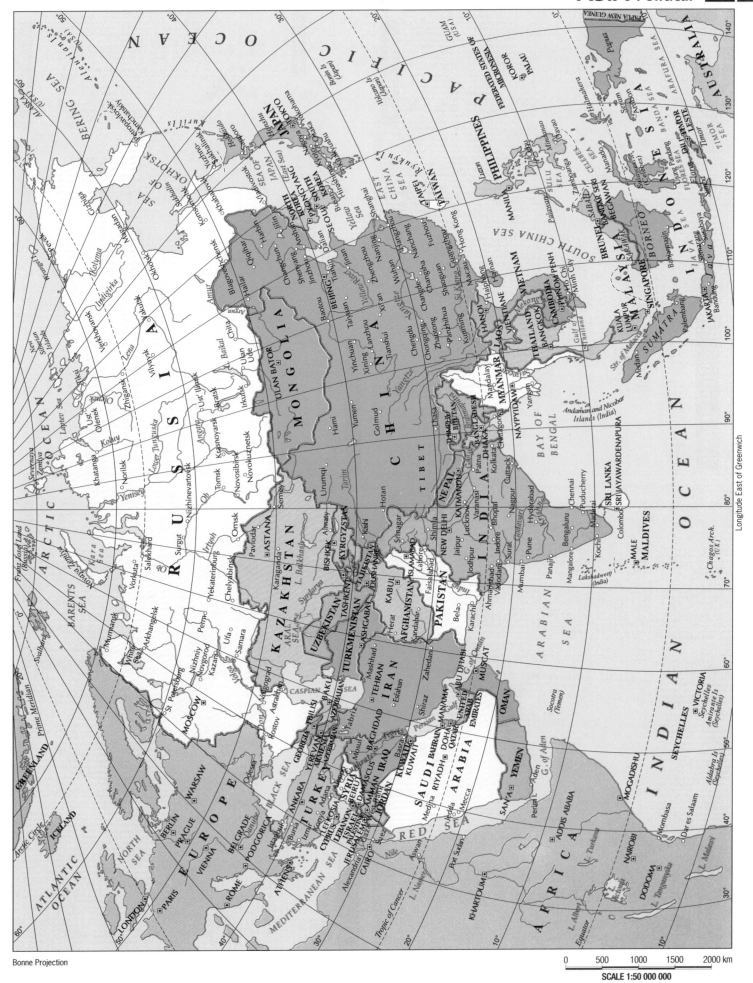

Bonne Projection

Longitude East of Greenwich

| 0 | 500 | 1000 | 1500 | 2000 km |

SCALE 1:50 000 000

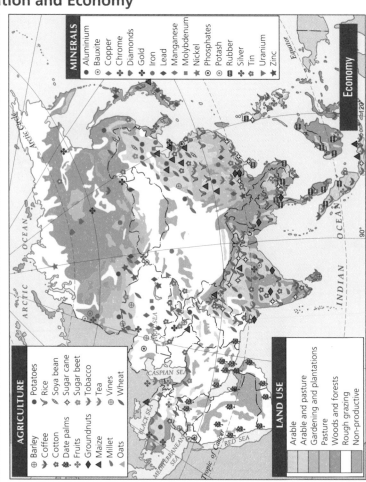

Natural Vegetation

NATURAL VEGETATION

- Alpine tundra and high plateau
- Broad-leaved forest and meadow
- Coniferous forest
- Desert
- Evergreen trees and shrubs
- Grassland
- Monsoon woodland and jungle
- Steppe and semi-desert
- Subtropical and temperate rainforest
- Tropical rainforest

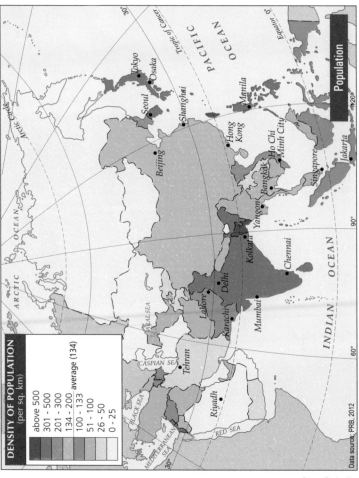

Economy

MINERALS

- Aluminium
- Bauxite
- Copper
- Chrome
- Diamonds
- Gold
- Iron
- Lead
- Manganese
- Molybdenum
- Nickel
- Phosphates
- Potash
- Rubber
- Silver
- Tin
- Uranium
- Zinc

AGRICULTURE

- Barley
- Coffee
- Cotton
- Date palms
- Fruits
- Groundnuts
- Maize
- Millet
- Oats
- Potatoes
- Rice
- Soya bean
- Sugar cane
- Sugar beet
- Tobacco
- Tea
- Vines
- Wheat

LAND USE

- Arable
- Arable and pasture
- Gardening and plantations
- Pasture
- Woods and forests
- Rough grazing
- Non-productive

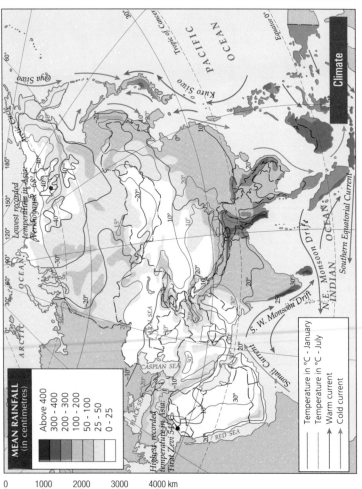

Climate

MEAN RAINFALL (in centimetres)

- Above 400
- 300 – 400
- 200 – 300
- 100 – 200
- 50 – 100
- 25 – 50
- 0 – 25

— Temperature in °C – January
— Temperature in °C – July
→ Warm current
→ Cold current

Lowest recorded temperature in Asia: Verkhoyansk -68°

Highest recorded temperature in Asia: Tirat Zevi 54°

Oya Siwo
Kuro Siwo
S.W. Monsoon Drift
N.E. Monsoon Drift
Somali Current
Southern Equatorial Current

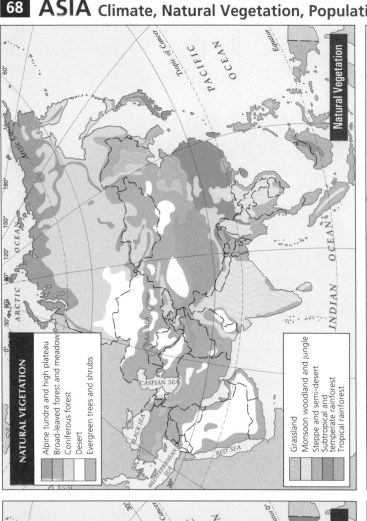

Population

DENSITY OF POPULATION (per sq. km)

- above 500
- 301 – 500
- 201 – 300
- 134 – 200 average (134)
- 100 – 133
- 51 – 100
- 26 – 50
- 0 – 25

Tokyo
Osaka
Seoul
Shanghai
Manila
Hong Kong
Beijing
Ho Chi Minh City
Bangkok
Jakarta
Singapore
Yangon
Kolkata
Chennai
Delhi
Lahore
Karachi
Mumbai
Tehran
Riyadh

Data source: PRB, 2012

0 1000 2000 3000 4000 km

SCALE 1:100 000 000

Bonne Projection

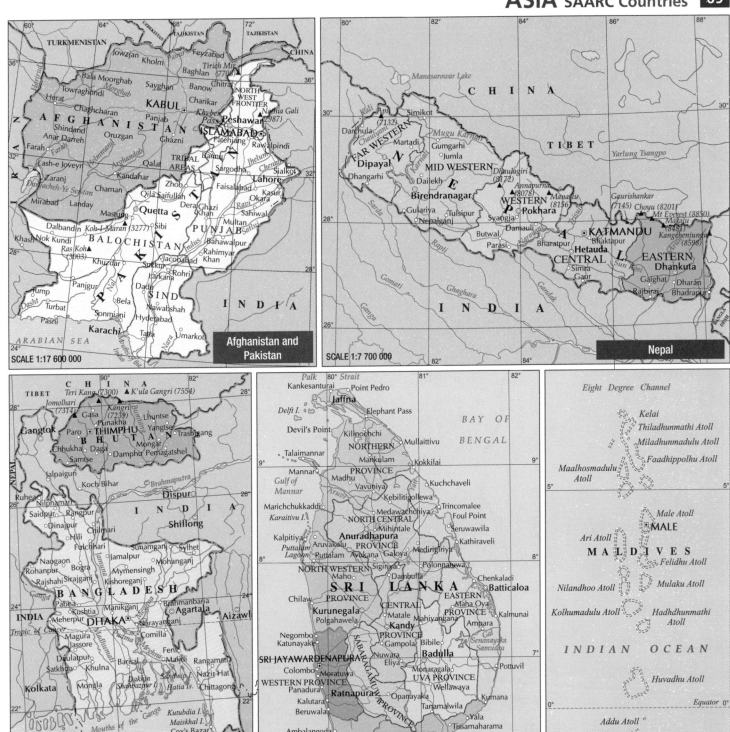

Afghanistan and Pakistan
SCALE 1:17 600 000

Nepal
SCALE 1:7 700 000

Bhutan and Bangladesh
SCALE 1:8 000 000

Sri Lanka
SCALE 1:4 300 000

Maldives
SCALE 1:10 000 000

HUMAN DEVELOPMENT INDEX OF SAARC MEMBER COUNTRIES

Source: HDR 2013

HDI RANK		HUMAN DEVELOPMENT COMPONENTS				ECONOMY	EDUCATION	HEALTH	POVERTY
HDI rank in world	Country	Human development index (HDI) value	GNI per capita (2005 PPP US$)	Life expectancy at birth (years)	Mean years of schooling (years)	GDP per capita (2005 PPP US$)	Adult literacy rate (%)	Expenditure on health (% of GDP)	Population below income poverty line (%) (PPP US$1.25 a day)
92	Sri Lanka	0.715	5,170	75.1	9.3	4,929	91.2	1.3	7.0
104	Maldives	0.688	7,478	77.1	5.8	7,834	98.4	3.8	…
136	India*	0.554	3,285	65.8	4.4	3,203	62.8	1.2	32.7
140	Bhutan	0.538	5,246	67.6	2.3	5,096	52.8	4.5	10.2
146	Bangladesh	0.515	1,785	69.2	4.8	1,568	56.8	1.2	43.3
146	Pakistan	0.515	2,566	65.7	4.9	2,424	54.9	0.8	21.0
157	Nepal	0.463	1,137	69.1	3.2	1,102	60.3	1.8	24.8
175	Afghanistan	0.374	1,000	49.1	3.1	1,083	…	0.9	…
…	**SOUTH ASIA**	**0.558**	**3,343**	**66.2**	**4.7**	**3,241**	**62.8**	**1.2**	…

*Map details of India are given in the preceding pages

Longitude East of Greenwich

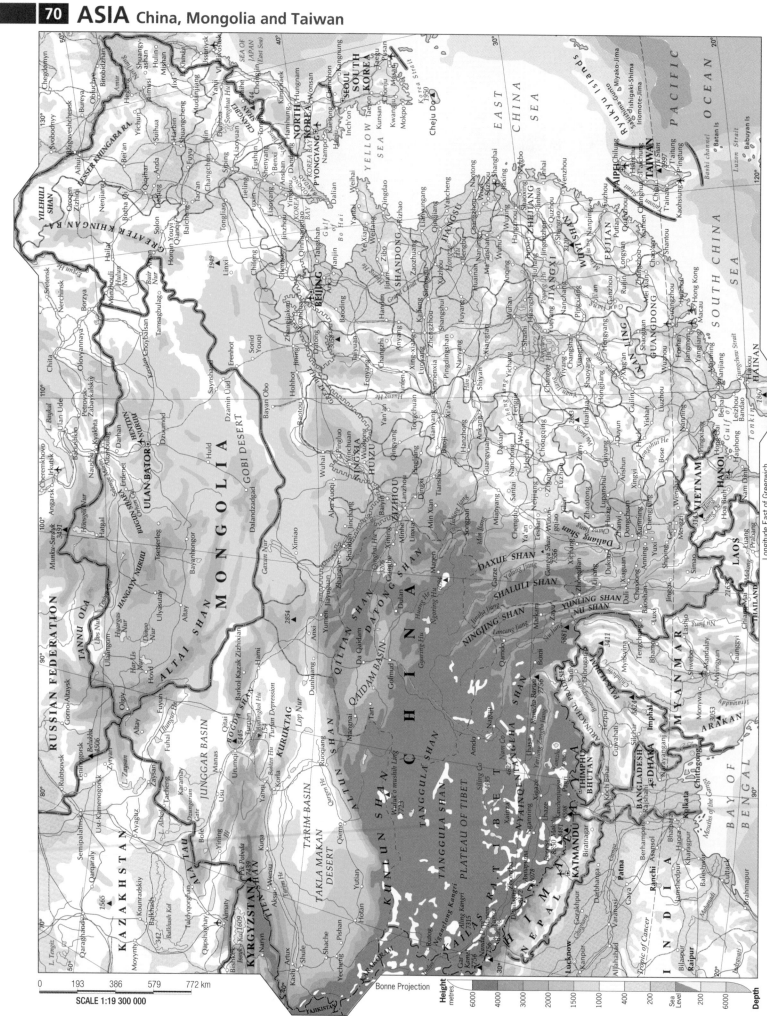

SCALE 1:19 300 000

0   193   386   579   772 km

Bonne Projection

Height metres
6000 4000 3000 2000 1500 1000 400 200 Sea Level

Depth
200 6000

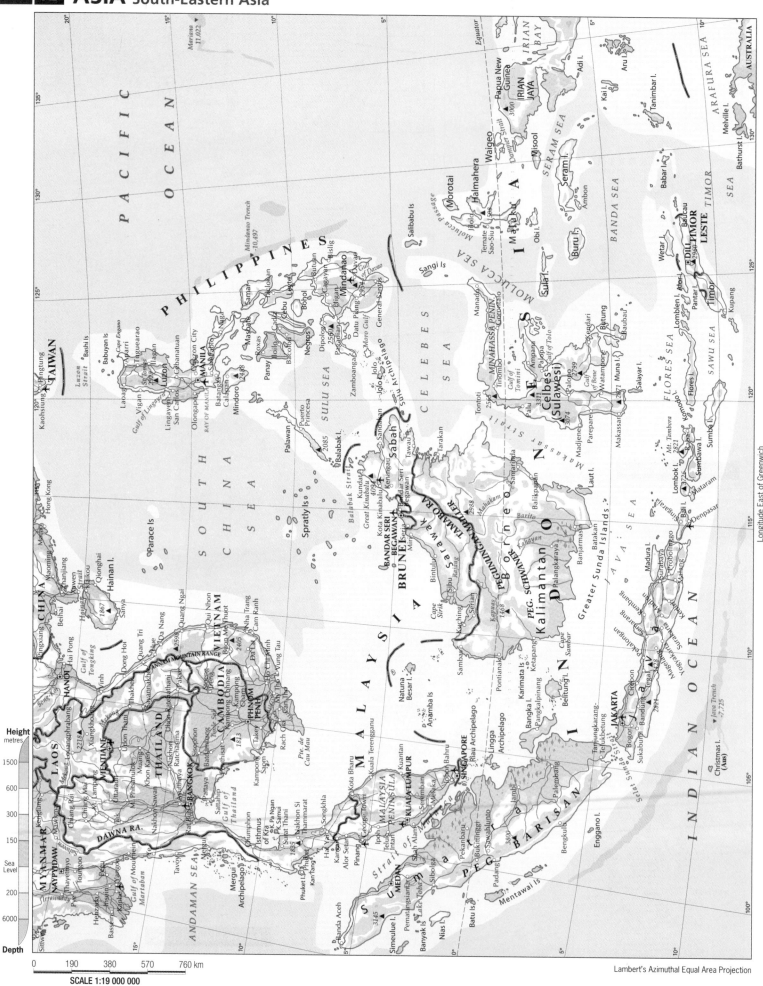

PACIFIC OCEAN

IRIAN BAY

ARAFURA SEA

AUSTRALIA

Equator

Papua New Guinea

IRIAN JAYA

SERAM SEA

BANDA SEA

TIMOR SEA

LESTE TIMOR

Mariana 11,022

Mindanao Trench –10,497

PHILIPPINES

MALUKU

CELEBES SEA

SULAWESI
Celebes

MOLUCCA SEA

TAIWAN

SOUTH CHINA SEA

SULU SEA

Sabah

BRUNEI
BANDAR SERI BEGAWAN

Sarawak

B o r n e o

Kalimantan

PEG. SCHWANER

CHINA

Hainan I.

MYANMAR
NAYPYIDAW

LAOS
VIENTIANE

VIETNAM
HANOI

THAILAND
BANGKOK

CAMBODIA
PHNOM PENH

MALAYSIA

KUALA LUMPUR

SINGAPORE

SUMATRA

MEDAN

PEG. BARISAN

JAVA SEA

JAKARTA

Java

FLORES SEA

SAWU SEA

INDIAN OCEAN

Java Trench –7,725

Christmas I. (Aus)

Height
metres

1500
600
300
150
Sea Level
200
6000

Depth

SCALE 1:19 000 000

0   190   380   570   760 km

Lambert's Azimuthal Equal Area Projection

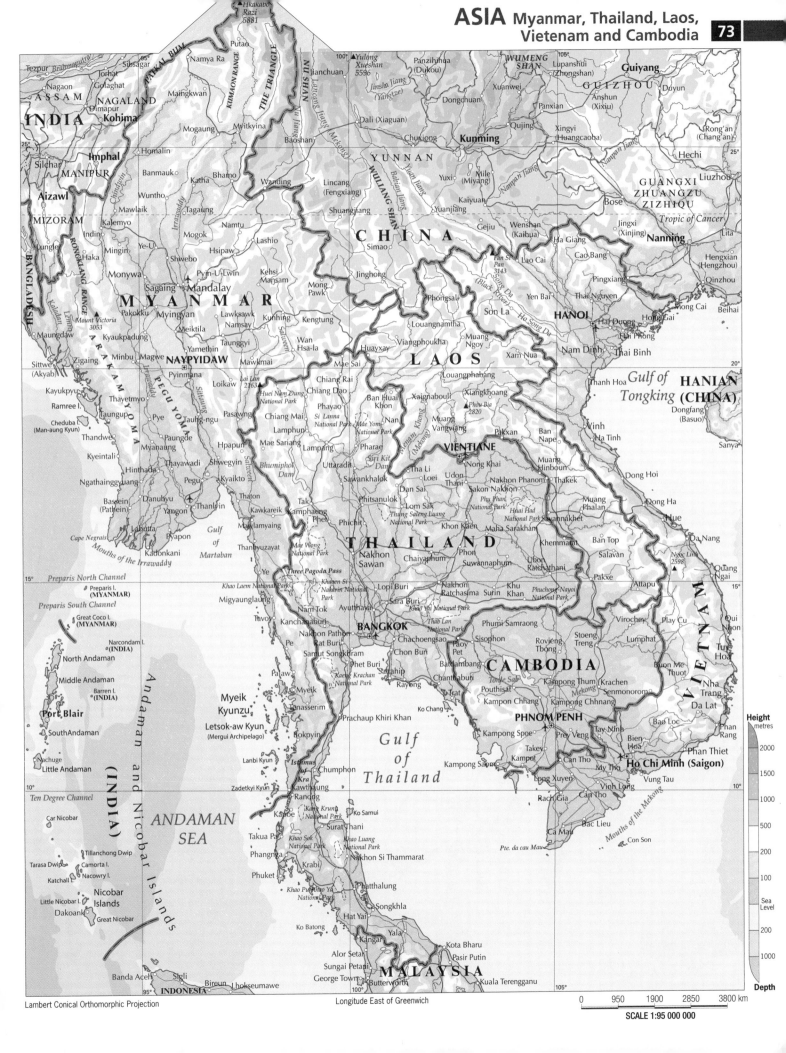

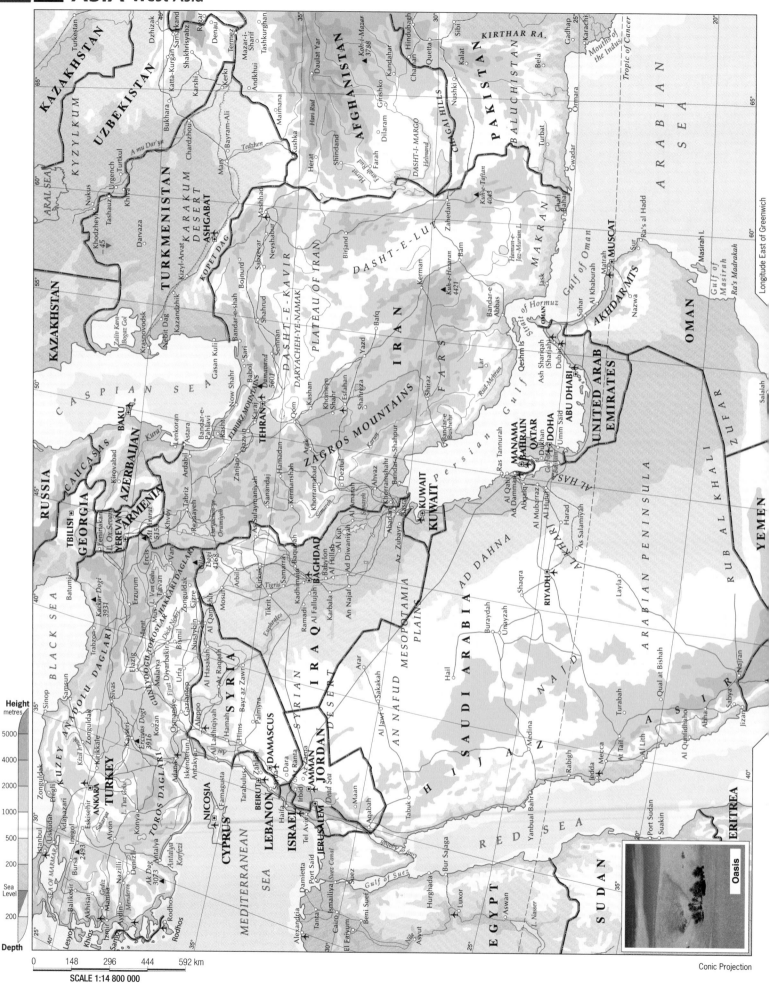

Height
metres

5000
4000
2000
1000
500
200
Sea
Level
200

Depth

0   148   296   444   592 km

SCALE 1:14 800 000

Conic Projection

Oasis

KAZAKHSTAN
UZBEKISTAN
TURKMENISTAN
ASHGABAT
AFGHANISTAN
PAKISTAN
BALUCHISTAN
KIRTHAR RA.
CHAGAI HILLS
Mouths of the Indus
Tropic of Cancer
ARABIAN SEA
KARAKUM DESERT
KOPET DAG
KYZYLKUM
ARAL SEA
RUSSIA
GEORGIA
TBILISI
CAUCASUS
AZERBAIJAN
BAKU
ARMENIA
YEREVAN
CASPIAN SEA
DASHT-E-KAVIR
DARYACHEH-YE-NAMAK
PLATEAU OF IRAN
DASHT-E-LUT
ELBURZ MOUNTAINS
TEHRAN
IRAN
MAKRAN
Strait of Hormuz
Gulf of Oman
MUSCAT
AKHDAR MTS
OMAN
Gulf of Masirah
Ra's Madrakah
UNITED ARAB EMIRATES
ABU DHABI
QATAR
DOHA
BAHRAIN
MANAMA
ZAGROS MOUNTAINS
FARS
Persian Gulf
KUWAIT
AL HASA
BLACK SEA
TURKEY
ANKARA
TOROS DAGLARI
KUZEY ANADOLU DAGLARI
GÜNEYDOGU TOROSLAR
HAKKARI DAGLARI
NICOSIA
CYPRUS
MEDITERRANEAN SEA
SEA OF MARMARA
SYRIA
DAMASCUS
LEBANON
BEIRUT
ISRAEL
JERUSALEM
Dead Sea
JORDAN
AMMAN
IRAQ
BAGHDAD
MESOPOTAMIA PLAIN
SYRIAN DESERT
Tigris
Euphrates
AN NAFUD
AD DAHNA
NAJD
SAUDI ARABIA
RIYADH
ARABIAN PENINSULA
RUB AL KHALI
ZUFAR
AL KHARJ
ASIR
HIJAZ
RED SEA
Mecca
Medina
Jedda
YEMEN
ERITREA
SUDAN
EGYPT
Cairo
Suez Canal
Gulf of Suez
Longitude East of Greenwich

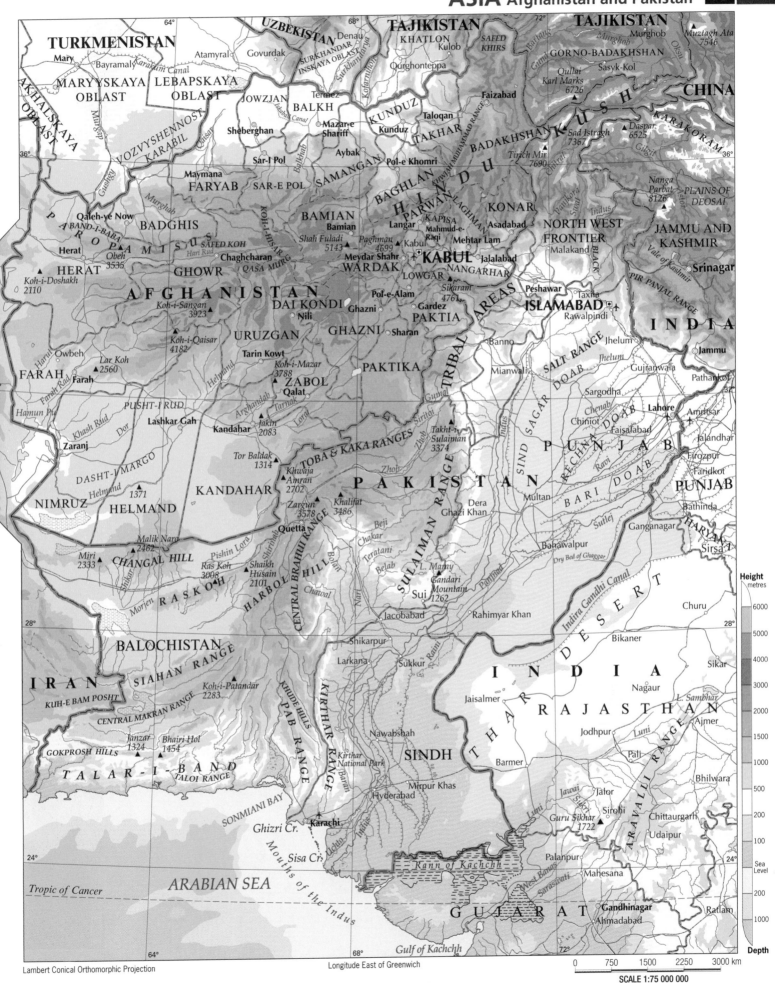

TURKMENISTAN

UZBEKISTAN

TAJIKISTAN

TAJIKISTAN

Mary
Bayramaly
Atamyral
Govurdak
Denau
SURKHANDAR
INSKAYA OBLAST
KHATLON
Kulob
SAFED
KHIRS
Murghob
Muztagh Ata
7546

MARYYSKAYA
OBLAST
LEBAPSKAYA
OBLAST
GORNO-BADAKHSHAN
CHINA

AKHALSKAYA
OBLAST
JOWZJAN
Termez
Kunduz
Qurghonteppa
Faizabad
Qullai
Karl Marks
6726
Sasyk-Kol

VOZVYSHENNOST
KARABIL
Sheberghan
Mazar-e
Shariff
Aybak
KUNDUZ
TAKHAR
Taloqan
KARAKORAM
Daspar
6525
Gilgit

Sar-i Pol
Pol-e Khomri
BADAKHSHAN
Sad Istragh
7367
Tirich Mir
7690
Chitral
Nanga
Parbat
8126
PLAINS OF
DEOSAI

Maymana
FARYAB
SAR-E POL
SAMANGAN
BAGHLAN
PARWAN-LAGHMAN
KONAR
NORTH WEST
FRONTIER
JAMMU AND
KASHMIR

Qaleh-ye Now
BADGHIS
BAMIAN
Bamian
Langar
KAPISA
Mahmud-e-
Raqi
Asadabad
Mehtar Lam
Malakand
Vale of Kashmir
Srinagar

BAND-I-BABA
SAFED KOH
Hari Rud
Paghman
4699
Kabul
Jalalabad
Peshawar
Taxila
PIR PANJAL RANGE

Herat
Obeh
3535
Chaghcharan
QASA MURG
Meydar Shahr
KABUL
NANGARHAR
ISLAMABAD

Koh-i-Doshakh
2110
GHOWR
WARDAK
LOWGAR
Sikaram
4761
TRIBAL
Rawalpindi
INDIA

AFGHANISTAN
DAI KONDI
Pol-e-Alam
Gardez
AREAS
Banno
Jhelum
Jammu

Koh-i-Sangan
3923
Nili
Ghazni
Sharan
PAKTIA
SALT RANGE
Pathankot

Owbeh
URUZGAN
GHAZNI
Mianwali
DOAB
Sargodha
Gujranwala

Koh-i-Qaisar
4182
Tarin Kowt
Koh-i-Mazar
3788
PAKTIKA
Jhelum
Chiniot
RECHNA
Faisalabad
Lahore
Amritsar

Lar Koh
2560
ZABOL
Qalat
SIND SAGAR DOAB
PUNJAB
DOAB
Jalandhar
Firozpur

Farah
FARAH
PUSHT-I RUD
Lashkar Gah
Kandahar
Jakin
2083
TOBA & KAKA RANGES
Takht-i-
Sulaiman
3374
SULAIMAN RANGE
Multan
BARI DOAB
PUNJAB
Faridkot
Bathinda

Zaranj
DASHT-I-MARGO
Tor Baldak
1314
Khwaja
Amran
2702
Khalifat
3486
Dera
Ghazi Khan
Ravi
HARYANA
Sirsa

NIMRUZ
HELMAND
1371
KANDAHAR
Zargun
3578
Quetta
Beji
Chakar
Sutlej
Bahawalpur
Ganganagar

Malik Naro
2462
CHANGAL HILL
Pishin Lora
Bolan
Teratani
Belab
L. Manu
Gandari
Mountain
1262
Panjnad
Dry Bed of Ghaggar
Indira Gandhi Canal
THAR DESERT
Churu

Miri
2333
Shaikh
Husain
2101
Ras Koh
3008
CENTRAL BRAHUI HILL
Chawal
Nari
Sui
Jacobabad
Rahimyar Khan
Bikaner
Sikar

RASKOH
Morjen
HARBOL HILL
SHIRINAB
Shikarpur
INDIA
Nagaur
L. Sambhar

BALOCHISTAN
SIAHAN RANGE
Larkana
Sukkur
RAJASTHAN
Ajmer

IRAN
Koh-i-Patandar
2283
KIRTHAR RANGE
Nawabshah
Jaisalmer
Jodhpur
Pali
ARAVALLI RANGE
Bhilwara

KUH-E BAM POSHT
CENTRAL MAKRAN RANGE
PAB RANGE
KHUDE HILLS
Barmer
Luni

Janzar
1324
Bhairi Hol
1454
Kirthar
National Park
SINDH
Guru Sikhar
1722
Sirohi
Chittaurgarh

GOKPROSH HILLS
Baran
Mirpur Khas
Jalor
Udaipur

TALAR-I-BAND
TALOI RANGE
Hyderabad

SONMIANI BAY
Karachi
Nawa Banas
Palanpur

Ghizri Cr.
Mouths of the Indus
Rann of Kachchh
Mahesana

Sisa Cr.
GUJARAT
Gandhinagar
Ratlam

Tropic of Cancer
ARABIAN SEA
Gulf of Kachchh
Ahmadabad

Height metres
6000
5000
4000
3000
2000
1500
1000
500
200
100
Sea Level
200
1000

Depth

Lambert Conical Orthomorphic Projection

Longitude East of Greenwich

0   750   1500   2250   3000 km

SCALE 1:75 000 000

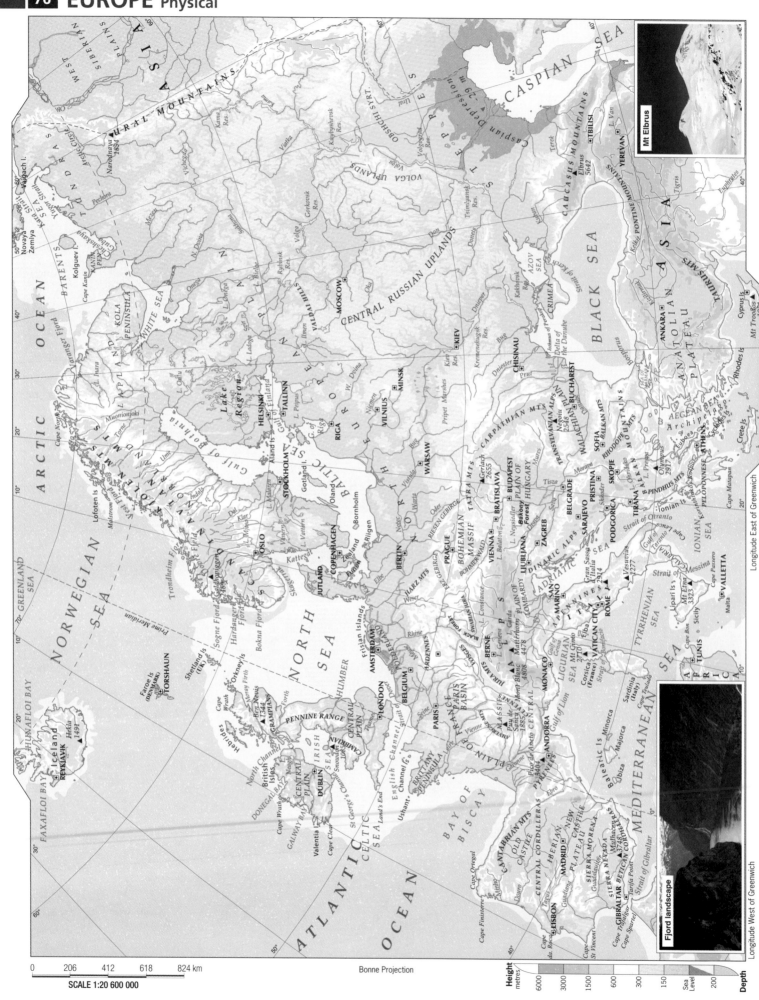

Mt Elbrus

Fjord landscape

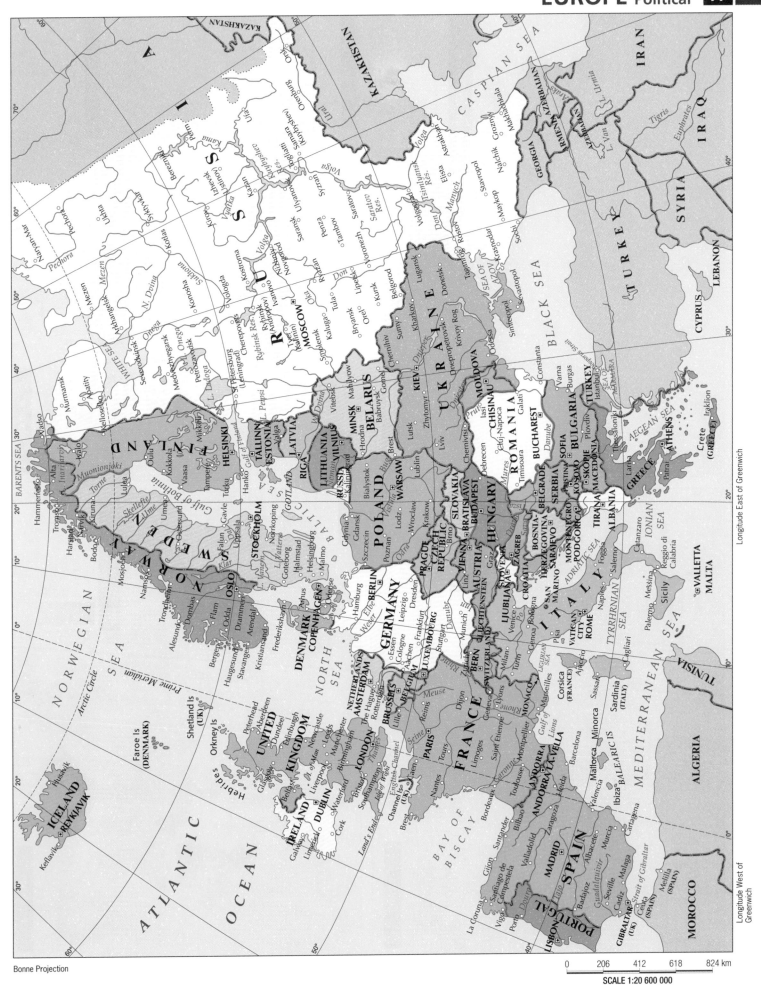

| 0 | 206 | 412 | 618 | 824 km |

SCALE 1:20 600 000

Longitude West of Greenwich

Longitude East of Greenwich

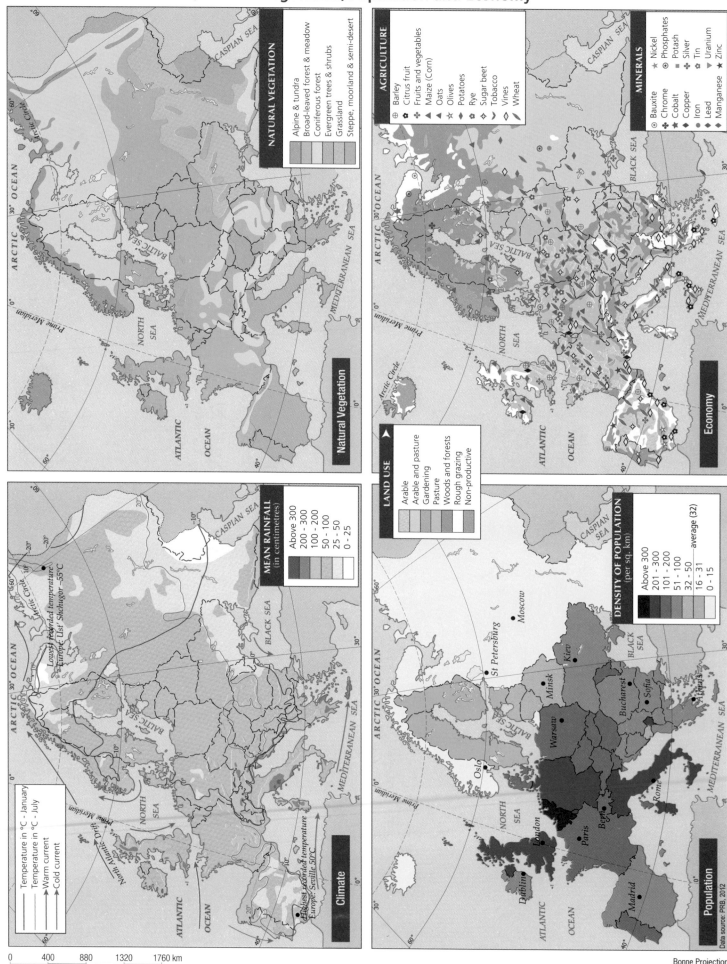

NATURAL VEGETATION

Alpine & tundra
Broad-leaved forest & meadow
Coniferous forest
Evergreen trees & shrubs
Grassland
Steppe, moorland & semi-desert

Natural Vegetation

AGRICULTURE

⊕ Barley
❀ Citrus fruit
♣ Fruits and vegetables
◀ Maize (Corn)
☆ Oats
◆ Olives
❀ Potatoes
▶ Rye
◇ Sugar beet
▽ Tobacco
◇ Vines
╲ Wheat

MINERALS

◎ Bauxite   ★ Nickel
❀ Chrome   ◉ Phosphates
● Cobalt   ■ Potash
◆ Copper   ✿ Silver
● Iron   ✿ Tin
◆ Lead   ✿ Uranium
◆ Manganese   ★ Zinc

Economy

LAND USE

Arable
Arable and pasture
Gardening
Pasture
Woods and forests
Rough grazing
Non-productive

MEAN RAINFALL
(in centimetres)

Above 300
200 - 300
100 - 200
50 - 100
25 - 50
0 - 25

Climate

Temperature in °C - January
Temperature in °C - July
Warm current
Cold current

Lowest recorded temperature
Europe: Ust' Shchugor -55°C

Highest recorded temperature
Europe: Seville 50°C

North Atlantic Drift

DENSITY OF POPULATION
(per sq. km)

Above 300
201 - 300
101 - 200
51 - 100
32 - 50
16 - 31
0 - 15
average (32)

Moscow
St Petersburg
Kiev
Minsk
Bucharest
Sofia
Athens
Warsaw
Oslo
Rome
London
Berlin
Paris
Dublin
Madrid

Population

Data source: PRB, 2012

SCALE 1:44 000 000

0   400   880   1320   1760 km

Bonne Projection

ATLANTIC OCEAN

NORTH SEA

Shetland Is
Yell
Unst
Fetlar
Mainland
Foula
Lerwick

Fair Isle

Westray
Sanday
Orkney Is
Stronsay
Mainland
Kirkwall
Hoy
South Ronaldsay
Pentland Firth

C. Wrath
Thurso
Wick

Outer Hebrides
North Minch
Helmsdale

Lewis
Stornoway
789
Laird
Golspie

St Kilda
Harris
Ben Wyvis
Tain
1046
Ullapool
Invergordon
Dingwall
Nairn
Elgin
Banff
Huntly
Fraserburgh
Peterhead

North Uist
Benbecula
Skye
Inverness
Spey
Inverurie
Aberdeen

Little Minch
South Uist
L. Ness
1182
Aviemore
Ben Macdhui
1311
Dee

Barra
Rhum
Eigg
Ben Nevis
1342
Fort William
GRAMPIAN MTS
Ballater
Stonehaven

Inner Hebrides
Coll
SCOTLAND
1214
Montrose

Tiree
Tobermory
Forfar

Mull
Oban
L. Lomond
973
Perth
Dundee
Firth of Tay
St Andrews

Colonsay
Stirling
Kirkcaldy
Glenrothes
Firth of Forth
Dunbar

Jura
Dunfermline
Edinburgh
St Abb's Head

Islay
Greenock
Clyde
Glasgow
Berwick-upon-Tweed
Holy I.
Paisley
Hamilton
Galashiels
East Kilbride
Arran
Irvine
Kilmarnock
SOUTHERN UPLANDS
840
Jedburgh
816
Alnwick

Campbeltown
Firth of Clyde
Ayr
Girvan
CHEVIOT HILLS
Newcastle-upon-Tyne

Malin Head
Rathlin I.
Dumfries
Hawick
South Shields

Buncrana
Coleraine
North Channel
Larne
Kirkcudbright
Hexham
Sunderland
Hartlepool

Aran I.
DONEGAL MTS
Letterkenny
Londonderry
Antrim
Stranraer
Carlisle
893
Durham

Lifford
Omagh
BELFAST
Mull of Galloway
Solway Firth
Workington
Darlington
Middlesbrough

Donegal
L. Lower
L. Neagh
Portadown
Lisburn
Whitehaven
CUMBRIAN MTS
Scarborough

DONEGAL BAY
Bundoran
Enniskillen
Armagh
Newry
Isle of Man
Scafell Pike
978
PENNINES
Flamborough Head
Bridlington

Erris Head
Sligo
Clones
Douglas
Barrow-in-Furness
Lancaster
Harrogate

Ballina
Leitrim
Dundalk
MORECAMBE BAY
York
Kingston upon Hull

Achill
L. Conn
Castlebar
Cavan
DUNDALK BAY
Blackpool
Burnley
Leeds
Spurn Head

MAYO MTS
Westport
Roscommon
Longford
IRISH SEA
Preston
Bradford
Scunthorpe
Humber

L. Mask
Boyne
LIVERPOOL BAY
Halifax
Doncaster
Grimsby

CONNEMARA
L. Corrib
Athlone
Mullingar
Anglesey
Manchester
Oldham
Rotherham
Lincoln
Cromer

CONNACHT
Ballinasloe
Tullamore
Colwyn Bay
Liverpool
Warrington
Stockport
Sheffield
Skegness

GALWAY BAY
Galway
Birr
LEINSTER
DUBLIN
Holyhead
Bangor
Chester
Crewe
Chesterfield
Mansfield
Boston
The Wash

Aran Is
Port Laoise
Dun Laoghaire
Bray
Wrexham
Stoke on Trent
Derby
Nottingham
King's Lynn

Ennis
L. Derg
Athy
926
CAERNARFON BAY
Snowdon
1085
Shrewsbury
Telford
Grantham
Norwich
Great Yarmouth

Kilrush
Nenagh
Kilkenny
WICKLOW MTS
Arklow
Pwllheli
Stafford
Leicester
Peterborough
Lowestoft

Shannon
Limerick
REPUBLIC
Welshpool
Wolverhampton
Nuneaton
Corby
Ely
Thetford
Bury St Edmunds
Ipswich

Listowel
Tipperary
GALTY MTS
OF
CAMBRIAN MTS
Birmingham
Coventry
Rugby
Northampton
Cambridge

Tralee
Dingle
Mallow
IRELAND
Wexford
Aberystwyth
CARDIGAN BAY
Redditch
Royal Leamington Spa
Bedford
Colchester
Felixstowe

Killarney
Blackwater
MUNSTER
Waterford
Rosslare
Worcester
ENGLAND
Milton Keynes
Luton
Stevenage
Harlow
Harwich

Carrauntoohill
1041
Dungarvan
Carnsore Point
WALES
Hereford
COTSWOLD HILLS
Oxford
CHILTERN HILLS
Chelmsford

Macgillycuddy's Reeks
Kenmare
St David's Head
Haverfordwest
Carmarthen
Brecon
886
Cheltenham
Gloucester
Cwmbran
Newport
High Wycombe
Slough
Watford
Basildon
Southend-on-Sea

CAHA MTS
Bandon
Cork
Cobh
Milford Haven
Pembroke
Llanelli
Merthyr Tydfil
Rhondda
Cardiff
Bristol
Bath
Newbury
Reading
LONDON
Reigate
Canterbury
Margate

BANTRY BAY
Bantry
Kinsale
CARMARTHEN BAY
Swansea
Barry
Weston-super-Mare
MENDIP HILLS
SALISBURY PLAIN
Basingstoke
Guildford
Crawley
Dover
Str of Dover
Folkestone
Oostende

C. Clear
St George's Channel
Bristol Channel
QUANTOCK HILLS
Taunton
Salisbury
Winchester
Fareham
Brighton
Hastings
Dunkerque
Calais
Gris Nez

Fishguard
BIDEFORD BAY
Barnstaple
Yeovil
Southampton
Bournemouth
Poole
Worthing
Eastbourne
Boulogne-sur-Mer
St-Omer
Lille

CELTIC SEA
Bude
618
Exeter
Exmouth
Weymouth
Isle of Wight
Newport
Le Touquet-Paris-Plage
Bruay-la-Buissiere
Bethune

Newquay
BODMIN MOOR
DARTMOOR
Torbay
LYME BAY
Lens

Truro
St Austell
Plymouth
Start Point
English Channel
FRANCE

Land's End
Penzance
Falmouth
Lizard Point
Isles of Scilly

NORTHERN IRELAND

UNITED KINGDOM

Prime Meridian

Longitude West of Greenwich
Longitude East of Greenwich

Conical With Two Standard Parallels

0 50 100 150 200 km
SCALE 1:50 000 000

Height
metres
1000
500
200
Sea Level
200
6000
Depth

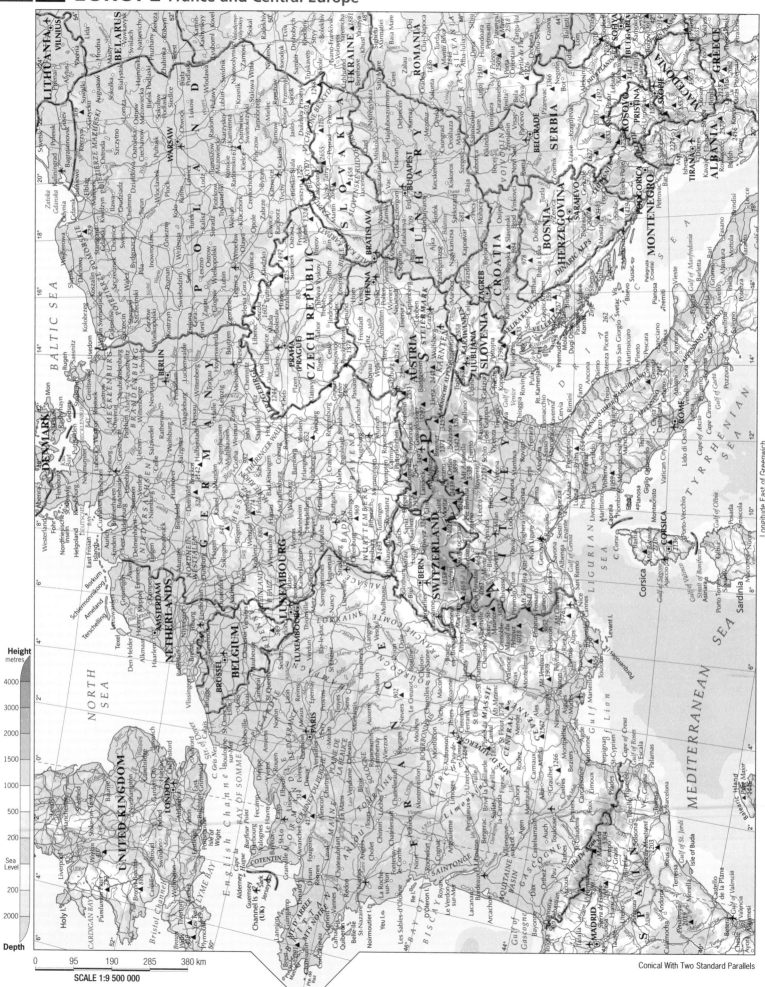

Height
metres

4000
3000
2000
1500
1000
500
200
Sea Level
200
2000

Depth

| 0 | 95 | 190 | 285 | 380 km |

SCALE 1:9 500 000

Conical With Two Standard Parallels

Longitude East of Greenwich

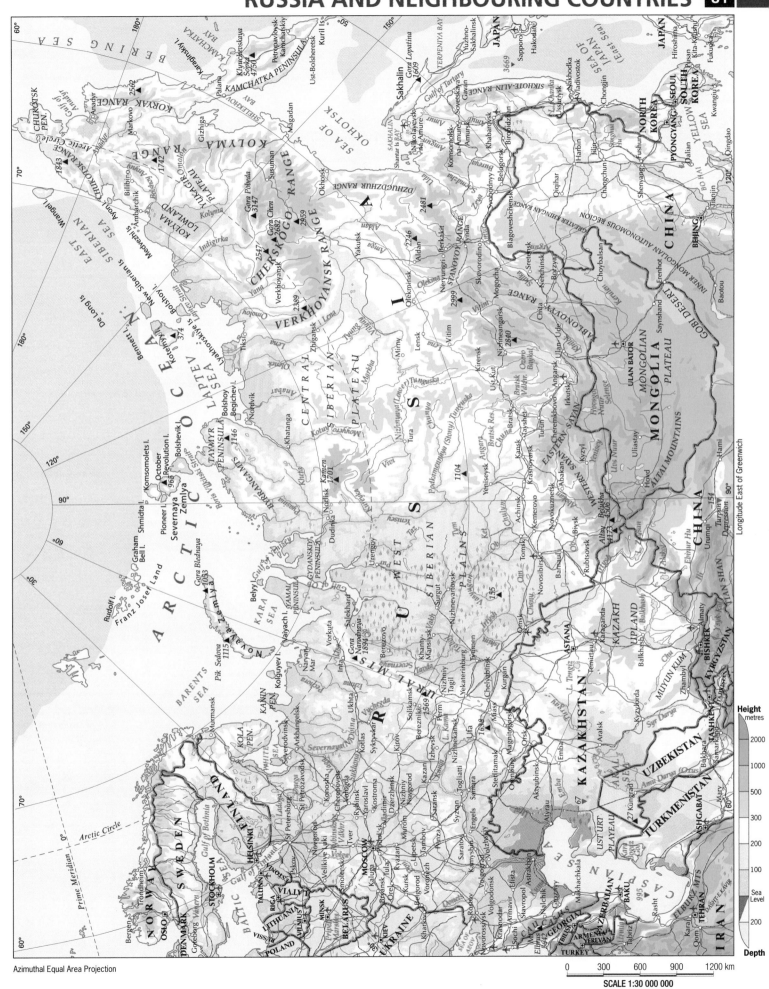

Azimuthal Equal Area Projection

Height	metres
2000
1000
500
300
200
100
Sea Level
200

Depth

SCALE 1:30 000 000

0   300   600   900   1200 km

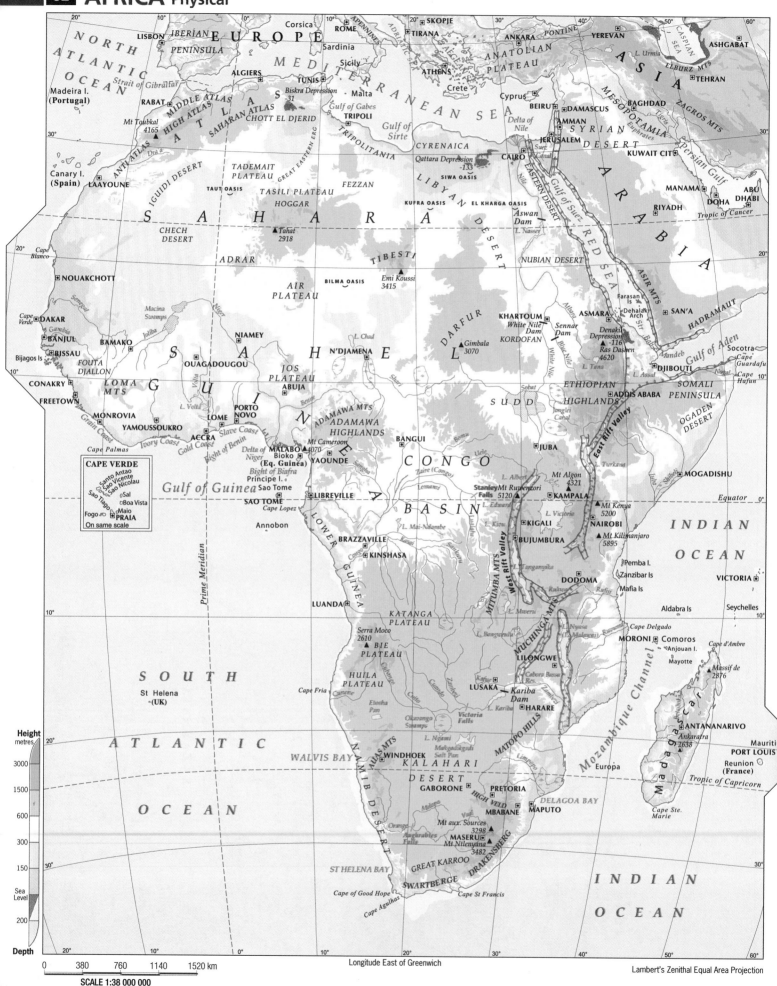

Height
metres

3000
1500
600
300
150
Sea
Level
200

Depth

0   380   760   1140   1520 km

SCALE 1:38 000 000

Longitude East of Greenwich

Lambert's Zenithal Equal Area Projection

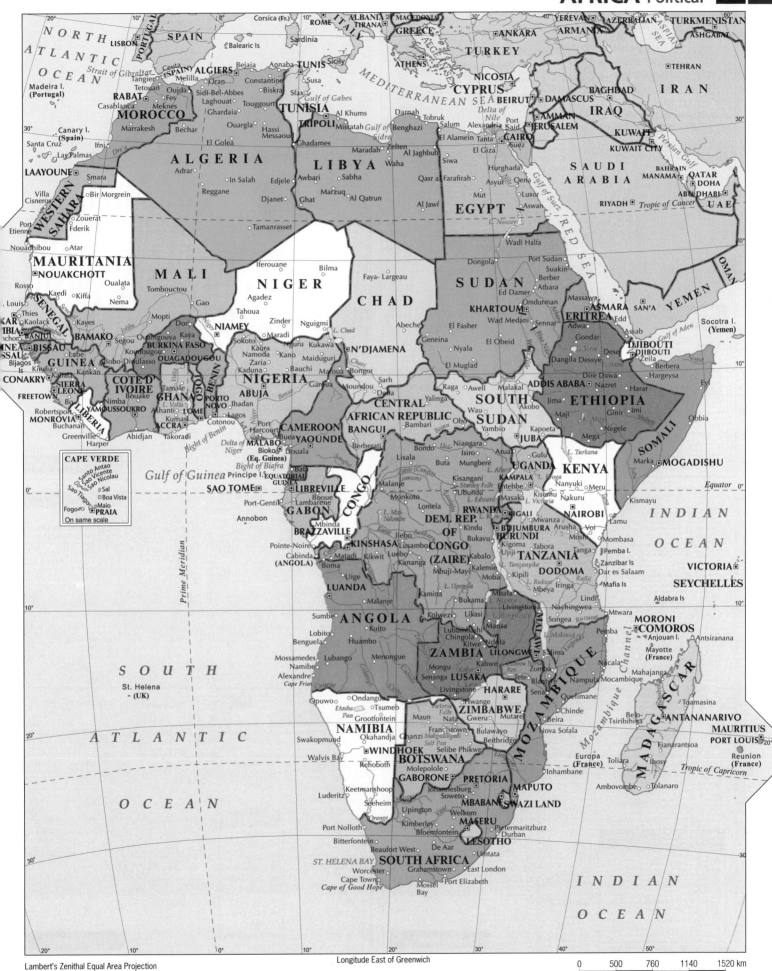

Lambert's Zenithal Equal Area Projection

Longitude East of Greenwich

SCALE 1:38 000 000

0   500   760   1140   1520 km

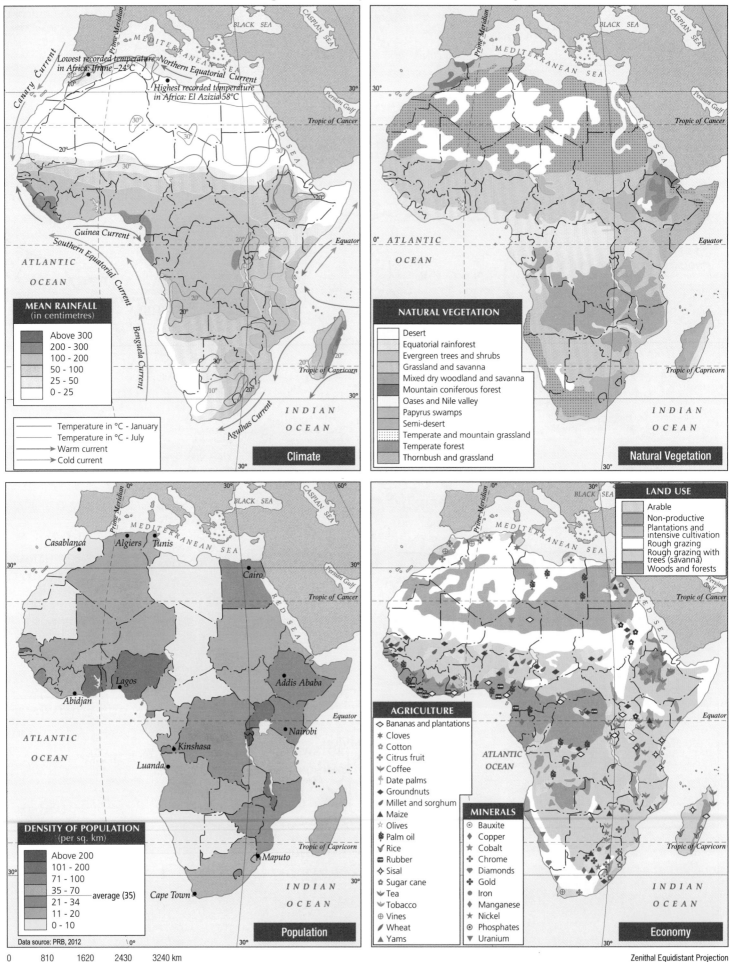

Climate

Lowest recorded temperature in Africa: Ifrane −24°C
Highest recorded temperature in Africa: El Azizia 58°C

Canary Current
Northern Equatorial Current
Guinea Current
Southern Equatorial Current
Benguela Current
Agulhas Current

ATLANTIC OCEAN
INDIAN OCEAN
MEDITERRANEAN SEA
BLACK SEA
CASPIAN SEA
Persian Gulf
RED SEA
Prime Meridian
Tropic of Cancer
Equator
Tropic of Capricorn

MEAN RAINFALL
(in centimetres)

- Above 300
- 200 - 300
- 100 - 200
- 50 - 100
- 25 - 50
- 0 - 25

— Temperature in °C - January
— Temperature in °C - July
→ Warm current
→ Cold current

Natural Vegetation

NATURAL VEGETATION

- Desert
- Equatorial rainforest
- Evergreen trees and shrubs
- Grassland and savanna
- Mixed dry woodland and savanna
- Mountain coniferous forest
- Oases and Nile valley
- Papyrus swamps
- Semi-desert
- Temperate and mountain grassland
- Temperate forest
- Thornbush and grassland

Population

Casablanca
Algiers Tunis
Cairo
Lagos
Abidjan
Addis Ababa
Nairobi
Kinshasa
Luanda
Maputo
Cape Town

DENSITY OF POPULATION
(per sq. km)

- Above 200
- 101 - 200
- 71 - 100
- 35 - 70 average (35)
- 21 - 34
- 11 - 20
- 0 - 10

Data source: PRB, 2012

Economy

LAND USE

- Arable
- Non-productive
- Plantations and intensive cultivation
- Rough grazing
- Rough grazing with trees (savanna)
- Woods and forests

AGRICULTURE

- ◇ Bananas and plantations
- ✳ Cloves
- ✿ Cotton
- ✤ Citrus fruit
- ⤳ Coffee
- ⸙ Date palms
- ◆ Groundnuts
- ⫟ Millet and sorghum
- ▲ Maize
- ☆ Olives
- ⚑ Palm oil
- ⤳ Rice
- ▭ Rubber
- ◇ Sisal
- ✿ Sugar cane
- ⤳ Tea
- ⤳ Tobacco
- ⊕ Vines
- ⟋ Wheat
- ▲ Yams

MINERALS

- ⊙ Bauxite
- ◆ Copper
- ★ Cobalt
- ✤ Chrome
- ▼ Diamonds
- ◆ Gold
- ● Iron
- ◆ Manganese
- ★ Nickel
- ⊙ Phosphates
- ▽ Uranium

0 810 1620 2430 3240 km

SCALE 1:81 000 000

Zenithal Equidistant Projection

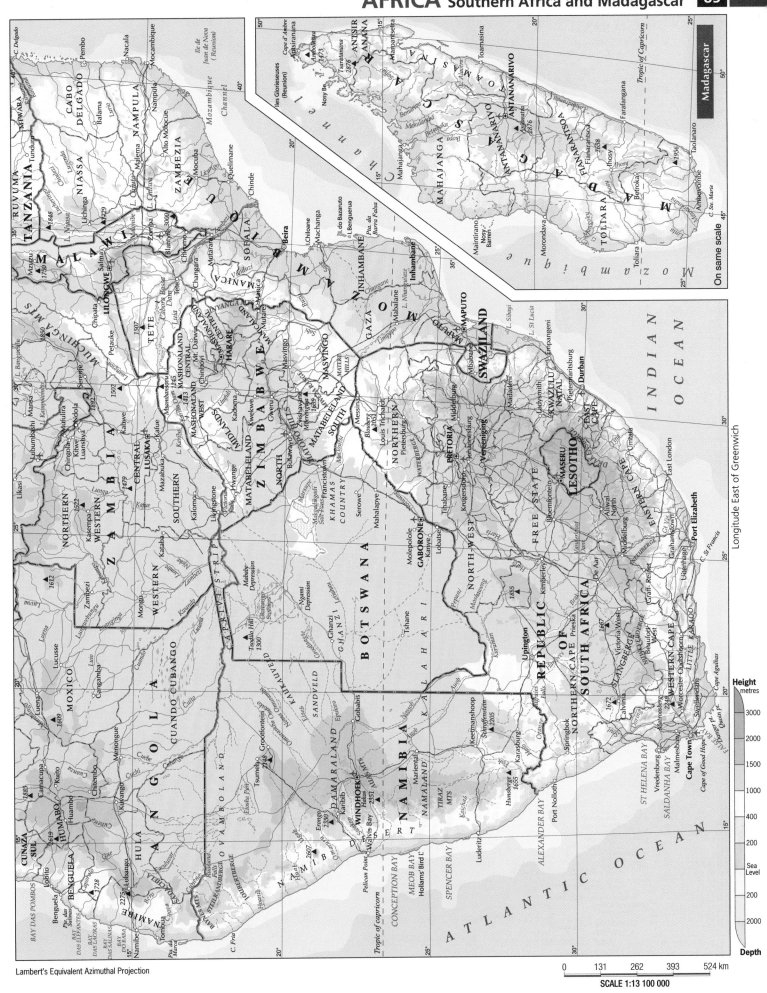

Madagascar

On same scale

Lambert's Equivalent Azimuthal Projection

Height	metres
	3000
	2000
	1500
	1000
	400
	200
	Sea Level
	200
	2000

Depth

0   131   262   393   524 km

SCALE 1:13 100 000

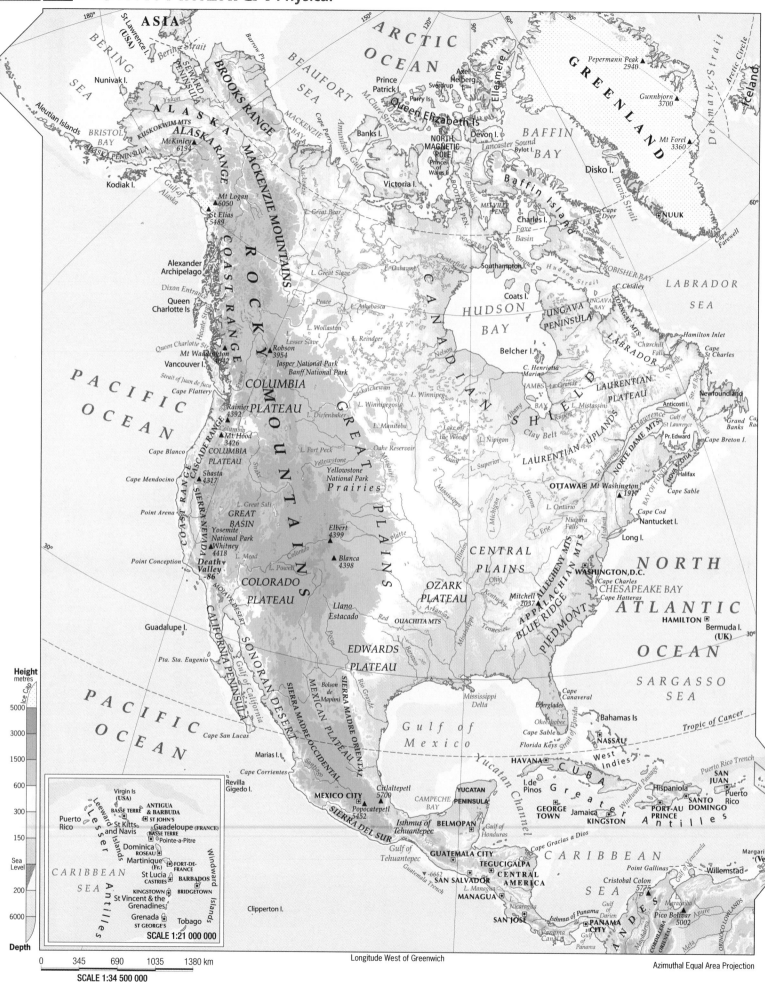

ASIA

ARCTIC OCEAN

GREENLAND
Pepermann Peak 2940
Gunnbjorn 3700
Mt Forel 3360
NUUK
Denmark Strait
Iceland

BERING SEA
St Lawrence I. (USA)
SEWARD PENINSULA
Bering Strait
Barrow Pt.
BEAUFORT SEA
Prince Patrick I.
Sverdrup
Axel Heiberg
Arctic Circle

Nunivak I.
BROOKS RANGE
ALASKA
ALASKA RANGE
McKinley 6194
KUSKOKWIM MTS
Aleutian Islands
BRISTOL BAY
ALASKA PENINSULA
Kodiak I.
Gulf of Alaska

MACKENZIE BAY
Cape Parry
Banks I.
Amundsen Gulf
McClure Strait
NORTH MAGNETIC POLE
Prince of Wales I.
Victoria I.
Prince Patrick I.
Queen Elizabeth Is
Parry Is
Devon I.
Lancaster Sound
Bylot I.
BAFFIN BAY

Mt Logan 6050
St Elias 5489
Alexander Archipelago
Dixon Entrance
Queen Charlotte Is
Mt Waddington 4042
Vancouver I.
Queen Charlotte Str.
Strait of Juan de Fuca
Cape Flattery

MACKENZIE MOUNTAINS
ROCKY MOUNTAINS
Robson 3954
Jasper National Park
Banff National Park
COLUMBIA PLATEAU

L. Great Bear
L. Great Slave
Peace
L. Athabasca
L. Wollaston
Lesser Slave
L. Reindeer
Saskatchewan
L. Winnipegosis
L. Diefenbaker
L. Fort Peck
L. Manitoba

MELVILLE PEN.
BOOTHIA PEN.
Foxe Basin
Southampton I.
Coats I.
Chesterfield Inlet
L. Dubawnt
HUDSON BAY
Belcher I.
C. Henrietta Maria
JAMES BAY
Albany
La Grande
Nelson

Charles I.
Foxe Channel
Cape Dyer
Cumberland Sound
FROBISHER BAY
Hudson Strait
C. Chidley
UNGAVA BAY
TORNGAT MTS
LABRADOR
Hamilton Inlet
Churchill Falls
Cape St Charles
LABRADOR SEA

Baffin Island
Disko I.
Cape Farewell

UNGAVA PENINSULA
CANADIAN SHIELD
Clay Belt
L. Mistassini
LAURENTIAN PLATEAU
Newfoundland
Anticosti I.
Gulf of St Lawrence
Grand Banks

PACIFIC OCEAN

CASCADE RANGE
Rainier 4392
Mt Hood 3426
COLUMBIA PLATEAU
Columbia
Snake
COAST RANGE
Cape Blanco
Shasta 4317
Cape Mendocino
Point Arena
SIERRA NEVADA
Yosemite National Park
Whitney 4418
GREAT BASIN
L. Great Salt
Point Conception
Death Valley -86
L. Mead
L. Powell
Colorado
COLORADO PLATEAU
Guadalupe I.
MOJAVE DESERT

GREAT PLAINS
Oahe Reservoir
Yellowstone National Park
Prairies
Elbert 4399
Blanca 4398
Llano Estacado
Red
Platte
Arkansas
Pecos

Missouri
Mississippi
L. Superior
L. Michigan
L. Huron
L. Nipigon
L. Winnipeg
Lake of the Woods
Rainy
Illinois
Ohio
Kentucky
Tennessee

CENTRAL PLAINS
OZARK PLATEAU
OUACHITA MTS
L. Erie
L. Ontario
Niagara Falls
Mitchell 2037
ALLEGHENY MTS
APPALACHIAN MTS
BLUE RIDGE
PIEDMONT
WASHINGTON,D.C.
CHESAPEAKE BAY
Cape Charles
Cape Hatteras

OTTAWA
Mt Washington 1916
St Lawrence
NORTE DAME MTS
NOVA SCOTIA
Halifax
Cape Sable
BAY OF FUNDY
Cape Cod
Nantucket I.
Long I.
Cape Breton I.
Pr. Edward

NORTH ATLANTIC OCEAN
SARGASSO SEA
HAMILTON
Bermuda I. (UK)

Pta. Sta. Eugenio
CALIFORNIA PENINSULA
Gulf of California
SONORAN DESERT
Cape San Lucas
Marias I.
Cape Corrientes
Revilla Gigedo I.
Clipperton I.

SIERRA MADRE OCCIDENTAL
MEXICAN PLATEAU
Bolson de Mapimi
SIERRA MADRE ORIENTAL
EDWARDS PLATEAU
Rio Grande
MEXICO CITY
Citlaltepetl 5700
Popocatepetl 5452
SIERRA DEL SUR
Isthmus of Tehuantepec
Gulf of Tehuantepec
Balsas
Santiago

Mississippi Delta
Gulf of Mexico
Everglades
Cape Canaveral
Cape Sable
Florida Keys
Strait of Florida
Bahamas Is
Tropic of Cancer
HAVANA
CUBA
West Indies
Puerto Rico Trench
I. de Pinos
YUCATAN PENINSULA
CAMPECHE BAY
BELMOPAN
GUATEMALA CITY
TEGUCIGALPA
CENTRAL AMERICA
SAN SALVADOR
-6662
Guatemala Trench
L. Managua
MANAGUA
Nicaragua
SAN JOSE
PANAMA CITY
Isthmus of Panama
Panama Canal
Gulf of Panama
Gulf of Honduras
NASSAU
GEORGE TOWN
Jamaica
KINGSTON
Greater Antilles
Hispaniola
SANTO DOMINGO
PORT-AU-PRINCE
Yucatan Channel
Windward Passage
Cape Gracias a Dios
CARIBBEAN SEA
SAN JUAN
Puerto Rico
Point Gallinas
Cristobal Colon 5775
ANDES
CORDILLERA ORIENTAL
Pico Bolivar 5002
Maracaibo
ORINOCO LOWLANDS
Apure
Meta
Willemstad
Margarita (Ve
Gulf of Venezuela
Gulf of Darien

Height metres

Ice Cap	
5000	
3000	
1500	
600	
300	
150	
Sea Level	
200	
6000	

Depth

Caribbean inset:
Virgin Is (USA)
Leeward Islands
Puerto Rico
BASSE TERRE
ANTIGUA & BARBUDA
ST JOHN'S
St Kitts and Navis
Guadeloupe (FRANCE)
BASSE TERRE
Pointe-a-Pitre
Dominica
ROSEAU
Martinique (Fr.)
FORT-DE-FRANCE
St Lucia
CASTRIES
BARBADOS
BRIDGETOWN
St Vincent & the Grenadines
KINGSTOWN
Grenada
ST GEORGE'S
Tobago
Lesser Antilles
Windward Islands
CARIBBEAN SEA
SCALE 1:21 000 000

SCALE 1:34 500 000

0   345   690   1035   1380 km

Longitude West of Greenwich

Azimuthal Equal Area Projection

ASIA

ARCTIC OCEAN

GREENLAND (Denmark)

BEAUFORT SEA

BAFFIN BAY

LABRADOR SEA

Point Hope
Bering Strait
Wales
Shishmaref
Wainwright
Point Barrow
St Lawrence I. (USA)
Nome
Kotzebue
Prudhoe Bay
Nunivak I.
Nulato
Beaver
Holy Cross
Tanana
Fairbanks
Fort Yukon
Circle
Bethel
Aniak
UNITED STATES
ALASKA
Anchorage
Dawson
Aleutian Islands
Shumagin Is
Kodiak I.
Afognak I.
Seward
Cordova
Mayo
Ft. Good Hope
BRISTOL BAY
L. Iliamna
ALASKA PENINSULA
Gulf of Alaska
Stewart

Prince Patrick I.
M'Clure Strait
Queen Elizabeth Islands
Ellesmere Is.
Axel Heiberg I.
Parry Is
Bathurst I.
Banks I.
Stefansson I.
Devon I.
Lancaster Sound
Somerset I.
Bylot I.
Disko I.
NORTH MAGNETIC POLE
FRANKLIN DISTRICT
Prince of Wales
Victoria I.
Cambridge Bay
Prince Charles I.
Foxe Basin
Frobisher Bay
Holsteinsborg
Godthaab
NUUK

Amundsen Gulf
Mackenzie
Coppermine
Port Radium
Baker Lake
Coral Southampton I.
Coats I.
Mansel I.
Cumberland Sound
FROBISHER BAY
Davis Strait
Arctic Circle

YUKON TERRITORY
Whitehorse
Skagway
Gustavus
Sitka
Juneau
Alexander Archipelago
Ketchikan
Queen Charlotte I.
Prince Rupert
BRITISH COLUMBIA
Aklavik
Inuvik
Norman Wells
L. Great Bear
Yellowknife
NORTH WEST TERRITORY
MACKENZIE DISTRICT
Hay River
Fort Resolution
Pine Point
L. Great Slave
Hay R.
Back
Churchill
NUNAVUT
HUDSON BAY
Ottawa Is
Belcher I.
JAMES BAY
Nain
Hopedale
Coast of Labrador
Goose Bay
NEWFOUNDLAND
Corner Brook
Gander
St John's
Anticosti I.
Port aux Basques

PACIFIC OCEAN

CANADA

Uranium City
Fort Chipewyan
L. Athabasca
Peace river
Peace R.
Prince George
Dawson Creek
ALBERTA
Edmonton
Jasper
Red Deer
Calgary
Medicine Hat
Lethbridge
Kamloops
Vancouver I.
Vancouver
Victoria
Strait of Juan de fuca
Hecate Strait

SASKATCHEWAN
Saskatoon
Prince Albert
Regina
Brandon
L. Reindeer
Thompson
Lynn Lake
York Factory
Nelson
MANITOBA
L. Winnipeg
Winnipeg
Manitoba

Scheferville
QUEBEC
Sept-Iles
Chibougamau
Chicoutimi
Jonquiere
Cochrane
Trois-Rivieres
Quebec
Montreal
St Lawrence
Charlottetown
NEW BRUNSWICK
Moncton
Sydney
NOVA SCOTIA
Fredericton
Saint John
Halifax
Dartmouth
MAINE
Augusta
Gulf of St Lawrence

ONTARIO
Moosonee
Nakina
Timmins
Sudbury
Thunder Bay
L. Nipigon
Sault Ste. Marie
Sault Ste Marie
Toronto
Kitchener
Hamilton
London
Windsor
Oshawa
L. Ontario
L. Erie
L. Huron
L. Superior
L. Michigan

Seattle
Tacoma
Olympia
WASHINGTON
Portland
Salem
Eugene
OREGON
Klamath Falls
Spokane
Columbia
Helena
Great Falls
MONTANA
Fort Peck
IDAHO
Boise
WYOMING
Casper
NORTH DAKOTA
Bismarck
L. Sakakawea
MINNESOTA
Duluth
Minneapolis
St Paul
WISCONSIN
Madison
Milwaukee
Green Bay
MICHIGAN
Lansing
Detroit
Cleveland
OHIO
Columbus
Toledo

UNITED STATES

NEVADA
Carson City
Sacramento
San Francisco
San Jose
CALIFORNIA
Fresno
Las Vegas
Los Angeles
San Bernardino
San Diego
Tijuana
Mexicali
Salt Lake City
UTAH
Great Salt L.
L. Mead
Hoover Dam
L. Powell
Colorado
ARIZONA
Phoenix
Tucson
NEW MEXICO
Roswell
El Paso
Albuquerque
Santa Fe
COLORADO
Denver
Colorado Springs
Pueblo
Raton
WYOMING
Cheyenne
SOUTH DAKOTA
Pierre
L. Oahe
Sioux Falls
NEBRASKA
Platte
Omaha
KANSAS
Topeka
Wichita
IOWA
Des Moines
ILLINOIS
Chicago
Gary
Peoria
Springfield
INDIANA
Indianapolis
Cincinnati
St Louis
MISSOURI
Kansas City
Jefferson City
KENTUCKY
Louisville
Nashville
TENNESSEE
Memphis
Knoxville
Raleigh
NORTH CAROLINA
Charlotte
Columbia
SOUTH CAROLINA
Charleston
Savannah
GEORGIA
Atlanta
Montgomery
ALABAMA
Birmingham
MISSISSIPPI
Jackson
LOUISIANA
Baton Rouge
New Orleans
Shreveport
ARKANSAS
Little Rock
OKLAHOMA
Oklahoma City
Tulsa
Wichita Falls
Fort Worth
Dallas
Abilene
TEXAS
Austin
San Antonio
Houston
Galveston
Corpus Christi
Laredo
Pecos
Red R.
Brazos R.
Rio Grande

PENNSYLVANIA
Pittsburgh
Buffalo
NEW YORK
Albany
New York
Philadelphia
NEW JERSEY
DELAWARE
MARYLAND
WASHINGTON, D.C.
CHESAPEAKE BAY
Baltimore
Richmond
WEST VIRGINIA
VIRGINIA
Newport News
Norfolk
Wilmington
NEW HAMPSHIRE
Boston
MASSACHUSETTS
Providence
RHODE ISLAND
CONNECTICUT
VERMONT
Portland

ATLANTIC OCEAN

BERMUDA
HAMILTON

SARGASSO SEA

Tropic of Cancer

Guadalupe I. (Mexico)
Sebastian Vizcaino Bay
LOWER CALIFORNIA
Gulf of California
La Paz
Mazatlan
Hermosillo
Ciudad Obregon
Ciudad Juarez
Chihuahua
Ciudad Delicias
Los Mochis
Topolobampo
Culiacan
Durango
Torreon
Saltillo
Monterrey
Matamoros
Ciudad Victoria
San Luis Potosi
Tampico
Aguascalientes
Tepic
Guadalajara
Leon
Morelia
Netzahualcoyotl
Colima
Manzanillo
Balsas R.
MEXICO CITY
Puebla
Veracruz
Coatzacoalcos
Acapulco
Chilpancingo
Oaxaca
Salina Cruz
Tuxtla Gutierrez
Villahermosa
Merida
Cancun
CAMPECHE BAY
Campeche
Chetumal
YUCATAN

MEXICO

Clipperton I.
Revilla Gigedo Is (Mexico)

PACIFIC OCEAN

Mississippi Delta
Mississippi R.
Mobile
Tallahassee
FLORIDA
Jacksonville
Daytona Beach
Orlando
St Petersburg
Tampa
L. Okeechobee
Miami
Freeport
Strait of Florida
THE BAHAMAS
NASSAU
Turks & Caicos Is (UK)
HAVANA
Santa Clara
CUBA
Camaguey
Holguin
Santiago de Cuba
Guantanamo
JAMAICA
KINGSTON
Juventud I.
CAYMAN (UK)
GEORGE TOWN
HAITI
PORT-AU-PRINCE
DOMINICAN REP
SANTO DOMINGO
PUERTO RICO (USA)
SAN JUAN
WEST INDIES

Gulf of Mexico

CARIBBEAN SEA

Aruba (Neth.)
Curacao (Neth.)
Orangestad
Willemstad

Belize City
BELMOPAN
BELIZE
Puerto Barrios
GUATEMALA CITY
GUATEMALA
SAN SALVADOR
EL SALVADOR
TEGUCIGALPA
HONDURAS
NICARAGUA
Leon
MANAGUA
L. Managua
L. Nicaragua
SAN JOSE
COSTA RICA
Limon
Colon
PANAMA CITY
PANAMA
David
Gulf of Panama
Coiba I.
SOUTH AMERICA
COLOMBIA
VENEZUELA
Lesser Antilles

Longitude West of Greenwich

Azimuthal Equal Area Projection

Inset (lower left):

CARIBBEAN SEA

Puerto Rico
Virgin Is (USA)
Leeward Islands
BASSE TERRE
ANTIGUA & BARBUDA
ST JOHN'S
St Kitts and Navis
Guadeloupe (FRANCE)
BASSE TERRE
Pointe-a-Pitre
Dominica
ROSEAU
Martinique (FRANCE)
FORT-DE-FRANCE
St Lucia
CASTRIES
BARBADOS
BRIDGETOWN
St Vincent & the Grenadines
KINGSTOWN
Grenada
ST GEORGE'S
Tobago
Windward Islands
Lesser Antilles

SCALE 1:21 000 000

Scale bar: 0 345 690 1035 1380 km

SCALE 1:34 500 000

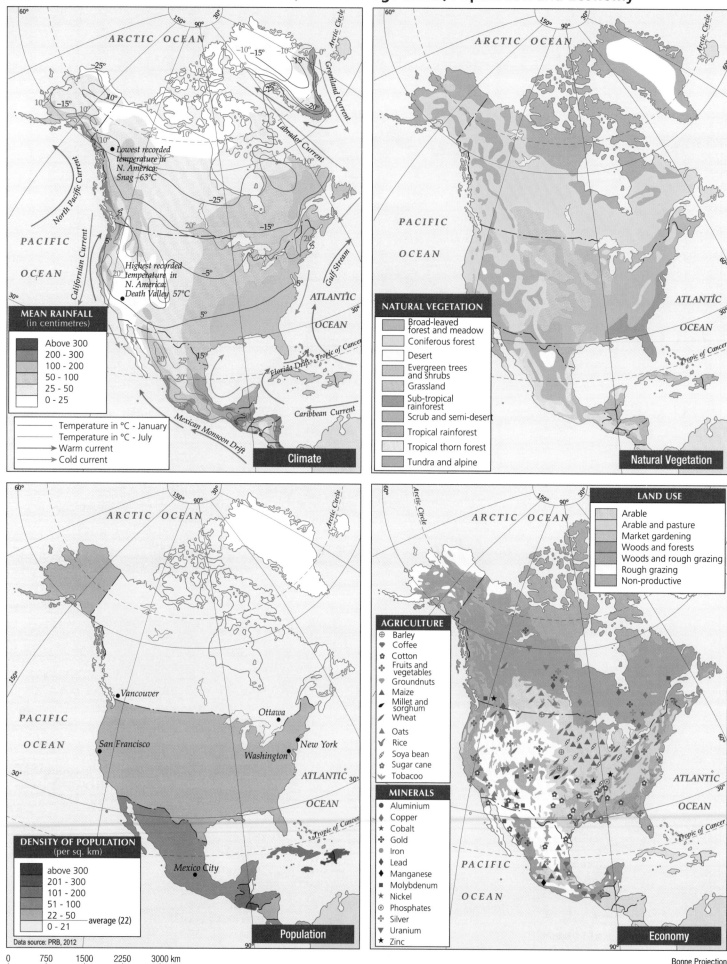

Climate

ARCTIC OCEAN

Greenland Current
Labrador Current

North Pacific Current

Californian Current

PACIFIC OCEAN

Lowest recorded temperature in N. America: Snag −63°C

Highest recorded temperature in N. America: Death Valley 57°C

Gulf Stream

ATLANTIC OCEAN

Tropic of Cancer

Florida Drift

Mexican Monsoon Drift

Caribbean Current

MEAN RAINFALL (in centimetres)

- Above 300
- 200 - 300
- 100 - 200
- 50 - 100
- 25 - 50
- 0 - 25

- —— Temperature in °C - January
- —— Temperature in °C - July
- → Warm current
- → Cold current

Natural Vegetation

ARCTIC OCEAN

PACIFIC OCEAN

ATLANTIC OCEAN

Tropic of Cancer

NATURAL VEGETATION

- Broad-leaved forest and meadow
- Coniferous forest
- Desert
- Evergreen trees and shrubs
- Grassland
- Sub-tropical rainforest
- Scrub and semi-desert
- Tropical rainforest
- Tropical thorn forest
- Tundra and alpine

Population

ARCTIC OCEAN

PACIFIC OCEAN

Vancouver

San Francisco

Ottawa

Washington

New York

ATLANTIC OCEAN

Tropic of Cancer

Mexico City

DENSITY OF POPULATION (per sq. km)

- above 300
- 201 - 300
- 101 - 200
- 51 - 100
- 22 - 50 — average (22)
- 0 - 21

Data source: PRB, 2012

Economy

ARCTIC OCEAN

PACIFIC OCEAN

ATLANTIC OCEAN

Tropic of Cancer

LAND USE

- Arable
- Arable and pasture
- Market gardening
- Woods and forests
- Woods and rough grazing
- Rough grazing
- Non-productive

AGRICULTURE

- ⊕ Barley
- ♥ Coffee
- ✿ Cotton
- ❖ Fruits and vegetables
- ♥ Groundnuts
- ▲ Maize
- ◣ Millet and sorghum
- ⫽ Wheat
- ▲ Oats
- ⩔ Rice
- ⌀ Soya bean
- ✿ Sugar cane
- ⚘ Tobacco

MINERALS

- ● Aluminium
- ◆ Copper
- ★ Cobalt
- ❖ Gold
- ● Iron
- ◆ Lead
- ◆ Manganese
- ■ Molybdenum
- ★ Nickel
- ◉ Phosphates
- ✦ Silver
- ▼ Uranium
- ★ Zinc

0	750	1500	2250	3000 km

SCALE 1:75 000 000

Bonne Projection

Conical Orthomorphic Projection

Hawaiian Islands

SCALE 1 : 3 800 000

Alaska

SCALE 1:30 500 000

Height
metres
3000
2000
1500
1000
400
200
Sea Level
200
6000

Depth

0   188   376   564   752 km

SCALE 1:18 800 000

Height
metres

6000
3000
1500
600
300
150
Sea Level
200
6000

Depth

0   345   690   1035   1380 km

SCALE 1:34 500 000

Longitude West of Greenwich

Lambert Equal Area Projection

CARIBBEAN SEA

NORTH ATLANTIC OCEAN

BELMOPAN
GUATEMALA CITY
TEGUCIGALPA
SAN SALVADOR
MANAGUA
SAN JOSE
PANAMA CITY

Cocos I. (COSTA RICA)
Malpelo I. (COLOMBIA)

Santa Marta
Barranquilla
Cartagena
Monteria
Sincelejo
Gulf of Darien
Maracaibo
L. Maracaibo
Valencia
Barquisimeto
Pto. Cabello
Margarita I. (VEN.)
Scarborough
TRINIDAD & TOBAGO
PORT OF SPAIN

CARACAS
Maturin
Tucupita
Delta of the Orinoco

Merida
Cucuta
San Cristobal
Bucaramanga
Pto. Berrio
Arauca
San Fernando
Ciudad Bolivar
Ciudad Guayana
Guri Res.
GEORGETOWN
PARAMARIBO
CAYENNE

Medellin
Manizales
Pereira
BOGOTA
Tunja
Ibague
Buenaventura
VENEZUELA
Puerto Ayacucho
Barticao
Linden
New Amsterdam
Kwakoegron
SURINAME
FRENCH GUIANA (France)
Oiapoque

Cali
Popayan
Neiva
COLOMBIA
San Carlos
Boa Vista
Lethem
GUYANA
Amapa
Maraca I.

Tumaco
Pasto
Esmeraldas
Ibarra
Mitu
Cucui
Icana
Haupes
Catrimani
Terezinha
Macapa
Mouths of the Amazon

Equator

Portoviejo
QUITO
Ambato
Manta
ECUADOR
Guayaquil
Cuenca
La Libertad
Gulf of Guayaquil
Iquitos
S. Paulo de Olivenca
Leticia
Forte Boa
Manaus
Borba
Santarem
Itaituba
Obidos
Marajo I.
Belem
Sao Luis
Parnaiba
Camocim
Fortaleza
Rocas I.

Galapagos I. (ECUADOR)

Talara
Loja
Sullana
Piura
Paita
Moyobamba
Chachapoyas
Carauari
Humaita
Barra de Sao Manuel
Tucurui Res.
Jatobal
Bacabal
Caxias
Maraba
Teresina
Sobral
Macau
Natal
Sousa

Chiclayo
Cajamarca
Pucallpa
Trujillo
Huanuco
PERU
Rio Branco
Porto Velho
Aripuana
BRAZIL
Boa Esperanca Res.
Paulistana
Crato
Joao Pessoa
Recife

Chimbote
Cerro de Pasco
Cobija
Guajara Mirim
Sobradinho Res.
Juazeiro
Petrolina
Barreiros
Maceio

Huancayo
Callao
Ayacucho
LIMA
Huancavelica
Riberalta
Jacobina
Aracaju
Alagoinhas

Pisco
Ica
Cuzco
Santa Ana
Trinidad
Mato Grosso
Aruana
Cachoeira
Salvador
Ilheus

Juliaca
L. Titicaca
Puno
BOLIVIA
Cuiaba
Goias
Anapolis
BRASILIA
Januaria
Montes Claros

Arequipa
LA PAZ
El Alto
Cochabamba
Santa Cruz
Rondonopolis
Coxim
Goiania
Piracpora
Diamantina

Matarani
Mollendo
Oruro
L. Poopo
Sucre
Pto. Suarez
Corumba
Pto Esperance
Araguari
Uberaba
Governador Valadares
Caravelas

Tacna
Arica
Potosi
Villa Montes
Fuerte Olimpo
Campo Grande
Penapolis
Ribeirao Preto
Belo Horizonte
Nova
Juiz de Fora
Victoria

Iquique
Uyuni
Tarija
PARAGUAY
Concepcion
Guaira
Sao Paulo
Londrina
Iguacu
Campinas
Campos
Duque de Caxias
Rio de Janeiro
Niteroi

Tocopila
Calama
Filadelfia
San Pedro
Ciudad del Este
Ponta Grossa
Santos

Tropic of Capricorn

Antofagasta
Jujuy
ASUNCION
San Lorenzo
Villarrica
Curitiba
Joinville

Salta
Formosa
Encarnacion
Passo Fundo
Blumenau

Taltal
San Miguel de Tucuman
Resistencia
Corrientes
Posadas
Santa Rosa
Florianopolis

Chanaral
Copiapo
Catamarca
Santiago del Estero
Porto Alegre

S. Felix I. (CHILE)
S. Ambrosio I. (CHILE)

La Serena
La Rioja
Mar Chiquita
Santa Fe
Uruguaiana
Santa Maria
Patos Lagoon

Coquimbo
San Juan
Cordoba
Parana
Rosario
Salto
Bage
Pelotas
Rio Grande

Juan Fernandez Is (CHILE)

Vina del Mar
Valparaiso
SANTIAGO
San Fernando
Mendoza
San Luis
Pergamino
Ibicuy
Fray Bentos
Mercedes
URUGUAY
MONTEVIDEO
Rocha

Curico
Talca
Trenque Lauquen
Chivilcoy
Ayellaneda
Lanus
La Plata
BUENOS AIRES

Talcahuano
Chillan
Santa Rosa
San Carlos de Bolivar
Azul
Mar del Plata

Concepcion
Zapala
Olavarria
Tandil

Temuco
Neuquen
Bahia Blanca
Tres Arroyos
Bahia Blanca

Valdivia
San Antonio Oeste

Osorno
San Carlos de Bariloche
Viedma
Carmen de Patagones
Gulf of San Matias

Puerto Montt
Ancud
Chiloe I.
Esquel
Rawson

Corcovado Gulf
Chonos Archipelago
ARGENTINA
Comodoro Rivadavia
Gulf of San Jorge

Coihaique
Puerto Deseado

Gulf of Penas

Gt. Wellington I.
Calafate
Santa Cruz
GRANDE BAY
Rio Turbio
Rio Gallegos
Falkland Is (UK)
STANLEY

Madre de Dios I.

Magellan Strait
Punta Arenas
Tierra Del Fuego
Ushuaia
Staten I.
Beagle Channel
Magellan Strait
South Georgia Is (UK)

SOUTH PACIFIC OCEAN

SOUTH ATLANTIC OCEAN

SOUTHERN OCEAN

Lambert Equal Area Projection

Longitude West of Greenwich

0   345   690   1035   1380 km

SCALE 1:34 500 000

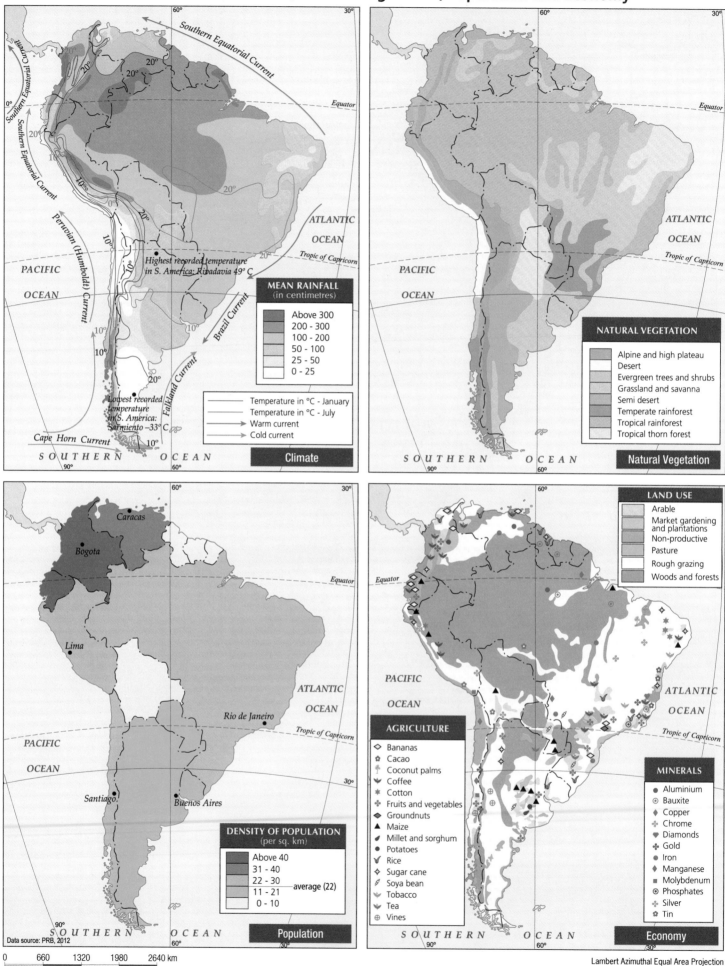

Southern Equatorial Current

Southern Equatorial Current

Southern Equatorial Current

Equator

Peruvian (Humboldt) Current

PACIFIC
OCEAN

Brazil Current

ATLANTIC
OCEAN

Tropic of Capricorn

Highest recorded temperature
in S. America: Rivadavia 49° C

Falkland Current

Lowest recorded
temperature
in S. America:
Sarmiento –33° C

Cape Horn Current

SOUTHERN   OCEAN

MEAN RAINFALL
(in centimetres)

Above 300
200 – 300
100 – 200
50 – 100
25 – 50
0 – 25

Temperature in °C – January
Temperature in °C – July
Warm current
Cold current

Climate

PACIFIC
OCEAN

ATLANTIC
OCEAN

Equator

Tropic of Capricorn

SOUTHERN   OCEAN

NATURAL VEGETATION

Alpine and high plateau
Desert
Evergreen trees and shrubs
Grassland and savanna
Semi desert
Temperate rainforest
Tropical rainforest
Tropical thorn forest

Natural Vegetation

Caracas
Bogota
Lima

PACIFIC
OCEAN

Equator

ATLANTIC
OCEAN

Rio de Janeiro

Tropic of Capricorn

Santiago
Buenos Aires

SOUTHERN   OCEAN

DENSITY OF POPULATION
(per sq. km)

Above 40
31 – 40
22 – 30   average (22)
11 – 21
0 – 10

Data source: PRB, 2012

Population

LAND USE

Arable
Market gardening
and plantations
Non-productive
Pasture
Rough grazing
Woods and forests

Equator

Equator

PACIFIC
OCEAN

ATLANTIC
OCEAN

Tropic of Capricorn

AGRICULTURE

◇ Bananas
✿ Cacao
🌴 Coconut palms
✶ Coffee
✳ Cotton
✤ Fruits and vegetables
◆ Groundnuts
▲ Maize
● Millet and sorghum
● Potatoes
✔ Rice
✧ Sugar cane
✤ Soya bean
✉ Tobacco
✾ Tea
⊕ Vines

MINERALS

● Aluminium
◉ Bauxite
◆ Copper
◢ Chrome
▼ Diamonds
✤ Gold
● Iron
◆ Manganese
■ Molybdenum
◉ Phosphates
✤ Silver
✿ Tin

SOUTHERN   OCEAN

Economy

0   660   1320   1980   2640 km

SCALE 1:66 000 000

Lambert Azimuthal Equal Area Projection

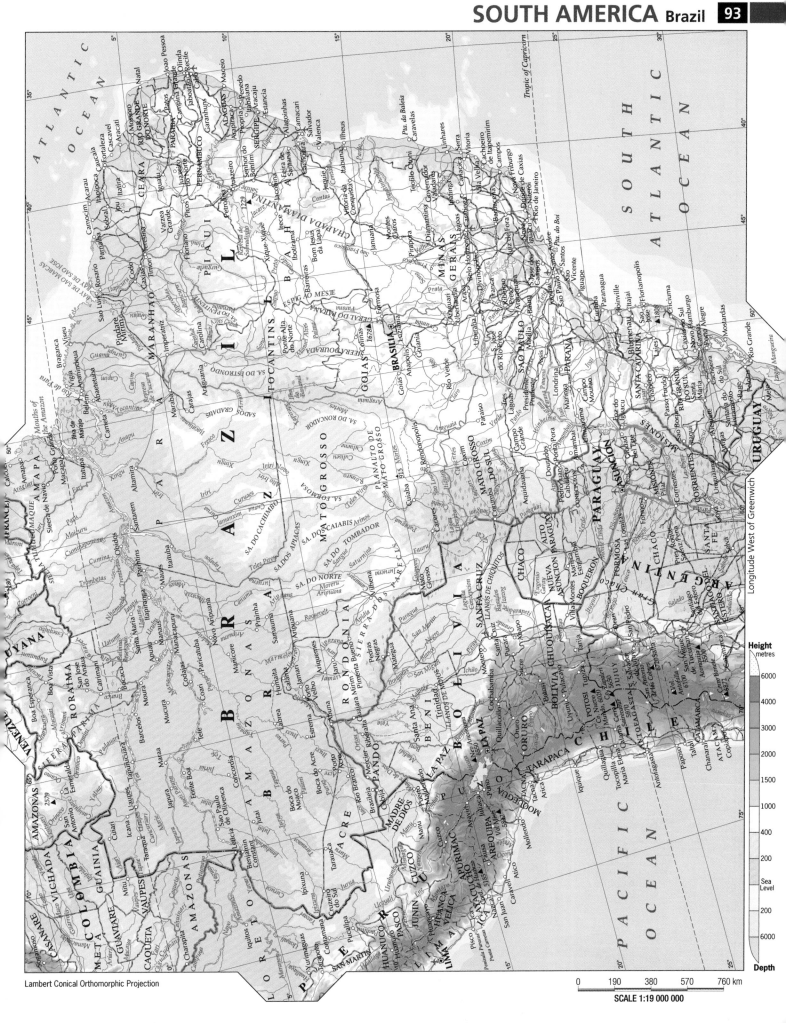

Lambert Conical Orthomorphic Projection

SCALE 1:19 000 000

0   190   380   570   760 km

Height
metres
6000
4000
3000
2000
1500
1000
400
200
Sea Level
200
6000

Depth

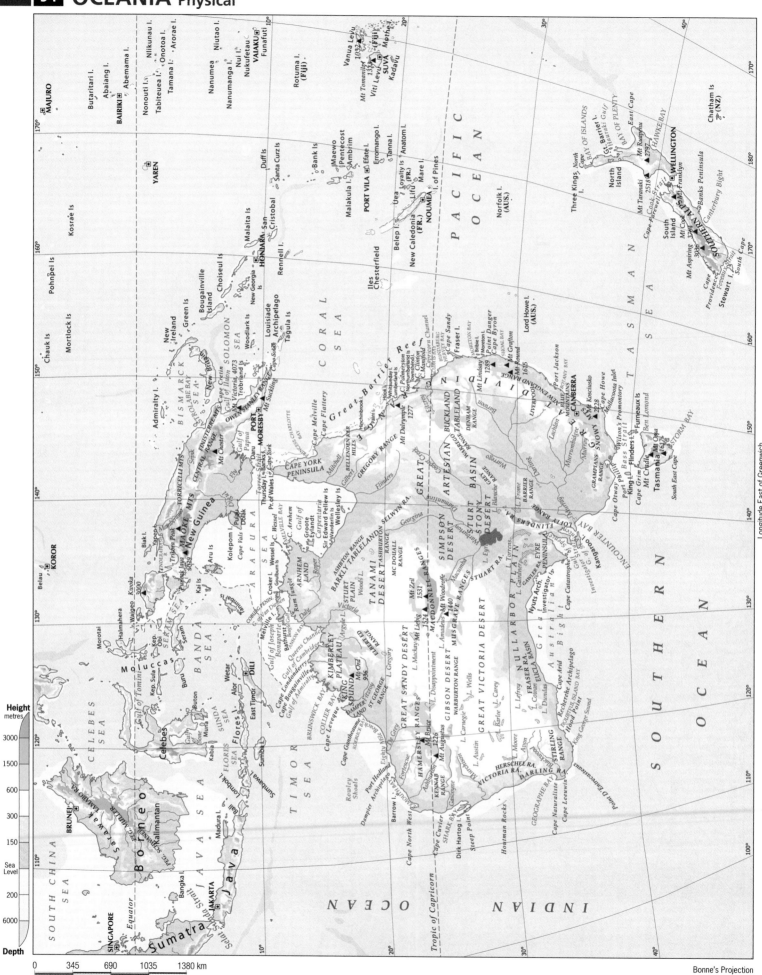

Height
metres

3000

1500

600

300

150

Sea
Level

200

6000

Depth

0   345   690   1035   1380 km

SCALE 1:34 500 000

Longitude East of Greenwich

Bonne's Projection

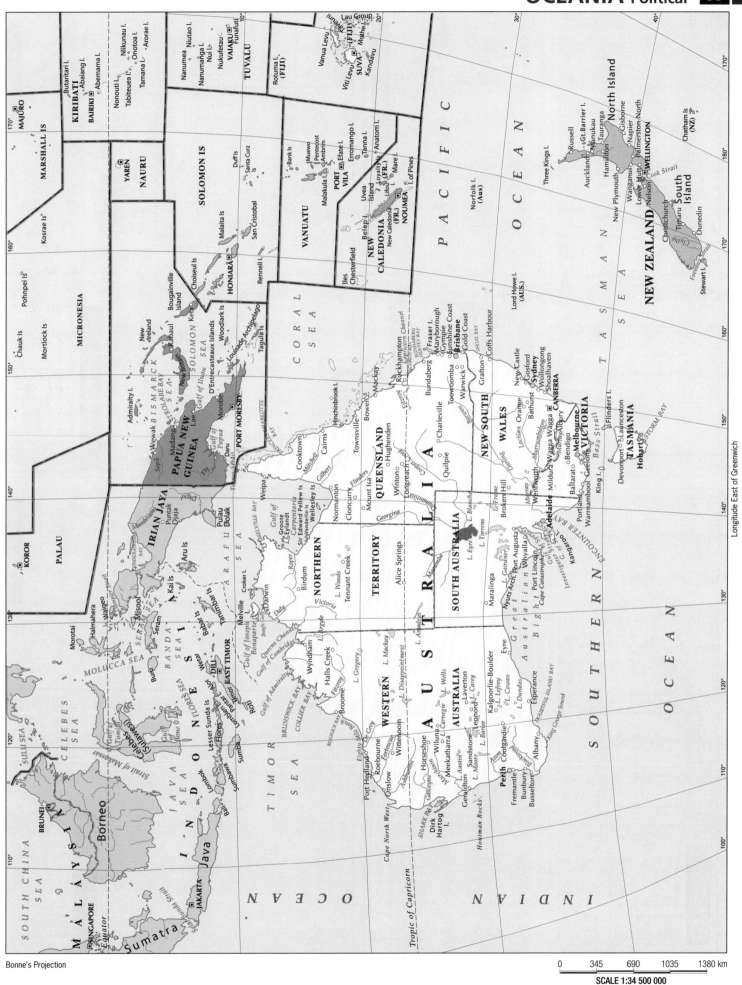

Bonne's Projection

Longitude East of Greenwich

| 0 | 345 | 690 | 1035 | 1380 km |

SCALE 1:34 500 000

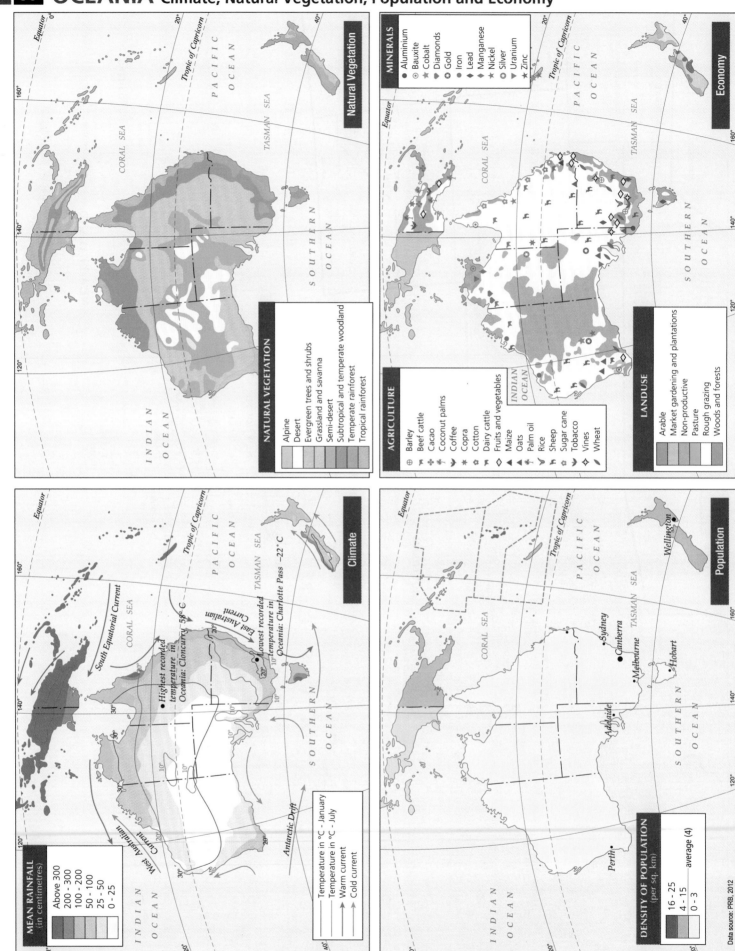

Natural Vegetation

NATURAL VEGETATION

Alpine
Desert
Evergreen trees and shrubs
Grassland and savanna
Semi-desert
Subtropical and temperate woodland
Temperate rainforest
Tropical rainforest

Economy

MINERALS
● Aluminium
◉ Bauxite
★ Cobalt
◇ Diamonds
✪ Gold
● Iron
◆ Lead
✦ Manganese
★ Nickel
✪ Silver
▼ Uranium
★ Zinc

AGRICULTURE
⊕ Barley
✚ Beef cattle
✿ Cacao
✦ Coconut palms
✿ Coffee
✧ Copra
⚘ Cotton
⋔ Dairy cattle
◇ Fruits and vegetables
◀ Maize
▲ Oats
✾ Palm oil
⚲ Rice
⚹ Sheep
⚙ Sugar cane
◇ Tobacco
✦ Vines
◥ Wheat

LANDUSE
Arable
Market gardening and plantations
Non-productive
Pasture
Rough grazing
Woods and forests

Climate

Highest recorded temperature in Oceania: Cloncurry 53°C
Lowest recorded temperature in Oceania: Charlotte Pass –22°C

South Equatorial Current
East Australian Current
West Australian Current
Antarctic Drift

MEAN RAINFALL
(in centimetres)
Above 300
200 - 300
100 - 200
50 - 100
25 - 50
0 - 25

Temperature in °C - January
Temperature in °C - July
Warm current
Cold current

0   620   1240   1860   2480 km

SCALE 1:62 000 000

Population

Wellington
Sydney
Canberra
Melbourne
Hobart
Adelaide
Perth

DENSITY OF POPULATION
(per sq. km)
16 - 25
4 - 15 — average (4)
0 - 3

Data source: PRB, 2012

Bonne Projection

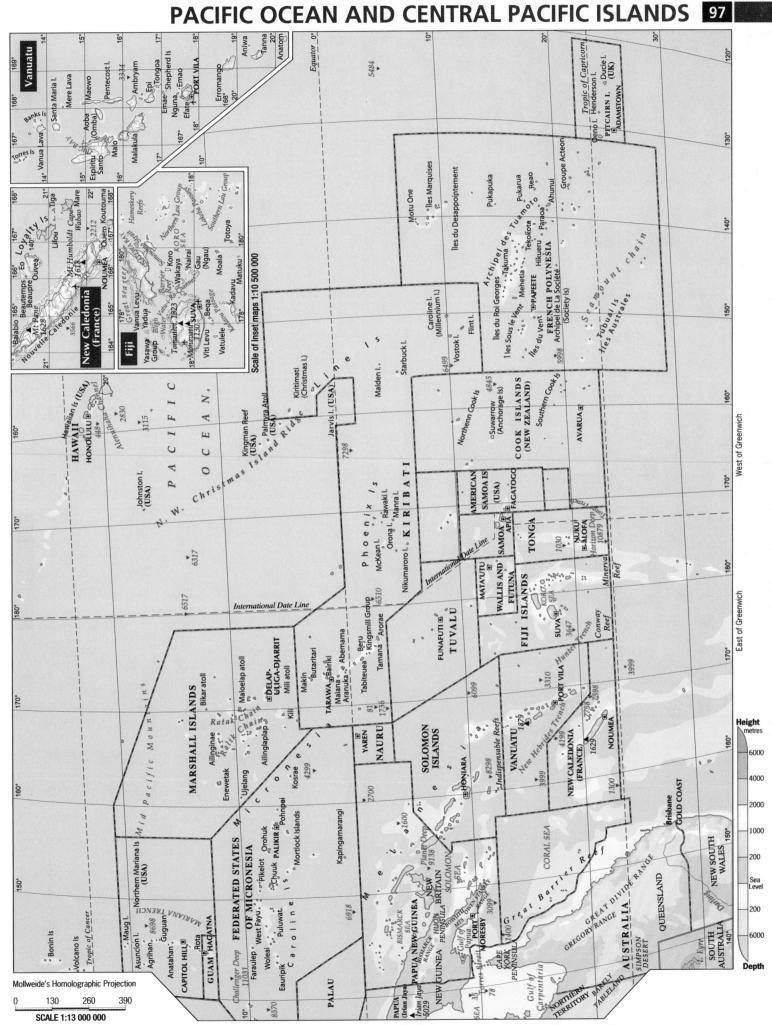

Vanuatu

Santa Maria I. · Banks Is · Mere Lava · Maewo · Pentecost I. · Aniwa · Tanna · Aoba (Omba) · Malo · Malakula · Espiritu Santo · Epi · Shepherd Is · Nguna, · Emao · Efate · Erromango · PORT VILA · Emae · Tongoa · Ambrym · 3334 · Torres Is · Vanua Lava · Torres Is

New Caledonia (France)

Loyalty Is · Lifou · Eo · Ouvéa · Tiga · Maré · Wabao · Ouém Koutouma · Balabio · Beautemps · Beaupré · Mt Panie 1628 · Mt Humboldt 1618 · NOUMEA · 2212 · Nouvelle Calédonie · 3566

Fiji

Hamaskery Reefs · Northern Lau Group · Yasawa Group · Yadua · Vanua Levu · KORO SEA · Koro · Wakaya · Nairai · Gau (Ngau) · Moala · Totoya · Southern Lau Group · Lakeba Passage · Viti Levu · SUVA 1323 · Beqa · Vatulele · Kadavu · Matuku · Great sea reef · Bligh Water · Tomanivi 1323 · Monasavu 714

Scale of inset maps 1:10 500 000

HAWAII · Hawaiian Is (USA) · HONOLULU · Alinahaha Channel · 2830 · 3115 · Kiritimati (Christmas I.) · Palmyra Atoll (USA) · Kingman Reef · Starbuck I. · Malden I. · Motu One · Îles Marquises · Pukapuka · Pukarua · Reao · Ahunui · Groupe Acteon · Oeno I. · Henderson I. · Ducie I. (UK) · PITCAIRN I. (UK) · ADAMSTOWN · Tropic of Capricorn

PACIFIC OCEAN · N.W. Christmas Island Ridge · Johnston I. (USA) · Jarvis I. (USA) · 7298 · Line Is · Caroline I. (Millennium I.) · Vostok I. · Flint I. · Archipel des Tuamoto · Takuma · Hikueru · Paraoa · Tekokota · Mehetia · PAPEETE · FRENCH POLYNESIA · Archipel de La Société (Society Is) · Îles du Roi Georges · Îles Sous le Vent · Îles du Vent · Tubuaï Is · Îles Australes · Seamount chain · 5998

6317 · 6517 · Phoenix Is · McKean I. · Orona I. · Rawaki I. · Manra I. · Nikumaroro I. · KIRIBATI · Northern Cook Is · Suwarrow (Anchorage Is) · COOK ISLANDS (NEW ZEALAND) · Southern Cook Is · AVARUA · 4845 · 6499

International Date Line · AMERICAN SAMOA IS (USA) · FAGATOGO · SAMOA · APIA · MATA'UTU · WALLIS AND FUTUNA · TONGA · NUKU'ALOFA · Horizon Deep 10879 · 1030 · Minerva Reef

MARSHALL ISLANDS · Bikar atoll · Maloelap atoll · DELAP-ULIGA-DJARRIT · Mili atoll · Makin · Butaritari · Marakei · TARAWA · Bairiki · Maiana · Abemama · Aranuka · Kingsmill Group · Beru · Tabiteuea · Tamaná · Arorae · 87 · 1735 · 6510 · FUNAFUTI · TUVALU · Ratak Chain · Ralik Chain · Alinginae · Enewetak · 'Ujelang · Allinglaplap · Kili · Kosrae · 4299 · YAREN · NAURU · 2700 · SOLOMON ISLANDS · HONIARA · 8298 · Indispensable Reefs · 3310 · 1879 · VANUATU · PORT VILA · New Hebrides Trench · Hunter Trench · 4758 · 2598 · Conway Reef · 3647 · FIJI ISLANDS · SUVA · KORO · 914 · 3999 · 6099 · 4199 · 3999 · NEW CALEDONIA (FRANCE) · 1629 · NOUMEA · 1300

FEDERATED STATES OF MICRONESIA · Northern Mariana Is (USA) · CAPITOL HILL · GUAM · HAGATNA · Maug I. · Asuncion I. · 8698 · Agrihan · Guguan · Anatahan · Pikelot · Orohuk · Farauleip · West Fayu · PALIKIR · Chuuk · Pohnpei · Mortlock Islands · Eauripik · Woleai · Puluwat · Kapingamarangi · Bonin Is · Volcano Is · Tropic of Cancer · MARIANA TRENCH · Challenger Deep 11031 · 8570 · 6918 · Caroline Is · Micronesia · Melanesia · Mid Pacific Mountains

PALAU · PAPUA (Irian Jaya) · 5029 · Planet Deep 9138 · BISMARCK SEA · PAPUA NEW GUINEA · NEW GUINEA · NEW BRITAIN · HUON PENINSULA · SOLOMON SEA · PORT MORESBY · 3099 · 1400 · Owen Stanley Range · Gulf of Papua · Torres Strait · CAPE YORK PENINSULA · Gulf of Carpentaria · CORAL SEA · Great Barrier Reef · Brisbane · GOLD COAST · QUEENSLAND · AUSTRALIA · NEW SOUTH WALES · GREAT DIVIDE RANGE · GREGORY RANGE · BARKLY TABLELAND · NORTHERN TERRITORY · SOUTH AUSTRALIA · SIMPSON DESERT · L. Eyre · Darling

Equator 0° · 5484 · International Date Line · Tropic of Capricorn · West of Greenwich · East of Greenwich

Mollweide's Homolographic Projection

0 · 130 · 260 · 390

SCALE 1:13 000 000

Height
metres
6000
4000
2000
1000
200
Sea Level
200
6000
Depth

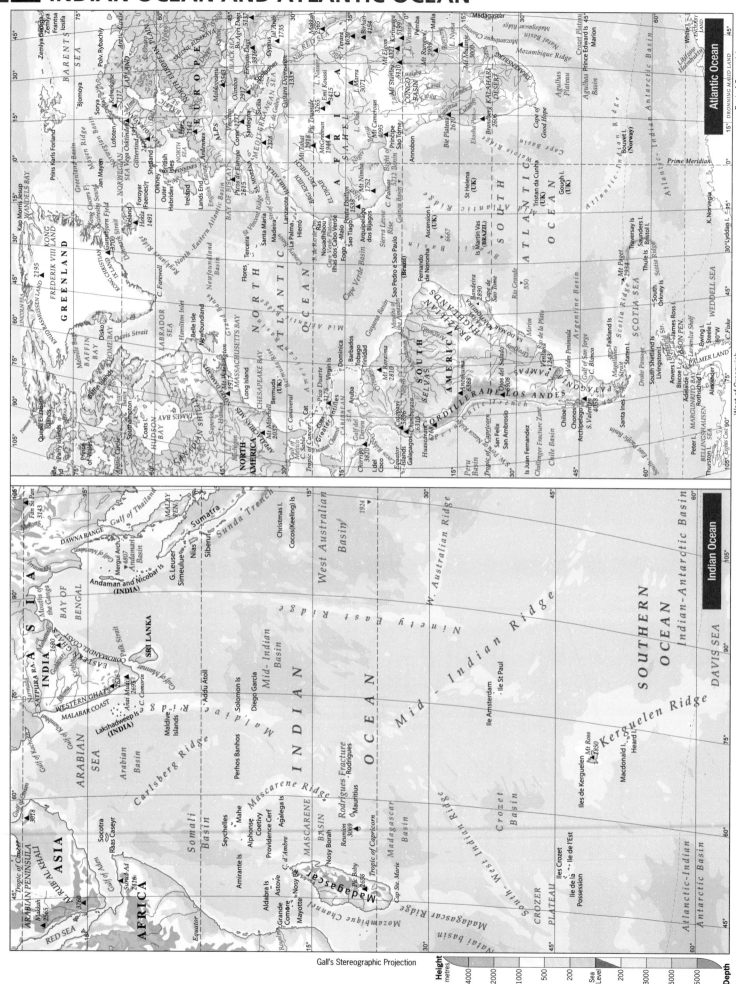

Atlantic Ocean

Indian Ocean

Gall's Stereographic Projection

Height
metres
4000
2000
1000
500
200
Sea Level
200
3000
5000
6000
Depth

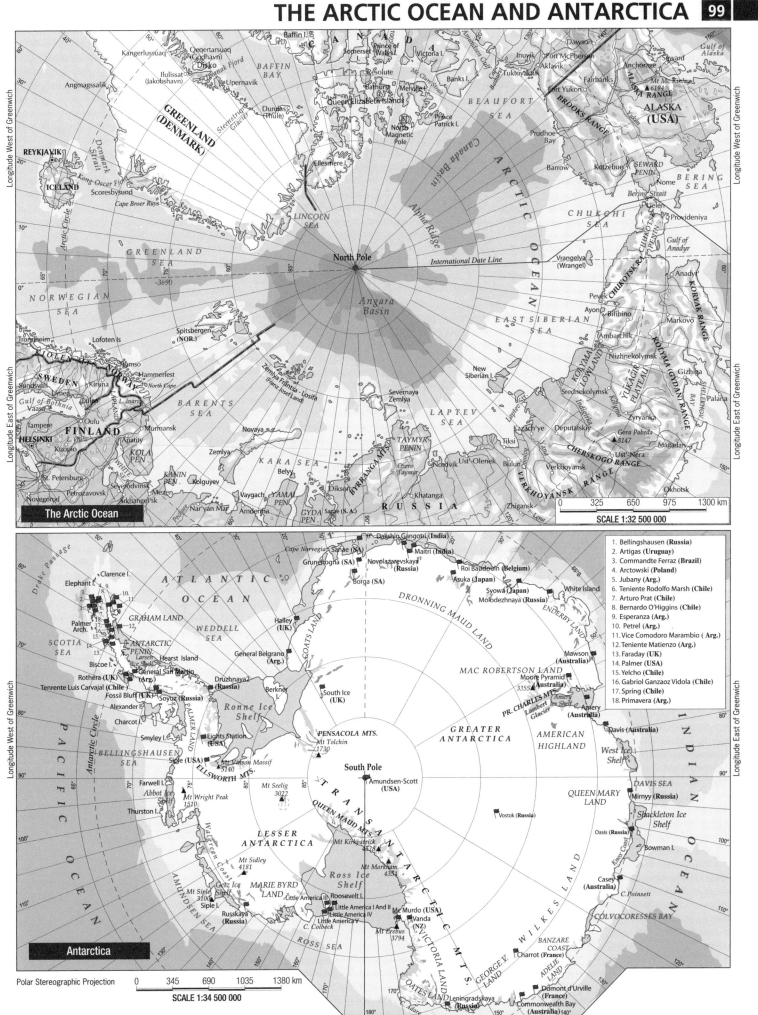

The Arctic Ocean

Longitude West of Greenwich

Longitude East of Greenwich

Kangerlussuaq
Qeqertarsuaq (Godhavn)
Disko
Ilulissat (Jakobshavn)
Upernavik
Angmagssalik
GREENLAND (DENMARK)
Steenstrup Glacier
Uummannaq Fjord
Dundas (Thule)
Baffin I.
Somerset I.
Prince of Wales I.
Victoria I.
Banks I.
C A N A D A
Resolute
Bathurst
Melville I.
Prince Patrick I.
BAFFIN BAY
Queen Elizabeth Islands
North Magnetic Pole
Ellesmere I.
Amundsen Gulf
Inuvik
Fort McPherson
Aklavik
Tuktoyaktuk
Dawson
Mt Mc Kinley
▲6194
Seward
Anchorage
Gulf of Alaska
ALASKA RANGE
Fairbanks
Fort Yukon
ALASKA (USA)
BROOKS RANGE
Prudhoe Bay
Barrow
Kotzebue
Nome
SEWARD PENIN.
Providentiya
CHUKCHI SEA
BERING SEA
Bering Strait
Uelen
CHUKOTSKI RA.
CHUKOT. PENIN.
Gulf of Anadyr
Anadyr
KORYAK RANGE

REYKJAVIK
ICELAND
Denmark Strait
Kong Oscar Fjd.
Scoresbysund
Cape Broer Ruys
GREENLAND SEA
LINCOLN SEA
-3690
North Pole
International Date Line
ARCTIC OCEAN
Canada Basin
Alpha Ridge
Angara Basin
EAST SIBERIAN SEA
Vrangelya (Wrangel)
Pevek
Ayon
Bilibino
Markovo
KOLYMA LOWLAND
YUKAGIR PLATEAU
SHELIKHOV BAY
Palana
Gizhiga

Trondheim
Lofoten Is
Tromso
Hammerfest
North Cape
NORWAY
Spitsbergen (NOR.)
BARENTS SEA
Zemlya Franta -Iosifa (Franz Josef Land)
Severnaya Zemlya
New Siberian I.
Nizhnekolymsk
Srednekolymsk
Zyryanka
Gora Pobeda ▲3147
Magadan
CHERSKOGO RANGE
KOLYMA (GYDAN) RANGE

SWEDEN
Sundsvall
Umea
FINLAND
Kiruna
L. Inari
Oulu
Apatity
Murmansk
Novaya
Zemlya
KARA SEA
Belyy
Diksson
TAYMYR PENIN.
Ozero Taymyr
BYRRANGA MTS.
Nordvik
Ust'-Olenek
Tiksi
Kazach'ye
Deputatskiy
Verkhoyansk
Ust'-Nera
VERKHOYANSK RANGE
Okhotsk

HELSINKI
Vaasa
Tampere
Gulf of Bothnia
Kuopio
St. Petersburg
WHITE SEA
KOLA PEN.
Severodvinsk
Arkhangel'sk
Mezen
KANIN PEN.
Kolguyev
Vaygach
YAMAL PEN.
GYDA PEN.
Khatanga
Zhigansk
R U S S I A
Lena
NORWEGIAN SEA

Petrozavovsk
Novegorod
Nar'yan Mar
Amderma
Pechora
Sanga (S.A.)

| 0 | 325 | 650 | 975 | 1300 km |

SCALE 1:32 500 000

Antarctica

Longitude West of Greenwich

Longitude East of Greenwich

Drake Passage
Clarence I.
Elephant I.
Palmer Arch.
GRAHAM LAND
ATLANTIC OCEAN
Cape Norvegia
Sanae (SA)
Grunehogna (SA)
Novolazarevskaya (Russia)
Borga (SA)
Dakshin Gangotri (India)
Maitri (India)
Roi Baudouin (Belgium)
Asuka (Japan)
Syowa (Japan)
Molodezhnaya (Russia)
White Island
DRONNING MAUD LAND
ENDERBY LAND

SCOTIA SEA
Biscoe Is
ANTARCTIC PENIN.
Halley (UK)
WEDDELL SEA
COATS LAND
Mawson (Australia)
MAC ROBERTSON LAND
Moore Pyramid 3355▲
PR. CHARLES MTS.
Lambert Glacier
Amery Ice Shelf
Amery (Australia)

Rothera (UK)
Tenrente Luis Carvajal (Chile)
Fossil Bluff (UK)
Alexander I.
Charcot I.
General San Martin (Arg.)
Soyuz (Russia)
General Belgrano (Arg.)
Hearst Island
Larsen Ice Shelf
Druzhnaya 2 (Russia)
Berkner I.
RONNE ICE SHELF
South Ice (UK)
PALMER LAND
GREATER ANTARCTICA
AMERICAN HIGHLAND
Davis (Australia)
West Ice Shelf

PACIFIC OCEAN
Smyley I.
Eights Station (USA)
Siple (USA)
Mt Tolchin 1730
PENSACOLA MTS.
South Pole
Amundsen-Scott (USA)
T R A N S A N T A R C T I C
QUEEN MARY LAND
DAVIS SEA
Mirnyy (Russia)
INDIAN OCEAN

BELLINGSHAUSEN SEA
Mt Vinson Massif 5140
ELLSWORTH MTS.
Farwell I.
Abbot Ice Shelf
Thurston I.
Mt Seelig 3022
Mt Wright Peak 1510
LESSER ANTARCTICA
QUEEN MAUD MTS.
Mt Kirkpatrick 4528
Vostok (Russia)
Oasis (Russia)
Shackleton Ice Shelf
Bowman I.

Walgreen Coast
Mt Sidley 4181
Getz Ice Shelf
Mt Siple 3100
Siple I.
Russkaya (Russia)
MARIE BYRD LAND
Little America III
Roosevelt I.
Little America I AND II
Little America IV
Little America V
C. Colbeck
ROSS ICE SHELF
Mt Markham 4351
Mc Murdo (USA)
Vanda (NZ)
Mt Erebus 3794
ROSS SEA
VICTORIA LAND
WILKES LAND
OATES LAND
C. Adare
Leningradskaya (Russia)
Charcot (France)
GEORGE V LAND
ADELIE LAND
BANZARE COAST
Dumont d'Urville (France)
Commonwealth Bay (Australia)
COLVOCORESSES BAY
C. Poinsett
Casey (Australia)

1. Bellingshausen (**Russia**)
2. Artigas (**Uruguay**)
3. Commandte Ferraz (**Brazil**)
4. Arctowski (**Poland**)
5. Jubany (**Arg.**)
6. Teniente Rodolfo Marsh (**Chile**)
7. Arturo Prat (**Chile**)
8. Bernardo O'Higgins (**Chile**)
9. Esperanza (**Arg.**)
10. Petrel (**Arg.**)
11. Vice Comodoro Marambio (**Arg.**)
12. Teniente Matienzo (**Arg.**)
13. Faraday (**UK**)
14. Palmer (**USA**)
15. Yelcho (**Chile**)
16. Gabriol Ganzaoz Vidola (**Chile**)
17. Spring (**Chile**)
18. Primavera (**Arg.**)

Polar Stereographic Projection

| 0 | 345 | 690 | 1035 | 1380 km |

SCALE 1:34 500 000

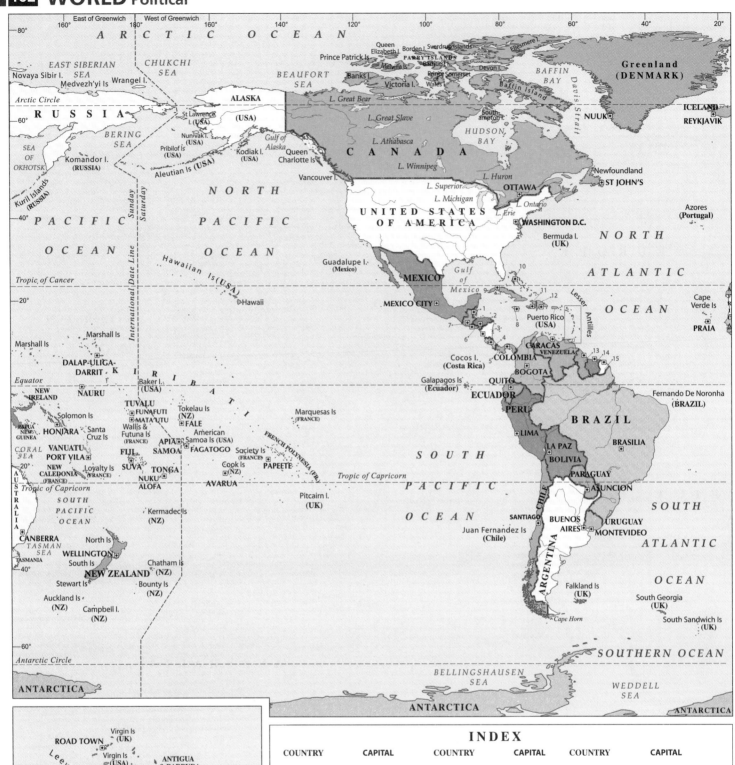

INDEX

COUNTRY	CAPITAL	COUNTRY	CAPITAL	COUNTRY	CAPITAL
1. BELIZE	BELMOPAN	17. THE NETHERLANDS	THE HAGUE	33. UAE	ABU DHABI
2. HONDURAS	TEGUCIGALPA	18. DENMARK	COPENHAGEN	34. ERITREA	ASMARA
3. NICARAGUA	MANAGUA	19. LITHUANIA	VILNIUS	35. DJIBOUTI	DJIBOUTI
4. COSTA RICA	SAN JOSE	20. LATVIA	RIGA	36. RAWANDA	KIGALI
5. PANAMA	PANAMA CITY	21. ESTONIA	TALLINN	37. BURUNDI	BUJUMBURA
6. EL SALVADOR	SAN SALVADOR	22. CYPRUS	LEFKOSIA	38. MALAWI	LILONGWE
7. GUATEMALA	GUATEMALA CITY	23. LEBANON	BEIRUT	39. SWAZILAND	MBABANE
8. JAMAICA	KINGSTON	24. ISRAEL	JERUSALEM	40. LESOTHO	MASERU
9. CUBA	HAVANA	25. PALESTINE	GAZA	41. EQUATORIAL GUINEA	MALABO
10. BAHAMAS	NASSAU	26. JORDAN	AMMAN	42. BHUTAN	THIMPHU
11. HAITI	PORT-AU-PRINCE	27. GEORGIA	TBILISI	43. BANGLADESH	DHAKA
12. DOMINICAN REP.	SANTO DOMINGO	28. ARMENIA	YEREVAN	44. BRUNEI	BANDAR SERI BEGAWAN
13. GUYANA	GEORGETOWN	29. AZERBAIJAN	BAKU	45. CAMBODIA	PHNOM PENH
14. SURINAME	PARAMARIBO	30. KUWAIT	KUWAIT	46. GIBRALTER	GIBRALTER
15. FRENCH GUIANA	CAYENNE	31. BAHRAIN	MANAMA	47. ANDORRA	ANDORRA LA VELLA
16. BELGIUM	BRUSSELS	32. QATAR	DOHA	48. LIECHTENSTEIN	VADUZ

SCALE 1:124 200 000

| 0 | 1210 | 2420 | 3630 | 4840 km |

SCALE 1:121 000 000

Robinson Projection

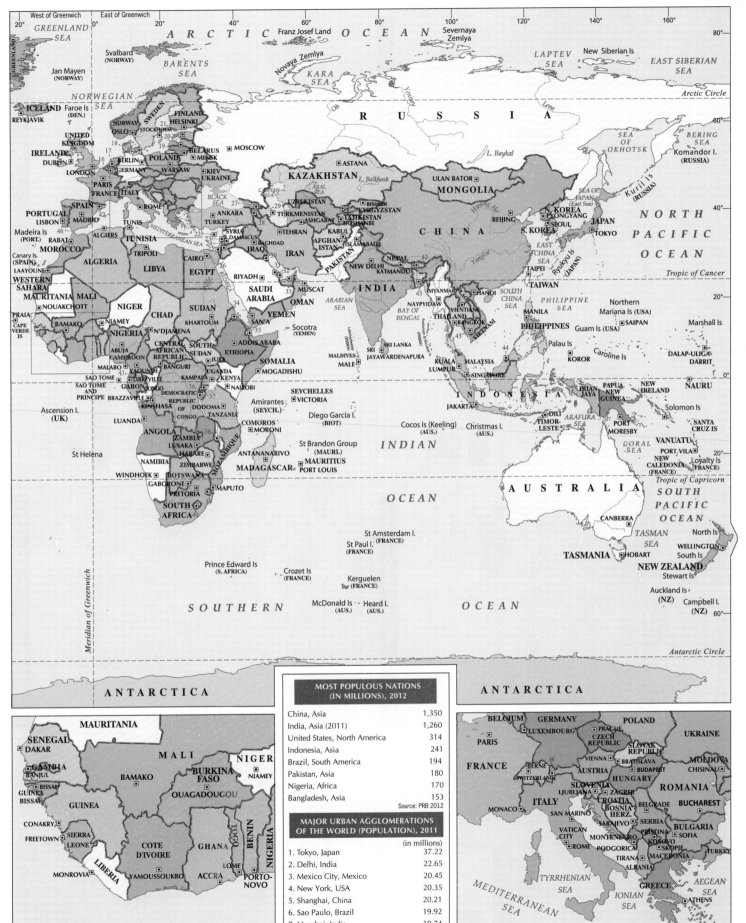

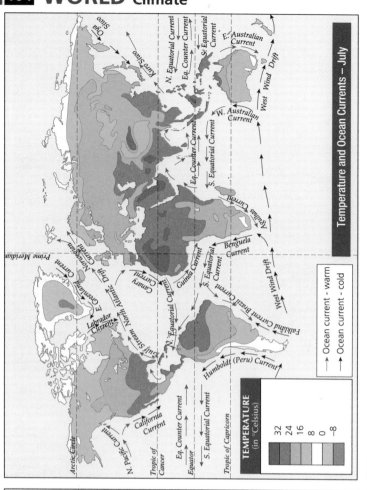

Temperature and Ocean Currents – July

Ocean current - warm
Ocean current - cold

TEMPERATURE
(in °Celsius)

32
24
16
8
0
-8

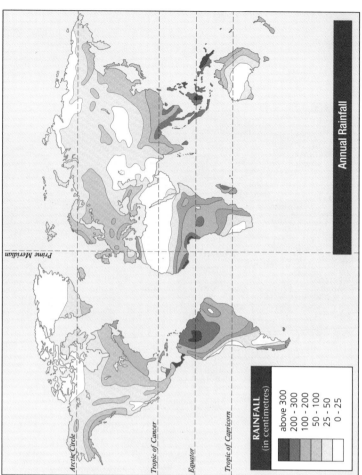

Annual Rainfall

RAINFALL
(in centimetres)

above 300
200 - 300
100 - 200
50 - 100
25 - 50
0 - 25

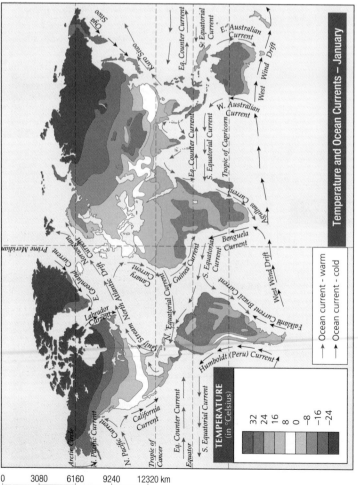

Temperature and Ocean Currents – January

Ocean current - warm
Ocean current - cold

TEMPERATURE
(in °Celsius)

32
24
16
8
0
-8
-16
-24

0   3080   6160   9240   12320 km

SCALE 1:308 000 000

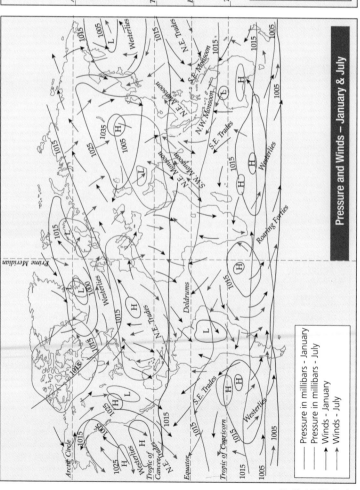

Pressure and Winds – January & July

Pressure in millibars - January
Pressure in millibars - July
Winds - January
Winds - July

Modified Gall Projection

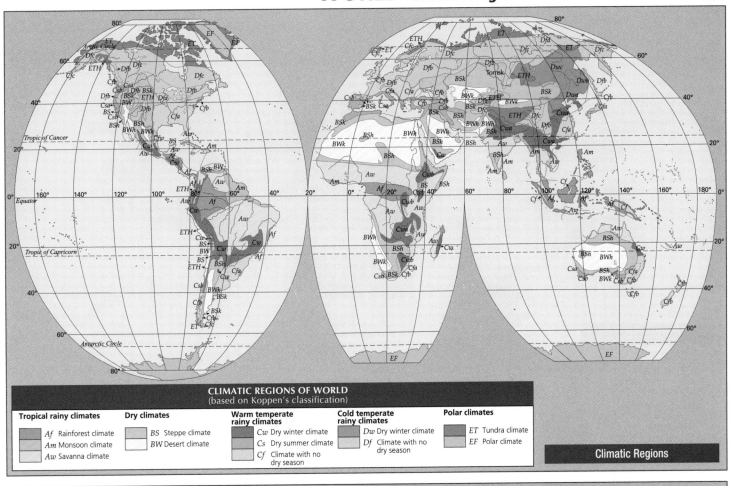

CLIMATIC REGIONS OF WORLD
(based on Koppen's classification)

Tropical rainy climates
- *Af* Rainforest climate
- *Am* Monsoon climate
- *Aw* Savanna climate

Dry climates
- *BS* Steppe climate
- *BW* Desert climate

Warm temperate rainy climates
- *Cw* Dry winter climate
- *Cs* Dry summer climate
- *Cf* Climate with no dry season

Cold temperate rainy climates
- *Dw* Dry winter climate
- *Df* Climate with no dry season

Polar climates
- *ET* Tundra climate
- *EF* Polar climate

Climatic Regions

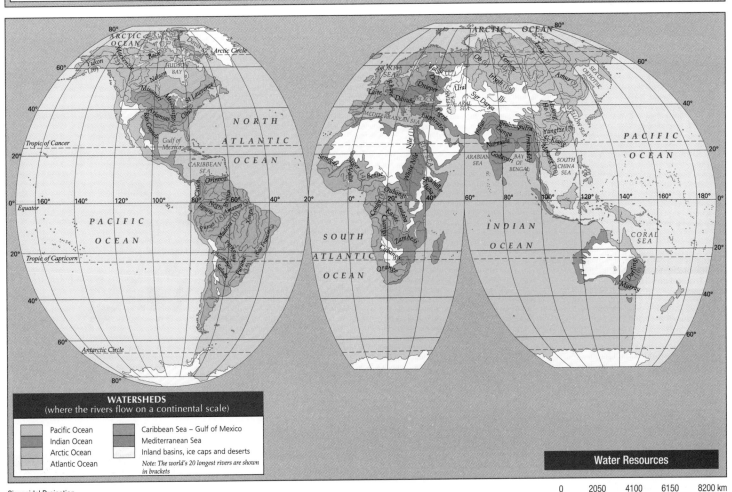

WATERSHEDS
(where the rivers flow on a continental scale)

- Pacific Ocean
- Indian Ocean
- Arctic Ocean
- Atlantic Ocean
- Caribbean Sea – Gulf of Mexico
- Mediterranean Sea
- Inland basins, ice caps and deserts

Note: The world's 20 longest rivers are shown in brackets

Water Resources

Sinusoidal Projection

0 2050 4100 6150 8200 km

SCALE 1:205 000 000

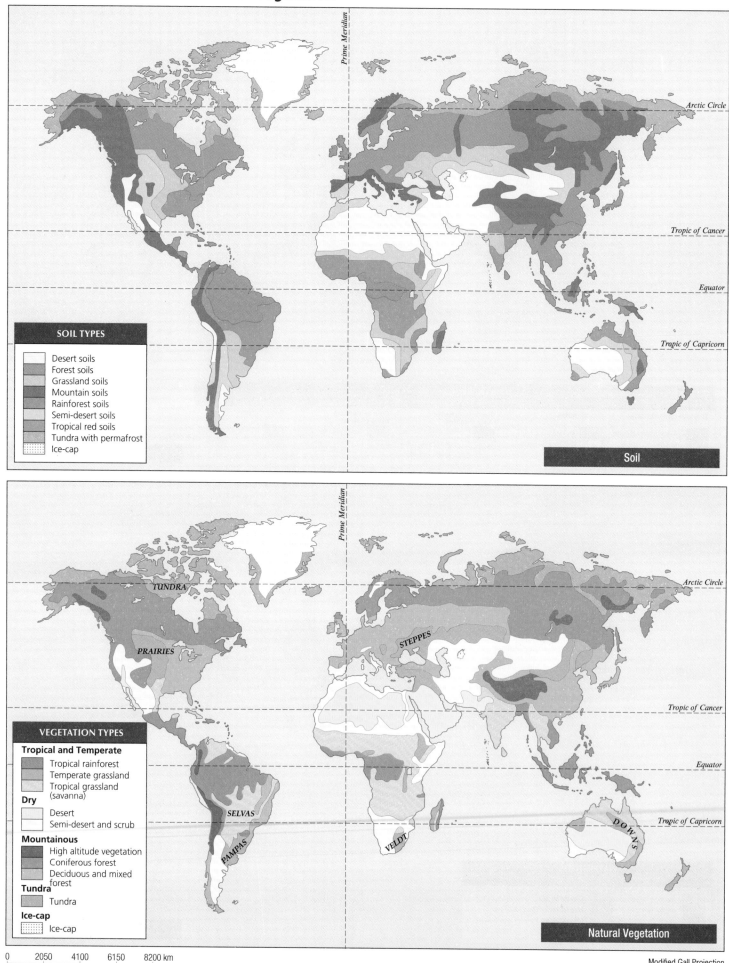

SOIL TYPES

Desert soils
Forest soils
Grassland soils
Mountain soils
Rainforest soils
Semi-desert soils
Tropical red soils
Tundra with permafrost
Ice-cap

Soil

VEGETATION TYPES

Tropical and Temperate
Tropical rainforest
Temperate grassland
Tropical grassland (savanna)

Dry
Desert
Semi-desert and scrub

Mountainous
High altitude vegetation
Coniferous forest
Deciduous and mixed forest

Tundra
Tundra

Ice-cap
Ice-cap

Natural Vegetation

TUNDRA
PRAIRIES
SELVAS
PAMPAS
STEPPES
VELDT
DOWNS

Prime Meridian
Arctic Circle
Tropic of Cancer
Equator
Tropic of Capricorn

0   2050   4100   6150   8200 km
SCALE 1:205 000 000

Modified Gall Projection

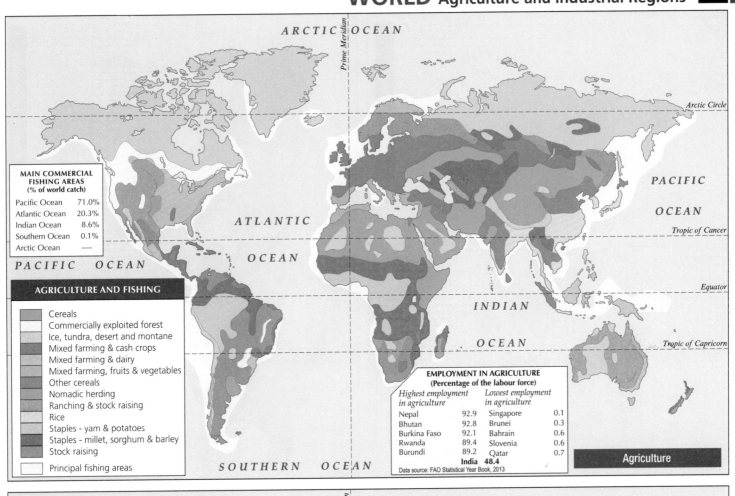

ARCTIC OCEAN

Prime Meridian

Arctic Circle

PACIFIC OCEAN

ATLANTIC OCEAN

Tropic of Cancer

PACIFIC OCEAN

Equator

INDIAN OCEAN

Tropic of Capricorn

SOUTHERN OCEAN

MAIN COMMERCIAL FISHING AREAS
(% of world catch)

Pacific Ocean	71.0%
Atlantic Ocean	20.3%
Indian Ocean	8.6%
Southern Ocean	0.1%
Arctic Ocean	----

AGRICULTURE AND FISHING

- Cereals
- Commercially exploited forest
- Ice, tundra, desert and montane
- Mixed farming & cash crops
- Mixed farming & dairy
- Mixed farming, fruits & vegetables
- Other cereals
- Nomadic herding
- Ranching & stock raising
- Rice
- Staples - yam & potatoes
- Staples - millet, sorghum & barley
- Stock raising
- Principal fishing areas

EMPLOYMENT IN AGRICULTURE
(Percentage of the labour force)

Highest employment in agriculture		Lowest employment in agriculture	
Nepal	92.9	Singapore	0.1
Bhutan	92.8	Brunei	0.3
Burkina Faso	92.1	Bahrain	0.6
Rwanda	89.4	Slovenia	0.6
Burundi	89.2	Qatar	0.7
India	**48.4**		

Data source: FAO Statistical Year Book, 2013

Agriculture

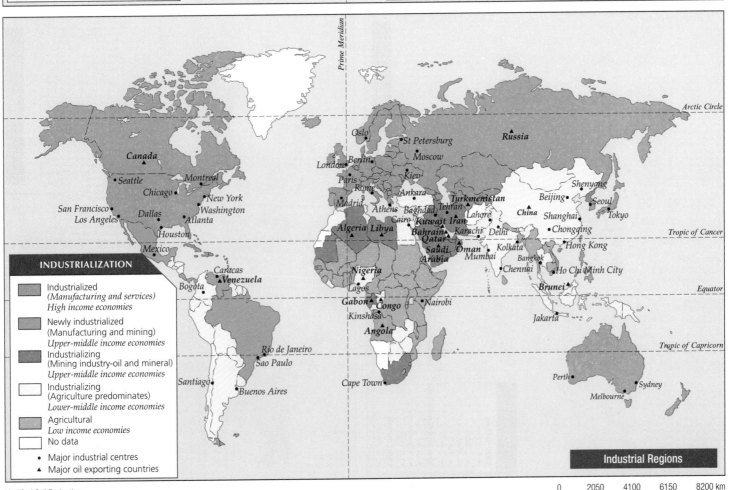

Prime Meridian

Arctic Circle

Oslo • St Petersburg • Russia

Canada ▲ London • Berlin • Moscow

Seattle • Paris • Kiev • Shenyang

Montreal • Rome • Ankara • Beijing • Seoul

Chicago • New York • Madrid • Athens • Baghdad • Tehran • Turkmenistan • China • Shanghai • Tokyo

San Francisco • Washington • Cairo • Kuwait Iran • Lahore • Chongqing

Dallas • Atlanta • Algeria Libya • Bahrain • Karachi • Delhi • Hong Kong Tropic of Cancer

Los Angeles • Houston • Qatar • Kolkata

Mexico • Saudi Arabia • Oman • Mumbai • Bangkok

Caracas ▲ Venezuela • Nigeria • Chennai • Ho Chi Minh City

Bogota • Lagos • Brunei Equator

Gabon ▲ Congo • Nairobi

Kinshasa • Jakarta

Angola ▲

Rio de Janeiro

Sao Paulo

Santiago • Cape Town • Perth • Sydney

Buenos Aires • Melbourne

Tropic of Capricorn

INDUSTRIALIZATION

- Industrialized (Manufacturing and services) *High income economies*
- Newly industrialized (Manufacturing and mining) *Upper-middle income economies*
- Industrializing (Mining industry-oil and mineral) *Upper-middle income economies*
- Industrializing (Agriculture predominates) *Lower-middle income economies*
- Agricultural *Low income economies*
- No data
- • Major industrial centres
- ▲ Major oil exporting countries

Industrial Regions

Modified Gall Projection

0	2050	4100	6150	8200 km

SCALE 1:205 000 000

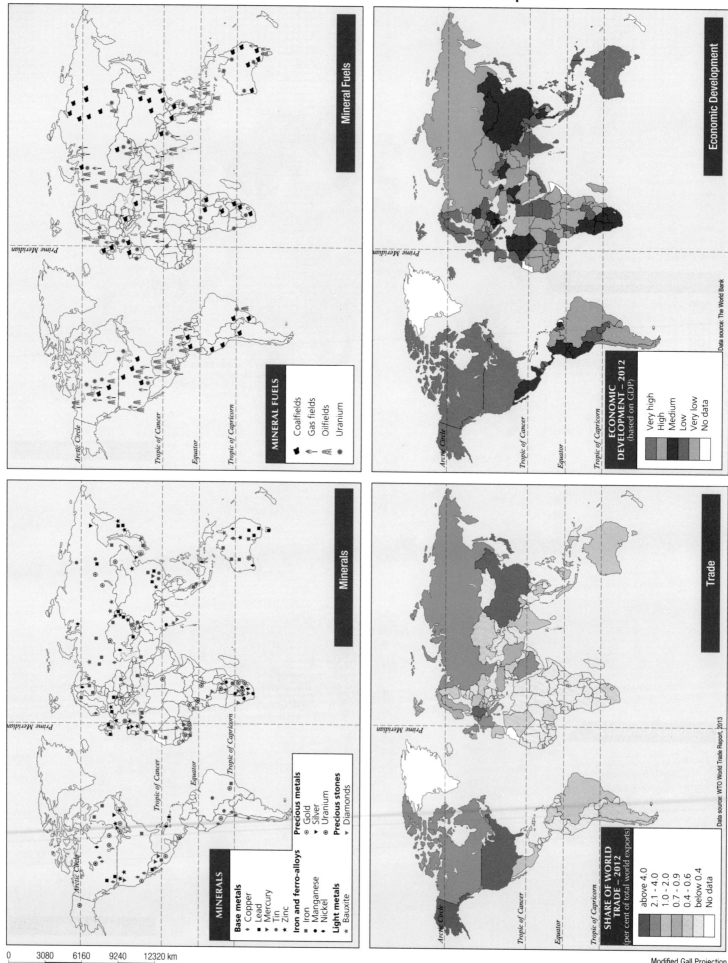

Mineral Fuels

MINERAL FUELS

	Coalfields
	Gas fields
	Oilfields
	Uranium

Economic Development

ECONOMIC DEVELOPMENT – 2012
(based on GDP)

- Very high
- High
- Medium
- Low
- Very low
- No data

Data source: The World Bank

Minerals

MINERALS

Base metals
- Copper
- Lead
- Mercury
- Tin
- Zinc

Iron and ferro-alloys
- Iron
- Manganese
- Nickel

Light metals
- Bauxite

Precious metals
- Gold
- Silver
- Uranium

Precious stones
- Diamonds

Trade

SHARE OF WORLD TRADE – 2012
(per cent of total world exports)

- above 4.0
- 2.1 - 4.0
- 1.0 - 2.0
- 0.7 - 0.9
- 0.4 - 0.6
- below 0.4
- No data

Data source: WTO World Trade Report, 2013

Modified Gall Projection

0   3080   6160   9240   12320 km

SCALE 1:308 000 000

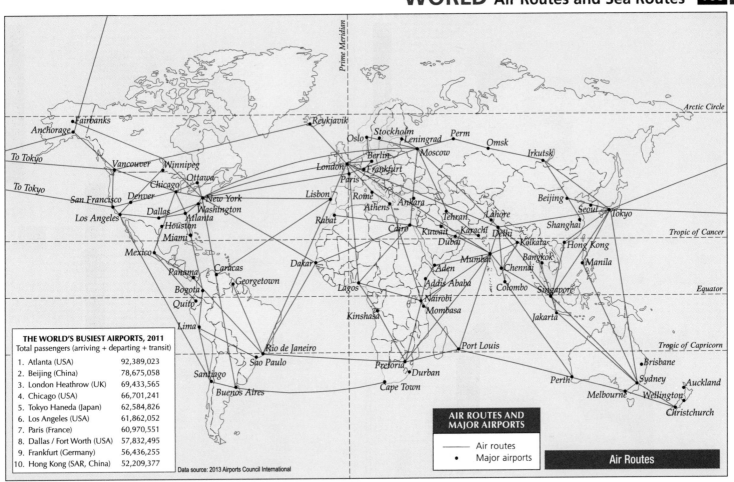

THE WORLD'S BUSIEST AIRPORTS, 2011
Total passengers (arriving + departing + transit)

1.	Atlanta (USA)	92,389,023
2.	Beijing (China)	78,675,058
3.	London Heathrow (UK)	69,433,565
4.	Chicago (USA)	66,701,241
5.	Tokyo Haneda (Japan)	62,584,826
6.	Los Angeles (USA)	61,862,052
7.	Paris (France)	60,970,551
8.	Dallas / Fort Worth (USA)	57,832,495
9.	Frankfurt (Germany)	56,436,255
10.	Hong Kong (SAR, China)	52,209,377

Data source: 2013 Airports Council International

AIR ROUTES AND MAJOR AIRPORTS

— Air routes
• Major airports

Air Routes

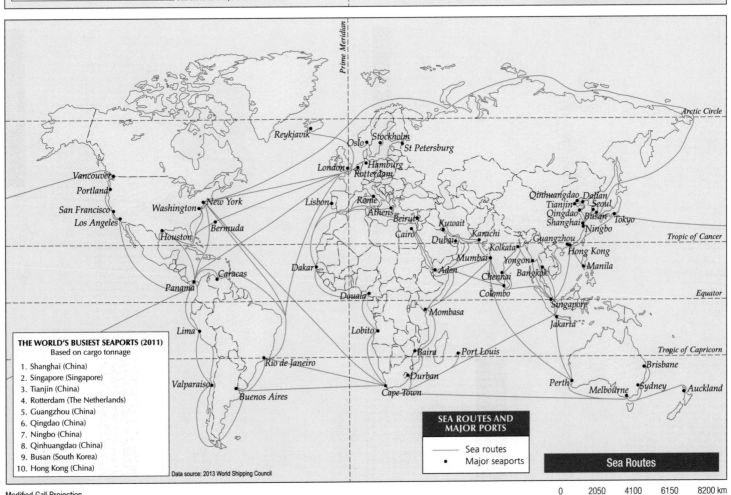

THE WORLD'S BUSIEST SEAPORTS (2011)
Based on cargo tonnage

1. Shanghai (China)
2. Singapore (Singapore)
3. Tianjin (China)
4. Rotterdam (The Netherlands)
5. Guangzhou (China)
6. Qingdao (China)
7. Ningbo (China)
8. Qinhuangdao (China)
9. Busan (South Korea)
10. Hong Kong (China)

Data source: 2013 World Shipping Council

SEA ROUTES AND MAJOR PORTS

— Sea routes
• Major seaports

Sea Routes

Modified Gall Projection

0 2050 4100 6150 8200 km

SCALE 1:205 000 000

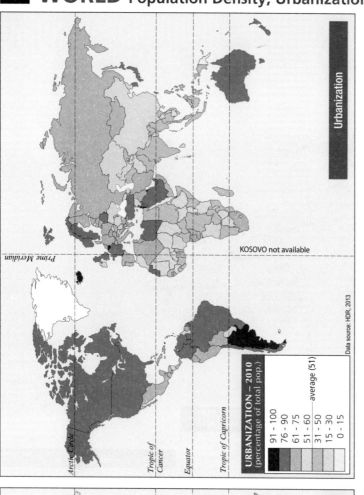

Urbanization

KOSOVO not available

Data source: HDR, 2013

URBANIZATION – 2010
(percentage of total pop.)

- 91 - 100
- 76 - 90
- 61 - 75
- 51 - 60   average (51)
- 31 - 50
- 15 - 30
- 0 - 15

Prime Meridian
Arctic Circle
Tropic of Cancer
Equator
Tropic of Capricorn

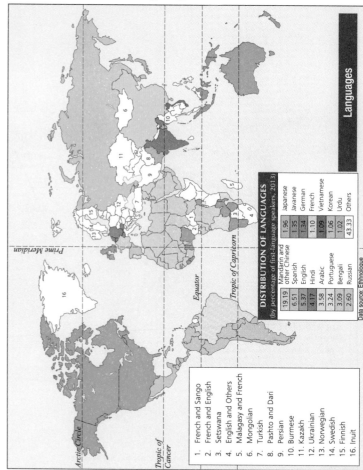

Languages

DISTRIBUTION OF LANGUAGES
(by percentage of first-language speakers, 2013)

Mandarin and other Chinese	19.19	Japanese	1.96
Spanish	6.51	Javanese	1.35
English	5.37	German	1.34
Hindi	4.17	French	1.10
Arabic	3.58	Vietnamese	1.09
Portuguese	3.24	Korean	1.06
Bengali	3.09	Urdu	1.02
Russian	2.60	Others	43.33

Data source: Ethnologue

1. French and Sango
2. French and English
3. Setswana
4. English and Others
5. Malagasy and French
6. Mongolian
7. Turkish
8. Pashto and Dari
9. Persian
10. Burmese
11. Kazakh
12. Ukrainian
13. Norwegian
14. Swedish
15. Finnish
16. Inuit

Prime Meridian
Arctic Circle
Tropic of Cancer
Equator
Tropic of Capricorn

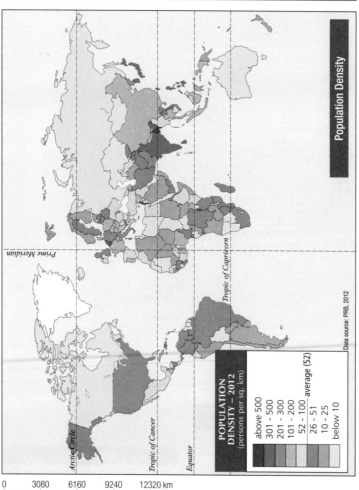

Population Density

Data source: PRB, 2012

POPULATION DENSITY – 2012
(persons per sq. km)

- above 500
- 301 - 500
- 201 - 300
- 101 - 200
- 52 - 100   average (52)
- 26 - 51
- 10 - 25
- below 10

Prime Meridian
Arctic Circle
Tropic of Cancer
Equator
Tropic of Capricorn

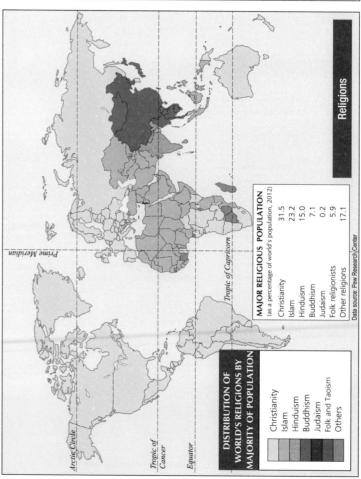

Religions

MAJOR RELIGIOUS POPULATION
(as a percentage of world's population, 2012)

Christianity	31.5
Islam	23.2
Hinduism	15.0
Buddhism	7.1
Judaism	0.2
Folk religionists	5.9
Other religions	17.1

Data source: Pew Research Center

DISTRIBUTION OF WORLD'S RELIGIONS BY MAJORITY OF POPULATION

- Christianity
- Islam
- Hinduism
- Buddhism
- Judaism
- Folk and Taoism
- Others

Prime Meridian
Arctic Circle
Tropic of Cancer
Equator
Tropic of Capricorn

0   3080   6160   9240   12320 km

SCALE 1:308 000 000

Modified Gall Projection

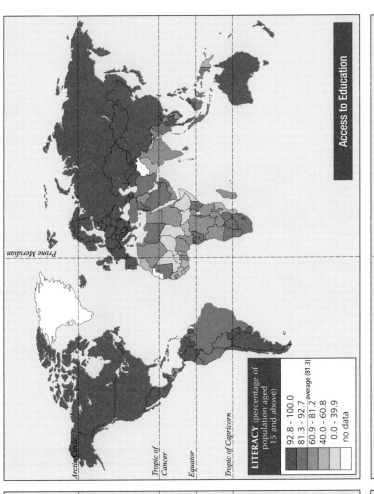

Access to Education

LITERACY (percentage of population aged 15 and above)

- 92.8 - 100.0
- 81.3 - 92.7
- 60.9 - 81.2 average (81.3)
- 40.0 - 60.8
- 0.0 - 39.9
- no data

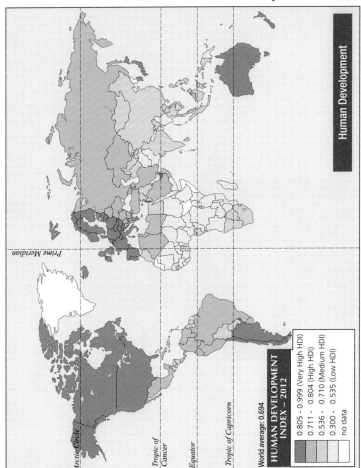

Human Development

HUMAN DEVELOPMENT INDEX – 2012

- 0.805 - 0.999 (Very High HDI)
- 0.711 - 0.804 (High HDI)
- 0.536 - 0.710 (Medium HDI)
- 0.300 - 0.535 (Low HDI)
- no data

World average: 0.694

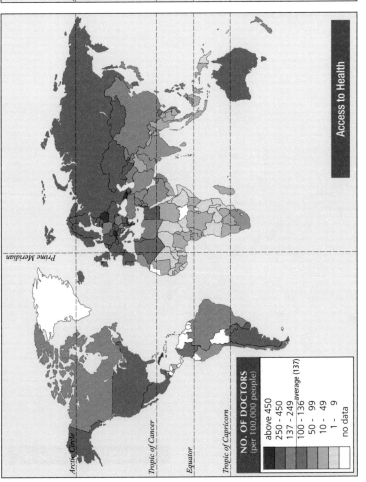

Access to Health

NO. OF DOCTORS (per 100,000 people)

- above 450
- 250 - 450
- 137 - 249
- 100 - 136 average (137)
- 50 - 99
- 10 - 49
- 1 - 9
- no data

Modified Gall Projection

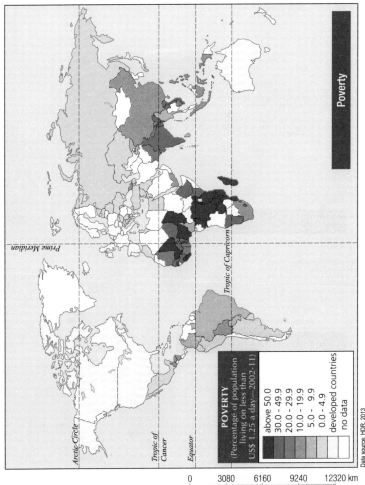

Poverty

POVERTY (Percentage of population living on less than US$ 1.25 a day—2002-11)

- above 50.0
- 30.0 - 49.9
- 20.0 - 29.9
- 10.0 - 19.9
- 5.0 - 9.9
- 0.0 - 4.9
- developed countries
- no data

Data source: HDR, 2013

0   3080   6160   9240   12320 km

SCALE 1:308 000 000

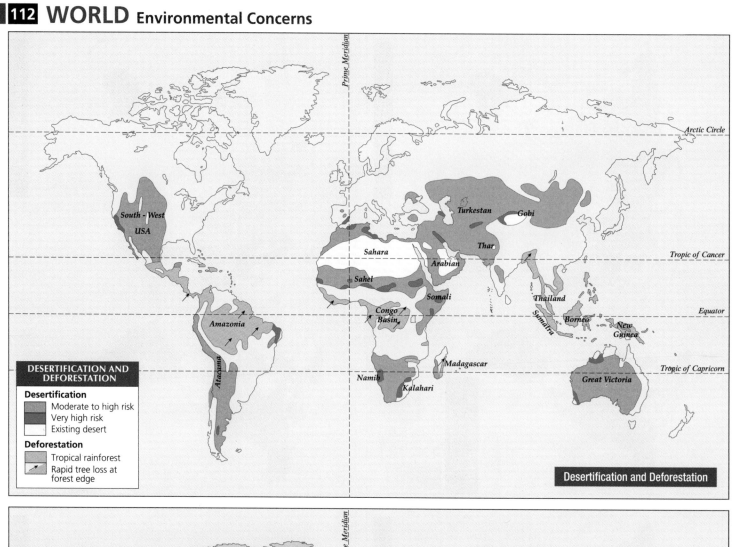

DESERTIFICATION AND DEFORESTATION

Desertification
- Moderate to high risk
- Very high risk
- Existing desert

Deforestation
- Tropical rainforest
- Rapid tree loss at forest edge

Arctic Circle

Tropic of Cancer

Equator

Tropic of Capricorn

Prime Meridian

South - West USA

Amazonia

Atacama

Sahara

Sahel

Turkestan

Gobi

Thar

Arabian

Somali

Congo Basin

Namib

Kalahari

Madagascar

Thailand

Sumatra

Borneo

New Guinea

Great Victoria

Desertification and Deforestation

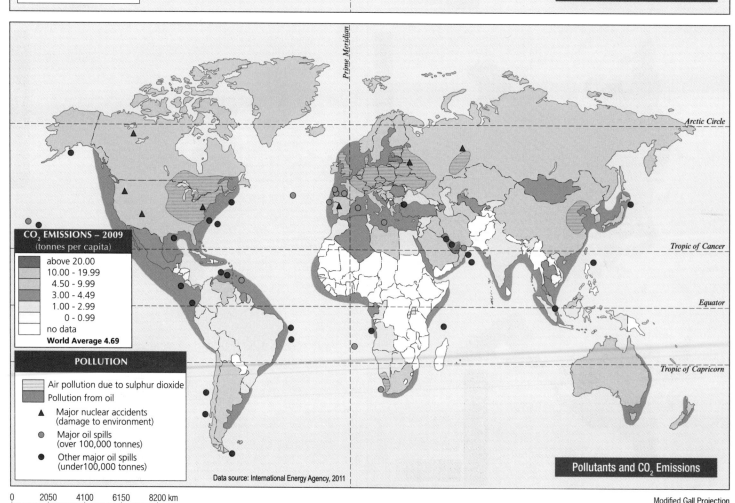

CO_2 EMISSIONS – 2009
(tonnes per capita)
- above 20.00
- 10.00 - 19.99
- 4.50 - 9.99
- 3.00 - 4.49
- 1.00 - 2.99
- 0 - 0.99
- no data

World Average 4.69

POLLUTION
- Air pollution due to sulphur dioxide
- Pollution from oil
- ▲ Major nuclear accidents (damage to environment)
- ● Major oil spills (over 100,000 tonnes)
- ● Other major oil spills (under 100,000 tonnes)

Arctic Circle

Tropic of Cancer

Equator

Tropic of Capricorn

Prime Meridian

Data source: International Energy Agency, 2011

Pollutants and CO_2 Emissions

0   2050   4100   6150   8200 km

SCALE 1:205 000 000

Modified Gall Projection

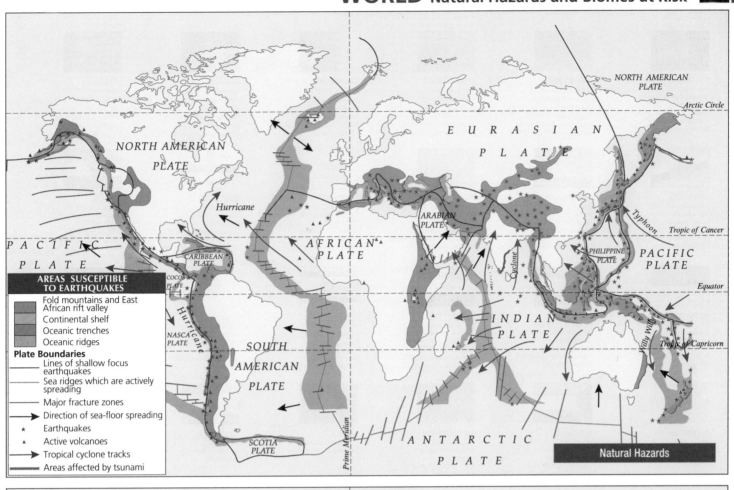

AREAS SUSCEPTIBLE TO EARTHQUAKES
- Fold mountains and East African rift valley
- Continental shelf
- Oceanic trenches
- Oceanic ridges

Plate Boundaries
- Lines of shallow focus earthquakes
- Sea ridges which are actively spreading
- Major fracture zones
- → Direction of sea-floor spreading
- ★ Earthquakes
- ▲ Active volcanoes
- → Tropical cyclone tracks
- Areas affected by tsunami

Natural Hazards

NORTH AMERICAN PLATE
EURASIAN PLATE
ARABIAN PLATE
AFRICAN PLATE
PHILIPPINE PLATE
PACIFIC PLATE
INDIAN PLATE
CARIBBEAN PLATE
COCOS PLATE
NASCA PLATE
SOUTH AMERICAN PLATE
SCOTIA PLATE
ANTARCTIC PLATE

Hurricane
Typhoon
Cyclone
Willy willy

Arctic Circle
Tropic of Cancer
Equator
Tropic of Capricorn
Prime Meridian

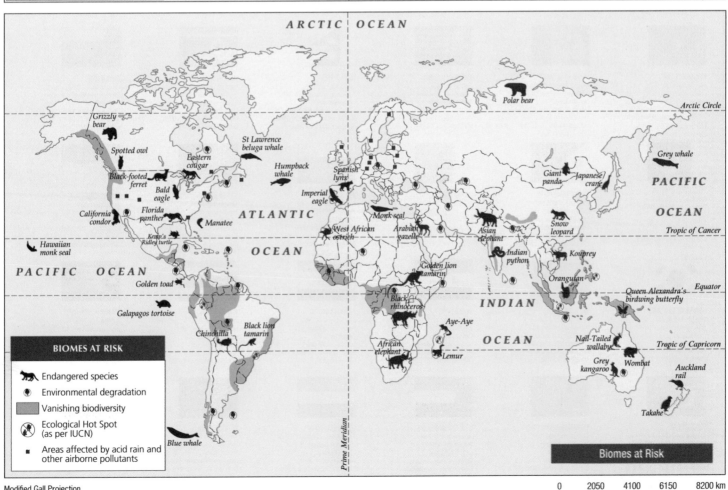

BIOMES AT RISK
- 🐾 Endangered species
- Environmental degradation
- Vanishing biodiversity
- Ecological Hot Spot (as per IUCN)
- ■ Areas affected by acid rain and other airborne pollutants

Biomes at Risk

ARCTIC OCEAN
ATLANTIC OCEAN
PACIFIC OCEAN
INDIAN OCEAN

Polar bear
Grizzly bear
Spotted owl
Eastern cougar
St Lawrence beluga whale
Humpback whale
Spanish lynx
Grey whale
Giant panda
Japanese crane
Black-footed ferret
Bald eagle
Imperial eagle
Snow leopard
California condor
Florida panther
Manatee
Monk seal
Arabian gazelle
Asian elephant
Kouprey
Hawaiian monk seal
West African ostrich
Indian python
Orangutan
Kemp's Ridley turtle
Golden lion tamarin
Queen Alexandra's birdwing butterfly
Golden toad
Black rhinoceros
Aye-Aye
Nail-Tailed wallaby
Galapagos tortoise
Chinchilla
Black lion tamarin
African elephant
Lemur
Grey kangaroo
Wombat
Auckland rail
Blue whale
Takahe

Arctic Circle
Tropic of Cancer
Equator
Tropic of Capricorn
Prime Meridian

Modified Gall Projection

0   2050   4100   6150   8200 km

SCALE 1:205 000 000

ASIA Flag, Area, Population, Capital, Language, Monetary Unit and GDP

AFGHANISTAN (AF)
Area (sq. km): 652,225
Population (million): 33.4
Capital: Kabul
Language: Dari Persian, Pushtu
Monetary Unit: Afghani (AFA)
GDP (per capita US$): NA

ARMENIA (AM)
Area (sq. km): 29,800
Population (million): 3.1
Capital: Yerevan
Language: Armenian, Yezidi
Monetary Unit: Dram (AMD)
GDP (per capita US$): 3,337.9

AZERBAIJAN (AZ)
Area (sq. km): 86,600
Population (million): 9.4
Capital: Baku
Language: Azerbaijani, Armenian
Monetary Unit: Az. Manat (AZM)
GDP (per capita US$): 7,227.5

BAHRAIN (BH)
Area (sq. km): 691
Population (million): 1.4
Capital: Manama
Language: Arabic, English
Monetary Unit: Bahraini Dinar (BHD)
GDP (per capita US$): NA

BANGLADESH (BD)
Area (sq. km): 143,998
Population(million): 152.4
Capital: Dhaka
Language: Bengali, English
Monetary Unit: Taka (BDT)
GDP (per capita US$): 747.3

BHUTAN (BT)
Area (sq. km): 38,394
Population (million): 0.8
Capital: Thimphu
Language: Dzongkha, Nepali
Monetary Unit: Ngultrum (BTN)
GDP (per capita US$): 2,398.9

BRUNEI (BN)
Area (sq. km): 5,765
Population (million): 0.4
Capital: Bandar Seri Begawan
Language: Malay, English
Monetary Unit: Br. Dollar (BND)
GDP (per capita US$): 41,126.6

CAMBODIA (KH)
Area (sq. km): 181,000
Population (million): 14.5
Capital: Phnom Penh
Language: Khmer, French
Monetary Unit: Riel (KHR)
GDP (per capita US$): 946.0

CHINA (CN)
Area (sq. km): 9,562,000
Population (million): 1353.6
Capital: Beijing
Language: Mandarin, Wu
Monetary Unit: Yuan Renminbi (CNY)
GDP (per capita US$): 6,091.0

CYPRUS (CY)
Area (sq. km): 9,251
Population (million): 1.1
Capital: Nicosia
Language: Greek, Turkish
Monetary Unit: Euro (EUR)
GDP (per capita US$): 26,315.5

GEORGIA (GE)
Area (sq. km): 69,700
Population (million): 4.3
Capital: T'bilisi
Language: Georgian, Russian
Monetary Unit: Lari (GEL)
GDP (per capita US$): 3,508.4

INDIA (IN)
Area (sq. km): 3,287,263
Population (million): 1,210.2 (2011)
Capital: New Delhi
Language: Hindi, English
Monetary Unit: Ind. Rupee (INR)
GDP (per capita US$): 1,489.2

INDONESIA (ID)
Area (sq. km): 1,919,445
Population (million): 244.8
Capital: Jakarta
Language: Indonesian
Monetary Unit: Rupiah (IDR)
GDP (per capita US$): 3,556.8

IRAN (IR)
Area (sq. km): 1,648,000
Population (million): 75.6
Capital: Tehran
Language:Farsi, Azeri
Monetary Unit: Iranian Rial (IRR)
GDP (per capita US$): NA

IRAQ (IQ)
Area (sq. km): 438,317
Population (million): 33.7
Capital: Baghdad
Language: Arabic, Kurdish
Monetary Unit: Iraqi Dinar (IQD)
GDP (per capita US$): 6,454.6

ISRAEL (IL)
Area (sq. km): 20,770
Population (million): 7.7
Capital: Jerusalem
Language: Hebrew, Arabic
Monetary Unit: Sheqel (ILS)
GDP (per capita US$): NA

JAPAN (JP)
Area (sq. km): 377,727
Population (million): 126.4
Capital: Tokyo
Language: Japanese
Monetary Unit: Yen (JPY)
GDP (per capita US$): 46,720.4

JORDAN (JO)
Area (sq. km): 89,206
Population (million): 6.5
Capital: Amman
Language: Arabic
Monetary Unit: Jord. Dinar (JOD)
GDP (per capita US$): 4,945.1

KAZAKHSTAN (KZ)
Area (sq. km): 2,717,300
Population (million): 16.4
Capital: Astana
Language: Kazakh, Russian
Monetary Unit: Tenge (KZT)
GDP (per capita US$): 12,006.6

KUWAIT (KW)
Area (sq. km): 17,818
Population (million): 2.9
Capital: Kuwait City
Language: Khalka (Mongolian)
Monetary Unit: Kuwaiti Dinar (KWD)
GDP (per capita US$): NA

KYRGYZSTAN (KG)
Area (sq. km): 198,500
Population (million): 5.4
Capital: Bishkek
Language: Kyrgyz, Russian
Monetary Unit: Ky. Som (KGS)
GDP (per capita US$): 1,159.6

LAOS (LA)
Area (sq. km): 236,800
Population (million): 6.4
Capital: Vientiane
Language: Lao
Monetary Unit: Kip (LAK)
GDP (per capita US$): 1,399.2

LEBANON (LB)
Area (sq. km):10,452
Population (million): 4.3
Capital: Beirut
Language: Arabic, Armenian
Monetary Unit: Leb. Pound (LBP)
GDP (per capita US$): 9,705.4

MALAYSIA (MY)
Area (sq. km): 332,965
Population (million): 29.3
Capital: Kuala Lumpur/Putrajaya
Language: Malay, English
Monetary Unit: Ringgit (MYR)
GDP (per capita US$): 10,380.5

MALDIVES (MV)
Area (sq. km): 298
Population (million): 0.3
Capital: Male
Language: Divehi (Maldivian)
Monetary Unit: Rufiyaa (MVR)
GDP (per capita US$): 6,566.6

MONGOLIA (MN)
Area (sq. km): 1,565,000
Population (million): 2.8
Capital: Ulan Bator
Language: Mongolian, Kazakh
Monetary Unit: Tugrik (MNT)
GDP (per capita US$): 3,673.0

MYANMAR (MM)
Area (sq. km): 676,577
Population (million): 48.7
Capital: Naypyidaw
Language: Burmese, Karen
Monetary Unit: Kyat (MMK)
GDP (per capita US$): NA

NEPAL (NP)
Area (sq. km): 147,181
Population (million): 26.5 (2011)
Capital: Katmandu
Language: Nepali, Maithili
Monetary Unit: Nep. Rupee (NPR)
GDP (per capita US$): 706.6

NORTH KOREA (KP)
Area (sq. km): 120,538
Population (million): 24.6
Capital: Pyongyang
Language: Korean
Monetary Unit: N. K. Won (KPW)
GDP (per capita US$): NA

OMAN (OM)
Area (sq. km): 309,500
Population (million): 2.9
Capital: Muscat
Language: Arabic, Baluchi
Monetary Unit: Rial Omani (OMR)
GDP (per capita US$): NA

PAKISTAN (PK)
Area (sq. km): 803,940
Population (million): 180.0
Capital: Islamabad
Language: Urdu, Punjabi
Monetary Unit: Pak. Rupee (PKR)
GDP (per capita US$): 1,290.4

PHILIPPINES (PH)
Area (sq. km): 300,000
Population (million): 96.5
Capital: Manila
Language: Filipino, English
Monetary Unit: Ph. Peso (PHP)
GDP (per capita US$): 2,587.9

QATAR (QA)
Area (sq. km): 11,437
Population (million): 1.9
Capital: Doha
Language: Arabic
Monetary Unit: Qatari Riyal (QAR)
GDP (per capita US$): NA

RUSSIA (RU)
Area (sq. km): 17,075,400
Population (million): 142.7
Capital: Moscow
Language: Russian, Tatar
Monetary Unit: Rouble (RUB)
GDP (per capita US$): 14,037.0

SAUDI ARABIA (SA)
Area (sq. km): 2,200,000
Population (million): 28.7
Capital: Riyadh
Language: Arabic
Monetary Unit: Saudi Rial (SAR)
GDP (per capita US$): NA

SINGAPORE (SG)
Area (sq. km): 639
Population (million): 5.3
Capital: Singapore
Language: Chinese, English
Monetary Unit: Sin. Dollar (SGD)
GDP (per capita US$): 51,709.5

SOUTH KOREA (KR)
Area (sq. km): 99,274
Population (million): 48.6
Capital: Seoul
Language: Korean
Monetary Unit: S. K. Won (KRW)
GDP (per capita US$): 22,590.2

SRI LANKA (LK)
Area (sq. km): 65,610
Population (million): 21.2
Capital: Sri Jayawardenapura
Language: Sinhalese, Tamil
Monetary Unit: Sri L. Rupee (LKR)
GDP (per capita US$): 2,923.1

SYRIA (SY)
Area (sq. km): 185,180
Population (million): 21.1
Capital: Damascus
Language: Arabic, Kurdish
Monetary Unit: Syrian Pound (SYP)
GDP (per capita US$): 3,289.1

TAJIKISTAN (TJ)
Area (sq. km): 143,100
Population (million): 7.1
Capital: Dushanbe
Language: Tajik, Uzbek
Monetary Unit: Tajik Rouble (TJR)
GDP (per capita US$): 872.3

THAILAND (TH)
Area (sq. km): 513,115
Population (million): 69.9
Capital: Bangkok
Language: Thai, Lao
Monetary Unit: Baht (THB)
GDP (per capita US$): 5,473.7

TIMOR-LESTE (TP)
Area (sq. km): 14,874
Population (million): 1.2
Capital: Dili
Language: Portuguese, Tetun
Monetary Unit: US Dollar (USD)
GDP (per capita US$): 1,068.1

TURKEY (TR)
Area (sq. km): 779,452
Population (million): 74.5
Capital: Ankara
Language: Turkish, Kurdish
Monetary Unit: Turkish Lira (TRL)
GDP (per capita US$):10,666.1

TURKMENISTAN (TM)
Area (sq. km): 488,100
Population (million): 5.2
Capital: Ashgabat
Language: Turkmen, Uzbek
Monetary Unit: Turk. Manat (TMM)
GDP (per capita US$): 6,510.6

U. A. EMIRATES (AE)
Area (sq. km): 77,700
Population (million): 8.1
Capital: Abu Dhabi
Language: Arabic, English
Monetary Unit: Dirham (AED)
GDP (per capita US$): NA

UZBEKISTAN (UZ)
Area (sq. km): 447,400
Population (million): 28.1
Capital: Tashkent
Language: Uzbek, Russian
Monetary Unit: Uzb. Som (UZS)
GDP (per capita US$): 1,716.5

VIETNAM (VN)
Area (sq. km): 329,565
Population (million): 89.7
Capital: Hanoi
Language: Vietnamese, Thai
Monetary Unit: Dong (VND)
GDP (per capita US$): 1,595.8

YEMEN (YE)
Area (sq. km): 527,968
Population (million): 25.6
Capital: San'a
Language: Arabic
Monetary Unit: Riyal (Yer)
GDP (per capita US$): 1,494.4

Gross Domestic Product (GDP) is the total value of goods and services produced in a country and are given in US$ per person, adjusted for the localcost of living.
Country codes and currency codes are given in brackets along with country names and monetary units respectively.
Two major official languages are given for each country.

Data source
Population - HDR 2013
GDP - World Bank 2012

ALBANIA (AL)
Area (sq. km): 28,748
Population (million): 3.2
Capital: Tirana
Language: Albanian, Greek
Monetary Unit: Lek (ALL)
GDP (per capita US$): 41,48.9

ANDORRA (AD)
Area (sq. km): 465
Population (million): 0.1
Capital: Andorra la vella
Language: Spanish, Catalan
Monetary Unit: Euro (EUR)
GDP: NA

AUSTRIA (AT)
Area (sq. km): 83,855
Population (million): 8.4
Capital: Vienna
Language: German, Croatian
Monetary Unit: Euro (EUR)
GDP (per capita US$): 47,226.2

BELARUS (BY)
Area (sq. km): 207,600
Population (million): 9.5
Capital: Minsk
Language: Belarusian, Russian
Monetary Unit: Belarussian Rouble (BYR)
GDP (per capita US$): 6,685.0

BELGIUM (BE)
Area (sq. km): 30,520
Population (million): 10.8
Capital: Brussels
Language: Dutch , French
Monetary Unit: Euro (EUR)
GDP (per capita US$): 43,412.5

BOSNIA-HERZEGOVINA (BA)
Area (sq. km): 51,130
Population (million): 3.7
Capital: Sarajevo
Language: Bosnian, Serbian
Monetary Unit: Convertible Mark (BAM)
GDP (per capita US$): 4,446.5

BULGARIA (BG)
Area (sq. km): 110,994
Population (million): 7.4
Capital: Sofia
Language: Bulgarian, Turkish
Monetary Unit: Lev (BGL)
GDP (per capita US$): 6,986.0

CROATIA (HR)
Area (sq. km): 56,538
Population (million): 4.4
Capital: Zagreb
Language: Croatian, Serbian
Monetary Unit: Kuna (HRK)
    Croatian Dinar (HRD)
GDP (per capita US$): 13,227.5

CZECH REPUBLIC (CZ)
Area (sq. km): 78,864
Population (million): 10.6
Capital: Prague
Language: Czech, Moravian
Monetary Unit: Czech Koruna (CZK)
GDP (per capita US$): 18,607.7

DENMARK (DK)
Area (sq. km): 43,075
Population (million): 5.6
Capital: Copenhagen
Language: Danish
Monetary Unit: Danish Krone (DKK)
GDP (per capita US$): 56,210.2

ESTONIA (EE)
Area (sq. km): 45,200
Population (million): 1.3
Capital: Tallinn
Language: Estonian, Russian
Monetary Unit: Kroon (EEK)
GDP (per capita US$): 16,316.5

FINLAND (FI)
Area (sq. km): 338,145
Population (million): 5.4
Capital: Helsinki
Language: Finnish, Swedish
Monetary Unit: Euro (EUR)
GDP (per capita US$): 46,178.6

FRANCE (FR)
Area (sq. km): 543,965
Population (million): 63.5
Capital: Paris
Language: French
Monetary Unit: Euro (EUR)
GDP (per capita US$): 39,771.8

GERMANY (DE)
Area (sq. km): 357,022
Population (million): 82.0
Capital: Berlin
Language: German, Turkish
Monetary Unit: Euro (EUR)
GDP (per capita US$): 41,514.2

GREECE (GR)
Area (sq. km): 131,957
Population (million): 11.4
Capital: Athens
Language: Greek
Monetary Unit: Euro (EUR)
GDP (per capita US$): 22,082.9

HOLY SEE (VA)
Area (sq. km): 0.5
Population (million): NA
Capital: Vatican City
Language:
Monetary Unit: Euro (EUR)
GDP (per capita US$): NA

HUNGARY (HU)
Area (sq. km): 93,030
Population (million): 9.9
Capital: Budapest
Language: Hungarian
Monetary Unit: Forint (HUF)
GDP (per capita US$): 12,621.7

ICELAND (IS)
Area (sq. km): 102,820
Population (million): 0.3
Capital: Reykjavik
Language: Icelandic
Monetary Unit: Icelandic Krona (ISK)
GDP (per capita US$): 42,658.4

IRELAND (IE)
Area (sq. km): 70,282
Population (million): 4.6
Capital: Dublin
Language: English, Irish
Monetary Unit: Euro (EUR)
GDP (per capita US$): 45,835.7

ITALY (IT)
Area (sq. km): 301,245
Population (million): 61.0
Capital: Rome
Language: Italian
Monetary Unit: Euro (EUR)
GDP (per capita US$): 33,048.8

KOSOVO (XK)*
Area (sq. km): 10,908
Population (million): 2.3
Capital: Pristina
Language: Albanian, Serbian
Monetary Unit: Euro (EUR)
GDP (per capita US$): 3,453.1

LATVIA (LV)
Area (sq. km): 63,700
Population (million): 2.2
Capital: Riga
Language: Latvian, Russian
Monetary Unit: Lats (LVL)
GDP (per capita US$): 14,008.5

LIECHTENSTEIN (LI)
Area (sq. km): 160
Population (million): 0.04
Capital: Vaduz
Language: German
Monetary Unit: Swiss franc (CHF)
GDP: NA

LITHUANIA (LT)
Area (sq. km): 65,200
Population (million): 3.3
Capital: Vilnius
Language: Lithuanian, Russian
Monetary Unit: Litas (LTL)
GDP (per capita US$): 14,150.2

LUXEMBOURG (LU)
Area (sq. km): 2,586
Population (million): 0.5
Capital: Luxembourg
Language: Luxembourgish, German
Monetary Unit: Euro (EUR)
GDP (per capita US$): 107,475.9

MACEDONIA (MK)
Area (sq. km): 25,713
Population (million): 2.1
Capital: Skopje
Language: Macedonian, Albanian
Monetary Unit: Dinar (MKD)
GDP (per capita US$): 4,589.3

MALTA (MT)
Area (sq. km): 316
Population (million): 0.4
Capital: Valletta
Language: Maltese, English
Monetary Unit: Euro (EUR)
GDP (per capita US$): 20,847.6

MOLDOVA (MD)
Area (sq. km): 33,700
Population (million): 3.5
Capital: Chisinau
Language: Romanian, Ukrainian
Monetary Unit: Moldavian Leu (MDL)
GDP (per capita US$): 2,037.9

MONACO (MC)
Area (sq. km): 2
Population (million): 0.04
Capital: Monaco
Language: French, Monegasque
Monetary Unit: Euro (EUR)
GDP (per capita US$): NA

MONTENEGRO
Area (sq. km): 13.812
Population (million): 0.6
Capital: Podgorica
Language:
Monetary Unit: Euro (EUR)
GDP (per capita US$): 6,813.0

NETHERLANDS (NL)
Area (sq. km): 41,526
Population (million): 16.7
Capital: Amsterdam, The Hague
Language: Dutch, Frisian
Monetary Unit: Euro (EUR)
GDP (per capita US$): 46,054.4

NORWAY (NO)
Area (sq. km): 323,878
Population (million): 5.0
Capital: Oslo
Language: Norwegian
Monetary Unit: Norwegian Krone, (NOK)
GDP (per capita US$): 99,557.7

POLAND (PL)
Area (sq. km): 312,683
Population (million): 38.3
Capital: Warsaw
Language: Polish, German
Monetary Unit: New Zloty (PLL)
GDP (per capita US$): 12,707.9

PORTUGAL (PT)
Area (sq. km): 88,940
Population (million): 10.7
Capital: Lisbon
Language: Portuguese
Monetary Unit: Euro (EUR)
GDP (per capita US$): 20,182.4

ROMANIA (RO)
Area (sq. km): 237,500
Population (million): 21.4
Capital: Bucharest
Language: Romanian, Hungarian
Monetary Unit: Romanian Leu (ROL)
GDP (per capita US$): 7,942.8

SAN MARINO (SM)
Area (sq. km): 61
Population (million): 0.03
Capital: San Marino
Language: Italian
Monetary Unit: Euro (EUR)
GDP (per capita US$): NA

SERBIA (RS)
Area (sq. km): 88,361
Population (million): 7.1
Capital: Belgrade
Language: Serbian, Albanian
Monetary Unit: Serbian Dinar (CSD)
GDP (per capita US$): 5,189.6

SLOVAKIA (SK)
Area (sq. km): 49,035
Population (million): 5.5
Capital: Bratislava
Language: Slovakian, Hungarian
Monetary Unit: Slovak Koruna (SKK)
GDP (per capita US$): 16,934.3

SLOVENIA (SI)
Area (sq. km): 20,251
Population (million): 2.0
Capital: Ljubljana
Language: Slovenian, Croatian
Monetary Unit: Tolar (SIT)
GDP (per capita US$): 22,092.3

SPAIN (ES)
Area (sq. km): 504,782
Population (million): 46.8
Capital: Madrid
Language: Spanish, Castilian
Monetary Unit: Euro (EUR)
GDP (per capita US$): 29,195.4

SWEDEN (SE)
Area (sq. km): 449,964
Population (million): 9.5
Capital: Stockholm
Language: Swedish
Monetary Unit: Swedish Krona (SEK)
GDP (per capita US$): 55,244.6

SWITZERLAND (CH)
Area (sq. km): 41,293
Population (million): 7.7
Capital: Berne
Language: German, French
Monetary Unit: Swiss Franc (CHF)
GDP (per capita US$): 79,052.3

UKRAINE (UA)
Area (sq. km): 603,700
Population (million): 44.9
Capital: Kiev
Language: Ukrainian, Russian
Monetary Unit: Hryvnia (UAH)
    Karbovanet (UAK)
GDP (per capita US$): 3,867.0

UNITED KINGDOM (GB)
Area (sq. km): 243,609
Population (million): 62.8
Capital: London
Language: English, Welsh
Monetary Unit: Pound Sterling (GBP)
GDP (per capita US$): 38,514.5

*XK: assigned as a temporary code to Kosovo under UN security council resolution 1244/99.

ALGERIA (DZ)
Area (sq. km): 2,381,741
Population (million): 36.5
Capital: Algiers
Language: Arabic, French
Monetary Unit: Alg. Dinar (DZD)
GDP (per capita US$): 5,404.0

ANGOLA (AO)
Area (sq. km): 1,246,700
Population (million): 20.2
Capital: Luanda
Language: Portuguese, Bantu
Monetary Unit: New Kwanza (AON)
GDP (per capita US$): 5,484.8

BENIN (BJ)
Area (sq. km): 112,620
Population (million): 9.4
Capital: Porto-Novo
Language: French, Fon
Monetary Unit: CFA Franc (XAF)
GDP (per capita US$): 751.9

BOTSWANA (BW)
Area (sq. km): 581,370
Population (million): 2.1
Capital: Gaborone
Language: Yoruba, Adja
Monetary Unit: Pula (BWP)
GDP (per capita US$): 7,191.4

BURKINA FASO (BF)
Area (sq. km): 274,200
Population (million): 17.5
Capital: Ouagadougou
Language: French, Moore
Monetary Unit: CFA Franc (XAF)
GDP (per capita US$): 634.3

BURUNDI (BI)
Area (sq. km): 27,835
Population (million): 8.7
Capital: Bujumbura
Language: Kirundi (Hutu, Tutsi)
Monetary Unit: Bur. Franc (BIF)
GDP (per capita US$): 251.0

CAMEROON (CM)
Area (sq. km): 475,442
Population (million): 20.5
Capital: Yaoundé
Language: French English, Fang
Monetary Unit: CFA Franc (XAF)
GDP (per capita US$): 1,151.4

CAPE VERDE (CV)
Area (sq. km): 4,033
Population (million): 0.5
Capital: Praia
Language: Portuguese, Creole
Monetary Unit: C. V. Escudo (CVE)
GDP (per capita US$) 3,837.7

CENTRAL AFRICAN REP. (CF)
Area (sq. km): 622,436
Population (million): 4.6
Capital: Bangui
Language: French, Sangho
Monetary Unit: CFA Franc (XAF)
GDP (per capita US$): 472.7

CHAD (TD)
Area (sq. km):1,284,000
Population (million): 11.8
Capital: N'Djamena
Language: Arabic, French
Monetary Unit: CFA Franc (XAF)
GDP (per capita US$): 885.1

CONGO (CG)
Area (sq. km): 342,000
Population (million): 4.2
Capital: Brazzaville
Language: French, Kongo
Monetary Unit: CFA Franc (XAF)
GDP (per capita US$): 3,153.7

COMOROS
Area (sq. km):
Population (million): 0.8
Capital: Moroni
Language: Comorian, Arabic, French
Monetary Unit: Cedi (GHC)
GDP (per capita US$): 830.5

COTE D'IVOIRE (CI)
Area (sq. km): 322,464
Population (million): 20.6
Capital: Yamoussoukro
Language: French, Creole
Monetary Unit: CFA Franc (XAF)
GDP (per capita US$): 1,244.0

DEMOCRATIC REPUBLIC OF THE CONGO
Area (sq. km):
Population (million): 69.6
Capital: Kinshasa
Language:English, Hausa
Monetary Unit: Cedi (GHC)
GDP (per capita US$): 272.0

DJIBOUTI (DJ)
Area (sq. km): 23,200
Population (million): 0.9
Capital: Djibouti
Language: Somali, Afar
Monetary Unit: Djib. Franc (DJF)
GDP (per capita US$): NA

EGYPT (EG)
Area (sq. km): 1,000,250
Population (million): 84.0
Capital: Cairo
Language: Arabic
Monetary Unit: Egyptian Pound (EGP)
GDP (per capita US$): 3,187.3

EQUATORIAL GUINEA
Area (sq. km): 28,051
Population (million): 0.7
Capital: Malabo
Language:English, Hausa
Monetary Unit: Cedi (GHC)
GDP (per capita US$): 24,035.7

ERITREA (ER)
Area (sq. km): 117,400
Population (million): 5.6
Capital: Asmara
Language:Tigrinya, Tigre
Monetary Unit: E. Nakfa (ERN, ETB)
GDP (per capita US$): 504.3

ETHIOPIA (ET)
Area (sq. km): 1,133,880
Population (million): 86.5
Capital: Addis Ababa
Language: Oromo, Amharic
Monetary Unit: Eth. Birr (ETB)
GDP (per capita US$): 470.2

GABON (GA)
Area (sq. km): 267,667
Population (million): 1.6
Capital: Libreville
Language: French, Fang
Monetary Unit: CFA Franc (XAF)
GDP (per capita US$): 11,430.5

GAMBIA (GM)
Area (sq. km): 11,295
Population (million): 1.8
Capital: Banjul
Language:English, Mandinka
Monetary Unit: Dalasi (GMD)
GDP (per capita US$): 512.1

GHANA (GH)
Area (sq. km): 238,537
Population (million): 25.5
Capital: Accra
Language:English, Hausa
Monetary Unit: Cedi (GHC)
GDP (per capita US$): 1,604.9

GUINEA-BISSAU
Area (sq. km):
Population (million): 1.6
Capital: Bissau
Language:English, Hausa
Monetary Unit: Cedi (GHC)
GDP (per capita US$): 539.5

GUINEA (GN)
Area (sq. km): 245,857
Population (million): 10.5
Capital: Conakry
Language: French, Fulani
Monetary Unit: G. Syli (Franc) (GNS)
GDP (per capita US$): 591.0

KENYA (KE)
Area (sq. km): 582,646
Population (million): 42.7
Capital: Nairobi
Language:Kiswahili, English
Monetary Unit: Ken. Shilling (KES)
GDP (per capita US$): 862.2

LESOTHO (LS)
Area (sq. km): 30,355
Population (million): 2.2
Capital: Maseru
Language:Sesotho, English
Monetary Unit: LSL, LSM, ZAR
GDP (per capita US$): 1,193.0

LIBERIA (LR)
Area (sq. km): 111,369
Population (million): 4.2
Capital: Monrovia
Language: English, Creole
Monetary Unit: Lib. Dollar (LRD)
GDP (per capita US$): 421.7

LIBYA (LY)
Area (sq. km): 1,759,540
Population (million): 6.5
Capital: Tripoli
Language:Arabic, Berber
Monetary Unit: Libyan Dinar (LYD)
GDP (per capita US$): NA

MADAGASCAR (MG)
Area (sq. km): 587,041
Population (million): 21.9
Capital: Antananarivo
Language: Malagasy, French
Monetary Unit: Malagasy Franc (MGF)
GDP (per capita US$): 447.4

MALAWI (MW)
Area (sq. km): 118,484
Population (million): 15.9
Capital: Lilongwe
Language:Chichewa, English
Monetary Unit: M. Kwacha (MWK)
GDP (per capita US$): 268.1

MALI (ML)
Area (sq. km): 1,240,140
Population (million): 16.3
Capital: Bamako
Language: French, Bambara
Monetary Unit: CFA Franc (XAF) Malian Franc (MLF)
GDP (per capita US$): 694.0

MAURITANIA (MR)
Area (sq. km): 1,030,700
Population (million): 3.6
Capital: Nouakchott
Language:Arabic, French
Monetary Unit: Ouguiya (MRO)
GDP (per capita US$): 1,106.1

MAURITIUS (MU)
Area (sq. km): 2,040
Population (million): 1.3
Capital: Port Louis
Language: English, Creole
Monetary Unit: Mau. Rupee (MUR)
GDP (per capita US$): 8,124.2

MOROCCO (MA)
Area (sq. km): 446,550
Population (million):32.6
Capital: Rabat
Language: Arabic, Berber
Monetary Unit: Mor. Dirham (MAD)
GDP (per capita US$): 2,924.9

MOZAMBIQUE (MZ)
Area (sq. km): 799,380
Population (million): 24.5
Capital: Maputo
Language: Portuguese, Makhuwa
Monetary Unit: Metical (MZM)
GDP (per capita US$): 578.8

NAMIBIA (NA)
Area (sq. km): 824,292
Population (million): 2.4
Capital: Windhoek
Language:English, Afrikaans
Monetary Unit: Namibiyan Dollar (NAD)
GDP (per capita US$): 5,668.4

NIGER (NE)
Area (sq. km): 1,267,000
Population (million): 16.6
Capital: Niamey
Language:French, Hausa
Monetary Unit: W. A.Frane (XOF) CFA Franc (XAF)
GDP (per capita US$): 382.8

NIGERIA (NG)
Area (sq. km): 923,768
Population (million): 166.6
Capital: Abuja
Language:English, Hausa
Monetary Unit: Naira (NGN)
GDP (per capita US$): 1,555.4

RWANDA (RW)
Area (sq. km): 26,338
Population (million): 11.3
Capital: Kigali
Language: Kinyarwanda, French
Monetary Unit: Rw. Franc (RWF)
GDP (per capita US$): 619.9

SAO TOME AND PRINCIPE
Area (sq. km): 964
Population (million): 0.2
Capital: São Tomé
Language:English, Hausa
Monetary Unit: Cedi (GHC)
GDP (per capita US$): 1,402.1

SIERRA LEONE
Area (sq. km): 71,740
Population (million): 6.1
Capital: Freetown
Language:English, Hausa
Monetary Unit: Cedi (GHC)
GDP (per capita US$): 634.9

SENEGAL (SN)
Area (sq. km): 196,720
Population (million): 13.1
Capital: Dakar
Language:French, Wolof
Monetary Unit: CFA Franc (XAF)
GDP (per capita US$): 1,031.6

SEYCHELLES (SC)
Area (sq. km): 455
Population (million): 0.1
Capital: Victoria
Language:English, French
Monetary Unit: Sey. Rupee (SCR)
GDP (per capita US$): 11,758.0

SOMALIA (SO)
Area (sq. km): 637,657
Population (million): 9.8
Capital: Mogadishu
Language:Somali, Arabic
Monetary Unit: S. Shilling (SOS)
GDP: NA

SOUTH AFRICA (ZA)
Area (sq. km): 1,219,090
Population (million): 50.7
Capital: Pretoria/Cape Town
Language: Afrikaans, English
Monetary Unit: Rand (ZAR)
GDP (per capita US$): 7,507.7

SOUTH SUDAN
Area (sq. km): 644,329
Population (million): 10.7
Capital: Juba
Language:English, Hausa
Monetary Unit: Cedi (GHC)
GDP (per capita US$): 861.6

SUDAN (SD)
Area (sq. km): 1,886,068
Population (million):35.0
Capital: Khartoum
Language: Arabic, Dinka
Monetary Unit: S. Pound (SDG)
GDP (per capita US$): 1,580.0

SWAZILAND (SZ)
Area (sq. km): 17,364
Population (million): 1.2
Capital: Mbabane
Language:Swazi, English
Monetary Unit: Lilangeni (SZL)
GDP (per capita US$): 3,043.5

TANZANIA (TZ)
Area (sq. km): 945,087
Population (million): 47.7
Capital: Dodoma
Language:Swahili, English
Monetary Unit: Tan. Shilling (TZS)
GDP (per capita US$): 608.9

TOGO
Area (sq. km): 56,785
Population (million): 6.3
Capital: Lomé
Language:English, Hausa
Monetary Unit: Cedi (GHC)
GDP (per capita US$): 574.1

TUNISIA (TN)
Area (sq. km): 164,150
Population (million): 10.7
Capital: Tunis
Language:Arabic, French
Monetary Unit: Tunisian Dinar (TND)
GDP (per capita US$): 4,236.8

UGANDA
Area (sq. km): 241,038
Population (million): 35.6
Capital: Kampala
Language:English, Hausa
Monetary Unit: Cedi (GHC)
GDP (per capita US$): 547.0

ZAMBIA (ZM)
Area (sq. km): 752,614
Population (million): 13.9
Capital: Lusaka
Language: English, Bemba
Monetary Unit: Zam. Kwacha (ZMK)
GDP (per capita US$): 1469.1

ZIMBABWE (ZW)
Area (sq. km): 390,759
Population (million): 13.0
Capital: Harare
Language: English, Shona
Monetary Unit: Zimbabwean Dollar (ZWD)
GDP (per capita US$): 787.9

NORTH AMERICA

ANTIGUA & BARBUDA (AG)
Area (sq. km): 442
Population (million): 0.1
Capital: St John's
Language: English, Creole
Monetary Unit: East C. Dollar (Xcd)
GDP (per capita US$): 13,207.2

BAHAMAS (BS)
Area (sq. km): 13,939
Population (million): 0.4
Capital: Nassau
Language: English, Creole
Monetary Unit: Bah. Dollar (Bsd)
GDP (per capita US$): NA

BARBADOS (BB)
Area (sq. km): 430
Population (million): 0.3
Capital: Bridgetown
Language: English, Creole
Monetary Unit: Bar. Dollar (BBD)
GDP (per capita US$): 14,426

BELIZE (BZ)
Area (sq. km): 22,965
Population (million): 0.3
Capital: Belmopan
Language: English, Spanish
Monetary Unit: Belize Dollar (BZD)
GDP (per capita US$): NA

CANADA (CA)
Area (sq. km): 9,984,670
Population (million): 34.7
Capital: Ottawa
Language: English, French
Monetary Unit: Can. Dollar (CAD)
GDP (per capita US$): 52,219.0

COSTA RICA (CR)
Area (sq. km): 51,100
Population (million): 4.8
Capital: San José
Language: Spanish
Monetary Unit: C. R. Colón (CRC)
GDP (per capita US$): 9,391.2

CUBA (CU)
Area (sq. km): 110,860
Population (million): 11.2
Capital: Havana
Language: Spanish
Monetary Unit: Cuban Peso (CUP)
GDP (per capita US$): NA

DOMINICA (DM)
Area (sq. km): 750
Population (million): 0.1
Capital: Roseau
Language:English, Creole
Monetary Unit: East C. Dollar (XCD)
GDP (per capita US$): 6,691.0

DOMINICAN REP. (DO)
Area (sq. km): 48,442
Population (million): 10.2
Capital: Santo Domingo
Language: Spanish, Creole
Monetary Unit: Dom. Rep. Peso (DOP)
GDP (per capita US$): 5,736.4

EL SALVADOR (SV)
Area (sq. km): 21,041
Population (million): 6.3
Capital: San Salvador
Language:Spanish
Monetary Unit: US Dollar (USD)
GDP (per capita US$): 3,777.2

GREENLAND (GL)
Area (sq. km): 2,175,600
Population (million): NA
Capital: Nuuk
Language:Kalaallisut
Monetary Unit: Danish Krone (GLK)
GDP (per capita US$): NA

GRENADA (GD)
Area (sq. km): 378
Population (million): 0.1
Capital: St George's
Language: English, Creole
Monetary Unit: East C. Dollar (XCD)
GDP (per capita US$): 7,485.0

GUATEMALA (GT)
Area (sq. km): 108,890
Population (million): 15.1
Capital: Guatemala City
Language:Spanish
Monetary Unit: Quetzal (GTQ)
GDP (per capita US$): 3,368.5

HAITI (HT)
Area (sq. km): 27,750
Population (million): 10.3
Capital: Port-au-Prince
Language:French, Creole
Monetary Unit: Gourde (HTG)
GDP (per capita US$): 771.0

HONDURAS (HN)
Area (sq. km): 112,088
Population (million): 7.9
Capital: Tegucigalpa
Language: Spanish
Monetary Unit: Lempira (HNL)
GDP (per capita US$): 2,264.1

JAMAICA (JM)
Area (sq. km): 10,991
Population (million): 2.8
Capital: Kingston
Language: English, Creole
Monetary Unit: Jam. Dollar (JMD)
GDP (per capita US$): 5,471.7

MEXICO (MX)
Area (sq. km): 1,972,545
Population (million): 116.1
Capital: Mexico City
Language: Spanish
Monetary Unit: M. New Peso (MXN)
GDP (per capita US$): 9,741.8

NICARAGUA (NI)
Area (sq. km): 130,000
Population (million): 6.0
Capital: Managua
Language:Spanish
Monetary Unit: Córdoba (NIC)
GDP (per capita US$): 1,753.6

PANAMA (PA)
Area (sq. km): 77,082
Population (million): 3.6
Capital: Panama City
Language:Spanish, English
Monetary Unit:Balboa (PAB)/US Dollor (USD)
GDP (per capita US$): 9,534.4

ST KITTS & NEVIS (KN)
Area (sq. km): 261
Population (million): 0.1
Capital: Basseterre
Language:English, Creole
Monetary Unit: East Car. Dollar (XCD)
GDP (per capita US$): 13,968.5

ST LUCIA (LC)
Area (sq. km): 616
Population (million): 0.2
Capital: Castries
Language:English, Creole
Monetary Unit: East Car. Dollar (XCD)
GDP (per capita US$): 6,558.4

ST VINCENT & GRE. (VC)
Area (sq. km): 389
Population (million): 0.1
Capital: Kingstown
Language:English, Creole
Monetary Unit: East Car. Dollar (XCD)
GDP (per capita US$): 6,515.2

TRINIDAD & TOBAGO (TT)
Area (sq. km): 5,130
Population (million): 1.4
Capital: Port of Spain
Language:English, Creole, Hindi
Monetary Unit: Tri. & Tob. Dollar (TTD)
GDP (per capita US$): 17,934.1

U. S. OF AMERICA (US)
Area (sq. km): 9,826,635
Population (million): 315.8
Capital: Washington DC
Language:English, Spanish
Monetary unit: US Dollar (USD)
GDP (per capita US$): 49,965.3

SOUTH AMERICA

ARGENTINA (AR)
Area (sq. km): 2,766,889
Population (million): 41.1
Capital: Buenos Aires
Language: Spanish, Italian,
Monetary Unit: Argentine Peso (ARS)
GDP (per capita US$): 11,557.6

BOLIVIA (BO)
Area (sq. km): 1,098,581
Population (million): 10.2
Capital: La Paz/Sucre
Language: Spanish, Quechua
Monetary Unit :Boliviano (BOB)/Bol. Peso (BOP)
GDP (per capita US$): 2,575.7

BRAZIL (BR)
Area (sq. km): 8,514,879
Population (million): 198.4
Capital: Brasília
Language: Portuguese
Monetary Unit: Cruzeiro Real (BRR)
GDP (per capita US$): 11,339.5

CHILE (CL)
Area (sq. km): 756,945
Population (million): 17.4
Capital: Santiago
Language: Spanish
Monetary Unit: Chilean Peso (CLP)
GDP (per capita US$): 15,363.1

COLOMBIA (CO)
Area (sq. km): 1,141,748
Population (million): 457.6
Capital: Bogotá
Language:Spanish
Monetary Unit: Col. Peso (COP)
GDP (per capita US$): 7,752.2

ECUADOR (EC)
Area (sq. km): 272,045
Population (million): 14.9
Capital: Quito
Language: Spanish, Quechua
Monetary Unit: US Dollar (USD)
GDP (per capita US$): 5,456.4

GUYANA (GY)
Area (sq. km): 214,969
Population (million): 0.8
Capital: Georgetown
Language: English, Creole
Monetary Unit: Gu. Dollar (GYD)
GDP (per capita US$): 3,584.4

PARAGUAY (PY)
Area (sq. km): 406,752
Population (million): 6.7
Capital: Asunción
Language: English, Creole
Monetary Unit: Guaraní (PYG)
GDP (per capita US$): 3,813.5

PERU (PE)
Area (sq. km): 1,285,216
Population (million): 29.7
Capital: Lima
Language: Spanish, Quechua
Monetary Unit: Inti (PEI) New Sol (PEN)
GDP (per capita US$): 6,573.0

SURINAME (SR)
Area (sq. km): 163,820
Population (million): 0.5
Capital: Paramaribo
Language: Dutch, Surinamese
Monetary Unit: S. Guilder (SRG)
GDP (per capita US$): 8,864.0

URUGUAY (UY)
Area (sq. km): 176,215
Population (million): 3.4
Capital: Montevideo
Language: Spanish
Monetary Unit: Ur. New Peso (UYU)
GDP (per capita US$): 14,449.5

VENEZUELA (VE)
Area (sq. km): 912,050
Population (million): 29.9
Capital: Caracas
Language: Spanish, Amerindian
Monetary Unit: Bolivar Fuerte (VEF)
GDP (per capita US$): 12,766.7

OCEANIA

AUSTRALIA (AU)
Area (sq. km): 7,692,024
Population (million): 22.9
Capital: Canberra
Language: English
Monetary Unit: Aus. Dollar (AUD)
GDP (per capita US$): 67,035.6

FIJI (FI)
Area (sq. km): 18,330
Population (million): 0.9
Capital: Suva
Language: English, Fijian
Monetary Unit: Fiji Dollar (FJD)
GDP (per capita US$): 4,437.8

KIRIBATI (KI)
Area (sq. km): 717
Population (million): 0.1
Capital: Tarawa
Language:Gilbertese, English
Monetary Unit: Aus. Dollar (AUD)
GDP (per capita US$): 1,743.4

MARSHALL IS (MH)
Area (sq. km): 181
Population (million): 0.1
Capital: Majuro
Language: English, Marshallese
Monetary Unit: US Dollar (USD)
GDP (per capita US$): 3,556.3

MICRONESIA (FM)
Area (sq. km): 701
Population (million): 0.1
Capital: Palikir
Language: English, Chuukese
Monetary Unit: US Dollar (USD)
GDP (per capita US$): 3,164.6

NAURU (NR)
Area (sq. km): 21
Population (million): 0.01
Capital: Yaren
Language: Nauruan, English
Monetary Unit: Aus. Dollar (AUD)
GDP (per capita US$): NA

NEW ZEALAND (NZ)
Area (sq. km): 270,534
Population (million): 4.5
Capital: Wellington
Language: English, Maori
Monetary Unit: New Z. Dollar (NZD)
GDP (per capita US$): NA

PALAU
Area (sq. km): 458
Population (million): 0.02
Capital: Melekeoky
Language:
Monetary Unit: US Dollar (USD)
GDP (per capita US$): 11,005.9

PAPUA NEW GUINEA (PG)
Area (sq. km): 462,840
Population (million): 7.2
Capital: Port Moresby
Language: English, Tok Pisin
Monetary Unit: Kina (PGK)
GDP (per capita US$): 2,184.2

SAMOA
Area (sq. km): 2831
Population (million): 0.2
Capital: Apia
Language:
Monetary Unit: tala
GDP (per capita US$): 3,584.3

SOLOMON IS (SB)
Area (sq. km): 28,370
Population (million): 0.6
Capital: Honiara
Language: English, Creole
Monetary Unit: Sol. Is. Dollar (SBD)
GDP (per capita US$): 1,834.8

TONGA (TO)
Area (sq. km): 748
Population (million): 0.1
Capital: Nuku'alofa}
Language: Tongan, English
Monetary Unit: Pa'anga (TOP)
GDP (per capita US$): 4,493.9

TUVALU (TV)
Area (sq. km): 25
Population (million): 0.01
Capital: Funafuti
Language: Tuvaluan, English
Monetary Unit: Aus. Dollar (AUD)
GDP (per capita US$): 3,739.8

VANUATU (VU)
Area (sq. km): 12,190
Population (million): 0.3
Capital: Port Vila
Language: English, Bislama
Monetary Unit: Vatu (VUV)
GDP (per capita US$): 3,176.2

GDP per capita, 2012

Gross domestic product (GDP) in US$ per person, adjusted for the local cost of living

Highest GDP per capita	(in US $)
Luxembourg	107,476
Norway	99,558
Switzerland	79,052
Macao SAR, China	78,275
Australia	67,036
Denmark	56,210
Sweden	55,245
Canada	52,219
Singapore	51,709

Lowest GDP per capita	(in US$)
Burundi	251
Malawi	268
Congo, Dem. Rep.	272
Niger	383
Liberia	422
Madagascar	447
Ethiopia	470
Central African Republic	473
Eritrea	504
The Gambia	512

INDIA 1,489

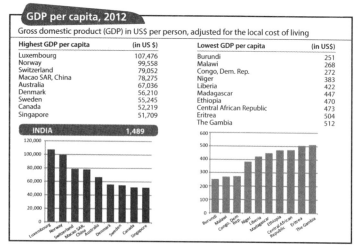

Data Source: World Bank

Life expectancy, 2012

Average expected lifespan of babies born in 2012 (years)

Highest life expectancy	
Japan	83.6
Hong Kong, China (SAR)	83.0
Switzerland	82.5
Australia	82.0
Italy	82.0
Iceland	81.9
Israel	81.9

Lowest life expectancy	
Chad	49.9
Zambia	49.4
Central African Republic	49.1
Afghanistan	49.1
Swaziland	48.9
Lesotho	48.7
Congo, Dem. Rep.	48.7
Guinea-Bissau	48.6
Sierra Leone	48.1

INDIA 65.8

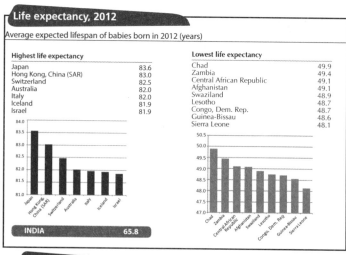

Literacy and Schooling, 2005-2010

Percentage of people aged 15 and above who can, with understanding, both read and write a short, simple statement on their everyday life

Highest literacy levels	
Norway	100
Australia	100
United States	100
Netherlands	100
Germany	100
New Zealand	100
Ireland	100
Sweden	100
Switzerland	100
Japan	100

Lowest literacy levels	
Niger	28.7
Burkina Faso	28.7
Mali	31.1
Chad	34.5
Ethiopia	39.0
Guinea	41.0
Sierra Leone	42.1
Benin	42.4
Haiti	48.7
Senegal	49.7
Gambia	50.0

INDIA 62.8

Health care, 2005 – 2010

Number of doctors per 1 000 people

Most doctors per 1 000 people	
Cuba	6.4
Greece	6.0
Belarus	4.9
Austria	4.7
Georgia	4.5
Russian Federation	4.3
Italy	4.2
Norway	4.1
Switzerland	4.1

Fewest doctors per 1 000 people	
Mali	0.05
Guinea-Bissau	0.05
Chad	0.04
Gambia	0.04
Burundi	0.03
Mozambique	0.03
Rwanda	0.02
Ethiopia	0.02
Malawi	0.02
Niger	0.02
Sierra Leone	0.02
Liberia	0.01
Tanzania	0.01

INDIA 0.06

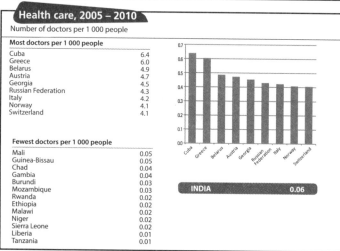

Human Development Index (HDI), 2012

HDI measures the relative social and economic progress of a country. It combines life expectancy, adult literacy, average number of years of schooling and purchasing power.

Highest HDI	
Norway	0.955
Australia	0.938
United States	0.937
Netherlands	0.921
Germany	0.920
New Zealand	0.919
Ireland	0.916
Sweden	0.916

Lowest HDI	
Eritrea	0.351
Mali	0.344
Burkina Faso	0.343
Chad	0.340
Mozambique	0.327
Niger	0.304
Congo, Dem. Rep.	0.304

INDIA 0.6

Population below income poverty line (PPP US$1.25 a day), 2002-2011

The proportion of the population with a standard of living below the national poverty line

Highest percentage of population	
Congo, Dem. Rep.	87.7
Liberia	83.8
Burundi	81.3
Madagascar	81.3
Malawi	73.9
Zambia	68.5
Nigeria	68.0
Tanzania	67.9
Rwanda	63.2

INDIA 32.7

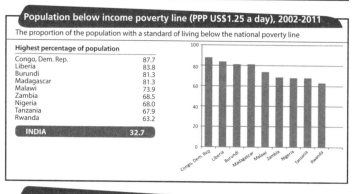

Gross National Income (GNI), 2012

The decent standard of living component of a country is measured by Gross National Inclome (GNI) per capita (2005 PPP US$).

Highest GNI	
Qatar	87,478
Liechtenstein	84,880
Kuwait	52,793
Singapore	52,613
Norway	48,688
Luxembourg	48,285

Lowest GNI	
Malawi	774
Central African Republic	722
Niger	701
Burundi	544
Eritrea	531
Liberia	480
Zimbabwe	424
Congo, Dem. Rep.	319

INDIA 3,285

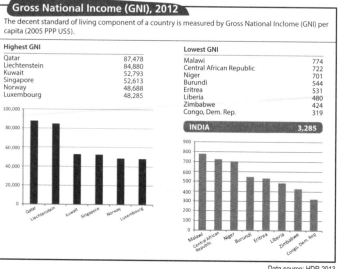

Fertility Rate, 2012 (births per woman)

Average number of children born to childbearing woman

Largest families	
Niger	7.0
Zambia	6.3
Mali	6.2
Afghanistan	6.0
Malawi	6.0
Timor Leste	6.0
Uganda	6.0
Chad	5.8
Burkina Faso	5.8
Congo, Demo. Rep.	5.5
Tanzania	5.5
Nigeria	5.5

INDIA 2.6

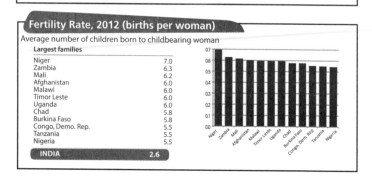

Data source: HDR 2013

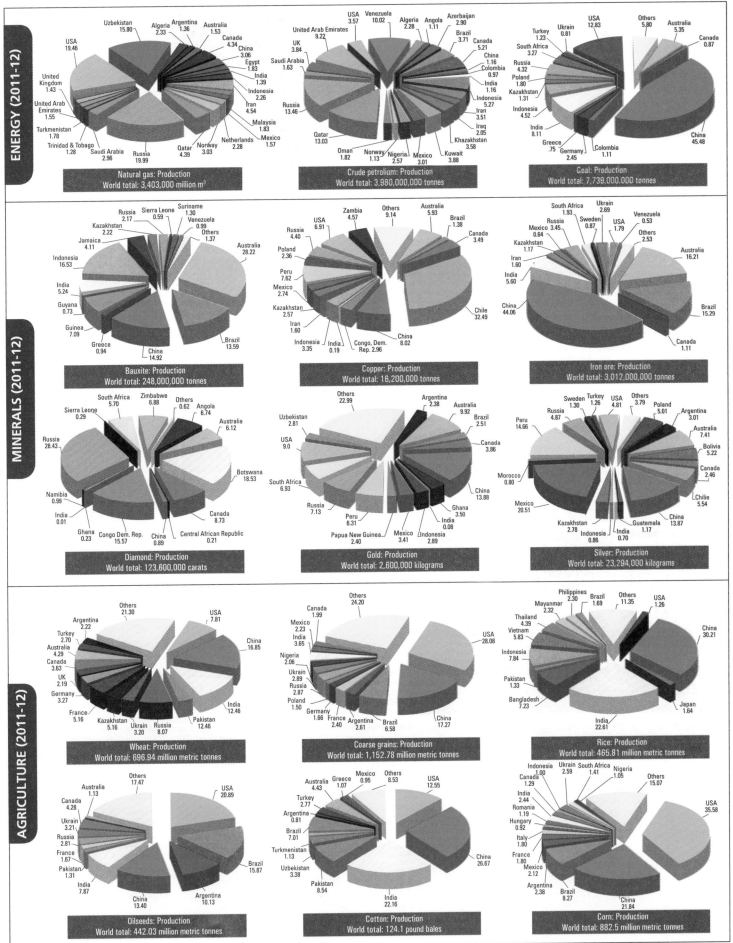

ENERGY (2011-12)

Natural gas: Production
World total: 3,403,000 million m³

- Uzbekistan 15.80
- Algeria 2.33
- Argentina 1.36
- Australia 1.53
- Canada 4.34
- China 3.06
- Egypt 1.83
- India 1.39
- Indonesia 2.26
- Iran 4.54
- Malaysia 1.83
- Mexico 1.57
- Netherlands 2.28
- Norway 3.03
- Qatar 4.39
- Russia 19.99
- Saudi Arabia 2.96
- Trinidad & Tobago 1.28
- Turkmenistan 1.78
- United Arab Emirates 1.55
- United Kingdom 1.43
- USA 19.46

Crude petrolium: Production
World total: 3,980,000,000 tonnes

- USA 3.57
- Venezuela 10.02
- Algeria 2.28
- Angola 1.11
- Azerbaijan 2.90
- Brazil 3.71
- Canada 5.21
- China 1.16
- Colombia 0.97
- India 1.16
- Indonesia 5.27
- Iran 3.51
- Iraq 2.05
- Khazakhstan 3.58
- Kuwait 3.88
- Mexico 3.01
- Nigeria 2.57
- Norway 1.13
- Oman 1.82
- Qatar 13.03
- Russia 13.46
- Saudi Arabia 1.63
- UK 3.84
- United Arab Emirates 9.22

Coal: Production
World total: 7,739,000,000 tonnes

- USA 12.83
- Others 5.80
- Australia 5.35
- Canada 0.87
- China 45.48
- Colombia 1.11
- Germany 2.45
- Greece .75
- India 8.11
- Indonesia 4.52
- Kazakhstan 1.31
- Poland 1.80
- Russia 4.32
- South Africa 3.27
- Turkey 1.23
- Ukrain 0.81

MINERALS (2011-12)

Bauxite: Production
World total: 248,000,000 tonnes

- Russia 2.17
- Sierra Leone 0.59
- Suriname 1.30
- Venezuela 0.99
- Others 1.37
- Australia 28.22
- Brazil 13.59
- China 14.92
- Greece 0.94
- Guinea 7.09
- Guyana 0.73
- India 5.24
- Indonesia 16.53
- Jamaica 4.11
- Kazakhstan 2.22

Copper: Production
World total: 16,200,000 tonnes

- Zambia 4.57
- Others 9.14
- Australia 5.93
- Brazil 1.38
- Canada 3.49
- Chile 32.49
- China 8.02
- Congo, Dem. Rep. 2.96
- India 0.19
- Indonesia 3.35
- Iran 1.60
- Kazakhstan 2.57
- Mexico 2.74
- Peru 7.62
- Poland 2.36
- Russia 4.40
- USA 6.91

Iron ore: Production
World total: 3,012,000,000 tonnes

- South Africa 1.93
- Ukrain 2.69
- Venezuela 0.53
- Sweden 0.87
- USA 1.79
- Others 2.53
- Australia 16.21
- Brazil 15.29
- Canada 1.11
- China 44.06
- India 5.60
- Iran 1.60
- Kazakhstan 1.17
- Mexico 0.64
- Russia 3.45

Diamond: Production
World total: 123,600,000 carats

- South Africa 5.70
- Zimbabwe 6.88
- Others 0.62
- Angola 6.74
- Australia 6.12
- Botswana 18.53
- Canada 8.73
- Central African Republic 0.21
- China 0.89
- Congo Dem. Rep. 15.57
- Ghana 0.23
- India 0.01
- Namibia 0.99
- Russia 28.43
- Sierra Leone 0.29

Gold: Production
World total: 2,600,000 kilograms

- Others 22.99
- Argentina 2.38
- Australia 9.92
- Brazil 2.51
- Canada 3.86
- China 13.88
- Ghana 3.50
- India 0.08
- Indonesia 2.89
- Mexico 3.41
- Papua New Guinea 2.40
- Peru 6.31
- Russia 7.13
- South Africa 6.93
- USA 9.0
- Uzbekistan 2.81

Silver: Production
World total: 23,294,000 kilograms

- Sweden 1.30
- Turkey 1.26
- USA 4.81
- Others 3.79
- Poland 5.01
- Argentina 3.01
- Australia 7.41
- Bolivia 5.22
- Canada 2.46
- Chilie 5.54
- China 13.87
- Guatemala 1.17
- India 0.70
- Indonesia 0.86
- Kazakhstan 2.78
- Mexico 20.51
- Morocco 0.80
- Peru 14.66
- Russia 4.87

AGRICULTURE (2011-12)

Wheat: Production
World total: 696.94 million metric tonnes

- Others 21.30
- USA 7.81
- China 16.85
- India 12.46
- Pakistan 12.46
- Russia 8.07
- Ukrain 3.20
- Kazakhstan 5.16
- France 5.16
- Germany 3.27
- UK 2.19
- Canada 3.63
- Australia 4.29
- Turkey 2.70
- Argentina 2.22

Coarse grains: Production
World total: 1,152.78 million metric tonnes

- Others 24.20
- Canada 1.99
- Mexico 2.23
- India 3.65
- Nigeria 2.06
- Ukrain 2.89
- Russia 2.87
- Poland 1.50
- Germany 1.66
- France 2.40
- Argentina 2.61
- Brazil 6.58
- China 17.27
- USA 28.08

Rice: Production
World total: 465.81 million metric tonnes

- Philippines 2.30
- Brazil 1.69
- Others 11.35
- USA 1.26
- China 30.21
- Japan 1.64
- India 22.61
- Bangladesh 7.23
- Pakistan 1.33
- Indonesia 7.84
- Vietnam 5.83
- Thailand 4.39
- Mayanmar 2.32

Oilseeds: Production
World total: 442.03 million metric tonnes

- Others 17.47
- Australia 1.13
- USA 20.89
- Brazil 15.87
- Argentina 10.13
- China 13.40
- India 7.87
- Pakistan 1.31
- France 1.67
- Russia 2.81
- Ukrain 3.21
- Canada 4.28

Cotton: Production
World total: 124.1 pound bales

- Australia 4.43
- Greece 1.07
- Mexico 0.95
- Others 8.53
- USA 12.55
- China 26.67
- India 22.16
- Pakistan 8.54
- Uzbekistan 3.38
- Turkmenistan 1.13
- Brazil 7.01
- Argentina 0.81
- Turkey 2.77

Corn: Production
World total: 882.5 million metric tonnes

- Indonesia 1.00
- Ukrain 2.59
- South Africa 1.41
- Nigeria 1.05
- Others 15.07
- USA 35.58
- China 21.84
- Brazil 8.27
- Argentina 2.38
- Mexico 2.12
- France 1.80
- Italy 1.80
- Hungary 0.92
- Romania 1.19
- India 2.44
- Canada 1.29

Note: Figures in the graphs are in per cent.

Data source - Energy and Minerals: British Geological Survey
Agriculture: Food and Agricultural Organization (FAO)

Earth-Fact File

Situation	Milky Way Galaxy	Orbital speed (around Sun)	29.79 km/sec.
Age	4.6 billion years	Period of revolution	365 days 5 hrs.
Mass	5,940,000,000,000,000,000,000 Metric tones	Axial tilt	23.45º
Equatorial circumference	40,066 km	Average surface temperatures	13º C
Polar circumference	39,992 km	Surface area	510,100,500 sq km
Equatorial diameter	12,756 km	Land surface	148,950,800 sq km
Polar diameter	12,710 km	No. of satellites	1 (Moon)
Equatorial radius	6,376 km	Nearest star	Sun
Polar radius	6,355 km	Solar light reaches Earth in	8 min. 20 sec.
Distance from Sun	149 407 000 km	Escape velocity	11.2 km/sec.

Earth from Moon

Composition of the Earth and Moon

	Earth (in per cent)	Moon (in per cent)
Iron	34.6	9.3
Oxygen	29.5	42.0
Silicon	15.2	19.6
Magnesium	12.7	18.7
Carbon	1.1	4.3
Aluminum	1.1	4.2
Nickel	2.4	0.6
Sodium	0.6	0.07
Sulphur	1.9	0.3

World, Continents and Oceans

	Area - Sq. km	Area - Miles	%
World			
The World	484,510,420	207,934,764	
Land	148,800,420	57,412,764	30.71
Water	335,710,000	150,522,000	69.29
Continents			
Asia	45,036,492	17,388,686	30.27
Africa	30,343,578	11,715,721	20.39
North America	24,680,331	9,529,129	16.59
South America	17,815,420	6,878,572	11.97
Antarctica	12,093,000	4,669,133	8.13
Europe	9,908,599	3,825,731	6.66
Australia and Oceania	8,923,000	3,405,792	6.00
World Land	**148,800,420**	**57,412,764**	**100.00**
Oceans			
Pacific Ocean	166,241,000	64,186,000	49.52
Atlantic Ocean	86,557,000	33,420,000	25.78
Indian Ocean	73,427,000	28,350,000	21.87
Arctic Ocean	9,485,000	24,566,000	2.83
World Water	**335,710,000**	**150,522,000**	**100.00**

Highest Waterfalls of the World

Name(s)	Location	Source/River	Height (in metres)
Angel	Canaima National Park, Venezuela	Upper tributary of Rio Caroni	979
Tugela	NatalNat'l Park, South Africa	Tugela	947
Utigord	Norway	Glacier stream	800
Monge	Marstein, Norway	Mongebeck	774
Gocta Cataracts	Chachapoyas, Peru	--	771
Mutarazi	Nyanga National Park, Zimbabwe	Mutarazi	762
Yosemite	Yosemite National Park, California	Yosemite Creek	739

Angel Fall

World's largest deserts

Desert	Location	Sq. km
Sahara	North Aftrica	9,065,000
Gobi	Mongolia-China	1,295,000
Kalahari	Southern Africa	582,000
Great Victoria	Australia	338,500
Great Sandy	Australia	338,500

Sahara Desert

Mount Everest

Highest Peaks and Longest Rivers in the World

Peak	Location	Height (in meters / feet)	River	Country	Length (in kilometers)
Mount Everest	Nepal/China	8,850 / 29,035	Nile	Egypt/Africa	6,695
K2	India	8,611 / 28,251	Amazon	Brazil/South America	6,516
Kangchenjunga	India/Nepal	8,586 / 28,169	Chang Jiang (Yangtze)	China/Asia	6,380
Lhotse	Nepal	8,516 / 27,939	Mississippi-Missouri	USA/North America	5,969
Makalu	Nepal	8,463 / 27,765	Ob'-Irtysh	Asia	5,568
Cho Oyu	Nepal/China	8,201 / 26,906	Yenisei-Angara	Russia/Asia	5,550
Dhaulagiri	Nepal	8,167 / 26,794	Huang He (Yellow)	China/Asia	5,464
Manaslu	Nepal	8,163 / 26,781	Congo	Africa	4,667
Nanga Parbat	India	8,126 / 26,660	Parana (Rio de la Plata)	South America	4,500
Annapurna I	Nepal	8,091 / 26,545	Mekong	Asia	4,425

Continental extremes

Continent	Asia	Europe	North America	South America	Africa	Oceania	Antarctica
Area (in sq. km)	45,036,492	9,908,599	24,680,331	17,815,420	30,343,578	8,923,000	12,093,000
Estimated Population (in thousand)	3,679,737	727,986	315,915	349,510	795,671	31,043	--
No. of Countries	49	50	23	12	54	14	--
Highest Point	Mt Everest, Nepal/China; 29,035 ft (8,850 m)	Mt Elbrus, Russia/Georgia; 18,510 ft (5,642 m)	Mt McKinley, Alaska; 20,320 ft (6,194 m)	Mt Aconcagua, Argentina; 22,834 ft (6,960 m)	Mt Kilimanjaro, Tanz.; 19,340 ft (5,895 m)	Kosciusko, Australia; 7,316 ft (2,228 m)	Vinson Massif, Ellsworth Mts; 16,066 ft (4,897 m)
Lowest Point	Dead Sea; 1341 ft below sea level (409 m bsl)	Caspian Sea Shore; 92 ft below sea level (28 m bsl)	Death Valley; 282 ft below sea level (86 m bsl)	Valdes Peninsula; 131 ft below sea level (40 m bsl)	Lake Assal; 512 ft below sea level (156 m bsl)	Lake Eyre; 52 ft below sea level (16 m bsl)	8327 ft below sea level (2,538 m bsl)
Largest Island	Borneo; 745,561 sq. km	Great Britain; 218,476 sq. km	Greenland; 2,175,600 sq. km	Tierra del Fuego; 47,000 sq. km	Madagascar; 587,040 sq. km	New Guinea; 808,510 sq. km	--
Longest river	Chang Jiang (Yangtze); 6,380 km	Volga; 3,688 km	Mississippi-Missouri; 5,969 km	Amazonas (Amazon); 6,516 km	Nile; 6,695 km	Murray-Darling; 3,750 km	--
Largest lake	Caspean Sea; 371,000 sq. km	Lake Ladoga; 18,390 sq. km	Lake Superior; 82,100 sq. km	Lake Titicaca; 8,340 sq. km	Lake Victoria; 68,800 sq. km	Lake Eyre; 9,000 sq. km	--

Tanz.: Tanzania

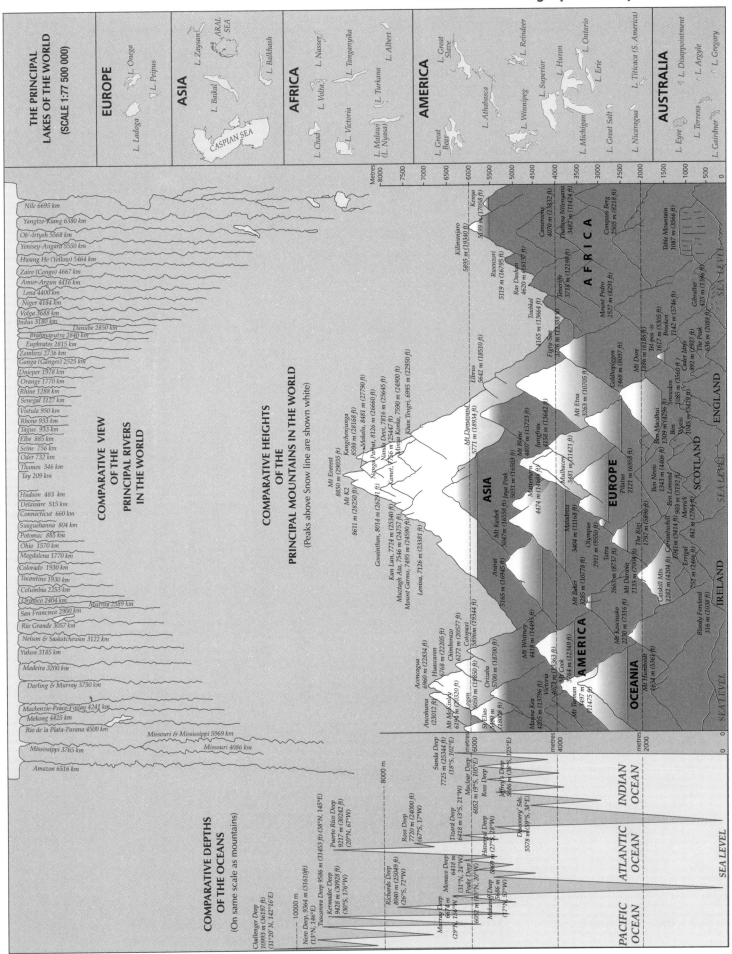

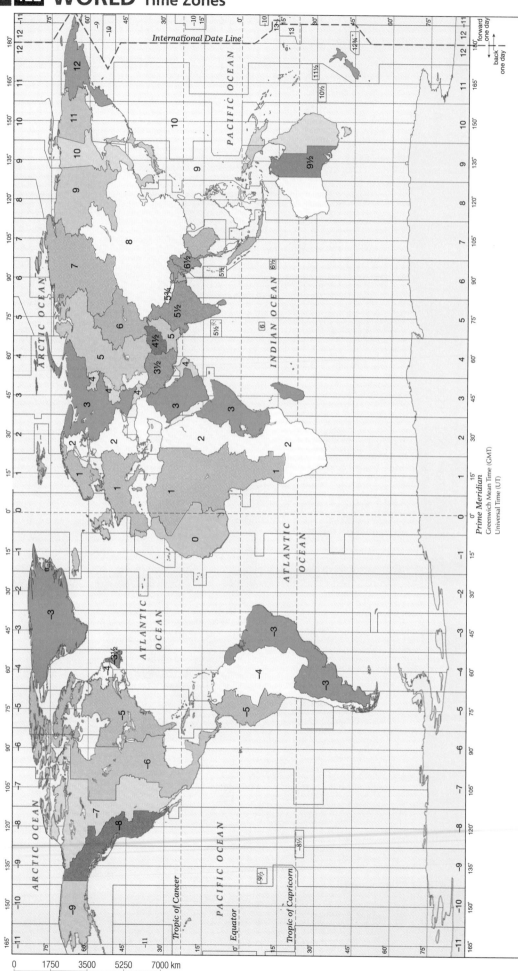

THE WORLD CLOCK: The earth is a globe which rotates and spins on its axis, and the sun and stars appear to revolve around it from east to west, because the earth is rotating from west to east. In twenty four hours the earth makes a complete rotation on its axis. The velocity of the earth's rotation is 360° in twenty four hours, or 15° in one hour, or 1° in four minutes. A clock is simply a machine to indicate the speed of the earth's rotation and inform us of the subdivisions of time. We see at a glance that at any place on the meridian 15° east of Greenwich the clock is one hour later than at Greenwich, because the sun has risen one hour earlier, and at any place 15° west of Greenwich the clock is an hour earlier, because the sun is an hour later in rising.

The 180° longitude is taken as the International Date Line where one calendar day ends and another begins. While crossing from east to west one gains a day and loses the same while travelling from west to east. The line is not straight in order to avoid the landmasses which would be divided in terms of time and add to the complexity of time zones.

Standard Time is the time kept on land. Countries may adopt a uniform or multiple time zones keeping in mind the extent of its boundaries longitudinally. Many countries also vary their time seasonally on account of the varying amount of daylight throughout the year. Such seasonal changes as 'Daylight Saving Time' is not shown on this map. Standard Time is measured in relation to the zero time zone, which is centered on the Greenwich or the Prime Meridian. The time in this zone is known as the Greenwich Mean Time or Universal Time.

Robinson Projecrion

SCALE 1:175 000 000

How to use this Index

The place names or features in this index are arranged in alphabetical order. Each entry in the index starts with the name of the place or feature, followed by the name of the country or region in which it is located. This is followed by the number of the most appropriate page on which the name appears, usually the largest scale map. Next comes the coordinate reference i.e., latitude and longitude, which gives a more exact description of the position of a name or feature. For example, the index entry for Aachen is given as follows:

Aachen Germany (77) 50.47N 6.05E

Aachen is in Germany and appears on page 77. Its latitude is 50 degrees and 47 minutes north of the equator and its longitude is 6 degrees and 05 minutes east of the prime meridian.

Names of the physical features such as rivers, lakes, mountains, etc. are followed by a description, which has been shortened to one or two or three letters, e.g. Everest mountain is written as Everest, Mt The names of rivers have been indexed either according to their origins or according to their mouths.

Where there is more than one place with the same name, the country name is used to decide the order.

Abbreviations used in the index

Arch.	Archipelago	Pt	Point
C.	Cape	R.	River
E.	East	Ra.	Range
I.	Island	Rep.	Republic
Is	Islands	Res.	Reservoir
L.	Lake	S.	South
Mt	Mount	S.E.	South east
Mts	Mountains	Str.	Strait
N.	North	Terr.	Territory
N.W.	North West	UK	United Kingdom
N.S.W.	New South Wales	USA	United States of America
Pen.	Peninsular/Peninsula	Vol.	Volcano
Prov.	Province	W.	West

Names	Country/Region	P. No.	Lat.	Long.
A				
Aachen	Germany	77	50.47N	6.05E
Abadan	Iran	74	30.27N	48.25E
Abaetetuba	Brazil	93	1.45S	48.54W
Abapo	Bolivia	91	18.50S	63.27W
Abashiri	Japan	71	44.00N	144.15E
Abbottabad	Pakistan	14	34.09N	73.15E
Aberdeen	Scotland	79	57.09N	2.05W
Aberystwyth	Wales	79	52.24N	4.05W
Abha	Saudi Arabia	74	18.00N	42.34E
Abidjan	Cote d' Ivoire	83	5.26N	3.58W
Abquaiq	Saudi Arabia	74	26.00N	49.45E
Abu Dhabi	United Arab Emirates	67	24.28N	54.25E
Abu Hills	Rajasthan	10	24.35N	72.42E
Abu	Rajasthan	23	24.40N	72.45E
Abuja	Nigeria	83	9.06N	7.19E
Abuna	Brazil	93	9.41S	65.20W
Acapulco	Mexico	87	17.00N	100.00W
Acarau	Brazil	93	2.55S	40.05W
Accra	Ghana	83	5.31N	0.15W
Achalpur	Maharashtra	20	21.18N	77.33E
Achill, Is.	Rep. of Ireland	79	53.57N	10.00W
Aconcagua, Mt	Argentina	90	32.30S	67.30W
Ad Damman	Saudi Arabia	74	26.20N	50.05E
Adam's Bridge	Sri Lanka	21	9.05N	79.35E
Adam's Peak	Sri Lanka	21	6.49N	80.30E
Addanki	Andhra Pradesh	20	15.49N	80.01E
Addis Ababa	Ethiopia	83	9.02N	38.44E
Adelaide	South Australia	95	35.57S	136.38E
Aden	Yemen	74	12.45N	45.04E
Adilabad	Andhra Pradesh	27	19.40N	78.32E
Adirampattinam	Tamil Nadu	21	10.21N	79.25E
Adoni	Andhra Pradesh	27	15.38N	77.19E
Adriatic Sea	Italy, etc.	76	43.00N	15.00E
Aegean Sea	Greece	77	39.00N	25.00E
AFGHANISTAN	Asia	67	34.00N	65.00E
Africa, Continent	**World**	**101**		
Agartala	Tripura	13	23.50N	91.16E
Agartala	Tripura	25	23.50N	91.25E
Agra	Uttar Pradesh	24	27.18N	78.02E
Ahmadabad	Gujarat	12	23.03N	72.40E
Ahmadnagar	Maharashtra	27	19.05N	74.48E
Ahmadpur East	Pakistan	14	29.06N	71.18E
Ahwa	Gujarat	23	20.44N	73.42E
Aizawl	Mizoram	25	23.36N	93.00E
Ajaccio	Corsica	77	41.55N	8.40E
Ajanta Range	Maharashtra	20	20.20N	77.10E
Ajanta	Maharashtra	27	20.33N	75.48E
Ajmer	Rajasthan	23	26.27N	74.42E
Akalkot	Maharashtra	20	17.31N	76.51E
Akbarpur	Uttar Pradesh	24	26.26N	79.57E
Akita	Japan	71	39.40N	140.00E
Akola	Maharashtra	27	20.42N	77.02E
Akot	Maharashtra	20	21.06N	77.06E
Akron	Ohio, USA	89	41.07N	81.31W
Aksu	China	70	41.04N	80.05E
Akyab	Myanmar	73	20.09N	92.57E
Al Amarah	Iraq	74	31.55N	47.15E
Alagoinhas	Brazil	93	12.09S	38.21W
Alappuzha	Kerala	28	9.30N	76.23E
Alaska	USA	89	65.00N	150.00W
Alaska, Gulf of	Alaska, USA	89	58.30N	145.00W
ALBANIA	S. Europe	77	41.00N	20.00E
Albany	W. Australia	95	35.00S	118.00E
Albany, R.	Canada	86	51.30N	83.35W
Albert, L.	Uganda, etc.	82	1.50N	31.00E
Albuquerque	New Mexico, USA	89	35.00N	106.40W
Aldershot	England	79	51.17N	0.45W
Alegrete	Brazil	93	29.45S	55.40W
Alessandria	Italy	80	44.54N	8.39E
Aleutian, Is.	Bering Sea, USA	89	51.00N	180.00E
Alexandria	Egypt	83	34.12N	29.53E
ALGERIA	N.W. Africa	83	28.30N	2.00E
Algiers	Algeria	83	36.50N	3.00E
Alhillah	Iraq	74	32.30N	44.25E
Alhufuf	Saudi Arabia	74	22.25N	49.48E
Alibag	Maharashtra	27	18.39N	72.55E
Aligarh	Uttar Pradesh	24	27.30N	79.40E
Alipur Duar	W. Bengal	25	26.30N	89.35E
Alipur	W. Bengal	25	22.32N	88.24E
Alipura	Madhya Pradesh	16	25.10N	79.22E
Alirajpur	Madhya Pradesh	26	22.16N	74.24E
Aliwal	South Africa	85	30.41S	26.42E
Aljawf	Saudi Arabia	74	29.55N	39.45E
Allahabad	Uttar Pradesh	24	25.28N	81.54E
Almaty	Kazakhstan	81	43.12N	76.45E
Almora	Uttarakhand	24	29.37N	79.40E
Almubarraz	Saudi Arabia	74	25.30N	49.40E
Along	Arunachal Pradesh	25	28.08N	94.43E
Alps, Southern	New Zealand	95	44.00S	170.00E
Alps, The	Switzerland	80	46.00N	7.00E
Alqatif	Saudi Arabia	74	26.35N	50.00E
Alqunfidha	Saudi Arabia	74	19.03N	41.04E
Altai, Mts	Mongolia	70	47.00N	90.00E
Altamira	Brazil	93	3.13S	52.15W
Altyn Tagh, Mts	China	70	38.40N	90.00E
Aluva	Kerala	28	10.07N	76.24E
Alwar	Rajasthan	23	27.34N	76.38E
Amambai	Brazil	93	23.04S	55.16W
Amapa	Brazil	93	2.00N	50.50W
Amarapura	Myanmar	73	21.55N	96.04E
Amaravati	Andhra Pradesh	27	16.50N	80.15E
Amarnath Cave	Jammu & Kashmir	22	34.12N	75.30E
Amazon, R.	S. America	90	3.00S	60.00W
Amb	Pakistan	14	34.20N	72.52E
Ambala	Haryana	22	30.21N	76.52E
Ambala	Haryana	22	30.21N	76.52E
Ambasamudram	Tamil Nadu	21	8.43N	77.29E
Ambassa	Tripura	25	23.51N	91.48E
Ambikapur	Chhattisgarh	26	23.10N	83.15E
Ambovombe	Madagascar	85	25.11S	46.08E
Amethi	Uttar Pradesh	24	26.08N	81.50E
Amindivi, Is.	Arabian Sea	29	10.00N	73.00E
Amirante, Is.	Indian Ocean	98	6.00S	53.00E
Amlekhganj	Nepal	15	27.15N	85.00E
Amman	Jordan	67	31.57N	35.56E
Ampani	Odisha	17	19.43N	82.40E
Amrawati	Maharashtra	27	20.56N	77.48E
Amreli	Gujarat	23	21.37N	71.14E
Amreli	Gurajat	23	21.36N	71.15E
Amritsar	Punjab	22	31.37N	74.55E
Amroha	Uttar Pradesh	24	28.54N	78.31E
Amsterdam	The Netherlands	77	52.22N	4.53E
Amu Darya	Turkmenistan	81	38.00N	65.00E
Amur, R.	Russia	81	50.30N	127.30E
Anadyr, Gulf of	Russia	81	65.00N	178.00W
Anaimalai Hills	Tamil Nadu	21	10.24N	76.40W
Anand	Gujarat	23	22.34N	72.56E
Anandpur	Punjab	14	31.15N	76.34E
Ananindeua	Brazil	93	1.22S	48.20W
Anantapur	Andhra Pradesh	27	14.41N	77.36E
Anantapur	Andhra Pradesh	27	14.41N	77.39E
Anantnag	Jammu & Kashmir	22	33.43N	75.17E
Anapolis	Brazil	93	16.19S	48.58W
Ancohuma, Mt	Bolivia	90	16.00S	68.50W
Ancona	Italy	80	43.36N	13.31E
Andaman & Nicobar Is.,Union Territory	India	13	12.00N	92.40E
Andes, Mts	S. America	90	10.00S	77.00W
Andhra Pradesh, State	India	13	16.00N	80.0E
Andkhui	Afghanistan	75	36.56N	65.05E
Andorra	South Europe	77	42.31N	1.32E
Andorra-la-Vella	Andorra	77	42.31N	1.32E
Angel Falls	Venezuela	90	6.00N	63.00W
Angers	France	80	47.28N	0.33W
ANGOLA	S. Africa	83	13.00S	15.00E
Angouleme	France	80	45.39N	0.10E
Angul	Odisha	26	24.50N	85.06E
Angul	Odisha	26	20.48N	85.05E
Anini	Arunachal Pradesh	25	28.47N	95.54E
Anju	N. Korea	71	39.32N	125.32E
Ankara	Turkey	74	39.57N	32.54E
Ankleshwar	Gujarat	23	21.38N	73.02E
Annam	Vietnam	72	15.00N	108.00E
Annapurna, Mt	Nepal	15	28.35N	83.57E
Anqing	China	70	30.34N	117.81E
Anshan	China	70	41.03N	122.58E
Antalya	Turkey	74	36.52N	30.45E
Antananarivo	Madagascar	83	18.54S	47.33E
Antarctica, Continent	**World**	**101**		
ANTIGUA & BARBUDA	West Indies	87	17.20N	61.48W
Antilles, Greater	West Indies	86	18.00N	74.00W
Antofagasta	Chile	93	23.40S	70.23W
Antsiranana	Madagascar	85	12.19S	49.17E
Antwerp	Belgium	80	51.13N	4.24E
Anupgarh	Rajasthan	23	29.07N	73.06E
Anuppur	Madhya Pradesh	26	23.05N	81.43E
Anuradhapura	Sri Lanka	69	8.22N	80.23E
Anxi	China	70	40.21N	96.10E
Anyang	China	70	36.07N	114.26E
Apennine, Mts	Italy	76	44.00N	12.00E
Apia	Samoa	97	13.50S	171.44W
Appalachian, Mts	USA	86	38.30N	80.00E
Aqaba	Jordan	74	29.31N	35.00E
Aquidauana	Brazil	93	20.27S	55.45W
Ara	Bihar	24	25.34N	84.32E
Arabia, Pen.	S.W. Asia	74	25.00N	45.00E
Arabian Sea	Indian Ocean	66	17.00N	66.00E
Aracaju	Brazil	93	10.54S	37.07W
Aracati	Brazil	93	4.32S	37.45W
Arad	Romania	80	46.11N	21.19E
Arafura Sea	Pacific Ocean	94	10.50N	132.00E
Araguania	Brazil	93	7.16S	48.18W
Araguari	Brazil	93	18.38S	48.13W
Arakan Yoma	Myanmar	73	20.00N	94.20E
Arakkonam	Tamil Nadu	28	13.05N	79.43E
Aral Sea	Kazakhstan	81	45.00N	60.00E
Arambagh	W. Bengal	25	22.53N	87.50E
Aran, I.	Rep. of Ireland	79	53.05N	9.35W
Arantangi	Tamil Nadu	21	10.10N	79.02E
Arapiraca	Brazil	93	9.45S	36.40W
Araraquara	Brazil	93	21.46S	48.08W
Araria	Bihar	24	26.11N	87.32E
Aravali Range	Rajasthan	10	25.00N	73.10E
Araxa	Brazil	93	19.37S	46.50W
Arcot	Tamil Nadu	21	12.56N	79.24E
Arctic Ocean	**World**	**101**		
Ardnamurchan, Pt	Scotland	79	56.43N	6.09W
Arequipa	Peru	91	16.28S	71.30W
ARGENTINA	South America	91	35.00S	65.00W
Arica	Chile	93	18.30S	70.20W
Aripuana	Brazil	93	7.00S	60.30W
Ariquemes	Brazil	93	9.55S	63.06W
Ariyalur	Tamil Nadu	28	11.11N	79.03E
Arkansas, R.	USA	86	38.20N	100.00W
Arkhangelsk	Russia	81	64.33N	40.33E
Arles	France	80	43.40N	4.38E
Armagh	N. Ireland	79	54.22N	6.39W
ARMENIA	Asia	67	40.00N	45.00E
Armur	Andhra Pradesh	20	18.48N	78.16E
Arni	Tamil Nadu	21	12.40N	79.19E
Arran, I.	Scotland	79	55.35N	5.15W
Artigas	Uruguay	93	30.25S	56.28W
Arunachal Pradesh, State	India	13	28.00N	95.00E
Aruppukkottai	Tamil Nadu	21	9.31N	78.08E
Arwal	Bihar	24	25.14N	84.40E
Asansol	W. Bengal	18	23.42N	87.01E
Ashgabat	Turkmenistan	67	37.45N	58.30E
Ashoknagar	Madhya Pradesh	26	24.35N	77.43E
Ashti	Maharashtra	20	21.12N	78.14E
Asia, Continent	**World**	**101**		
Asir	Saudi Arabia	74	20.00N	42.00E
Asmar	Afghanistan	75	35.03N	71.30E
Asmara	Eritrea	83	15.20N	38.56E
Assam, State	India	25	26.00N	93.00E
Assis	Brazil	93	22.37S	50.25W
Astana	Kazakhstan	67	51.10N	71.30E
Astrakhan	Russia	81	46.15N	48.04E
Asuncion	Paraguay	93	25.15S	57.40W
Aswan	Egypt	83	24.05N	32.57E
Asyut	Egypt	83	27.14N	31.07E
Atacama Desert	Chile	90	24.00S	69.20W
Athabasca, L. & R.	Canada	86	59.00N	110.00W
Athens	Greece	77	37.54N	23.52N
Athgarh	Odisha	17	20.32N	85.41E
Athlone	Rep. of Ireland	79	53.26N	7.56E
Athni	Karnataka	20	16.44N	75.06E
Atico	Peru	93	16.12S	73.38W
Atlanta	Georgia, USA	89	33.45N	84.21W
Atlantic Ocean	**World**	**100**		
Atlas, Mts	Morocco	82	32.00N	5.00W
Atmakur	Andhra Pradesh	20	14.37N	79.40E
Attock	Pakistan	14	33.53N	72.17E
Attur	Tamil Nadu	21	11.36N	78.39E
Atur	Tamil Nadu	21	10.16N	77.53E
Auckland	New Zealand	95	36.52S	174.42E
Augsburg	Germany	80	48.22N	10.53E
Augusta	Georgia, USA	89	33.29N	81.59W
Augusta	Maine, USA	89	44.20N	69.45W
Auraiya	Uttar Pradesh	24	26.26N	79.32E
Aurangabad	Bihar	24	24.45N	84.25E
Aurangabad	Maharashtra	27	19.53N	75.23E
Austin	Texas, USA	89	30.16N	97.43W
AUSTRALIA	Oceania	95	25.00S	135.00E
AUSTRIA	Europe	77	47.00N	14.00E
Avignon	France	80	43.57N	4.49E
Ayaviri	Peru	93	14.53S	70.35W
Aydin	Turkey	74	37.45N	27.40E
Ayodhya	Uttar Pradesh	24	26.48N	82.14E
Ayr	Scotland	79	55.28N	4.39W
Ayutthaya	Thailand	72	14.23N	100.35E
Azamgarh	Uttar Pradesh	24	26.03N	83.13E
AZERBAIJAN	Asia	67	40.00N	47.00E
B				
Babol	Iran	74	36.30N	52.49E
Badami	Karnataka	28	15.55N	75.45E
Badanah	Saudi Arabia	74	30.58N	41.30E
Badarinath	Uttarakhand	24	30.44N	79.32E
Bad-el-Mandeb	Str. of Africa, etc.	82	13.00N	43.10E
Badgam	Jammu & Kashmir	22	34.06N	74.44E
Badnur	Madhya Pradesh	16	21.80N	77.90E
Badulla	Sri Lanka	69	6.59N	81.05E
Baffin, Bay & I.	Canada	86	73.00N	65.00W
Bagalkot	Karnataka	28	16.12N	75.45E
Bagdogra	West Bengal	18	26.42N	88.19E
Bage	Brazil	93	31.22S	54.06W
Bageshwar	Uttarakhand	24	29.50N	79.49E
Baghdad	Iraq	67	33.20N	44.27E
Baghelkhand	Madhya Pradesh	17	24.10N	82.00E
Baghmara	Meghalaya	25	25.11N	90.38E
Baghpat	Uttar Pradesh	24	28.56N	77.17E
BAHAMAS	North America	87	24.00N	75.00W
Baharampur	West Bengal	25	24.06N	88.15E
Baharampur	W. Bengal	25	24.06N	88.19E
Bahawalpur	Pakistan	75	28.24N	71.47E
Bahia Blanca	Argentina	91	38.40S	62.13W
Bahraich	Uttar Pradesh	24	27.34N	81.38E
BAHRAIN	Persian Gulf	74	26.00N	50.35E
Baikal, L.	Russia	66	54.00N	108.00E
Baikunthpur	Chhattisgarh	26	23.16N	82.33E
Bairiki	Kiribati	97	01.20N	172.59E
Baku	Azerbaijan	67	40.22N	49.50E
Balaghat	Madya Pradesh	26	21.48N	80.15E
Balaghat, Ra.	Maharashtra	10	18.37N	76.14E
Balama	Mozambique	85	13.20S	38.35E
Balaton, L.	Hungary	80	46.50N	17.40E
Balearic, Is.	Spain	77	39.30N	2.00E
Baleshwar	Odisha	26	21.30N	86.54E
Bali, I.	Indonesia	72	8.20S	115.00E
Balia	Bangladesh	18	25.09N	89.18E
Balikesir	Turkey	74	39.35N	27.58E
Balkan, Mts	Bulgaria	76	42.45N	24.20E
Balkhash	Kazakhstan	81	46.50N	74.50E
Balkhash, L.	Kazakhstan	66	46.30N	75.00E
Balkonda	Andhra Pradesh	20	19.05N	78.20E
Ballarat	Australia	95	37.35S	143.55E
Ballarshah	Maharastra	27	19.55N	79.23E
Ballary	Karanataka	28	15.09N	76.55E
Ballia	Uttar Pradesh	24	25.44N	84.11E
Balochistan	Pakistan	75	28.00N	65.00E
Balrampur	Uttar Pradesh	24	27.25N	82.15E
Baltic Sea	N. Europe	77	56.00N	16.00E
Baltimore	Maryland, USA	89	39.18N	76.37W
Baltistan	Jammu & Kashmir	14	35.30N	76.00E
Balurghat	W. Bengal	25	25.14N	88.47E
Bamako	Mali	83	12.34N	7.55W
Bamberg	Germany	80	49.54N	10.53E
Banas, R.	Rajsthan	19	26.13N	76.13E
Banda Atjeh	Sumatra	72	5.30N	95.00E
Banda	Uttar Pradesh	24	25.20N	80.22E
Banda, Is. and Sea	Indonesia	72	5.00S	128.00E
Bandar Abbas	Iran	74	27.12N	56.15E
Bandar Seri Begawnan	Brunei	72	4.56N	114.58E
Bandar-e-Pahlavi	Iran	74	37.30N	49.30E
Bandipore	Jammu & Kashmir	22	34.25N	74.39E
Bandjarmasin	Borneo	72	3.20S	114.35E
Bandra	Maharashtra	27	19.03N	72.52E
Banff	Scotland	79	57.31N	2.32W
Banganapalle	Andhra Pradesh	27	15.19N	78.17E
Bangkok	Thailand	72	13.42N	100.30E
BANGLADESH	South Asia	67	24.00N	90.00E
Bangui	Central African Re	83	4.23N	18.37E
Bangweulu, L.	Zimbabwe	82	12.00S	30.00E
Banjul	Gambia	83	13.28N	16.40W
Banka	Bihar	24	24.53N	86.55E
Banki	Odisha	17	20.21N	85.33E
Bankipore	Bihar	17	25.40N	85.12E

Names	Country/Region	P. No.	Lat.	Long.
Banks, I.	Canada	86	73.30N	120.00W
Bankura	W. Bengal	25	23.14N	87.07E
Bannu	Pakistan	75	33.00N	70.39E
Bansi	Uttar Pradesh	17	27.10N	82.56E
Banswara	Rajasthan	23	23.30N	74.24E
Bantval	Karnataka	21	12.53N	75.05E
Bara Banki	Uttar Pradesh	24	26.53N	81.12E
Baragarh	Odisha	26	21.20N	83.37E
Baraj	Uttar Pradesh	17	26.16N	83.46E
Baramba	Odisha	17	20.25N	85.23E
Baramula	Jammu & Kashmir	22	34.10N	74.30E
Baran	Rajasthan	23	25.05N	76.33E
Barannda	Madhya Pradesh	17	25.03N	80.40E
Barasat	West Bengal	25	22.43N	88.29E
Barbacena	Brazil	93	21.13S	43.47W
BARBADOS	West Indies	87	10.10N	59.30W
Barcelona	Spain	77	41.22N	2.10E
Barcelos	Brazil	93	00.59S	62.58W
Barddhaman	W. Bengal	25	23.16N	87.54E
Bardi	Madhya Pradesh	17	24.30N	82.26 E
Bareilly	Uttar Pradesh	24	28.22N	79.27E
Barents Sea	Arctic Ocean	99	73.00N	42.00E
Bargarh	Odisha	26	21.20N	83.37E
Baripada	Odisha	26	21.56N	86.46E
Barisal	Bangladesh	18	22.43N	90.24E
Barmer	Rajasthan	23	25.45N	71.25E
Barnala	Punjab	14	30.25N	75.35E
Barnaul	Russia	81	53.23N	83.40E
Barnstaple	England	79	51.05N	4.15W
Barpeta	Assam	25	26.19N	91.00E
Barrackpur	W. Bengal	18	22.46N	88.24E
Barranquilla	Colombia	91	10.50N	74.48
Barreiras	Brazil	93	12.09S	44.58W
Barrow	England	79	54.07N	3.15W
Barrow, Pt	Alaska, USA	89	71.22N	156.30W
Barshi	Maharashtra	27	18.13N	75.44E
Barwani	Madhya Pradesh	26	22.03N	74.57E
Basavana Bagevadi	Karnataka	28	16.32N	76.03E
Basra	Iraq	74	30.28N	47.51E
Bass , Str.	Australia	95	39.20S	145.00E
Bassein	Myanmar	73	16.54N	94.50E
Basseterre	St Kitts & Nevis	87	17.18N	62.44W
Basti	Uttar Pradesh	24	26.48N	82.46E
Batala	Punjab	14	31.49N	75.14E
Batan, Is.	Philippines	72	20.25N	121.59E
Bath	England	79	51.24N	2.20W
Bathinda	Punjab	22	30.11N	75.00E
Bathurst	N.S.W., Australia	95	33.30S	149.35E
Batticaloa	Sri Lanka	74	7.43N	81.44E
Battle Harbour	Labrador, Canada	87	52.19N	55.57W
Batumi	Georgia	74	41.41N	41.38E
Baudh	Odisha	26	20.50N	84.19E
Baurul	Brazi	93	22.20S	49.05W
Bay of Bengal	South Asia	66	16.00N	88.00E
Bayonne	France	80	43.29N	1.28W
Bayreuth	Germany	80	49.57N	11.34E
Beachy Head	England	79	50.44N	0.15E
Bear Great, L.	Canada	86	66.00N	120.00W
Beaufort Sea	Canada	86	72.00N	140.0W
Beaumont	Texas, USA	89	30.05N	94.08W
Beawar	Rajasthan	23	26.06N	74.21E
Begusarai	Bihar	24	25.26N	86.13E
Beijing	China	70	39.55N	116.24E
Beira	Mozambique	85	19.50S	34.52E
Beirut	Lebanon	74	33.50N	35.25E
Bela	Pakistan	14	26.20N	66.20E
Bela	Uttar Pradesh	24	25.56N	82.02E
BELARUS	Europe	77	53.00N	30.00E
Beldanga	W. Bengal	18	23.58N	88.20E
Belem (Para)	Brazil	93	1.27S	48.27W
Belem	Brazil	93	1.20S	48.30W
Belfast	N. Ireland	79	54.35N	5.56W
Belfort	France	80	47.38N	6.52E
Belgaum	Karnataka	28	15.52N	74.34E
BELGIUM	W. Europe	77	51.00N	5.00E
Belgrade	Serbia	77	44.50N	20.30E
Belitung, I.	Indonesia	72	2.30S	108.10E
BELIZE	Central America	87	17.29N	88.14W
Bellary	Karnataka	28	15.09N	76.56E
Belle Ile	France	80	47.20N	3.10W
Bellinghausen Sea	Antarctica	99	66.00S	81.00W
Belmopan	Belize	87	17.14N	88.46W
Belo Horizonte	Brazil	93	19.55S	43.56W
Ben Nevis	Scotland	79	56.48N	5.00W
Bendigo Victoria	Australia	95	36.46S	144.17E
Bengaluru	Karnataka	28	12.58N	77.38E
Benghazi	Libya	83	32.10N	20.10E
Benguela	Angola	83	12.37S	13.25E
BENIN	West Africa	83	8.00N	2.00E
Benjamin Constant	Brazil	93	4.23S	69.58W
Benxi	China	70	41.16N	123.45E
Berber	Sudan	83	18.01N	34.04E
Berbera	Somali Rep	83	10.27N	45.01E
Bergamo	Italy	80	45.42N	9.41E
Bering , Str.	Asia - N. America	66	65.00N	169.00W
Bering Sea	East Asia	66	58.00N	179.00E
Berlin	Germany	77	52.32N	13.25E
Bermuda	Atlantic Ocean	98	32.19N	64.50W
Bern	Switzerland	77	46.55N	7.30E
Berwick on Tweed	England	79	55.48N	2.00W
Besancon	France	80	47.14N	6.02E
Betroka	Madagascar	85	23.16S	46.05E
Bettiah	Bihar	24	26.48N	84.33E
Betul	Madhya Pradesh	26	21.88N	77.98E
Beypore	Kerala	21	11.10N	75.50E
Beziers	France	80	43.21N	3.14E
Bhabua	Bihar	24	25.01N	83.43E
Bhadohi	Uttar Pradesh	17	25.24N	82.38E
Bhadra	Rajasthan	19	29.15N	75.30E
Bhadrachalam	Andhra Pradesh	27	17.40N	80.56E
Bhadrak	Odisha	26	21.03N	86.33E
Bhadravati	Karnataka	28	13.52N	75.40E
Bhadreswar	W. Bengal	25	22.49N	88.20E
Bhagalpur	Bihar	24	25.15N	87.02E
Bhalki	Karnataka	20	18.04N	77.10E
Bhamo	Myanmar	73	24.16N	97.17E
Bhandara	Maharashtra	27	21.09N	79.42E
Bharatpur	Rajasthan	23	27.15N	77.30E
Bharuch	Gujarat	23	21.41N	73.01E
Bhatgaon	Nepal	15	27.39N	85.22E
Bhatpara	W. Bengal	18	22.54N	88.25E
Bhavnagar	Gujarat	23	21.46N	72.11E
Bhawanipatna	Odisha	26	19.58N	83.12E
Bhilwara	Rajasthan	23	25.21N	74.40E
Bhind	Madhya Pradesh	26	26.36N	78.46E
Bhinmal	Rajasthan	23	25.00N	72.19E
Bhiwani	Haryana	22	28.46N	76.18E
Bhopal	Madhya Pradesh	13	23.16N	77.36E
Bhubaneshwar	Odisha	13	20.15N	85.52E
Bhuj	Gujarat	23	23.15N	69.49E
Bhusawal	Maharashtra	27	21.02N	75.47E
BHUTAN	Asia	67	27.30N	90.00E
Biagoveshchensk	Russia	81	50.20N	127.39E
Bialystok	Poland	77	53.06N	23.18E
Biaora	Madhya Pradesh	26	23.55N	76.57E
Bibao	Spain	80	43.16N	2.56W
Bid	Maharashtra	27	19.00N	75.50E
Bidar	Karnataka	28	17.57N	77.39E
Bihar Sharif	Bihar	24	25.10N	85.36E
Bihar, State	India	24	25.37N	85.32E
Bijapur	Karnataka	28	16.49N	75.43E
Bijapur	Chhattisgarh	26	18.50N	80.50E
Bijawar	Madhya Pradesh	17	24.38N	79.32E
Bijna	Madhya Pradesh	17	25.27N	79.05E
Bijnor	Uttar Pradesh	24	29.23N	79.11 E
Bikaner	Rajasthan	23	28.01E	73.22E
Bilaspur	Himachal Pradesh	22	31.19N	76.50E
Bilaspur	Chhattisgarh	26	22.05N	82.13E
Bingerville	Cote D Ivoire	83	5.18N	3.53W
Birjand	Iran	74	32.57N	59.10E
Birkenhead	England	79	53.24N	3.02W
Birmingham	Alabama, USA	89	33.30N	86.49W
Birmingham	England	79	52.30N	1.55W
Biscay, Bay of	France, etc	80	45.00N	2.30W
Bishkek	Kyrgystan	81	42.59N	74.00E
Bishnupur	W. Bengal	25	23.05N	87.23E
Bismarck	N. Dakota, USA	89	46.49N	100.49W
Bissau	Guinea Bissau	83	11.53N	15.38W
Black Sea	S.E. Europe	76	43.00N	33.00E
Blackpool	England	79	53.50N	3.02W
Blanco, C.	W. Africa	83	21.00N	16.59W
Blantyre	Malawi	83	15.47S	35.02E
Bloemfontein	South Africa	85	29.07S	26.14E
Blue, Mts	N.S.W., Australia	95	34.00S	150.00E
Blumenau	Brazil	93	27.00S	49.00W
Boa Vista	Brazil	93	02.48N	60.30W
Bobbili	Andhra Pradesh	20	18.34N	83.25E
Bodh Gaya	Bihar	24	24.41N	85.02E
Bodinayakkanur	Tamil Nadu	21	10.01N	77.24E
Bogota	Colombia	91	4.43N	74.12W
Bogra	Bangladesh	18	24.51N	89.26E
Boise	Idaho, USA	89	43.36N	116.15W
Bokaro	Jharkhand	24	23.46N	85.58E
Bolangir	Odisha	26	20.41N	83.32E
BOLIVIA	South America	91	15.00S	65.00W
Bologna	Italy	80	44.30N	11.21E
Bolzano	Italy	80	46.31N	11.22E
Bom Jesus da Lapa	Brazil	93	13.14S	43.23W
Bomdila .	Arunachal Pradesh	25	27.20N	92.22E
Bongaigaon	Assam	25	26.26N	90.31E
Bonifacio, Str. of	Corsica-Sardinia	76	41.23N	9.08E
Bonn	Germany	80	40.44N	9.04E
Boothia, Gulf of and Pen.	Canada	86	71.00N	90.00W
Bordeaux	France	80	44.50N	0.34W
Borneo, I.	Indonesia	72	1.00N	115.00E
BOSNIA-HERZEGOVINA	S. Europe	77	44.00N	17.00E
Bosporus, Str.	Black Sea	76	41.10N	29.00E
Boston	USA	89	42.22N	71.02W
Botad	Gujarat	23	22.10N	71.40E
Bothnia, Gulf of	Baltic Sea	76	63.00N	21.00E
BOTSWANA	Africa	83	23.00S	22.00E
Boudh	Odisha	26	20.49N	84.24E
Bourges	France	80	47.05N	2.23E
Bournemouth	England	79	50.44N	1.50W
Boyne, R.	Rep. of Ireland	79	53.44N	6.15W
Bradford	England	79	53.46N	1.40W
Braganca	Brazil	93	1.02S	46.46W
Brahmanbaria	Bangladesh	18	23.58N	91.09E
Brahmaputra, R.	Assam	18	26.45N	93.30E
Brahmpur	Odisha	26	19.18N	84.51E
Brasileia	Brazil	93	10.59S	68.45W
Brasilia	Brazil	93	16.13S	44.29W
Bratislava	Slovakia	80	48.09N	17.07E
BRAZIL	South America	91	10.00S	55.00W
Brazilian Highlands	Brazil	93	18.00S	46.30W
Brazzaville	Congo	83	4.15S	15.20E
Bremen	Germany	80	53.05N	8.50E
Brescia	Italy	80	45.33N	10.15E
Brest	Poland	80	52.05N	23.42E
Bridgetown	Barbados	87	13.05N	59.30W
Brighton	England	79	50.50N	0.10W
Brisbane	Queensland, Aust.	95	27.30S	153.00E
Bristol	England	79	51.27N	2.35W
British Isles	N.W. Europe	79	55.00N	2.00W
British Isles	United Kingdom	79	53.00N	2.00W
Brno	Czech Republic	80	49.12N	16.37E
Broken Hill	N.S.W., Australia	94	30.58S	141.27E
Brownsville	Texas, USA	89	25.56N	97.25W
BRUNEI	S.E. Asia	67	4.55N	114.57E
Brussels	Belgium	80	50.52N	4.22E
Buchan Ness	Scotland	79	57.28N	1.46W
Bucharest	Romania	77	44.25N	26.07E
Budapest	Hungary	77	47.29N	19.03E
Budaun	Uttar Pradesh	24	28.02N	79.10E
Budejovice	Czech Republic	80	48.58N	14.28E
Buea	Cameroon	83	4.09N	9.06E
Buenaventura	Colombia	91	3.55N	77.11W
Buenos Aires	Argentina	91	34.35S	58.20W
Buffalo	New York, USA	89	42.53N	78.50W
Buir Nur	Mongolia	70	47.50N	117.35E
Bujumbura	Burundi	83	3.24S	29.22E
Bukhara	Uzbekistan	74	39.52N	64.30E
Bulandshahr	Uttar Pradesh	24	28.24N	77.54E
Bulawayo	Zimbabwe	85	20.10S	28.43E
Buldhana	Maharashtra	27	20.32N	76.14E
BULGARIA	S.E. Europe	80	42.10N	24.00E
Bundelkhand	Madhya Pradesh	17	24.40N	80.00E
Bundi	Rajasthan	23	25.27N	75.41E
Burgin	China	74	48.00N	86.70E
Burhanpur	Madhya Pradesh	16	21.17N	76.16E
BURKINA FASO	E. Africa	83	12.00N	2.00W
Bursa	Turkey	74	40.10N	29.01E
Buru, I.	Moluccas	72	3.20S	126.30E
BURUNDI	Africa	83	3.00S	30.00E
Busan	South Korea	71	35.07N	129.02E
Butte (But)	Montana, USA	89	46.00N	112.33W
Buxar	Bihar	24	25.34N	84.01E
Bydgoszcz	Poland	80	53.03N	18.00E
C				
Cabinda	Angola	83	5.00S	12.30E
Cabo	Brazil	93	8.14S	34.58W
Caceres	Spain	80	39.29N	6.23W
Cachoeira do Sul	Brazil	93	30.03S	52.52W
Cachoeira	Brazil	93	12.35S	39.59W
Cadiz	Spain	77	36.32N	6.17W
Caen	France	80	49.11N	0.22W
Caernarvon	Wales	79	53.08N	4.15W
Cagliari	Sardinia, Italy	77	39.15N	9.05E
Cairns	Queensland, Aust.	95	16.54S	145.44E
Cairo	Egypt	83	30.02N	31.15E
Calais	France	80	50.55N	1.50E
Calama	Chile	93	22.30S	68.55W
Calgary	Canada	87	51.02N	114.20W
Cali	Colombia	91	3.25N	76.35W
California	USA	89	40.00N	120.00W
California, Gulf of	Mexico	86	27.00N	111.00W
Callao	Peru	91	12.00S	77.00W
Calvinia	South Africa	85	31.25S	19.47E
Camacupa	Angola	83	12.03S	17.50E
Camaguey	Cuba	87	21.20N	78.00W
CAMBODIA	S.E. Asia	67	12.00S	105.00E
Cambrai	France	80	50.11N	3.14E
Cambrian, Mts	Wales	79	52.00N	3.50W
Cambridge	England	79	52.12N	0.10E
CAMEROON	West Africa	83	5.30N	13.00E
Cameroun, Mt	Cameroon	82	4.11N	9.09E
Cameta	Brazil	93	2.13S	49.30W
Camocim	Brazil	93	2.55S	40.50W
Campina Grande	Brazil	93	7.15S	35.50W
Campo Grande	Brazil	93	20.25S	54.40W
Campo Mourao	Brazil	93	24.01S	52.24W
Campos	Brazil	93	21.20S	41.20W
Canacona	Goa	20	14.50N	74.08E
CANADA	North America	87	60.00N	100.00W
Canadian, R.	USA	89	35.20N	100.00W
Canary, Is.	Atlantic Ocean	98	28.00N	15.30W
Canberra	Australia	95	35.17S	149.18E
Cangamba	Angola	85	13.41S	19.51E
Cannes	France	80	43.33N	6.59E
Canoas	Brazil	93	28.55S	51.10W
Canterbury Bight	New Zealand	95	44.10S	172.00E
Cape Comorin	India	11	8.03N	77.40E
Cape Lopez	Gabon	83	0.50S	8.30E
Cape Province	S. Africa	83	32.00S	24.00E
Cape Town	South Africa	85	33.56S	18.28E
CAPE VERDE	West Africa	83	17.00N	25.00W
Car Nicobar	Andaman & Nicobar Is	29	9.12N	92.48E
Carajas	Brazil	93	6.02S	50.10W
Caraoas	Venezuela	91	10.31N	67.05W
Caratinga	Brazil	93	19.50S	42.06W
Carcassonne	France	80	43.13N	2.21E
Cardamom Hills	Kerala	21	9.27N	76.52E
Cardiff	Wales	79	51.30N	3.10W
Cardigan, Bay	Wales	79	52.05N	4.39W
Cariacica	Brazil	93	20.15S	40.23W
Caribbean Sea	West Indies	86	15.00N	73.00W
Carlisle	England	79	54.54N	3.00W
Carolina	Brazil	93	7.21S	47.22W
Carpathian, Mts	S.E. Europe	76	49.00N	22.30E
Carpentaria, G. of	Queensland, Aust.	94	15.00S	139.00E
Carson City	Nevada, USA	89	39.08N	119.45W
Cartagena	Spain	77	37.39N	0.55W
Cartagena	Columbia	91	10.22N	75.32W
Casablanca	Morocco	83	33.39N	7.35W
Cascade, Ra.	N. America	86	47.00N	121.30W
Cascavel	Brazil	93	4.10S	38.15W
Caspian Sea	Europe-Asia	81	42.00N	52.00E
Cassel (Kassel)	Germany	80	51.20N	9.30E
Castries	St Lucia	87	14.01N	60.59W
Caucaia	Brazil	93	3.44S	38.45W
Caucasus, Mts	Georgia	66	43.00N	44.00E
Cavan	Rep. of Ireland	79	54.00N	7.30W
Caxias do Sul	Brazil	93	29.14S	51.10W
Caxias	Brazil	93	4.53S	43.20W
Cayenne	Fr. Guiana	91	4.58N	52.18W
Cayman's, Is.	West Indies	86	19.40N	80.30W
Celebes, I.	Indonesia	72	2.00S	120.00E
CENTRAL AFRICAN REPUBLIC	Africa	83	5.00N	20.00E
Ceuta	North Africa	83	35.53N	5.20W
CHAD	Africa	83	15.00N	17.15E
Chad, L.	Africa	83	13.20N	14.00E
Chagos, Arch.	Indian Ocean	66	6.00S	72.00E
Chaibasa	Jharkhand	24	22.33N	85.51E
Chakdarra	Pakistan	14	34.40N	72.06E
Chakwal	Pakistan	14	32.56N	72.53E
Chalgali	Chhattisgarh	17	23.18N	83.42E
Chalisgaon	Maharashtra	27	20.33N	75.10E
Chalons-sur-Saone	France	80	46.47N	4.52E
Chamarajanagar	Karnataka	28	11.55N	76.56E
Chamba	Himachal Pradesh	22	32.29N	76.10E
Chambal, R.	Madhya Pradesh	26	26.40N	76.20E
Chambery	France	80	45.34N	5.56E
Champa	Chhattisgarh	26	22.02N	82.43E
Champawat	Uttarakhand	24	29.21N	80.07E
Champhai	Mizoram	25	23.29N	93.17E
Chamrajnagar	Karnataka	28	11.56N	77.00E
Chanaral	Chile	93	26.23S	70.40W
Chandauli	Uttar Pradesh	24	25.15N	83.16E
Chandausi	Uttar Pradesh	17	28.27N	78.49E
Chandel	Manipur	25	24.17N	93.56E
Chanderi	Madhya Pradesh	16	24.42N	78.11E
Chandigarh, Union Territory	India	13	30.42N	76.54E
Chandrakona	W. Bengal	18	22.44N	87.33E
Chandrapur	Maharashtra	27	19.57N	79.21E
Chanduria	W. Bengal	18	22.56N	88.55E
Changara	Mozambique	85	16.50S	33.17E
Changchun	China	70	43.54N	125.20E
Changhua	Taiwan	70	24.02N	120.30E
Changlang .	Arunachal Pradesh	25	27.04N	95.39E
Changsha	China	70	28.09N	112.45E
Channapatna	Karnataka	21	12.38N	77.13E
Channel, Is.	English Channel	79	49.30N	2.30W
Charkhari	Uttar Pradesh	17	25.26N	79.45E
Charkhi Dadri	Punjab	14	28.37N	76.19E
Charleston	S. Carolina, USA	89	32.50N	79.58W
Charleston	W. Virginia, USA	89	38.23N	81.40W
Charsadda	Pakistan	14	34.08N	71.46E
Chartres	France	80	48.27N	1.30E
Chatra	Jharkhand	24	24.12N	84.56E
Cheduba, I.	Myanmar	73	18.40N	93.30E
Cheju Do, I.	S. Korea	71	33.29N	126.34E
Chelyuskin, C.	Russia	81	77.52N	104.30E
Chemnitz	Germany	80	50.50N	12.55E
Chenab, R.	India	22	32.00N	77.14E
Chengalpattu	Tamil Nadu	21	12.42N	80.01E
Chengde	China	70	40.59N	117.55E
Chengdu	China	70	30.40N	104.12E
Chennai	Tamil Nadu	28	13.04N	80.17E
Cherbourg	France	80	49.40N	1.40W
Chernivih	Ukraine	77	51.29N	31.19E
Chernivtsi (Cernauti)	Ukraine	80	48.18N	25.56E
Cherrapunji	Meghalaya	25	25.17N	91.47E
Chesapeake	Virginia, USA	89	38.00N	76.12W
Cheyenne	Wyoming, USA	89	41.09N	104.19W
Chhapra	Bihar	24	25.47N	84.47E
Chhatarpur	Madhya Pradesh	26	24.54N	79.38E
Chhatrapur	Odisha	26	19.21N	85.03E
Chhattisgarh, State	India	26	21.00N	81.00E
Chhindwara	Madhya Pradesh	26	22.03N	78.59E
Chhota Udepur Town	Gujarat	23	22.19N	74.01E
Chiang Mai	Thailand	72	18.50N	98.53E
Chicago	Illinois, USA	89	42.00N	87.40E
Chidambaram	Tamil Nadu	28	11.24N	79.44E
Chik Ballapur	Karnataka	28	13.29N	77.42E
Chikmagalur	Karnataka	28	13.18N	75.49E
Chiknayakanhalli	Karnataka	21	13.25N	76.40E
CHILE	South America	91	30.00S	71.00W
Chilika, L.	Odisha	26	9.50N	85.30E
Chiloe, I.	Chile	90	42.52S	74.00W
Chimbay	Uzbekistan	74	43.00N	59.43E
Chimborazo, Vol.	Equador	90	1.30S	79.11W
CHINA	S.E. Asia	72	33.00N	105.00E
Chinde	Mozambique	85	18.35S	36.28E
Chindwin, R.	Myanmar	73	22.30N	95.00E
Chingola	Zambia	85	12.31S	27.53E
Chinhoyi	Zimbabwe	85	17.21S	30.11E
Chiniot	Pakistan	75	31.44N	73.01E
Chinju	S. Korea	71	35.12N	128.02E
Chipata	Zambia	85	13.40S	32.42E
Chiromo	Malawi	85	16.33S	35.10E
Chisinau	Maldova	77	47.00N	28.55E
Chisinau	Moldova	81	47.02N	28.52E
Chita	Russia	81	53.10N	113.40E
Chitembo	Angola	83	13.32S	16.46E
Chitradurga	Karnataka	28	14.14N	76.26E

Names	Country/Region	P. No.	Lat.	Long.
Chitrakootdham	Uttar Pradesh	24	25.15N	80.41E
Chitral	Pakistan	14	35.48N	71.52E
Chittagong	Bangladesh	18	22.21N	91.53E
Chittaranjan	W. Bengal	25	23.50N	87.00E
Chittaurgarh	Rajasthan	23	24.54N	74.42E
Chittoor	Andhra Pradesh	27	13.13N	79.08E
Chittur	Kerala	21	10.42N	76.47E
Chongjin	N. Korea	71	41.51N	129.58E
Chongju	S. Korea	71	35.50N	127.04E
Chongqing	China	70	29.32N	106.50E
Chota Nagpur Plateau	Eastern India	11	23.21N	85.20E
Choybalsan	Mongolia	70	48.03N	114.28E
Christchurch	New Zealand	95	43.30S	172.40E
Chukchi Sea	Arctic Ocean	99	68.00N	175.00W
Chunar	Uttar Pradesh	25	25.08N	82.56E
Chunchura	W. Bengal	25	22.53N	88.27E
Chur	Switzerland	80	46.52N	9.22E
Churachandpur	Manipur	25	24.18N	93.39E
Churchill	Canada	87	58.44N	94.15W
Churu	Rajasthan	23	28.19N	75.01E
Cincinnati	Ohio, USA	89	39.07N	84.30W
Circars, Northern	Andhra Pradesh	20	17.00N	83.30E
Ciudad Bolivar	Venezuela	91	8.08N	63.57W
Ciudad del Este	Paraguay	93	25.32S	54.34W
Clermont Ferrand	France	80	45.46N	3.06N
Cleveland	Ohio, USA	89	41.28N	81.40W
Cluj-Napoca	Romania	77	46.46N	23.35E
Clyde, Firth of	Scotland	79	54.40N	4.30W
Coast, Ra.	N. America	86	40.00N	123.00W
Cobh	Rep. of Ireland	79	51.55N	8.19W
Cobija	Bolivia	91	11.01S	68.45W
Cochabamba	Bolivia	90	17.26S	66.10W
Cochrane	Ontario, Canada	89	49.00N	81.00W
Cocos-Keeling, Is.	Indian Ocean	98	12.12S	96.54E
Codajas	Brazil	93	3.55S	62.00W
Codo	Brazil	93	4.28S	43.51W
Coimbatore	Tamil Nadu	28	11.00N	77.00E
Colgong	Bihar	17	25.16N	87.17E
Cologne	Germany	80	50.56N	6.57E
COLOMBIA	South America	91	5.00N	75.00W
Colombo	Sri Lanka	67	6.56N	79.56E
Colon	Panama	87	9.21N	79.56W
Colorado, R.	Argentina	90	38.00S	65.00W
Colorado, R.	USA	89	37.30N	109.43W
Columbia	S. Carolina, USA	89	34.00N	81.00W
Columbia, R.	USA	89	48.25N	118.12W
Columbus	Georgia, USA	89	32.30N	84.56W
Columbus	Ohio, USA	89	39.57N	83.02W
Comilla	Bangladesh	18	23.25N	91.13E
Como	Italy	80	45.48N	9.05E
Comorin, C.	Tamil Nadu	28	8.04N	77.36E
COMOROS	Africa/Indian Oean	83	11.55S	44.30E
Conakry	Guinea	83	9.29N	13.42W
Concepcion	Chile	91	36.50S	73.10W
Concord	New Hampshire, USA	89	43.15N	71.34W
Conepcion	Paraguay	91	23.22S	57.26W
CONGO	W. Africa	83	1.00S	16.00E
CONGO, DEMOCRATIC REP.	Africa	83	5.00S	15.00E
Constanta	Romania	77	44.12N	28.38E
Cook, Str.	New Zealand	95	41.00S	171.30E
Cook, Is.	Pacific Ocean	97	20.00S	160.00W
Coolgardie	W. Australia	95	30.57S	121.10E
Copenhagen	Denmark	77	55.40N	12.30E
Copiapo	Chile	93	27.18S	70.24W
Coral Sea	Australia	94	15.00S	150.00E
Cordoba	Argentina	91	31.22S	64.15W
Cork	Rep. of Ireland	79	51.54N	8.29W
Coromandel Coast	Tamil Nadu	11	12.00N	80.30E
Corsica, I.	France	76	42.00N	9.00E
Corumba	Brazil	93	19.00S	57.30W
COSTA RICA	Central America	87	10.00N	85.00W
COTE D' IVOIRE	Africa	82	06.51N	5.18W
Cotswold Hills	England	79	51.40N	2.20W
Coventry	England	79	52.24N	1.30W
Covington	Kentucky, USA	89	39.05N	84.30W
Cox's Bazar	Bangladesh	18	21.27N	92.01E
Coxim	Brazil	93	18.30S	54.55W
Crete, Is	Greece	76	35.10N	25.00E
Crewe	England	79	53.07N	2.27W
Crimea	Ukraine	77	45.30N	35.00E
CROATIA	S. Europe	80	45.00N	16.00E
Crowlest Pass	Canada	86	49.40N	114.40W
Croydon	England	79	51.22N	0.06W
CUBA	West Indies	83	22.00N	80.00E
Cuddalore	Tamil Nadu	28	11.43N	79.49E
Cuddapah	Andhra Pradesh	27	14.30N	78.42E
Cuddapah	Andhra Pradesh	27	14.28N	78.52E
Cuiaba	Brazil	93	15.30S	56.00W
Curitiba	Brazil	93	25.26S	49.20W
Cuttack	Odisha	26	20.28N	85.54E
Cuxhaven	Germany	80	53.53N	8.42E
Cuzco	Peru	93	13.32S	72.05W
CYPRUS	Mediterranean	67	35.00N	33.00E
CZECH REPUBLIC	Central Europe	77	49.00N	16.00E
D				
Dabhoi	Gujarat	23	22.11N	73.25E
Dadra & Nagar Haveli, Union Terr.	India	12	20.10N	72.90E
Dahej	Gujarat	23	21.42N	72.38E
Dahod	Gujarat	23	22.46N	74.18E
Dakar	Senegal	83	14.34N	17.29W
Dakshin Gangotri	Antarctica	99	70.00S	12.00E
Dalandzadgad	Mongolia	70	43.37N	104.17E
Dalap-Uliga-Darrit	Marshall Is.	97	7.07N	171.22E
Dalian	China	70	38.51N	121.37E
Dallas	Texas, USA	89	34.45N	96.48W
Dalmau	Uttar Pradesh	17	26.07N	81.05E
Dalmianagar	Bihar	24	24.53N	84.09E
Daltenganj	Jharkhand	24	24.02N	84.04E
Daly Waters	N. Terr., Australia	94	16.19S	133.28E
Daman & Diu, Union Territory	Western India	12	20.25N	72.50E
Daman, Union Terr.	Western India	12	20.25N	72.53E
Damascus	Syria	67	33.30N	36.14E
Damavand, Mt	Iran	74	36.00N	52.00E
Damietta	Egypt	74	31.24N	31.48E
Damodar, R.	W. Bengal	25	23.17N	87.35E
Damoh	Madhya Pradesh	26	23.50N	79.29E
Danapur	Bihar	17	25.38N	85.05E
Dandot	Pakistan	14	32.41N	72.59E
Dantewara	Chhattisgarh	26	18.52N	81.26E
Danube, R.	Europe	76	44.00N	29.00E
Danzig (Gdansk)	Poland	80	54.20N	18.45E
Daporijo	Arunachal Pradesh	25	27.59N	94.18E
Dar es Salaam	Tanzania	83	6.50S	39.17E
Darbhanga	Bihar	24	26.10N	85.57E
Dargai	Pakistan	14	34.30N	71.53E
Darjiling	West Bengal	25	27.03N	88.18E
Darling, R.	Australia	94	33.00S	142.30E
Darlington	England	79	54.32N	1.33W
Darmstadt	Germany	80	49.52N	8.39E
Darrang	Assam	17	26.45N	92.40E
Dartmoor	England	79	50.40N	4.00W
Darwin	N. Terr., Australia	94	12.30S	131.00E
Daska	Pakistan	14	32.17N	74.24E
Datia	Madhya Pradesh	26	25.39N	78.27E
Daulatabad	Maharashtra	27	19.57N	75.15E
Daund	Maharashtra	27	18.32N	74.40E
Dausa	Rajasthan	23	26.50N	76.21E
Davangere	Karnataka	28	14.31N	75.58E
Davis, Str.	Canada-Greenland	86	67.00N	58.00W
Dawson	Canada	87	64.05N	139.20W
De Aar	South Africa	85	30.40S	24.00E
Dead Sea	Israel/Jordan	74	31.30N	35.00E
Debagarh	Odisha	26	21.32N	84.44E
Deccan	S. India	11	18.00N	77.00E
Dee, R.	Scotland	79	57.05N	2.15W
Dehra Dun	Uttarakhand	13	30.19N	78.04E
Delaram	Afghanistan	75	32.10N	65.30E
Delft, I.	Sri Lanka	21	9.30N	79.40E
Delgado, C.	Mozambique	82	10.45S	40.40E
Delhi, Union Territory	India	13	28.38N	77.12E
Denizli	Turkey	74	37.42N	29.02E
DENMARK	N.W. Europe	77	56.30N	8.00E
Denver	Colorado, USA	89	39.45N	105.00W
Deogarh	Jharkhand	24	24.29N	86.42E
Deogarh	Odisha	26	21.32N	84.46E
Deoghar	Jharkhand	24	24.29N	84.42E
Deoli	Maharashtra	20	20.39N	78.32E
Deoria	Uttar Pradesh	24	26.23N	83.42E
Dera Ghazi Khan	Pakistan	75	30.04N	70.49E
Dera	Syria	74	32.36N	36.07E
Derby	England	79	52.58N	1.25W
Des Moines	USA	89	41.35N	93.37W
Detroit	Michigan, USA	89	42.21N	83.03W
Devakottai	Tamil Nadu	21	9.57N	78.53E
Devarkonda	Andhra Pradesh	20	16.42N	78.58E
Devli	Rajasthan	23	25.46N	75.25E
Dewangiri	Bhutan	18	26.51N	91.27E
Dewas	Madhya Pradesh	26	22.58N	76.06E
Dezful	Iran	74	32.24N	48.32E
Dezhnev, C.	Russia	81	66.10N	169.03W
Dhaka	Bangladesh	18	23.43N	90.26E
Dhamra	Odisha	17	20.48N	86.56E
Dhamtari	Chhattisgarh	26	20.42N	81.34E
Dhanbad	Jharkhand	24	23.47N	86.30E
Dhandhuka	Gujarat	19	22.21N	72.02E
Dhankuta	Nepal	15	26.55N	87.20E
Dhanushkodi	Tamil Nadu	21	09.13N	79.24E
Dhar	Madhya Pradesh	26	22.35N	75.20E
Dharapuram	Tamil Nadu	21	10.45N	77.34E
Dharmapuri	Tamil Nadu	28	12.08N	78.13E
Dharmavaram	Andhra Pradesh	27	14.25N	77.00E
Dharmshala	Himachal Pradesh	22	32.16N	76.23E
Dharwad	Karnataka	28	15.27N	75.05E
Dhaulagiri	Nepal	11	29.11N	83.00E
Dhaulpur	Rajasthan	23	26.42N	77.53E
Dhebar, L.	Rajasthan	19	24.30N	74.00E
Dhemaji	Assam	25	27.32N	94.43E
Dhenkanal	Odisha	26	20.40N	85.38E
Dholadhar	India	10	32.30N	76.06E
Dholera	Gujarat	19	22.15N	72.15E
Dholka	Gujarat	19	22.44N	72.29E
Dhrangadhra	Gujarat	23	22.59N	71.31E
Dhubri	Assam	25	26.02N	90.02E
Dhule	Maharashtra	27	20.58N	74.47E
Diamantina	Brazil	93	18.17S	43.40W
Diamond Harbour	W. Bengal	25	22.11N	88.14E
Dibrugarh	Assam	25	27.27N	94.55E
Didwana	Rajasthan	23	27.17N	74.25E
Dieppe	France	80	49.58N	1.00E
Dig	Rajasthan	19	27.28N	77.20E
Digboi	Assam	25	27.33N	95.40E
Dijon	France	80	47.20N	5.03E
Dili	East Timor	67	08.34S	125.34E
Dimapur	Nagaland	25	25.51N	93.48E
Dinajpur	Bangladesh	18	25.37N	88.40E
Dinaric Alps	Croatia	76	44.00N	17.00E
Dindigul	Tamil Nadu	28	10.22N	78.00E
Dindori	Madhya Pradesh	26	22.57N	81.41E
Dingwall	Scotland	79	57.36N	4.26E
Diphu	Assam	25	25.49N	93.26E
Disa	Gujarat	23	24.14N	72.13E
Dispur	Assam	25	26.09N	91.50E
Diu, Union Terr.	Western India	12	20.42N	71.01E
Divinopolis	Brazil	93	20.08S	44.55W
Djibouti	E. Africa	83	11.34N	43.01E
Dnieper, R.	Ukraine-Belarus	76	50.00N	32.00E
Dnepropetrovsk	Ukraine	77	48.28N	35.02E
Dniester, R.	Ukraine	76	46.00N	29.50E
Doda	Jammu & Kashmir	22	33.08N	75.37E
Dodabetta, Mt	Tamil Nadu	11	11.25N	76.46E
Dod-Ballapur	Karnataka	21	13.14N	77.23E
Dodoma	Tanzania	83	06.10S	35.44E
Doha	Qatar	67	25.15N	51.36E
Dohad	Gujarat	23	22.52N	74.15E
Dolomites, Mts	Italy	80	46.15N	12.00E
DOMINICA	West Indies	87	15.20N	61.20W
DOMINICAN REP.	West Indies	87	19.00N	70.00W
Don, R.	Scotland	79	57.11N	2.05W
Don, R.	Russia	81	50.10N	40.00E
Donegal	Rep. of Ireland	79	54.39N	8.06W
Donegal, Bay	Rep. of Ireland	79	52.08N	10.16W
Donetsk (Stalino)	Ukraine	77	48.00N	37.38E
Dongargarh	Chhattisgarh	26	21.12N	80.50E
Dongola	Sudan	83	19.10N	30.26E
Doranda	Jharkhand	17	23.22N	85.22E
Dortmund	Germany	80	51.31N	7.27E
Douglas	Isle of Man., UK	79	54.12N	4.25W
Dourados	Brazil	93	22.09S	54.52W
Dover	England	79	51.08N	1.15E
Dover, Str. of	England/France	79	51.00N	1.30E
Drakensberg	Southern Africa	82	28.30S	29.00E
Dras	Jammu & Kashmir	14	34.22N	75.50E
Drazinda	Pakistan	14	31.47N	70.05E
Dresden	Germany	80	51.03N	13.45E
Drogheda	Rep. of Ireland	79	52.44N	6.23W
Duala (Douala)	Cameroon	83	4.05N	9.40E
Dublin	Ireland	77	53.21N	6.16W
Dublin	Rep. of Ireland	79	53.21N	6.16W
Duisburg	Germany	80	51.26N	6.45E
Duki	Pakistan	14	30.10N	68.35E
Duluth	Minnesota, USA	89	46.49N	92.09W
Dumfries	Scotland	79	55.05N	3.37W
Dumka	Jharkhand	24	24.15N	87.16E
Dun Laoghaire	Rep. of Ireland	79	53.17N	6.09W
Duncansby Head	Scotland	79	58.4	3.00W
Dundalk	Rep. of Ireland	79	54.00N	6.25W
Dundee	Scotland	79	56.29N	3.00W
Dunedin	New Zealand	95	54.40S	170.30E
Dunnet Head	Scotland	79	58.38N	3.22W
Durban	South Africa	85	29.53S	31.00E
Durg	Chhattisgarh	26	21.12N	81.18E
Durgapur	Bangladesh	18	25.30N	90.50E
Durgapur	W. Bengal	25	23.30N	87.20E
Dushanbe	Tajikistan	81	38.50N	69.20E
Dusseldorf	Germany	80	51.13N	6.47E
Dwarka	Gujarat	23	22.14N	69.01E
E				
East London	South Africa	85	33.00S	27.54E
East Sea	Asia	67	39.00N	137.00E
East Siberian Sea	Russia	81	73.00N	160.00E
ECUADOR	South America	91	2.00S	78.00E
Edinburgh	Scotland	79	55.56N	3.12W
Edmonton	Canada	87	55.35N	113.30W
EGYPT	N. Africa	83	25.00N	30.00E
El Alamein	Egypt	83	30.50N	28.57E
El Faiyum	Egypt	83	29.19N	30.50E
El Giza	Egypt	83	31.01N	31.13E
El Obeid	Sudan	83	13.16N	29.48E
El Paso	Texas, USA	89	31.49N	106.31W
EL SALVADOR	Central America	87	13.50N	89.00W
Elarish	Egypt	74	31.08N	33.50E
Elba, I.	Italy	80	42.45N	10.10E
Elbe, R.	Germany	76	53.50N	9.00E
Elbert, Mt	USA	89	39.05N	106.27W
Elbrus, Mt	Russia	74	42.23N	42.27E
Elburz, Mts	Iran	74	36.10N	52.00E
Elgin	Scotland	79	57.40N	3.20W
Ellenabad	Haryana	14	29.26N	74.54E
Ellesmere, I.	Canada	86	79.30N	80.00W
Ellora	Maharashtra	27	20.02N	75.13E
Eluru	Andhra Pradesh	27	16.43N	81.09E
Empangeni	South Africa	85	28.45S	31.55E
England	U.K.	77	53.00N	1.00W
English Channel	England/France	79	50.00N	2.00W
Ennore	Tamil Nadu	21	13.14N	80.22E
Entebbe	Uganda	83	0.02N	32.30E
EQUATORIAL GUINEA	Africa	82	03.45N	08.47E
Eregli	Turkey	74	41.15N	31.30E
Erfurt	Germany	80	50.58N	11.02E
Ernakulam	Kerala	28	10.00N	76.15E
Erode	Tamil Nadu	28	11.20N	77.46E
ERITREA	Africa	83	15.20N	38.55E
Erimala, Ra.	Andhra Pradesh	20	15.20N	78.00E
Erimo, C.	Japan	71	41.50N	143.15E
Erz Gebirge	Germany	80	50.40N	13.30E
Erzurum	Turkey	74	39.55N	41.10E
Eskisehir	Turkey	74	39.50N	30.35E
Essen	Germany	80	51.28N	7.01E
Estancia	Brazil	93	11.15S	37.28W
ESTONIA	Europe	77	58.20N	27.00E
Etah	Uttar Pradesh	24	27.35N	78.40E
Etawah	Uttar Pradesh	24	26.47N	79.02E
ETHIOPIA	N. E. Africa	83	10.00N	40.00E
Ethiopian Highlands	E. Africa	82	10.00N	37.00E
Etna, Mt	Sicily	76	37.45N	15.00E
Euphrates, R.	Iraq	74	33.30N	43.10E
Europe, Continent	World	101		
Everest, Mt	Nepal-China	15	27.59N	86.53E
Exeter	England	79	50.43N	3.30W
Eyre, L.	S. Australia	94	28.30S	137.20E
Eyre, Pen.	S. Australia	94	34.00S	137.00E
F				
Fairbanks	Alaska, USA	89	64.59N	148.10W
Faisalabad	Pakistan	75	31.30N	73.05E
Faizabad	Uttar Pradesh	24	26.47N	82.12E
Fale	Tokelau	97	9.22 S	171.14 W
Falkland, Is.	S. Atlantic Ocean	91	52.00S	59.00W
False Point	Odisha	17	20.20N	86.46E
Farafangana	Madagascar	85	22.48S	47.48E
Farah	Afghanistan	75	32.30N	62.10E
Farewell, C.	Greenland	87	59.47N	43.40W
Faridabad	Haryana	22	28.25N	77.22E
Faridkot	Punjab	22	30.40N	74.57E
Faroe, Is.	Denmark	77	62.00N	7.00W
Fatehabad	Haryana	22	29.31N	75.30E
Fatehgarh	Uttar Pradesh	24	27.23N	79.40E
Fatehgarh Sahib	Punjab	22	30.41N	76.28E
Fatehjang	Pakistan	14	33.34N	72.38E
Fatehpur	Rajasthan	23	28.00N	75.02E
Fatehpur	Uttar Pradesh	24	25.55N	80.52E
Fazilka	Punjab	22	30.25N	74.04E
Fderik	Mauritania	83	22.40N	12.45W
Ferrara	Italy	80	44.51N	11.28E
Fez	Morocco	83	34.08N	5.06W
Fianarantsoa	Madagascar	85	21.27S	47.07E
Fife Ness	Scotland	79	56.16N	2.35W
FIJI	Pacific Ocean/Oceania	97	16.00S	180.00E
FINLAND	N. Europe	77	62.00N	25.00E
Firozabad	Uttar Pradesh	24	27.09N	78.24E
Firozepur	Punjab	22	30.55N	74.40E
Fishguard	Wales	79	51.59N	4.59W
Fiume (Reijeka)	Croatia	80	45.20N	14.25E
Flamborough Head	England	79	54.07N	0.05W
Flores, I.	Indonesia	72	8.30S	121.00E
Floriano	Brazil	93	6.46S	42.59W
Florianopolis	Brazil	93	27.37S	48.27W
Florida	USA	89	27.00N	82.00W
Folkestone	England	79	51.04N	1.10E
Fongafale	Tuvalu	97	8.31S	179.13E
Forfar	Scotland	79	56.40N	2.50W
Formosa	Brazil	93	15.30S	47.22W
Fort Munro	Pakistan	14	29.55N	70.03E
Fort Smith	Canada	87	60.05N	112.00W
Fort Smith	Arkansas USA	89	35.25N	94.25W
Fort William	Scotland	79	56.48N	5.05W
Fort Worth	Taxas, USA	89	32.43N	97.20W
Fort Yukon	Alaska, USA	89	66.20N	145.00W
Fortaleza	Brazil	93	3.50S	38.28W
Fort-de-France	Martinique	97	14.36N	61.02W
Forth, Firth of	Scotland	79	56.03N	3.00W
Fouta Djallon	W. Africa	82	11.20N	12.10W
Foxe Basin	Canada	87	68.00N	78.00W
Foz do Iguacu	Argentina	91	25.33S	54.31W
Franca	Brazil	93	20.33S	47.27W
FRANCE	W. Europe	77	48.00N	2.00E
Franceville	Gabon	83	1.40S	13.31E
Francistown	Bostwana	85	21.11S	27.32E
Frankfort	Kentucky, USA	89	33.12N	85.44W
Frankfurt-am-Main	Germany	80	50.06N	8.40E
Frankfurt-an-der-Oder	Germany	80	52.22N	14.33W
Fraserburgh	Scotland	79	57.42N	2.00E
Fredericton	Canada	87	44.55N	66.32W
Freetown	Sierra Leone	83	8.30N	13.10W
Freiburg	Germany	80	48.00N	7.52E
Fremantle	W. Australia	95	32.05S	115.40E
French Guiana	South America	91	4.00N	53.00W
French Polynesia	Pacific Ocean	97	20.00S	145.00W
Frisian, Is.	Germany/Netherlands	80	53.40N	7.00E
Fuji San, Mt	Japan	71	35.20N	138.20E
Fukui	Japan	71	35.25N	135.09E
Fukuoka	Japan	71	33.30N	131.00E
Fundy, Bay of	Nova Scotia, Canada	86	45.00N	66.00W
Fushun	China	70	42.00N	123.59E
Fuzhou	China	70	26.07N	119.21E
G				
Gabes, Gulf of	Tunisia	83	34.00N	10.20E
GABON	Africa	83	1.00S	12.00E
Gaborone	Bostwana	83	24.45S	25.55E
Gadag	Karnataka	28	15.25N	75.42E
Gadchiroli	Maharashtra	27	20.11N	80.00E
Gadwel	Andhra Pradesh	27	16.13N	77.48E
Galapagos, I.	Ecuador	90	1.00S	90.00W
Galati	Romania	77	45.28N	28.04E
Galle	Sri Lanka	69	6.01N	80.14E
Galveston	Taxas, USA	89	29.19N	94.50W

Names	Country/Region	P. No.	Lat.	Long.
Galway (Gaillimh)	Rep. of Ireland	79	53.16N	9.05W
GAMBIA	W. Africa	83	13.25N	16.00W
Ganawati	Karnataka	20	15.30N	76.36E
Gandak, R.	Bihar	24	26.30N	84.30E
Ganderbal	Jammu & Kashmir	22	34.14N	74.47E
Gandhinagar	Gujarat	12	23.10N	72.41E
Ganga (Ganges), R.	India	11	21.30N	89.40E
Ganganagar	Rajasthan	23	29.49N	73.50E
Gangotri	Uttarakhand	24	30.54N	78.54E
Gangtok	Sikkim	25	27.20N	88.40E
Ganjam	Odisha	26	19.22N	85.06E
Gar	China	70	31.45N	80.21E
Garanhuns	Brazil	93	8.53S	36.28W
Garhwa	Jharkhand	24	24.10N	83.52E
Garo Hills	Meghalaya	11	25.30N	90.20E
Garo Hills	Meghalaya	11	25.30N	90.30E
Garonne, R.	France	80	44.34N	0.10E
Garrauli	Madhya Pradesh	17	25.05N	79.24E
Gartha	Madhya Pradesh	16	24.25N	78.03E
Gauriganj	Uttar Pradesh	24	26.13N	81.41E
Gaurihar	Madhya Pradesh	17	25.16N	80.12E
Gautemala City	Guatemala	87	14.38N	90.33W
Gavle	Sweden	77	60.40N	17.00E
Gawilgarh	Maharashtra	20	21.22N	77.25E
Gaya	Bihar	24	24.48N	85.00E
Gdynia	Poland	80	54.34N	18.35E
Geelong	Victoria, Australia	95	38.10S	144. 21E
Geneva	Switzerland	80	46.13N	6.07E
Genoa	Italy	80	44.24N	8.57E
Georgetown	Guyana	91	6.50N	58.12W
GEORGIA	Asia	67	41.40N	45.00E
Gereshk	Afghanistan	75	31.50N	64.38E
GERMANY	Europe	76	52.0N	12.00E
Gerona	Spain	80	41.59N	2.49E
Ghadames	Libya	83	30.10N	9.30E
Ghaghara, R.	Uttar Pradesh	17	27.30N	81.20E
GHANA	W. Africa	83	6.00N	1.00W
Ghanzi	Bostwana	85	21.42S	21.39E
Ghatampur	Uttar Pradesh	17	26.08N	80.13E
Ghats, Eastern	S. India	11	16.00N	80.00E
Ghats, Western	S. India	10	16.00N	74.00E
Ghaziabad	Uttar Pradesh	24	28.40N	77.28E
Ghazipur	Uttar Pradesh	24	25.34N	83.35E
Ghazni	Afghanistan	75	33.34N	68.17E
Ghent	Belgium	80	51.03N	3.45E
Ghotaru	Rajasthan	23	27.22N	70.02E
Gibraltar	Spain	77	36.08N	5.19W
Gifu	Japan	71	35.30N	135.45E
Gilgit	India	22	35.55N	74.22E
Gir	Gujarat	16	21.00N	71.00E
Gir, Ra.	Gujarat	10	21.03N	71.00E
Giridih	Jharkhand	24	24.10N	86.21E
Girvan	Scotland	79	55.15N	4.50W
Gisborne	New Zealand	95	38.40S	178.03E
Glasgow	Scotland	79	55.52N	4.15W
Gloucester	England	79	51.52N	2.15W
Goa, State	India	12	14.20N	74.00E
Goalpara	Assam	25	26.11N	90.41E
Gobabis	Namibia	85	22.30S	18.58E
Gobi, The	Mongolia	70	44.00N	108.00E
Gobindpur	Jharkhand	17	23.51N	86.34E
Godavari, R.	Andhra Pradesh	20	16.35N	82.15E
Godda	Jharkhand	24	24.50N	87.13E
Godhra	Gujarat	23	22.45N	73.40E
Godthaab	Greenland	87	64.10N	51.32W
Godwin Austen (K2), Mt	Jammu & Kashmir	11	35.30N	76.32E
Gogri	Bihar	17	25.28N	86.38E
Goiania	Brazil	93	16.43S	49.18W
Goias	Brazil	93	15.57S	50.07W
Gokak	Karnataka	28	16.11N	74.52E
Golaghat	Assam	25	26.30N	94.00E
Golconda	Andhra Pradesh	20	17.23N	78.27E
Gomati, R.	Uttar Pradesh	17	27.15N	80.38E
Gonda	Uttar Pradesh	24	27.28N	82.01E
Gondal	Gujarat	23	21.55N	70.52E
Gondar	Ethiopia	83	12.35N	37.28E
Gondia	Maharashtra	27	21.28N	80.29E
Good Hope, Cape of	S. Africa	83	34.12S	18.23E
Gooty	Andhra Pradesh	27	15.07N	77.41E
Gopalganj	Bihar	24	26.28N	84.26E
Gopalpur	Odisha	26	19.16N	84.57E
Gopeshwar	Uttarakhand	24	30.23N	79.24E
Gorakhpur	Uttar Pradesh	24	26.45N	83.24E
Gorlitz	Germany	80	51.09N	14.59E
Gorontalo	Celebes	72	0.32N	123.13E
Goteborg	Sweden	77	57.42N	12.00E
Gotland I.	Sweden	77	57.30N	18.30E
Gottingen	Germany	80	51.30N	10.00E
Goulburn	N.S.W., Australia	95	34.50S	149.45E
Grahamstown	South Africa	85	33.19S	26.32E
Grampians	Scotland	79	56.52N	4.00W
Gran Chaco, El	S. America	90	23.30S	60.00W
Grande Rio	Mexico, etc.	86	26.10N	98.30W
Graz	Austria	80	47.04N	15.26E
Great Barrier Reef	Queensland, Aust.	94	18.00S	148.00E
Great Himalaya	India-Nepal	11	28.00N	82.00E
Great Indian Desert	Rajasthan	10	27.00N	71.00E
Great Salt, L.	USA	89	41.15N	112.30W
GREECE	S. E. Europe	77	38.00N	23.00E
Green Bay	Wisconsin, USA	89	44.30N	88.00W
GREENLAND	N. America	87	72.15N	40.00W
Greenock	Scotland	79	55.57N	4.45W
GRENADA	West Indies	87	12.10N	61.40W
Grenadines	West Indies	87	13.00N	61.10W

Names	Country/Region	P. No.	Lat.	Long.
Grenoble	France	80	45.11N	5.43E
Grimsby	Great England	79	53.34N	0.04E
Groningen	Netherlands	80	53.13N	6.34E
Grootfontein	Namibia	85	19.32S	18.05E
Grossglockner	Austria	80	47.06N	12.35E
Groznyy	Russia	77	43.20N	45.45E
Guadalajara	Mexico	87	20.40N	103.20W
Guadalquivir, R.	Spain	76	36.45N	6.18W
Guadalupe, I.	Mexico	86	28.40N	118.12W
Guadeloupe, I.	West Indies	87	16.10N	61.45W
Guajara Mirim	Brazil	93	10.50S	65.20W
Guangzhou	China	70	23.11N	113.14E
GUATEMALA	Central America	87	14.38N	90.22W
Guayaquil	Ecuador	91	2.15S	79.52W
Gudiyatam	Tamil Nadu	21	12.57N	78.55E
Gudur	Andhra Pradesh	27	14.09N	79.54E
Guernsey	Channel Is.	80	49.30N	2.35W
Guiana Highlands	S. America	90	5.00N	60.00W
GUINEA	W. Africa	83	11.00N	12.00W
Guinea, Gulf of	W. Africa	82	3.00N	2.00E
GUINEA-BISSAU	W. Africa	83	12.00N	15.00W
Guiyang	China	70	26.33N	106.39E
Gujar Khan	Pakistan	14	33.16N	73.20E
Gujarat, State	W. India	12	23.00N	72.00E
Gujranwala	Pakistan	75	32.10N	74.14E
Gulbarga	Karnataka	28	17.20N	76.50E
Gulmarg	Jammu & Kashmir	22	34.15N	74.25E
Gumla	Jharkhand	24	23.03N	84.33E
Guna	Madhya Pradesh	26	24.40N	77.20E
Guntakal	Andhra Pradesh	27	15.11N	77.25E
Guntur	Andhra Pradesh	27	16.18N	80.29E
Gurdaspur	Punjab	22	32.03N	75.27E
Gurgaon	Haryana	22	28.37N	77.04E
Guryev	Kazakhstan	81	47.15N	51.52E
Guthrie	Oklahoma USA	89	35.55N	97.30W
Guwahati	Assam	25	26.12N	91.42E
GUYANA	South America	91	5.00N	60.00W
Guyenne	France	80	42.15N	1.00E
Gwallior	Madhya Pradesh	26	26.15N	78.10E
Gweru	Zimbabwe	85	19.27S	29.49E
Gyalshing	Sikkim	25	27.18N	88.16E
Gyor	Hungary	80	47.41N	17.38E
H				
Haarlem	Netherlands	80	52.24N	4.40E
Haeju	N. Korea	71	38.12N	125.41E
Haflong	Assam	25	25.08N	93.03E
Haifa	Israel	74	32.49N	36.00E
Hailakandi	Assam	25	24.39N	92.35E
Hainan, I.	China	70	19.00N	110.0E
HAITI	West Indies	87	19.00N	72.00W
Hajipur	Bihar	24	25.41N	85.14E
Hakodate	Japan	71	41.46N	140.44E
Halifax	Nova Scotia, Canada	87	44.38N	63.35W
Halle	Germany	80	51.28N	11.58E
Halmahera, I.	Moluccas	72	1.00N	128.00E
Hamadan	Iran	74	34.49N	48.27E
Hamah	Syria	74	35.05N	36.40E
Hamamatsu	Japan	71	34.45N	137.45E
Hamburg	Germany	80	53.35N	10.00E
Hami	China	70	42.54N	93.28E
Hamilton Inlet	Labrador, Canada	86	54.00N	59.00W
Hamilton	Ontario, Canada	89	43.16N	79.48W
Hamirpur	Himachal Pradesh	22	31.38N	76.35E
Hamirpur	Uttar Pradesh	24	25.58N	80.12E
Hammerfest	Norway	77	70.40N	23.30E
Hampi (Vijaynagar)	Karnataka	28	15.20N	76.30E
Hanamkonda	Andhra Pradesh	27	18.03N	79.32E
Hangayn Nuruu, Mt	Mongolia	70	48.00N	99.00E
Hangzhou	China	70	30.16N	120.08E
Hangzhou Wan	China	70	30.30N	121.03E
Hanoi	Vietnam	67	21.02N	105.52E
Hanover	Germany	80	52.23N	9.00E
Hansi	Haryana	14	29.06N	76.00E
Hanumangarh	Rajasthan	23	29.35N	74.21E
Haora	W. Bengal	25	22.35N	88.23E
Harappa	Pakistan	14	30.35N	72.58E
Harare	Zimbabwe	83	17.50S	31.03E
Harbin	China	70	45.40N	126.37E
Harda	Madhya Pradesh	26	22.20N	77.06E
Hardoi	Uttar Pradesh	24	27.23N	80.10E
Haridwar	Uttarakhand	24	29.58N	78.13E
Harihar	Karnataka	20	14.31N	75.52E
Haripur	Pakistan	14	34.00N	72.58E
Harnahalli	Karnataka	21	13.15N	76.12E
Harnai	Pakistan	14	30.08N	68.00E
Harpanahalli	Karnataka	28	14.47N	75.58E
Harrisburg	Penn., USA	89	40.18N	76.52E
Harrogate	England	79	54.00N	1.30W
Harwich	England	79	51.56N	1.15E
Haryana, State	India	12	30.30N	74.60E
Hassan	Karnataka	28	13.01N	76.10E
Hassan Abdal	Pakistan	14	33.48N	72.45E
Hathras	Uttar Pradesh	24	27.36N	78.06E
Hauraki, Gulf	New Zealand	94	36.25S	175.05E
Havana	Cuba	87	23.08N	82.22W
Haveri	Karnataka	28	14.45N	75.26E
Hawai	Arunachal Pradesh	25	27.04N	93.22E
Hawaiian, Is	Pacific Ocean	97	20.00N	155.00W
Hawick	Scotland	79	55.27N	2.47W
Hawke, Bay	New Zealand	95	39.30S	176.30E
Hazaribag	Jharkhand	24	23.59N	85.25E
Hazro	Pakistan	14	33.55N	72.32E
Hearst	Canada	89	49.40N	83.40W

Names	Country/Region	P. No.	Lat.	Long.
Hebrides, Is	Scotland	79	57.40N	7.00W
Hefei	China	70	31.51N	117.19E
Hegang	China	70	47.13N	130.13E
Heibronn	Germany	80	19.08N	9.13E
Heidelberg	Germany	80	49.24N	8.42E
Helder	Netherlands	80	52.58N	4.45E
Helena	Montana, USA	89	46.35N	112.01W
Heligoland, I.	Germany	80	54.11N	7.55E
Helmand, R.	Afghanistan	75	32.00N	61.00E
Helsinki	Finland	77	60.09N	24.57E
Hengyang	China	70	26.52N	112.33E
Herat	Afghanistan	75	34.22N	62.08E
Herat	Pakistan	75	34.20N	62.12E
Hijaz	Saudi Arabia	74	25.00N	39.00E
Himachal Pradesh, State	N. India	13	32.29N	76.10E
Himalayan, Ra.	N. India	11	28.00N	88.00E
Himatnagar	Gujarat	23	23.42N	73.02E
Hindol	Odisha	17	20.36N	85.14E
Hindu Kush, Mts	Afghanistan	75	36.10N	71.30E
Hinganghat	Maharashtra	27	20.34N	78.53E
Hinggan Ling	China	70	47.00N	120.00E
Hingoli	Maharashtra	27	19.43N	77.11E
Hirakud Dam and Res.	Odisha	17	21.30N	84.00E
Hiriyur	Karnataka	20	13.57N	76.40E
Hiroshima	Japan	71	34.30N	132.30E
Hisar	Haryana	22	29.10N	75.46E
Hispaniola	West Indies	87	19.00N	72.00W
Ho Chi Minh City	Vietnam	72	10.49N	106.00E
Hobart	Tasmania	95	42.53S	147.00E
Hoggar Plateau	Sahara	82	23.30N	6.00E
Hokkaido, I.	Japan	71	43.00N	140.00E
Hole Narsipur	Karnataka	21	12.47N	76.17E
HOLI SEE	S. Europe	77	41.55N	12.27E
Holo, Is	Philippines	72	5.00N	121.30E
Holyhead	Wales	79	53.20N	4.42W
Homer	Alaska, USA	89	59.40N	151.35W
Homnabad	Karnataka	28	17.43N	77.12E
Homs	Syria	74	34.40N	36.45E
Honavar	Karnataka	21	14.17N	74.29E
HONDURAS	Central America	87	14.40N	86.30W
Hong Kong	China	70	22.12N	114.12E
Honiara	Solomon Is.	97	9.26S	159.57E
Honnali	Karnataka	28	14.15N	75.41W
Honolulu	Hawaiian Is.	97	22.00N	156.00E
Honshu, I.	Japan	71	37.00N	139.00E
Horn, C.	S. America	90	55.58S	67.16W
Hosapete	Karnataka	28	15.16N	76.26E
Hosdurga	Karnataka	28	13.48N	76.20E
Hoshangabad	Madhya Pradesh	26	22.46N	77.45E
Hoshiarpur	Punjab	22	31.32N	75.57E
Hosur	Tamil Nadu	28	12.44N	77.52E
Hotan	China	70	37.07N	80.02E
Houston	Texas, USA	89	29.49N	95.20W
Hovd (Jirgalanta)	Mongolia	70	48.00N	91.40E
Hovsgol Nuur	Mongolia	70	51.00N	100.30E
Hradec Kraiove	Czech Republic	80	50.13N	15.49E
Hrodna	Belarus	77	53.41N	23.49E
Hsenwi	Myanmar	73	23.18N	98.00E
Hsinchu	Taiwan	70	24.55N	121.00E
Hualien	Taiwan	70	24.00N	121.30E
Huambo (Nova Lisboa)	Angola	83	13.20S	15.30E
Huambo	Angola	83	12.44S	15.47E
Huancayo	Peru	93	12.05S	75.12W
Huang He	China	70	37.40N	118.40E
Huanuco	Peru	93	09.55S	76.15W
Huascaren, Mt	Peru	90	9.08S	77.63W
Hubballi	Karnataka	28	15.20N	75.12E
Hudson, Bay	Canada	86	60.00N	88.00W
Hudson, Str.	Canada	86	62.00N	70.00W
Hue	Vietnam	72	16.27N	107.33E
Hugli, R.	W. Bengal	18	22.00N	88.00E
Hull	England	79	53.45N	0.20E
Humaita	Brazil	93	07.30S	63.01W
Humber, R.	England	79	54.35N	0.00E
HUNGARY	S.E. Europe	77	47.00N	19.00E
Hunsur	Karanataka	21	12.18N	76.19E
Hurghada	Egypt	83	27.15N	33.50E
Huron, L.	Canada-USA	86	44.30N	82.00W
Hwange	Zimbabwe	85	18.22S	26.29E
Hyderabad	Andhra Pradesh	13	17.22N	78.28E
Hyderabad	Andhra Pradesh	27	17.20N	78.30E
Hyderabad	Pakistan	75	25.25N	68.38E
I				
Iasi	Romania	77	47.12N	27.35E
Ibadan	Nigeria	83	7.23N	3.56E
Ibotirama	Brazil	93	12.13S	43.12W
Ica	Peru	93	14.00S	75.48W
Icana	Brazil	93	00.21N	67.19W
ICELAND	N.W. Europe	77	65.00N	17.00W
Ichak	Jharkhand	17	24.05E	85.25E
Ichchapuram	Andhra Pradesh	27	19.07N	84.44E
Ifni	N.W. Africa	83	29.10N	10.20W
Igatpuri	Maharashtra	20	19.40N	73.35E
Iguape	Brazil	93	24.37S	47.30W
Iguatu	Brazil	93	6.22S	39.17W
Ihosy	Madagascar	85	22.23S	46.09E
Ilebo	Congo Dem. Rep.	83	5.00S	21.10E
Ilheus	Brazil	93	14.49S	39.02W
Imperatriz	Brazil	93	5.32S	47.28W
Imphal	Manipur	13	24.44N	93.58E
INDIA	South Asia	67	20.00N	78.00E
INDIAN OCEAN	World	101		

Names	Country/Region	P. No.	Lat.	Long.
Indianapolis	Indian, USA	89	39.45N	86.16W
INDONESIA	S.E. Asia	72	5.00S	115.00E
Indore	Madhya Pradesh	26	22.44N	75.50E
Indravati, R.	Chhattisgarh	17	19.03N	81.00E
Indus, R.	Jammu & Kashmir	22	33.30N	78.00E
Ingraj Bazar	W. Bengal	25	25.00N	88.11E
Inhambane	Mozambique	85	23.51S	35.29E
Innsbruck	Austria	80	47.16N	11.23E
Inuvik	Canada	87	68.25N	135.05W
Invercargill	New Zealand	95	46.30S	168.30E
Inverness	Scotland	79	57.30N	4.15W
Ionian, Is	Greece	76	38.00N	20.00E
Ipatinga	Brazil	93	19.32S	42.30W
Ipswich	England	79	52.06N	1.10E
Ipu	Brazil	93	4.32S	40.44W
Iquique	Chile	93	20.19S	70.05W
Iquitos	Peru	91	3.45S	73.10W
IRAN	S.W. Asia	67	33.00N	55.00E
IRAQ	S.W. Asia	67	32.00N	45.00E
IRELAND	W. Europe	77	53.00N	8.00W
Irkutsk	Russia	81	52.36N	104.10E
Irrawaddy, R.	Myanmar	73	20.40N	95.00E
Irtysh, R.	Russia	81	53.36N	75.30E
Isa Khel	Pakistan	14	32.41N	71.19E
Isfahan	Iran	74	32.37N	51.38E
Ishinomaki	Japan	71	38.32N	141.20E
Islamabad	Pakistan	67	33.44N	73.10E
Isle of Man	Irish Sea	79	54.05N	4.37W
ISRAEL	W. Asia	67	32.30N	35.30E
Issyk Kul	Kyrgystan	81	42.30N	77.00E
Istanbul (Constantinople)	Turkey	74	41.00N	29.00E
Itabaiana	Brazil	93	10.42S	37.37W
Itabuna	Brazil	93	14.28S	39.19W
Itaituba	Brazil	93	4.15S	55.56W
Itajai	Brazil	93	26.50S	48.39W
ITALY	S. Europe	77	42.00N	12.00E
Itanagar	Arunachal Pradesh	13	27.08N	93.40E
Itapipoca	Brazil	93	3.29S	39.35W
Itaqui	Brazil	93	29.10S	56.30W
Itarsi	Madhya Pradesh	26	22.30N	77.55E
Iturup, I.	Russia	81	45.00N	148.00E
Izmir (Smyma)	Turkey	74	38.24N	27.06E
J				
Jabalpur	Madhya Pradesh	26	23.10N	79.59E
Jaboatao	Brazil	93	8.05S	35.00W
Jackson	Mississipi, USA	89	32.17N	90.08W
Jacksonville	Florida, USA	89	30.21N	81.40W
Jacobabad	Pakistan	75	28.17N	68.29E
Jacobina	Brazil	93	11.13S	40.30W
Jaffna	Sri Lanka	69	9.45N	80.02E
Jagannathganj	Bangladesh	18	24.39N	89.50E
Jagatsinghapur	Odisha	26	20.13N	86.18E
Jagdalpur	Chhattisgarh	26	19.05N	82.04E
Jaggayyapeta	Andhra Pradesh	20	16.52N	80.09E
Jaghbub	Libya	83	29.55N	24.00E
Jagtiyal	Andhrya Pradesh	27	18.48N	79.09E
Jahanabad	Bihar	24	25.13N	85.05E
Jahazpur	Rajasthan	23	25.38N	75.19E
Jaintia Hills	Meghalaya	11	25.27N	92.12E
Jaipur	Rajasthan	12	26.55N	75.52E
Jakarta	Indonesia	72	6.12S	106.50E
Jalalabad	Afghanistan	75	34.24N	70.26E
Jalalpur Pirwala	Pakistan	14	29.30N	71.16E
Jalandhar	Punjab	22	31.18N	75.40E
Jalaun	Uttar Pradesh	17	26.08N	79.23E
Jalgaon	Maharashtra	27	21.05N	75.40E
Jalna	Maharashtra	27	19.51N	75.56E
Jalor	Rajasthan	23	25.22N	72.58E
Jalpaiguri	W. Bengal	25	26.32N	88. 46E
JAMAICA	West Indies	87	18.00N	77.00W
Jamalpur	Bihar	17	25.19N	86.32E
Jamalpur	Bangladesh	18	24.56N	90.00E
Jamkhandi	Karnataka	20	16.30N	75.20E
Jamkhed	Maharashtra	27	18.43N	75.24E
Jammalamadugu	Andhra Pradesh	20	14.51N	78.25E
Jammu	Jammu & Kashmir	22	32.43N	74.54E
Jammu & Kashmir, State	India	13	32.44N	74.54E
Jamnagar	Gujarat	23	22.27N	70.07E
Jampur	Pakistan	14	29.39N	70.38E
Jamshedpur	Jharkhand	24	22.50N	86.10E
Jamtara	Jharkhand	24	23.57N	86.36E
Jamui	Bihar	24	24.55N	86.13E
Jamuna, R.	Bangladesh	18	24.25N	89.50E
Janakpur	Chhattisgarh	17	23.43E	81.50E
Jandiala	Punjab	14	31.51N	75.37E
Jangipur	W. Bengal	18	24.28N	88.05E
Jani Khel	Pakistan	14	32.48N	70.27E
Janjgir	Chhattisgarh	26	22.02N	82.35E
Janjira	Maharashtra	20	18.18N	73.00E
JAPAN	E. Asia	67	40.00N	135.00E
Japvo, Mt	Nagaland	18	25.32N	94.10E
Jaru	Brazil	93	10.24S	62.45W
Jasdan	Gujarat	23	22.04N	71.01E
Jashpurnagar	Chhattisgarh	26	22.53N	84.12E
Jaso	Madhya Pradesh	17	24.30N	80.32E
Jath	Maharashtra	27	17.03N	75.15E
Jaunpur	Uttar Pradesh	24	25.46N	82.44E
Java, I.	Indonesia	72	7.30S	110.00E
Javadi Hills	Tamil Nadu	21	12.40N	78.40E
Jawalamukhi	Himachal Pradesh	14	31.53N	76.22E
Jawhar	Maharashtra	20	19.52N	73.21E
Jaynagar	Bihar	24	26.35N	86.09E
Jaypur	Odisha	26	18.52N	82.38E

ames	Country/Region	P. No.	Lat.	Long.
efferson City	Missouri, USA	89	38.35N	92.11W
equie	Brazil	93	13.52S	40.06W
ersey	Channel Is.	80	49.15N	2.00W
erusalem	Israel	67	31.46N	35.14E
essore	Bangladesh	18	23.10N	89.10E
habua	Madhya Pradesh	26	22.45N	74.38E
hajjar	Haryana	22	28.36N	76.39E
hal	Pakistan	14	28.18N	67.30E
halawar	Rajasthan	23	24.35N	76.11E
hang	Pakistan	14	31.16N	72.22E
hansi	Uttar Pradesh	24	25.27N	78.37E
haria	Jharkhand	24	23.50N	86.33E
harkhand, State	India	13	24.02N	86.00E
harsuguda	Odisha	26	21.54N	84.05E
hunjhunun	Rajasthan	23	28.05N	75.29E
iamusi	China	70	46.47N	130.15E
iddah	Saudi Arabia	74	21.32N	39.10E
igni	Uttar Pradesh	17	25.44N	79.25E
ihlava	Czech Republic	80	49.24N	15.35E
ilin	China	70	43.53N	126.33E
inan	China	70	36.38N	117.01E
ind	Haryana	22	29.19N	76.23E
inzhou	China	70	41.10N	121.02E
oao Pessoa	Brazil	93	7.06S	34.53W
obat	Madhya Pradesh	16	22.29N	74.37E
odhpur	Rajasthan	23	26.18N	73.04E
og Falls	Karnataka	20	14.18N	74.55E
ogindernagar	Himachal Pradesh	14	31.50N	76.45E
ohannesburg	South Africa	85	26.10S	28.02E
oinville	Brazil	93	26.20S	48.55W
olarpettai	Tamil Nadu	21	12.34N	78.37E
ORDAN	W. Asia	67	32.00N	35.00E
orhat	Assam	25	26.46N	94.16E
owai	Meghalaya	25	25.18N	92.09E
uan Fernandez, Is.	Chile	91	33.36S	78.55W
uazeiro do Norte	Brazil	93	7.10S	39.18W
uba	South Sudan	83	4.56N	32.20E
uiz de Fora	Brazil	93	21.47S	43.23W
uliaca	Peru	93	15.29S	70.09W
umla	Nepal	15	29.17N	82.13E
unagadh	Gujarat	23	21.31N	70.36E
unagarh	Odisha	26	19.52N	82.59E
undiai	Brazil	93	23.10S	46.54W
uneau	Alaska, USA	89	58.21N	134.20W
unnar	Maharashtra	20	19.12N	73.58E
K				
Kabul	Afghanistan	67	34.30N	69.18E
Kabul, R.	Afghanistan	75	34.32N	69.20E
Kabwe	Zambia	85	14.29S	28.25E
Kachchh, Gt. Rann of	Gujarat	19	24.00N	70.00E
Kachchh, Gulf of	Gujarat	19	22.35N	69.40E
Kachchh, Little Rann of	Gujarat	19	23.26N	71.20E
Kadiri	Andhra Pradesh	20	14.07N	78.14E
Kadoma	Zimbabwe	85	18.21S	29.55E
Kaduna	Nigeria	83	10.30N	7.28E
Kaesong	N. Korea	71	38.01N	126.46E
Kafue	Zambia	85	15.44S	28.10E
Kagoshima	Japan	71	31.36N	130.33E
Kailash, Ra.	Tibet, China	11	31.40N	81.19E
Kailashahar	Tripura	25	24.22N	92.06E
Kaimur Hills	India	11	24.35N	82.04E
Kaintira	Odisha	17	20.45N	84.37E
Kaithal	Haryana	22	29.48N	76.26E
Kajalgaon	Assam	25	26.31N	90.31E
Kakinada	Andhra Pradesh	27	16.57N	82.15E
Kalabagh	Pakistan	14	32.58N	71.36E
Kalaburgi	Karanataka	28	17.19N	76.54E
Kalahandi	Odisha	26	20.05N	83.12E
Kalahari Desert	S. Africa	82	23.00S	22.00E
Kalam	Pakistan	14	35.27N	72.30E
Kalemie	Congo Dem. Rep.	83	7.00S	29.12E
Kalgoorlie	W. Australia	95	30.50S	121.20E
Kalingapatnam	Andhra Pradesh	21	18.20N	84.10E
Kaliningrad	Russia	81	54.42N	20.30E
Kalol	Gujarat	23	23.15N	72.33E
Kalomo	Zambia	85	17.02S	26.29E
Kalpetta	Kerala	28	11.37N	76.04E
Kaluga	Russia	77	54.30N	36.16E
Kalutara	Sri Lanka	69	6.34N	79.54E
Kalyan	Maharashtra	27	19.14N	73.10E
Kalyani	Karnataka	20	17.53N	76.59E
Kamachatka, Pen.	Russia	81	57.00N	158.00E
Kamalia	Pakistan	14	30.44N	72.42E
Kamareddi	Andhra Pradesh	27	18.17N	78.22E
Kambham	Andhra Pradesh	27	15.34N	79.19E
Kamet, Mt	Uttarakhand	15	30.56N	79.36E
Kampala	Uganda	83	0.19N	32.35E
Kampli	Andhra Pradesh	20	15.25N	76.39E
Kamptee	Maharashtra	20	21.14N	79.15E
Kanazawa	Japan	71	36.30N	136.38E
Kancheepuram	Tamil Nadu	28	12.50N	79.45E
Kandahar	Afghanistan	75	31.37N	65.30E
Kandla	Gujarat	23	23.00N	70.10E
Kandukur	Andhra Pradesh	20	15.12N	79.57E
Kandy	Sri Lanka	21	7.18N	80.40E
Kangaroo, I.	S. Australia	94	35.50S	137.20E
Kangchenjunga	India	18	27.42N	88.11E
Kangra	Himachal Pradesh	22	32.05E	76.18E
Kanigiri	Andhra Pradesh	27	15.23N	79.32E
Kanker	Chhattisgarh	26	20.15N	81.32E
Kankesanturai	Sri Lanka	69	9.51N	80.05 E
Kannauj	Uttar Pradesh	24	27.03N	79.58 E

Names	Country/Region	P. No.	Lat.	Long.
Kanniyakumari	Tamil Nadu	28	8.06N	77.35E
Kannur	Kerala	28	11.52N	75.25E
Kano	Nigeria	83	12.00N	8.30E
Kanpur	Uttar Pradesh	24	26.28N	80.24E
Kansas City	Kansas USA	89	39.05N	94.35W
Kanye	Botswana	85	24.59S	25.10E
Kapurthala	Punjab	22	31.23N	75.25E
Kara Sea	Arctic Ocean	99	75.00N	70.00E
Karabala	Iraq	74	32.35N	44.07E
Karachi	Pakistan	75	24.51N	67.04E
Karad	Maharashtra	27	17.15N	74.12E
Karaganda	Kazakhstan	81	49.50N	73.00E
Karaikal	Puducherry	28	10.55N	79.52E
Karakoram, Ra.	India	10	36.10N	75.00E
Karanja	Maharashtra	20	20.29N	77.32E
Karanjia	Odisha	17	21.43N	87.07E
Karasburg	Namibia	85	28.00S	18.43E
Karativo, I.	Sri Lanka	21	8.21N	79.52E
Karauli	Rajasthan	23	26.30N	77.04E
Kargil	Jammu & Kashmir	22	34.30N	76.13E
Kariba Dam	Zambia/Zimbabwe	83	16.51S	28.50E
Karibib	Namibia	85	21.59S	15.51E
Karimganj	Assam	25	24.40N	92.30E
Karimnagar	Andhra Pradesh	27	18.28N	79.06E
Karkala	Karnataka	21	13.12N	75.00E
Karlsruhe	Germany	80	49.01N	8.23E
Karnal	Haryana	22	29.42N	77.02E
Karnataka, State	India	12	15.00N	75.00E
Karshi	Uzbekistan	74	38.48N	65.48E
Karur	Tamil Nadu	28	10.58N	78.07E
Karwar	Karnataka	28	14.48N	74.11E
Kasaragod	Kerala	28	12.30N	75.00E
Kasauli	Himachal Pradesh	14	30.53N	77.01E
Kasempa	Zambia	85	13.28S	25.48E
Kasganj	Uttar Pradesh	24	27.49N	78.39E
Kashi	China	70	39.20N	74.04E
Kassel	Germany	80	51.19N	9.28E
Kasur	Pakistan	14	31.07N	74.31E
Kataba	Zambia	85	16.02S	25.03E
Katangi	Madhya Pradesh	26	21.47N	79.51E
Kathiawar, Pen.	Gujarat	10	22.00N	71.00E
Kathiawar, Pen.	Gujarat	10	21.48N	70.45E
Kathiraveli	Sri Lanka	69	8.13N	81.23E
Kathua	Jammu & Kashmir	22	32.17N	75.36E
Katihar	Bihar	24	25.30N	87.40E
Katmandu	Nepal	67	27.42N	85.12E
Katni	Madhya Pradesh	26	23.50N	80.26E
Katowice	Poland	80	50.16N	19.03E
Katoya	W. Bengal	18	23.39N	88.11E
Kaushambi	Uttar Pradesh	24	25.33N	81.33E
Kavali	Andhra Pradesh	27	14.55N	80.03E
Kavaratti	Lakshadweep	12	10.33N	72.39E
Kaveri, R.	Tamil Nadu, etc.	21	11.20N	77.50E
Kawardha	Chhattisgarh	26	22.00N	81.17E
Kayalpatnam	Tamil Nadu	21	8.34N	78.10E
Kayseri	Turkey	74	38.42N	35.25E
KAZAKHSTAN	Asia	67	48.00N	70.00E
Kazan	Russia	81	55.48N	49.10E
Kecskemet	Hungary	80	46.55N	19.35E
Keetmanshoop	Namibia	85	26.36S	18.08E
Keewatin	N.W. Terr., Canada	87	63.00N	94.00E
Kekirawa	Sri Lanka	21	8.02N	80.36E
Kekri	Rajasthan	23	25.56N	75.20E
Kellam	Kerala	28	8.53N	76.36E
Kendal	England	79	54.20N	2.45W
Kendrapara	Odisha	26	20.30N	86.28E
Kendujhar	Odisha	26	21.38N	85.37E
KENYA	East Africa	83	1.00N	38.00E
Kenya, Mt	E. Africa	82	0.10S	37.18E
Kerala, State	S. India	12	10.00N	76.25E
Kerguelen, I.	Indian Ocean	98	48.30S	69.40E
Kerki	Turkmenistan	74	37.50N	65.12E
Kermadec, Is	S. Pacific Ocean	97	30.03S	178.40W
Kerman	Iran	74	30.20N	57.10E
Key West	Florida, USA	89	24.40N	81.48W
Khabarovsk	Russia	81	48.40N	135.05E
Khagaria	Bihar	24	25.29N	86.31E
Khairagarh	Chhattisgarh	17	21.26N	81.02E
Khairpur	Pakistan	14	27.28N	68.44E
Khalilabad	Uttar Pradesh	24	26.46N	83.06E
Khambhalia	Gujarat	23	22.12N	69.39E
Khambhat	Gujarat	23	22.19N	72.38E
Khambhat, Gulf of	Gujarat	19	21.00N	72.30E
Khammam	Andhra Pradesh	27	17.15N	80.11E
Khandpara	Odisha	17	20.16N	85.13E
Khandwa	Madhya Pradesh	26	21.50N	76.23E
Khaniadhana	Madhya Pradesh	16	25.01N	78.07E
Khanka, L.	Russia	81	45.00N	132.30E
Khanpur	Pakistan	14	28.30N	70.40E
Khapa	Maharashtra	20	21.25N	79.02E
Kharagpur	W. Bengal	25	22.30N	87.20E
Khargone	Madhya Pradesh	26	21.48N	75.41E
Kharkiv	Ukraine	77	48.58N	36.11E
Kharsawan	Jharkhand	17	22.48N	85.52E
Khartoum	Sudan	83	15.35N	32.35E
Khasi and Jaintia Hills	Meghalaya	18	25.30N	91.30E
Khasi Hills	Meghalaya	11	25.35N	91.38E
Khed	Maharashtra	20	18.51N	73.56E
Kheda	Gujarat	23	22.45N	72.45E
Khedbrahma	Gujarat	23	24.03N	73.04E
Kheri	Uttar Pradesh	24	27.54N	80.48E
Kherson	Ukraine	77	46.38N	32.36E
Khilok	Russia	81	51.30N	110.45E
Khiva	Uzbekistan	74	41.30N	60.18E

Names	Country/Region	P. No.	Lat.	Long.
Khonsa	Arunachal Pradesh	25	26.57N	95.33E
Khordha	Odisha	26	20.11N	85.40E
Khorramshahr	Iran	74	30.30N	48.30E
Khulna	Bangladesh	18	22.49N	89.37E
Khunti	Jharkhand	24	23.01N	85.16E
Khurai	Madhya Pradesh	16	24.03N	78.23E
Khurja	Uttar Pradesh	17	28.15N	77.50E
Khurrambad	Iran	74	33.30N	48.25E
Khushab	Pakistan	14	32.18N	72.24E
Khyber Pass	Pakistan	10	34.06N	71.05E
Kidare	Rep. of Ireland	79	53.09N	6.54W
Kiev	Ukraine	77	50.28N	30.11E
Kigali	Rwanda	83	1.59S	30.05E
Kigoma	Tanzania	83	4.52S	29.36S
Kilabira	Odisha	17	21.49N	84.15E
Kilakarai	Tamil Nadu	21	9.14N	78.50E
Kilchu	N. Korea	71	41.00N	129.20E
Kilimanjaro, Mt	E. Africa	82	3.40S	37.00E
Kilkenny	Rep. of Ireland	79	52.39N	7.15W
Kilmarnock	Scotland	79	55.36N	4.30W
Kimberley	South Africa	85	28.45S	24.46E
Kingston	Jamaica	87	17.59N	76.50W
Kingston	Ontario, Canada	89	44.16N	76.30W
Kingstown	St Vincent & Grenadines	87	13.10N	61.14W
Kinshasa	Congo Dem. Rep.	83	4.20S	15.18E
Kiphire	Nagaland	25	25.54N	94.47E
KIRIBATI	Pacific Ocean	97	5.00S	180.00E
Kirkcaldy	Scotland	79	56.05N	3.10W
Kirkcudbright	Scotland	79	54.51N	4.03W
Kirkuk	Iraq	74	35.30N	44.21E
Kirkwall	Scotland	79	59.09N	3.00W
Kirov	Russia	77	58.35N	49.40E
Kisangani	Congo Dem. Rep.	83	0.30N	25.10W
Kishanganj	Bihar	24	26.08N	98.57E
Kishangarh	Rajasthan	19	27.53N	70.37E
Kishorganj	Bangladesh	18	24.26N	90.49E
Kishtwar	Jammu & Kashmir	22	33.19N	75.48E
Kismayu	Somali Rep.	83	0.03S	49.30E
Kitakyushu	Japan	71	33.50N	130.50E
Kitwe	Zambia	85	0.08S	30.30E
Kizil Irmak	Turkey	74	41.20N	35.40E
Klagenfurt	Austria	80	46.38N	14.18E
Klondike Goldfields	Canada	89	64.00N	139.20W
Kobdo	Mongolia	70	48.02N	91.39E
Kobe	Japan	71	34.41N	135.12E
Koch Bihar	W. Bengal	25	26.20N	89.29E
Kochi	Kerala	28	9.55N	76.14E
Kochi	Japan	71	33.30N	133.35E
Kodaikkanal	Tamil Nadu	28	10.13N	77.32E
Kodarma	Jharkhand	24	24.27N	85.36E
Kodiak, I.	Alaska, USA	89	57.30N	153.00W
Kodikkarai	Tamil Nadu	28	10.18N	79.52E
Kohat	Pakistan	14	33.36N	71.29E
Kohima	Nagaland	13	25.40N	94.07E
Kohima	Negaland	25	25.40N	94.08E
Kokrajhar	Assam	25	26.24N	90.16E
Kolar	Karnataka	28	13.09N	78.11E
Kolasib	Mizoram	25	24.10N	92.42E
Kolhapur	Maharashtra	27	16.42N	74.14E
Kolkata	West Bengal	13	22.34N	88.24E
Kollam	Kerala	28	08.53N	76.36E
Kollegal	Karnataka	21	12.09N	77.09E
Kolleru, L.	Andhra Pradesh	20	16.40N	81.10E
Kollur	Karnataka	28	13.53N	74.53E
Koluapur	Maharashtra	27	16.42N	74.16E
Komsomolsk	Russia	81	50.30N	137.00E
Konarka	Odisha	26	19.53N	86.08E
Kondalwadi	Maharashtra	20	18.15N	77.43E
Kondapalli	Andhra Pradesh	20	16.38N	80.36E
Kongwa	Tanzania	83	6.20S	36.30E
Konosha	Russia	77	60.58N	40.08E
Konya	Turkey	74	37.52N	32.28E
Koppal	Karnataka	28	15.21N	76.09E
Koraput	Odisha	26	18.49N	82.48E
Koratla	Andhra Pradesh	20	18.43N	78.41E
Korba	Chhattisgarh	26	22.21N	82.42E
Korea	South Asia	71	36.00N	128.00E
Korea, Str.	Korea-Japan	71	34.00N	129.30E
Koror	Palau	67	07.21N	134.28E
Korsakov	Russia	81	46.30N	142.42E
Korwai	Madhya Pradesh	16	24.07N	78.05E
Kosi, R.	Bihar	17	26.00N	87.06E
KOSOVO	Europe	77	42.36N	20.51E
Kostroma	Russia	77	57.45N	40.58E
Kot Kapura	Punjab	14	30.34N	74.52E
Kota	Rajasthan	23	25.10N	75.52E
Kota Kinabulu	Sabah	72	5.55N	116.12E
Kotapad	Odisha	17	19.04N	82.24E
Kothi	Madhya Pradesh	17	24.45N	80.40E
Kottagudem	Andhra Pradesh	20	17.30N	80.40E
Kottayam	Kerala	28	9.36N	76.34E
Kottbus	Germany	80	51.46N	14.20E
Kotturu	Karnataka	20	14.49N	76.16E
Koyna, R.	Maharashtra	20	17.30N	73.45E
Kozhikode	Kerala	28	11.15N	75.49E
Kragujevac	Serbia	80	44.01N	20.56E
Krakow	Poland	77	50.50N	19.50E
Krasnodar	Russia	77	45.03N	38.53E
Krasnovodsk	Turkmenistan	81	40.01N	52.52E
Krasnoyarsk	Russia	81	56.08N	93.00E
Krishnagiri	Tamil Nadu	28	12.32N	78.16E
Krishnanagar	W. Bengal	25	23.24N	88.33E
Krishnarajasagara, Res.	Karnataka	21	12.20N	76.32E
Krisnha, R.	Andhra Pradesh	20	15.55N	81.10E

Names	Country/Region	P. No.	Lat.	Long.
Kristiansand	Norway	77	58.08N	7.59E
Krugersdorp	South Africa	85	26.06S	27.46E
Kuala Lumpur	Malaysia	67	3.11N	101.40E
Kuching	Sarawak	72	1.30N	110.20E
Kudremukh, Peak	Karnataka	21	13.10N	75.15E
Kuito	Angola	83	12.25S	16.56E
Kukawa	Nigeria	83	12.55N	13.30E
Kukshi	Madhya Pradesh	16	22.13N	74.48E
Kulachi	Pakistan	14	31.56N	70.30E
Kulgam	Jammu & Kashmir	22	33.39N	75.01E
Kullu	Himachal Pradesh	22	31.57N	77.06E
Kumamoto	Japan	71	32.50N	130.40E
Kumbakonam	Tamil Nadu	28	10.58N	79.25E
Kumta	Karnataka	28	14.26N	74.27E
Kunashir	Russia	81	44.00N	146.00E
Kundapura	Karnataka	28	13.50N	74.40E
Kunlun, Mts	China	11	36.00N	84.00E
Kunlun, Mts	China, etc.	70	36.00N	85.00E
Kunming	China	70	25.02N	102.42E
Kunsan	S. Korea	71	35.59N	126.45E
Kupwara	Jammu & Kashmir	22	34.31N	74.20E
Kuril, Is	Russia	81	46.0N	160.00E
Kurnool	Andhra Pradesh	27	15.50N	78.05E
Kursk	Russia	77	51.42N	36.11E
Kurukshetra	Haryana	22	29.57N	76.52E
Kurunegala	Sri Lanka	21	7.31N	80.22E
Kushiro	Japan	71	43.00N	144.30E
Kushka	Turkmenistan	81	35.12N	62.30E
Kushtia	Bangladesh	18	23.55N	89.10E
Kusma	Nepal	15	28.16N	83.40E
Kutaisi	Georgia	74	42.19N	42.40E
Kutru	Chhattisgarh	17	19.03N	80.53E
Kuvango	Angola	83	14.27S	16.20E
KUWAIT	Asia	67	28.59N	47.52E
Kuwait City	Kuwait	67	29.12N	47.59E
Kuybyshev, Res.	Rusia	77	55.00N	50.00E
Kwekwe	Zimbabwe	85	18.55S	29.49E
Kyakhta	Russia	81	50.04N	106.20E
Kyelang	Himachal Pradesh	22	32.33N	77.05E
Kyle of Lochalsh	Scotland	79	7.16N	5.43W
Kyoto	Japan	71	35.01N	135.34E
KYRGYZSTAN	Asia	67	42.00N	75.00E
Kyushu, I.	Japan	71	32.30N	131.00E
Kyzyl	Russia	81	51.50N	94.30E
Kyzyl-Orda	Kazakhstan	81	44.50N	65.33E
L				
La Coruna	Spain	77	43.21 N	8.24 W
La Guaira	Venezuela	91	10.35N	67.02E
La Paz / Sucre	Bolivia	91	16.31S	67.58W
La Plata	Argentina	90	34.53S	58.00W
La Rochelle	France	80	46.10N	1.09W
Laayoune	Western Sahara	83	27.09 N	13.12 W
Labrador, Coast of	Canada	86	54.00 N	64.00 W
Labrea	Brazil	93	7.20S	64.46W
Ladakh, Ra.	Jammu & Kashmir	11	32.00N	80.00E
Ladakh, Ra.	Jammu and Kashmir	11	34.00N	78.00E
Ladysmith	South Africa	85	28.34S	29.47E
Ladysmith	Canada	87	48.57N	123.50W
Laghman	Afghanistan	75	34.30N	70.00E
Lagoas	Nigeria	83	6.27N	3.28E
Lagos	Nigeria	83	6.25N	3.27E
Lahara	Odisha	17	21.26N	85.14E
Lahore	Pakistan	75	31.37N	74.26E
Lajes	Brazil	93	27.48S	50.20W
Lakhimpur	Uttar Pradesh	24	27.57N	80.49E
Lakhimpur	Assam	25	27.32N	94.01E
Lakhisarai	Bihar	24	25.09N	86.07E
Lakhnadon	Madhya Pradesh	26	22.36N	79.39E
Lakhpat	Gujarat	23	23.49N	68.48E
Lakki	Pakistan	14	32.37N	70.57E
Lakshadweep, Union Territory	India	12	10.00N	73.00E
Lala Musa	Pakistan	14	32.40N	74.01E
Lalbagh	W. Bengal	18	24.13N	88.19E
Lalitpur	Uttar Pradesh	24	24.22N	78.28E
Lalsot	Rajasthan	23	26.34N	76.23E
Lamphelpat	Manipur	25	24.49N	93.54E
Land's End	England	79	50.04N	5.45W
Landshut	Germany	80	48.27N	12.10E
Lansing	Michigan, USA	89	42.44N	84.33W
Lanzhou	China	70	36.02N	103.50E
LAOS	S.E. Asia	67	19.00N	104.00E
Lapland	N. Europe	76	67.00N	25.00E
Laptev Sea	Arctic Ocean	81	76.00N	125.00E
Lar	Iran	74	27.40N	54.15E
Laredo	Texas, USA	89	27.30N	99.30W
Larentian Uplands	Canada	86	50.00N	75.00W
Larissa	Greece	77	39.36N	22.25E
Larkana	Pakistan	75	27.33N	68.15E
Larne	N. Ireland	79	54.51N	5.49W
Lashkar	Madhya Pradesh	16	26.10N	78.10E
Latakia	Syria	74	35.30N	35.45E
Latehar	Jharkhand	24	23.46N	84.35E
Latur	Maharashtra	27	18.24N	76.36E
LATVIA	Europe	77	57.00N	24.00E
Launceston	Tasmania	95	41.25S	147.10E
Lausanne	Switzerland	80	46.31N	6.38E
Laval	France	80	48.04N	0.46W
Lawngtlai	Mizoram	25	22.31N	92.57E
Laying-Yangte	Arunachal Pradesh	25	27.54N	93.21E
Leadville	Colorado, USA	89	39.17N	106.23W
LEBANON	W. Asia	67	33.00N	35.00E
Leeds	England	79	53.48N	1.30W

Names	Country/Region	P. No.	Lat.	Long.
Lefkosia (Nicosia)	Cyprus	67	35.10N	33.22E
Leh (Ladakh)	Jammu & Kashmir	22	34.09N	77.36E
Leiah	Pakistan	14	30.58N	70.58E
Leicester	England	79	52.38N	1.05W
Leipzig	Germany	80	51.20N	12.23E
Leith	Scotland	79	55.58N	3.10W
Lemans	France	80	48.01N	0.12E
Lena, R.	Russia	81	70.00N	126.00E
Lerwick	Scotland	79	60.10N	1.00W
LESOTHO	S. Africa	83	30.00S	28.00E
Lethbridge	Canada	89	49.43N	112.50W
Levis	Canada	89	46.48N	71.09W
Lewis, I.	Scotland	79	58.10N	6.40W
Leyte, I.	Philippines	72	11.25N	124.36E
Lhasa	Tibet, China	67	29.40N	91.05E
Liaqatabad	Pakistan	14	32.17N	71.24E
LIBERIA	W. Africa	83	6.00N	9.00W
Libreville	Gabon	83	0.26N	9.25E
LIBYA	N. Africa	83	25.00N	15.00E
Libyan, Desert	N. Africa	82	25.00N	26.00E
Lichinga	Mozambique	85	13.19S	35.13E
LIECHTENSTIEN	Centrral Europe	77	47.10N	9.50E
Liege	Belgium	80	50.38N	6.34E
Ligurian, Sea	Italy	80	53.30N	9.00E
Lille	France	80	50.40N	3.00E
Lilongwe	Malawi	83	13.58S	33.49E
Lima	Peru	91	12.02S	77.02W
Limbdi	Gujarat	23	22.34N	71.53E
Limerick	Rep. of Ireland	79	52.40N	8.37W
Limoges	France	80	45.50N	1.16E
Limpopo, R.	S. Africa	82	23.20S	30.00E
Lincoln	England	79	53.12N	0.30W
Lincoln	USA	89	40.50N	96.42W
Lingsugur	Karnataka	28	16.07N	76.34E
Lini	China	70	35.02N	118.10E
Linsia	China	70	35.50N	103.00E
Linz	Austria	80	48.18N	14.18E
Lions, G. of	France	80	43.10N	4.00E
Lisbon	Portugal	77	38.44N	9.09W
LITHUANIA	Europe	77	54.40N	25.30E
Little Rock	Arkansas, USA	89	34.41N	92.15W
Liverpool	England	79	53.24N	2.58W
Livingstone	Zambia	83	17.55S	25.48E
Livingstone	USA	89	45.40N	110.33W
Livingstonia	Malawi	83	10.35S	34.05E
Lizard, Pt	England	79	49.56N	5.15W
Ljubljana	Solvenia	80	46.03N	14.31E
Llano Estacado	USA	89	34.00N	100.03W
Lleida	Spain	80	41.38N	0.38E
Lobatse	Botswana	85	25.11S	25.40E
Lobito	Angola	83	12.20S	13.34E
Lodoga, L.	Russia	77	60.00N	32.00E
Lodz	Poland	80	51.46N	19.26E
Lofoten, Is	Norway	76	68.00N	12.30E
Lohardaga	Jharkhand	24	23.26N	84.42E
Loharu	Haryana	14	28.16N	75.45E
Loire, R.	France	80	47.17N	2.10W
Loktak, L.	Manipur	18	24.30N	93.55E
Lombok, I.	Indonesia	72	8.30S	116.20E
Lome	Togo	83	6.09N	1.13E
Lonavala	Maharashtra	27	18.44N	73.28E
Londa	Karnataka	20	15.60N	74.50E
London	United Kingdom	77	51.30N	0.05W
London	Canada	89	42.58N	81.15W
London	Ontario, Canada	89	43.00N	91.15W
Londonderry	N. Ireland	79	55.00N	7.20W
Londrina	Brazil	93	23.18S	51.13W
Long Beach	California, USA	89	33.46N	118.12W
Long, I.	USA	89	40.45N	73.00W
Longleng	Nagaland	25	26.31N	94.56E
Loralai	Pakistan	14	30.24N	68.36E
Lord Howe, I.	Pacific Ocean	94	31.46S	159.08E
Lorient	France	80	47.45N	3.21W
Los Angeles	California, USA	89	34.03N	118.17W
Louis Trichardt	South Africa	85	23.01S	29.43E
Louisiade, Arch.	New Guinea	94	11.30S	152.00E
Louisville	Kentucky, USA	89	38.16N	85.47W
Luanda	Angola	83	8.50S	13.14E
Luang Prabang	Laos	72	19.55N	102.05E
Luanshya	Zambia	85	13.09S	28.24E
Lubango	Angola	85	14.55S	13.30E
Lubeck	Germany	80	53.50N	10.40E
Lublin	Poland	80	51.15N	22.34E
Lubumbashi	Congo Dem. Rep.	83	11.40S	27.28E
Lucerne	Switzerland	80	47.03N	8.18E
Lucknow	Uttar Pradesh	13	26.55N	80.59E
Lucusse	Angola	85	12.33S	20.51E
Luderitz	Namibia	85	26.38S	15.10E
Luderitz .	S.W. Africa	83	27.00S	16.00E
Ludhiana	Punjab	22	30.55N	75.54E
Luena	Angola	85	11.47S	19.52E
Lulea	Sweden	77	65.35N	22.10E
Lunavada	Gujarat	23	23.08N	73.37E
Lunavada	Gujarat	23	23.08N	73.37E
Lundy, I.	England	79	51.12N	4.40W
Luneburg	Germany	80	53.16N	10.26E
Lunglei	Mizoram	25	22.56N	92.49E
Luni, R.	Rajasthan	19	26.01N	73.02E
Lusaka	Zambia	83	18.26S	28.20E
Luton	England	79	51.53N	0.25W
LUXEMBOURG	W. Europe	77	49.38N	6.10E
Luziania	Brazil	93	16.16S	47.57W
Luzon, I.	Philippines	72	16.00N	121.00E
Lviv	Ukraine	80	49.50N	24.00E

Names	Country/Region	P. No.	Lat.	Long.
Lyme, Bay	England	79	50.43N	2.56W
Lyons	France	77	45.25N	4.50E
M				
Ma'an	Jordan	74	30.11N	35.43E
Mabalane	Mozambique	85	23.51S	32.38E
Macapa	Brazil	93	0.04N	51.04W
Macau	China	70	22.15N	113.33E
MACEDONIA	S. Europe	77	42.00N	21.32E
Maceio	Brazil	93	1.32S	27.16E
Macgillicuddy's Reeks	Rep. of Ireland	79	52.10N	9.45W
Machilipatnam	Andhra Pradesh	27	16.09N	81.12E
Macias Nguema	W. Africa	83	3.30N	8.40E
Mackenzie, R.	Canada	86	67. 26N	131.00W
Macon	France	80	46.18N	4.50E
Macon	Georgia, USA	89	32.50N	83.37W
MADAGASCAR	Indian Ocean	83	20.00S	46.00E
Madakasira	Andhra Pradesh	20	13.57N	77.19E
Madaripur	Bangladesh	18	23.14N	90.15E
Madeira, Is	Atlantic Ocean	98	32.50N	17.00W
Madeira, R.	S. America	90	5.30S	61.20W
Madhepura	Bihar	24	25.57N	86.51E
Madhubani	Bihar	24	26.21N	86.07E
Madhupur	Jharkhand	24	24.18N	86.37E
Madhya Pradesh, State	India	26	23.30N	80.00E
Madicine Hat	Canada	87	50.00N	110.45W
Madikeri	Karnataka	28	12.26N	75.47E
Madison	Wisconsin, USA	89	43.05N	89.25W
Madre, Sierra	Mexico	86	25.00N	105.00W
Madrid	Spain	77	40.24N	3.42W
Madurai	Tamil Nadu	28	9.58N	78.10E
Madurantakam	Tamil Nadu	21	12.30N	79.56E
Magdeburg	Germany	80	53.08N	11.38E
Magellan	Strait of Chile	91	52.30S	69.00W
Magnitogorsk	Russia	81	53.30N	59.00E
Mahabaleshwar	Maharashtra	27	17.58N	73.43E
Mahabubnagar	Andhra Pradesh	27	16.42N	77.58E
Mahadeo Hills	Madhya Pradesh	11	22.24 N	78.00E
Mahajanga	Madagascar	85	15.40S	46.20E
Mahanadi, R.	Odisha	17	20.19N	86.45E
Maharajganj	Uttar Pradesh	24	27.11N	83.37E
Maharashtra, State	India	27	20.00N	76.00E
Mahasamund	Chhattisgarh	26	21.11N	82.10E
Mahe	Puducherry	28	11.41N	75.30E
Mahendragarh	Chhattisgarh	17	23.21N	82.21E
Mahesana	Gujarat	23	23.42N	72.37E
Maheshwar	Madhya Pradesh	26	22.11N	75.37E
Mahi, R.	Gujarat	23	22.20N	73.05E
Mahoba	Uttar Pradesh	24	25.17N	79.54E
Mahrajganj	Uttar Pradesh	24	27.08N	83.34E
Mahuva	Gujarat	23	21.10N	71.45E
Maihar	Madhya Pradesh	17	24.16N	80.49E
Maijdi	Bangladesh	18	22.48N	91.09E
Maikala, Ra.	Central India	11	22.30N	81.30E
Maimana	Afghanistan	75	35.55N	64.48E
Mainpuri	Uttar Pradesh	24	27.14N	79.03E
Majitha	Punjab	14	31.46N	75.01E
Majorca (Mallorca)	Balearic Is	76	39.30N	3.00E
Makasar (Makassar)	Celebes	72	5.05 S	119.30E
Makhach-Kala	Russia	81	42.52N	47.50E
Malabo	Equatorial Guinea	83	3.45N	8.48E
Malacca and Strait	Malaysia	72	2.10N	102.14E
Malaga	Spain	77	36.43N	4.25W
Malappuram	Kerala	28	11.03N	76.03E
Malatya	Turkey	74	38.20N	38.20E
MALAWI	East Africa	83	13.00S	34.00E
Malawi L.	East Africa	82	12.00 S	34.30E
MALAYSIA	S. E. Asia	67	5.00N	105.00E
Maldah	West Bengal	18	25.03N	88.09E
MALDIVES	Indian Ocean	67	5.30N	73.00E
MALDOVA	Europe	77	47.00N	28.55E
Male	Maldives	67	4.00N	73.28E
Malegaon	Maharashtra	20	20.30N	74.40E
Malema	Mozambique	85	14.57S	37.25E
Maler Kotla	Punjab	14	30.31N	75.59E
MALI	W. Africa	83	15.00N	5.00W
Malkangiri	Odisha	26	18.22N	81.56E
Malkapur	Maharashtra	20	20.53N	76.17E
Malmesbury	South Africa	85	33.28S	18.43E
Malmo	Sweden	77	55.40N	13.00E
MALTA	Mediterranean	77	36.00N	14.30E
Malvan	Maharashtra	27	16.03N	73.30E
Malwa Plateau	Madhya Pradesh	10	24.00N	76.00E
Mamallapuram	Tamil Nadu	28	12.37N	80.14E
Mamit	Mizoram	25	23.52N	92.32E
Manama	Bahrain	67	26.12N	50.35E
Manaus	Brazil	93	3.10 S	60.00W
Manchester	England	79	53.28N	2.12W
Manchouli	China	70	49.46N	117.24E
Mandalay	Myanmar	73	21.59N	96.08E
Mandav Hills	Gujarat	10	22.20N	75.25E
Mandi	Himachal Pradesh	22	31.39N	76.58E
Mandla	Madhya Pradesh	26	22.35N	80.23E
Mandsaur	Madhya Pradesh	26	24.03N	75.10E
Mandvi	Gujarat	23	22.51N	68.32E
Mandya	Karnataka	28	12.33N	76.53E
Mangalagiri	Andhra Pradesh	20	16.26N	80.36E
Mangaldai	Assam	25	26.27N	92.05E
Mangalore	Karnataka	28	12.52N	74.53E
Mangan	Sikkim	25	27.30N	88.32E
Mangaon	Maharashtra	20	18.15N	73.20E

Names	Country/Region	P. No.	Lat.	Long.
Mangyai	China	70	38.06N	91.37E
Manica	Mozambique	85	18.56S	32.52E
Manila	Philippines	72	14.30N	121.30E
Manipur, State	India	13	24.44N	93.58W
Manisa	Turkey	74	38.38N	27.30E
Manitoba, Prov.	Canada	87	52.00N	97.00W
Mankheri	Jharkhand	17	23.40N	84.33E
Manmad	Maharashtra	20	20.15N	74.29E
Mannar	Sri Lanka	69	8.59N	79.55E
Mannar, Gulf of.	India-Sri Lanka	11	8.50N	79.50E
Mannargudi	Tamil Nadu	21	10.40N	79.29E
Mansa	Punjab	22	29.58N	75.24E
Mansa	Zambia	85	11.10S	28.52E
Mansar	Maharashtra	20	21.24N	79.19E
Manugua	Nicaragua	91	12.10N	86.51W
Manvi	Karnataka	20	15.57N	76.58E
Manwat	Maharashtra	20	19.18N	76.30E
Manzai	Pakistan	14	32.12N	70.15E
Maputo	Mozambique	85	25.58S	32.35E
Mar Del Plata	Argentina	91	37.59 S	57.30W
Maraba	Brazil	93	5.23S	49.10W
Maracaibo	Venezuela	91	10.37N	71.41W
Mardan	Pakistan	75	34.10N	72.03E
Margao	Goa	27	15.15N	73.59E
Mariental	Namibia	85	24.36S	17.59E
Maringa	Brazil	93	23.26S	52.02W
Markham, Mt	Antarctica	99	83.00S	164.00E
Marmara, Sea of	Turkey	74	40.40N	27.35E
Marmugao	Goa	27	15.25N	73.43E
Marrakech	Morocco	83	31.38N	7.59W
Marseilles	France	77	43.20N	3.30E
MARSHALL IS.	Pacific Ocean	97	13.00N	170.00E
Martaban	Myanmar	73	16.30N	97.40E
Martaban, Gulf of	Myanmar	73	16.00N	97.00E
Martigny	Switzerland	80	46.07N	7.05E
Martinique	West Indies	87	14.40N	61.00W
Mary	Turkmenistan	81	37.32N	61.58E
Maryborough	Queensland, Aust.	95	25.35 S	152.43E
Maseru	Lesotho	85	29.30S	27.29E
Mashhad	Iran	74	36.16N	59.36E
Massawa	Ethiopia	83	15.36N	39.28E
Mastuj	Pakistan	14	36.16N	72.36E
Masvingo	Zimbabwe	85	20.50S	30.50E
Matadi	Congo Dem, Rep.	83	5.42 S	13.31E
Matale	Sri Lanka	69	7.28N	80.37E
Matanzas	Cuba	87	23.01N	81.39W
Matara	Sri Lanka	69	5.57N	80.33E
Matheran	Maharashtra	27	18.59N	73.18E
Mathura	Uttar Pradesh	24	27.28N	77.41E
Mato Grosso	Brazil	93	15.00S	60.00W
Mattancheri	Kerala	21	9.57N	76.17E
Mau	Madhya Pradesh	17	22.15N	80.13E
Mauganj	Madhya Pradesh	17	24.40N	81.56E
Maunath Bhanjan	Uttar Pradesh	24	25.57N	83.36E
MAURITANIA	West Africa	83	19.00N	13.00W
MAURITIUS	indian Ocean/Africa	83	20.00S	57.00E
Mawlaik	Myanmar	73	23.36N	94.26E
Mayiladutural	Tamil Nadu	21	11.06N	79.42E
Mayo	Canada	89	63.38N	135.57W
Mayotte	Indian Ocean	83	12.50S	45.10E
Mazabuka	Zambia	85	15.50S	27.47E
Mazalgaon	Maharashtra	20	19.08N	76.13E
Mazar-i-sharif	Afghanistan	75	36.45N	67.09E
Mazatlan	Mexico	87	23.15N	106.30W
Mbabane	Swaziland	85	26.20S	31.08E
Mecca	Saudi Arabia	74	21.25N	39.54E
Medak	Andhra Pradesh	27	18.01N	78.15E
Medan	Sumatra	72	3.40N	78.38E
Medellin	Colombia	91	6.15N	75.45W
Medina	Saudi Arabia	74	24.33N	39.53E
Medinipur	W. Bengal	25	22.25N	87.21E
Mediterranean Sea	S. Europe, etc.	80	37.00N	15.00E
Meerut	Uttar Pradesh	24	29.01N	77.45E
Meghalaya, State	India	13	25.30N	91.00E
Meherpur	Bangladesh	18	23.47N	88.40E
Mekong, R.	S.E. Asia	72	15.00N	106.00E
Melbourne	Victoria Australia	95	37.50 S	144.59E
Melilla	North Africa	83	35.21N	2.57W
Melo	Ururuay	91	32.22S	54.10W
Melville, I.	Canada	86	75.30N	113.00W
Memphis	Tennessee USA	89	35.08N	90.01W
Mendocino, C.	USA	89	40.26N	124.23W
Mendoza	Argentina	91	32.50 S	68.52W
Menongue	Angola	85	14.36S	17.48E
Mentawei, Is.	Sumatra	72	2.00 S	99.00E
Mergui, Arch.	Myanmar	11	12.32N	98.07E
Merida	Mexico	89	20.54N	89.40W
Merida	Venezuela	91	8.20N	71.08W
Merta	Rajasthan	23	26.39N	74.06E
Merthyr Tydfil	Wales	79	51.46N	3.20W
Messanjore	Jharkhand	17	24.05N	87.21E
Messina	Italy	77	38.13N	15.13E
Messina	South Africa	85	22.23S	30.00E
Mettupalaiyam	Tamil Nadu	22	11.18N	76.59E
Mettur Dam	Tamil Nadu	21	11.52N	77.50E
Metz	France	80	49.05N	6.12E
MEXICO	N. America	87	19.26N	99.01W
Mexico City	Mexico	87	19.26N	99.08W
Mexico, Gulf of	Mexico	86	26.00N	92.00W
Miami	Florida USA	89	25.46N	80.12W
Miani	Pakistan	14	32.32N	73.08E
Mianwali	Pakistan	75	32.35N	71.33E
Michigan, L.	USA	86	44.00N	87.00W

Names	Country/Region	P. No.	Lat.	Long.
MICRONESIA, FED. STATES OF	Oceania	95	6.55N	158.11E
Middelburg	South Africa	85	31.28S	25.01E
Middlesbrough	England	79	54.30N	1.15W
Mikir Hills	Assam	11	26.10N	93.30E
Milan	Italy	80	45.27N	9.10E
Milwaukee	Wisconsin, USA	89	43.09N	87.55W
Mindanao, I.	Philippines	72	8.00N	125.00E
Mindoro, I.	Philippines	72	13.00N	121.00E
Mingin	Myanmar	73	22.51N	94.34E
Minicoy, I.	India	12	8.10N	73.00E
Minneapolis	Minnesota, USA	89	44.59N	93.17W
Minorca	Balearic Is	76	40.00N	4.00E
Minsk	Belarus	77	53.55N	27.35E
Minyuwa	Myanmar	73	22.00N	94.06E
Miraj	Maharashtra	27	16.49N	74.43E
Miram Shah	Pakistan	14	33.00N	70.04E
Mirpur	Jammu & Kashmir	22	33.12N	73.51E
Mirzapur	Uttar Pradesh	24	25.10N	82.37E
Mishmi Hills	Arunachal Pradesh	11	28.22N	95.48E
Mississippi, R.	USA	89	34.00N	91.00W
Missouri, R.	USA	89	48.00N	107.00W
Mitchell, Mt	USA	89	35.44N	82.15W
Mito	Japan	71	36.20N	140.30E
Miyako	Japan	71	39.40N	141.75E
Miyazaki	Japan	71	32.00N	131.30E
Mizoram, State	India	13	23.30N	92.52E
Mobile	Alabama, USA	89	30.41N	88.03W
Mocambique	Mozambique	85	15.03S	40.45E
Mocuba	Mozambique	85	16.52S	36.57E
Modasa	Gujarat	23	23.28N	73.18E
Modena	Italy	80	44.38N	10.55E
Moga	Punjab	22	30.49N	75.14E
Mogadishu	Somali Rep.	83	2.05N	45.25E
Mohali	Punjab	14	30.78N	76.69E
Mokameh	Bihar	24	25.24N	85.55E
Mokokchung	Nagaland	25	26.18N	94.30E
Mokpo	S. Korea	71	35.50N	126.30E
Moldova	Europe	76	47.40N	28.00E
Molepolole	Botswana	85	24.25S	25.30E
Mollendo	Peru	93	17.00S	72.00W
Moluccas, Is.	Indonesia	72	2.00S	128.00E
Mombasa	Kenya	83	4.00S	39.40E
Mominabad	Maharashtra	20	18.44N	76.23E
Mon	Nagaland	25	26.40N	95.01E
MONACO	Europe	77	43.43N	07.25E
Monaco	Riviera, France	80	43.44N	7.24E
Monaco	Monaco, Europe	81	43.43N	7.25E
Monaragala	Sri Lanka	69	6.52N	81.22E
MONGOLIA	Asia	67	46.00N	105.00E
Mongu	Zambia	85	15.13S	23.09E
Monrovia	Liberia	83	6.18N	10.45W
Mons	Belgium	80	50.27N	3.57E
Mont Blanc	France	80	45.49N	6.52E
Montauban	France	80	44.02N	1.22E
MONTENEGRO	Europe	77	43.01N	19.05E
Montepelier	Vermont, USA	89	44.16N	72.35W
Monteral	Canada	87	45.31N	73.34W
Montero	Bolivia	91	17.20S	63.15W
Monterrey	Mexico	89	25.42N	100.14W
Montes Claros	Brazil	93	16.45S	43.52W
Montevideo	Uruguay	91	34.55S	56.11W
Montgomery	Alabama, USA	89	32.21N	85.20W
Montpellier	France	80	43.36N	3.53E
Montreal	Scotland	79	56.44N	2.28W
Montserrat	West Indies	87	16.40N	62.10W
Moradabad	Uttar Pradesh	24	28.51N	78.49E
Morar	Madhya Pradesh	16	26.13N	78.14E
Moratuwa	Sri Lanka	69	6.53N	79.56E
Moray Firth	Scotland	79	57.45N	3.45W
Morbi	Gujarat	23	22.49N	70.54E
Morbi	Gujarat	23	22.49N	70.50E
Morea	Greece	76	37.20N	22.00E
Morecambe, Bay	England	79	54.00N	3.00W
Morena	Madhya Pradesh	26	26.23N	78.04E
Morigaon	Assam	25	26.14N	92.23E
Morioka	Japan	71	39.45N	141.08E
MOROCCO	N.W. Africa	83	32.00N	5.00W
Morondava	Madagascar	85	20.19S	44.17E
Moroni	Comoros Is.	83	11.39S	43.14E
Moscow	Russian Federation	77	55.45N	37.37E
Mossamedes	Angola	83	15.07S	12.15E
Mossel Bay	South Africa	83	34.11S	22.09E
Mostar	Bosnia-Herzegovina	80	43.02N	17.49E
Mosul	Iraq	74	36.20N	43.05E
Motihari	Bihar	24	26.37N	84.57E
Moulmein	Myanmar	73	16.30N	97.38E
Mourne Mts	N. Ireland	79	54.10N	6.05W
MOZAMBIQUE	S. E. Africa	83	15.02 S	40.48E
Mozambique Channel	S. E. Africa	83	15.00 S	42.00E
Mucia	Spain	77	37.59N	1.07W
Muddedihal	Karnataka	20	16.20N	76.10E
Mudhol	Andhra Pradesh	20	19.00N	77.52E
Mudhol	Karnataka	28	16.20N	75.20E
Mufulira	Zambia	85	12.30S	28.12E
Mugal Sarai	Uttar Pradesh	17	25.17N	83.11E
Muhammadgarh	Madhya Pradesh	16	23.39N	78.13E
Mukher	Maharashtra	20	18.42N	77.24E
Muktinath	Nepal	15	28.54N	83.49E
Muktsar	Punjab	22	30.30N	74.43E
Mul	Maharashtra	20	20.04N	79.43E
Mulbagal	Karnataka	21	13.11N	78.14E
Mulhouse	France	80	47.45N	7.20E

Names	Country/Region	P. No.	Lat.	Long.
Mull, I.	Scotland	79	56.20N	6.00W
Mullaittivu	Sri Lanka	69	9.16N	80.48E
Mulshi, L.	Maharashtra	20	18.50N	73.50E
Multan	Pakistan	75	30.12N	71.28E
Mumbai	Maharashtra	27	18.55N	72.54E
Mundra	Gujarat	23	22.49N	69.52E
Munger	Bihar	24	25.23N	86.30E
Munich	Germany	77	48.08N	11.35E
Murmansk	Russia	77	68.50N	33.10E
Muroran	Japan	71	42.25N	141.00E
Murray, R.	Australia	94	35.25 S	139.30E
Murree	Pakistan	14	33.55N	73.27E
Murrumbidgee, R.	Australia	94	35.35 S	149.07E
Murshidabad	W. Bengal	25	24.11N	88.19E
Murud	Maharashtra	27	18.18N	72.59E
Murwara	Madhya Pradesh	26	23.51N	80.02E
Murzug	Libya	83	25.52N	14.10E
Musa Khel Bazar	Pakistan	14	30.53N	69.54E
Muscat	Oman	67	23.37N	58.36E
Muscogee	USA	89	35.50N	95.25W
Mushalpur	Assam	25	26.40N	91.22E
Mussoorie	Uttarakhand	24	30.27N	78.06E
Mutarara	Mozambique	85	17.30S	32.40E
Mutare	Zimbabwe	85	18.58S	32.40E
Muzaffarabad	Jammu & Kashmir	22	34.24N	73.22E
Muzaffargarh	Pakistan	14	30.05N	71.14E
Muzaffarnagar	Uttar Pradesh	24	29.28N	77.44E
Muzaffarpur	Bihar	24	26.07N	85.27E
Mwanza	Tanzania	83	2.35S	32.56E
MYANMAR	S. Asia	67	20.20N	96.00E
Myitkyina	Myanmar	73	25.24N	97.26E
Myittha, R.	Myanmar	73	23.12N	94.18E
Mymensingh	Bangladesh	18	24.45N	90.27E
Mysore	Karnataka	28	12.18N	76.42E
Mzuzu	Malawi	85	11.31S	34.00E

N

Names	Country/Region	P. No.	Lat.	Long.
N. Ireland	UK, British Isles	79	53.00N	2.00W
N'Djamena	Chad	83	12.10N	14.59E
Nabarangapur	Odisha	26	19.17N	82.37E
Nabha	Punjab	14	30.25N	76.09E
Nacala	Mozambique	85	14.34S	40.40E
Nachana	Rajasthan	19	27.29N	71.45E
Nadiad	Gujarat	23	22.41N	72.55E
Naga Hills	India-Myanmar	11	26.00N	95.00E
Naga Hills	Nagaland	18	26.00N	94.20E
Nagaland, State	India	13	26.00N	94.20E
Nagaon	Assam	25	26.21N	92.45E
Nagappattinam	Tamil Nadu	28	10.46N	79.51E
Nagar Karnul	Andhra Pradesh	20	16.30N	78.19E
Nagarcoil	Tamil Nadu	28	8.10N	77.26E
Nagarjunasagar Dam	Andhra Pradesh	20	16.50N	79.20E
Nagasaki	Japan	71	32.47N	129.52E
Nagaur	Rajasthan	23	27.11N	73.40E
Nagercoil	Tamil Nadu	28	8.11N	77.29E
Nagina	Uttar Pradesh	24	29.27N	78.29E
Nagod (Unchahra)	Madhya Pradesh	17	24.33N	80.37E
Nagoya	Japan	71	35.07N	136.56E
Nagpur	Maharashtra	27	21.09N	79.09E
Nagrota	Himachal Pradesh	14	32.07N	76.23E
Nahan	Himachal Pradesh	22	30.33N	77.17E
Naini Tal	Uttarakhand	24	29.23N	79.30E
Nairn	Scotland	79	57.36N	3.53W
Nairobi	Kenya	83	1.18S	36.52E
Najin	N. Korea	71	42.12N	130.15E
Nalbari	Assam	25	26.25N	91.29E
Naldrug	Maharashtra	20	17.49N	76.20E
Nalgonda	Andhra Pradesh	27	17.03N	79.02E
Nallamalai, Ra.	Andhra Pradesh	20	15.00N	78.38E
Namakkal	Tamil Nadu	28	11.13N	78.13E
Namchi	Sikkim	25	27.07N	88.23E
Namib Desert	S. W. Africa	82	22.30W	15.00E
Namibe	Angola	85	15.10S	12.09E
NAMIBIA	S. W. Africa	83	23.00S	15.00E
Nampula	Mozambique	85	15.09S	39.14E
Namur	Belgium	80	50.28N	4.53E
Nanchang	China	70	28.34N	115.48E
Nancy	France	80	48.40N	6.15E
Nanda Devi, Mt	Uttarakhand	24	30.23N	80.01E
Nanded	Maharashtra	27	19.09N	77.27E
Nandigama	Andhra Pradesh	20	16.46N	80.20E
Nandikotkur	Andhra Pradesh	20	15.52N	78.18E
Nandod	Gujarat	19	21.54N	73.34E
Nandurbar	Maharashtra	27	21.23N	74.19E
Nandyal	Andhra Pradesh	27	15.29N	78.32E
Nanga Parbat, Mt	Jammu & Kashmir	14	35.14N	74.35E
Nanguneri	Tamil Nadu	21	8.29N	77.44E
Nanjangud	Karnataka	28	12.07N	76.44E
Nanjing	China	70	32.04N	118.50E
Nanning	China	70	22.49N	108.24E
Nantes	France	80	47.13N	1.32W
Naoshera	Jammu & Kashmir	14	33.13N	74.17E
Napier	New Zealand	95	39.29S	176.55E
Naples	Italy	77	40.51N	14.26E
Naraina	Rajasthan	19	26.50N	74.11E
Narasapur	Andhra Pradesh	20	16.26N	81.45E
Narasaraopet	Andhra Pradesh	20	16.14N	80.06E
Narayanganj	Bangladesh	18	23.37N	90.32E
Narayanpet	Andhra Pradesh	20	16.46N	77.27E
Narayanpur	Chhattisgarh	26	19.43N	81.14E
Narbonne	France	80	43.11N	3.01E
Narmada, R.	India	16	21.48N	74.00E
Narnaul	Haryana	22	28.02N	76.14E
Narsinghgarh	Madhya Pradesh	26	23.44N	77.08E
Narsinghpur	Odisha	17	20.28N	85.07E
Narsinghpur	Madhya Pradesh	26	22.56N	79.12E
Narsipatnam	Andhra Pradesh	20	17.40N	82.39E
Narvik	Norway	77	68.25N	17.30E
Nashik	Maharashtra	27	20.02N	73.50E
Nashville	Tennessee, USA	89	36.11N	86.50W
Nasirabad	Pakistan	14	28.24N	68.28E
Nasirabad	Rajasthan	19	26.18N	74.46E
Nassau	Bahamas	87	25.04N	77.20W
Nasser, L.	Egypt	82	23.00N	32.30E
Natal	S. Africa	83	29.00 S	30.30E
Natuna, Is.	Indonesia	72	4.00N	108.00E
Naugarh	Uttar Pradesh	24	27.18N	83.06E
NAURU	Pacific Ocean	97	1.00S	166.00E
Navadwip	W. Bengal	18	23.24N	88.23E
Navsari	Gujarat	23	21.07N	73.40E
Nawabganj	Uttar Pradesh	17	26.56N	82.12E
Nawabshah	Pakistan	75	26.08N	68.28E
Nawada	Bihar	24	24.53N	85.35E
Nawanshahr	Punjab	22	31.06N	76.09E
Nayagarh	Odisha	26	20.08N	85.08E
Naypyidaw	Myanmar	67	19.45N	96.06E
Nazca	Peru	93	14.53S	74.54W
Nazwa	Oman	74	22.56N	57.31E
Ndola	Zambia	85	13.00S	28.39E
Neagh, L.	N. Ireland	79	54.36N	6.25W
Neemuch	Madhya Pradesh	26	24.26N	74.57E
Negombo	Sri Lanka	21	7.12N	79.50E
Negro, R.	S. America	90	40.00S	64.00W
Negros, I.	Philippines	72	10.00N	122.55E
Neijiang	China	70	29.35N	105.10E
Nejd	Saudi Arabia	74	25.40N	47.00E
Nellore	Andhra Pradesh	27	14.27N	80.02E
Nelma	Russia	81	47.30N	139.00E
Nelson	Canada	89	49.29N	117.20W
Nelson	New Zealand	95	41.15S	173.20E
Nelson, R.	Canada	86	55.20N	96.52W
Nemawar	Madhya Pradesh	16	22.30N	77.00E
Nemuro	Japan	71	43.20N	145.35E
NEPAL	Asia	67	28.00N	85.00E
Nepalganj	Nepal	15	27.59N	81.40E
NETHERLANDS	W. Europe	77	53.00N	5.00E
Netrakona	Bangladesh	18	24.53N	90.47E
Nevada	Sierra, USA	86	40.00N	120.00W
Nevers	France	80	47.00N	3.09E
New Brunswick	Canada	87	46.50N	66.30W
New Caledonia I.	Pacific Ocean	94	21.30S	166.00E
New Delhi	India	13	28.37N	77.12E
New Guinea	Pacific Ocean	97	5.00S	142.00E
New Haven	Connecticut, USA	89	41.20N	72.54W
New Orleans	Louisiana, USA	89	30.00N	90.00W
New Plymouth	New Zealand	95	39.05S	174.05E
New Port News	USA	89	37.02N	76.54W
New Siberian Is.	Russia	81	74.20N	148.00E
New South Wales, State	Australia	95	32.00 S	146.00E
New Tehri	Uttarakhand	24	30.23N	78.29E
New Westminster	Canada	89	49.13N	122.52W
New York	USA	89	40.43N	74.01W
NEW ZEALAND	Oceania	95	40.00S	175.00E
Newcastle	England	79	54.58N	1.35W
Newcastle	N. S. Wales, Aust.	95	33.00S	151.40E
Newfoundland	Canada	87	49.00N	57.00W
Newhaven	England	79	50.36N	0.05E
Neyveli	Tamil Nadu	28	11.31N	79.29E
Nguru	Nigeria	83	12.30N	10.00E
Nha-Trang	Vietnam	72	12.16N	109.10E
Niagara Falls	Canada-USA	86	43.07N	79.02W
Niamey	Niger	83	13.27N	2.06E
Nias, I.	Sumatra	72	1.00N	97.30E
NICARAGUA	Central America	87	12.00N	86.00W
Nicaragua, L.	Central America	86	12.00N	85.30W
Nice	France	80	43.41N	7.18E
Nicosia	Cyprus	67	35.10N	33.22E
NIGER	West Africa	83	18.00N	10.00E
Niger, R.	West Africa	82	15.00N	2.03E
NIGERIA	W. Africa	83	10.00N	8.00E
Nighasan	Uttar Pradesh	17	28.14N	80.55E
Nijgata	Japan	71	37.58N	139.04E
Nikolayevsk	Russia	81	53.18N	140.44E
Nilagiri	Odisha	17	21.27N	86.49E
Nile, R.	N. E. Africa	82	28.00N	32.00E
Nilgiri Hills	South India	11	11.28N	76.47E
Nimas	France	80	43.50N	4.22E
Nimbahera	Rajasthan	23	24.37N	74.45E
Ningbo	China	70	29.50N	121.30E
Nipigon, L.	Ontario, Canada	89	49.50N	88.30W
Nirmal	Andhra Pradesh	27	19.06N	78.25E
Niteroi	Brazil	93	22.54S	43.06W
Nizamabad	Andhra Pradesh	27	18.40N	78.10E
Nizampatnam	Andhra Pradesh	20	15.54N	80.43E
Nizhniy Novgorod	Russia	81	56.15N	43.38E
Nohar	Rajasthan	19	29.11N	74.49E
Noida	Uttar Pradesh	24	28.33N	77.37E
Nome	Alaska, USA	89	64.45N	165.25W
Nongpoh	Meghalaya	25	25.53N	91.55E
Nongstoin	Meghalaya	25	25.28N	91.17E
Norfolk	Virginia, USA	89	36.51N	76.18W
Norfolk, I.	Pacific Ocean	94	29.00S	170.00E
Norrkoping	Sweden	77	58.35N	16.15E
North America, Continent	**World**	**100**		
North Channel	Scotland-Ireland	79	55.10N	6.00W
NORTH KOREA	North Asia	67	40.00N	126.00E
North Lakhimpur	Assam	25	27.10N	94.07E
North Sea	N. W. Europe	76	55.00N	2.30E
North, C.	Norway	76	71.12N	25.45E
Northampton	England	79	52.41N	0.55W
Northern Ireland	Great Britain	79	55.00N	7.00W
Northern Marianas	Pacific Ocean	97	17.00N	145.00E
Northern Territory	Australia	95	15.00N	135.00E
Northwest Territories	Canada	87	65.00N	100.00W
NORWAY	N. W. Europe	77	62.00N	10.00E
Norwich	England	79	52.40N	1.15E
Nottingham	England	79	59.57N	1.10E
Nouakchott	Mauritania	83	18.06N	15.58W
Nova Scotia	Canada	87	45.00N	64.00W
Novaya Zemlya	Russia	81	73.00N	55.00E
Novi Sad	Serbia	80	45.16N	19.50E
Novosibirsk	Russia	81	55.20N	83.42E
Nowshera	Pakistan	14	34.00N	72.00E
Nuapara	Odisha	26	20.46N	82.35E
Nubian Desert	Sudan	82	21.00N	34.00E
Nuh	Haryana	22	28.07N	77.01E
Nuku'alofa	Tonga	97	21.80S	175.12W
Nukus	Uzbekistan	74	42.30N	59.40E
Numberg (Nuremberg)	Germany	80	49.27N	11.05E
Nuuk	Greenland	87	64.10N	51.44W
Nuwara Eliya	Sri Lanka	21	6.59N	80.47E
Nyaingentanglha, Ra.	China	70	30.30N	95.00E

O

Names	Country/Region	P. No.	Lat.	Long.
Oakland	California, USA	89	37.40N	122.19W
Oaxaca	Mexico	89	17.02N	96.40W
Ob, R.	Russia	81	68.00N	74.00E
Oban	Scotland	79	56.26N	5.28W
Obbia .	Somali Rep.	83	5.20N	48.30E
Obluch'ye	Russia	81	49.10N	130.50E
Oceania, Continent	**World**	**101**		
Odessa	Ukraine	77	46.27N	30.48E
Odisha, State	India	13	21.10N	85.00E
Offenbach	Germany	80	50.06N	8.45E
Oghi	Pakistan	14	34.32N	73.02E
Ohio, R.	USA	86	37.20N	88.00W
Okara	Pakistan	14	30.50N	73.30E
Okhotsk	Russia	81	59.30N	143.20E
Okhotsk, Sea of	Russia	81	55.00N	145.00E
Okinawa	Japan	71	26.40N	128.00E
Oklahoma City	Oklahoma, USA	89	35.29N	97.31W
Oldenburg	Germany	80	53.09N	8.13E
Olinda	Brazil	93	8.00S	34.51E
Olympia	Washington, USA	89	47.00N	122.58W
Omagh	N. Ireland	79	54.36N	7.19W
Omaha	Nebraska, USA	89	41.16N	95.58E
OMAN	Asia	67	23.00N	58.00E
Oman, Gulf of	Iran/Arabia	74	23.30N	57.00E
Omdurman	Sudan	83	15.36N	32.47E
Omsk	Russia	81	55.00N	73.38E
Onega, L.	Russia	81	61.30N	35.00E
Ongole	Andhra Pradesh	27	15.30N	80.06E
Ontario, L.	Canada-USA	89	43.40N	78.00W
Oppeln (Opole)	Poland	80	50.41N	17.55E
Orai	Uttar Pradesh	24	25.59N	79.30E
Oran	Algeria	83	35.45N	0.39W
Orange, R.	S. Africa	82	29.40S	16.22E
Oras	Maharashtra	27	16.04N	73.31E
Orchha	Madhya Pradesh	16	25.21N	78.38E
Orel	Russia	77	52.56N	36.05E
Orenburg	Russia	81	54.46N	55.07E
Orhon Gol	Mongolia	70	49.30N	106.00E
Orinoco, R.	Venezuela	90	6.00N	67.30W
Orizaba	Mexico	89	18.49N	97.04W
Orkney, Is.	Scotland	79	59.00N	3.00W
Orleans	France	80	47.54N	1.54E
Orsk	Russia	81	51.15N	58.34E
Osaka	Japan	71	34.39N	135.27E
Osend	Belgium	80	51.13N	2.57E
Oslo	Norway	77	59.54N	10.45E
Osmanabad	Maharashtra	27	18.09N	76.05E
Osnabruck	Germany	80	52.17N	8.03E
Ottawa	Canada	89	45.27N	75.42W
Ouagodougou	Burkina Faso	83	12.25N	1.30W
Oudtshoorn	South Africa	85	33.35S	22.12E
Oulu	Finland	77	65.03N	25.35E
Ouse, R.	England	79	52.40N	0.21E
Oxford	England	79	51.46N	1.15W

P

Names	Country/Region	P. No.	Lat.	Long.
Pabna	Bangladesh	18	24.01N	89.18E
Pachmarhi	Madhya Pradesh	26	22.30N	78.22E
Pachora	Maharashtra	27	20.38N	75.29E
Pacific Ocean	**World**	**100**		
Padang	Sumatra	72	0.55S	100.20E
Padmanabhapuram	Tamil Nadu	21	9.06N	76.50E
Padra	Gujarat	19	22.15N	73.07E
Padrauna	Uttar Pradesh	24	26.52N	84.01E
Padua (Padova)	Italy	80	45.23N	11.54E
Paharpur	Pakistan	14	32.07N	71.02E
Painavu	Kerala	28	9.46N	77.01E
Paisley	Scotland	79	55.51N	4.24W
Paithan	Maharashtra	27	19.29N	75.26E
Pakala	Andhra Pradesh	21	13.30N	79.00E
Pakaur	Jharkhand	24	24.38N	87.54E
PAKISTAN	S. Asia	67	30.00N	70.00E
Pakpattan	Pakistan	14	30.21N	73.26E
Pakur	Jharkhand	24	24.38N	87.51E
Palakkad	Kerala	28	10.46N	76.42E
Palakollu	Andhra Pradesh	20	16.31N	81.46E
Palamu	Jharkhand	24	23.52N	84.17E
Palani	Tamil Nadu	28	10.27N	77.33E
Palanpur	Gujarat	23	24.12N	72.28E
PALAU	Asia	67	07.21N	119.00E
Palawan, I.	Philippiness	72	10.00N	134.28E
Palayankottai	Tamil Nadu	28	8.43N	77.46E
Palembang	Sumatra	72	3.00S	104.39E
Palermo	Italy	77	38.07N	13.23E
Palestine	Asia	67	32.30N	35.30E
Pali	Rajasthan	23	25.46N	73.25E
Palikir	Micronesia, Fed. States of	97	06.55N	158.11E
Palitana	Gujarat	23	21.31N	71.53E
Palk, Str.	India-Sri Lanka	11	10.00N	80.00E
Palkonda	Andhra Pradesh	20	18.36N	83.48E
Palkonda, Ra.	Andhra Pradesh	20	13.50N	79.20E
Palkot	Jharkhand	17	22.52N	84.41E
Palladam	Tamil Nadu	21	10.59N	77.20E
Palmyras, Pt	Odisha	17	20.45N	87.02E
Palni Hills	Tamil Nadu	21	10.20N	77.10E
Palwal	Haryana	22		
Pamirs	Tajikistan	81	38.00N	73.00E
Pampas	S. America	90	30.00S	60.00W
Pamplona	Spain	80	42.50N	1.38W
Panaji	Goa	12	15.30N	73.55E
PANAMA	Central America	87	9.00N	79.35W
Panama City	Panama	87	8.59N	79.31W
Panay, I.	Philippines	72	11.10N	122.30E
Panchkula	Haryana	22	30.42N	76.53E
Pandaria	Chhattisgarh	17	22.15N	81.27E
Pandharpur	Maharashtra	27	17.41N	75.23E
Panikoili	Odisha	26	20.48N	86.24E
Panipat	Haryana	22	29.23N	77.10E
Panna	Madhya Pradesh	26	24.44N	80.14E
Panruti	Tamil Nadu	21	11.47N	79.35E
Papeete	Fr. Polynesia	97	17.32S	149.34W
PAPUA NEW GUINEA	Oceania	95	8.00S	145.00E
Parachinar	Pakistan	14	33.55N	70.00E
Paradwip	Odisha	26	20.30N	86.55E
PARAGUAY	South America	91	25.16S	57.40W
Paraguay and R.	South America	91	23.00S	58.00W
Paralakhemundi	Odisha	26	18.47N	84.08E
Paramakkudi	Tamil Nadu	21	9.31N	78.39E
Paramaribo	Suriname	91	5.42N	55.11W
Parana, R.	S. America	90	30.00S	60.00W
Parangipettai	Tamil Nadu	21	11.30N	79.48E
Parasnath, Mt	Bihar	17	24.00N	86.11E
Parbhani	Maharashtra	27	19.08N	76.50E
Parenda	Maharashtra	20	18.16N	75.30E
Paricatuba	Brazil	93	18.00S	49.00W
Paris	France	77	48.50N	2.20E
Parlakot	Chhattisgarh	17	19.45N	80.48E
Parli	Maharashtra	20	18.53N	76.36E
Parma	Italy	80	44.48N	10.21E
Parnaiba	Brazil	93	2.58S	41.46W
Paro	Bhutan	18	27.24N	89.14E
Paron	Madhya Pradesh	16	24.57N	76.50E
Partabgarh	Rajasthan	23	24.02N	74.40E
Partabpur	Chhattisgarh	17	19.59N	80.50E
Parvatipuram	Andhra Pradesh	20	18.47N	83.28E
Pashat	Afghanistan	75	34.42N	71.05E
Pasighat	Arunachal Pradesh	25	28.00N	95.22E
Pasrur	Pakistan	14	32.16N	74.43E
Passau	Germany	80	48.34N	13.27E
Passo Fundo	Brazil	93	28.16S	52.20W
Patagonia	Argentina	90	43.00S	70.00W
Patan	Nepal	15	27.38N	85.13E
Patan	Rajasthan	19	27.49N	76.01E
Patan	Gujarat	23	23.52N	72.10E
Patancheru	Andhra Pradesh	20	17.36N	78.20E
Pataudi	Haryana	16	28.18N	76.48E
Pathanamthitta	Kerala	28	9.18N	76.51E
Pathankot	Punjab	22	32.17N	75.42E
Pathari	Madhya Pradesh	16	23.56N	78.15E
Pathri	Maharashtra	20	19.20N	76.30E
Patiala	Punjab	22	30.20N	76.25E
Patkai Bum	N. E. India	11	27.00N	95.30E
Patna	Bihar	13	25.37N	85.13E
Patos	Brazil	93	6.55S	37.15W
Patrai	Greece	77	38.14N	21.48E
Pattikonda	Andhra Pradesh	20	15.24N	77.04E
Pattukkottai	Tamil Nadu	28	10.26N	79.22E
Patuakhali	Bangladesh	18	22.20N	90.22W
Pau	France	80	43.18N	0.22W
Pauni	Maharashtra	20	20.48N	79.40E
Pauri	Uttarakhand	24	30.10N	78.48E
Paysandu	Uruguay	91	32.19S	58.08W
Peace , R.	Canada	86	56.15N	117.18W
Peak, The	England	79	53.24N	1.50W
Pecs	Hungary	80	46.04N	18.13E
Peddapuram	Andhra Pradesh	20	17.05N	82.11E
Pegu	Myanmar	73	17.20N	96.29E
Pegu Yoma, Ra.	Myanmar	73	20.00N	96.00E
Pehowa	Haryana	14	29.57N	76.37E
Peipus, L.	Estonia-Russia	76	58.30N	27.30E
Pembroke	Wales	79	51.40N	4.55W
Penganga, R.	Maharashtra	20	20.00N	77.00E
Pennine Chain	England	79	54.00N	2.00W
Pensacola	Florida, USA	89	30.30N	87.10W

Names	Country/Region	P. No.	Lat.	Long.
Penukonda	Andhra Pradesh	27	14.05N	77.38W
Penza	Russia	77	53.10N	45.00E
Penzance	England	79	50.06N	5.35W
Peoria	USA	89	40.40N	89.40W
Perambalur	Tamil Nadu	28	11.14N	78.56E
Peren	Nagaland	25	25.31N	93.44E
Perigueux	France	80	45.11N	0.43E
Perim, I.	Red Sea	66	12.38N	43.25E
Periyakulam	Tamil Nadu	21	10.07N	77.35E
Periyar, R.	Kerala	21	10.00N	76.52E
Perm (Molotov)	Russia	81	58.00N	56.15E
Persian Gulf	Arabia, etc	74	27.00N	51.00E
Perth	Scotland	79	56.25N	3.28W
Perth	W. Australia	95	32.00S	115.50E
PERU	South America	91	10.00S	75.00W
Perugia	Italy	80	43.07N	12.23E
Peshawar	Pakistan	75	34.02N	71.37E
Petauke	Zambia	85	14.15S	31.20E
Peterhead	Scotland	79	57.31N	1.47W
Petlad	Gujarat	19	22.29N	72.50E
Petropavlovsk-Kamchatskiy	Russia	81	53.16N	159.00E
Petrozavodsk	Russia	77	61.41N	34.20E
Phalodi	Rajasthan	23	27.09N	72.24E
Phaltan	Maharashtra	20	18.00N	74.29E
Phek	Negaland	25	25.41N	94.32E
Philadelphia	Penn., USA	89	39.57N	75.10W
PHILIPINES	Pacific Ocean	67	14.00N	123.00E
Phnom-Penh	Cambodia	72	11.35N	104.56E
Phoenix	USA	89	33.25N	112.10W
Phulabani	Odisha	26	20.29N	84.20E
Phulera	Rajasthan	23	26.52N	75.16E
Phulijhar	Chhattisgarh	17	21.14N	82.54E
Phulpur	Uttar Pradesh	17	25.32N	82.07E
Picos	Brazil	93	7.05S	41.24W
Pidurutalagala	Sri Lanka	69	7.00N	80.46E
Pietermaritzburg	S. Africa	83	29.36S	30.23E
Pietersburg	South Africa	85	23.54S	29.23E
Pilar	Paraguay	93	26.51S	58.20W
Pilibhit	Uttar Pradesh	24	28.38N	79.51E
Pimenta Bueno	Brazil	93	11.40S	61.14W
Pinang, I.	Malaysia	72	5.25N	100.14E
Pind-Dadan-Khav	Pakistan	14	32.55N	73.47E
Pirpanjal	Jammu and Kashmir	10	33.54N	74.30E
Pisa	Italy	80	43.44N	10.26E
Pisco	Peru	93	13.36S	76.12W
Pitcairn, Is.	Pacific Ocean	97	25.05S	130.05W
Pithapuram	Andhra Pradesh	20	17.07N	82.19E
Pithoragarh	Uttarakhand	24	29.36N	80.18E
Pitihra	Madhya Pradesh	17	23.04N	79.20E
Pittsburgh	Penn., USA	89	40.26N	79.57W
Plata, Rio de la	S. America	90	35.00S	57.00W
Platte, R.	USA	89	41.00N	100.00W
Pleven	Bulgaria	80	43.26N	24.37E
Plodiv (Philippopolis)	Bulgaria	80	42.08N	24.44E
Plymouth	England	79	50.22N	4.07W
Plzon	Czech Republic	80	49.45N	13.23E
Po, R.	Italy	76	45.00N	12.00E
Pobedino	Russia	81	49.51N	142.49E
Podgorica	Montenegro	77	42.27N	19.17E
Podili	Andhra Pradesh	20	15.36N	79.39E
Pointe Noire	Congo Rep.	83	4.38S	11.50E
Poitiers	France	80	46.35N	0.20E
Pokaran	Rajasthan	23	26.55N	71.58E
Pokhara	Nepal	15	28.17N	83.56E
POLAND	Central Europe	77	52.00N	20.00E
Pollachi	Tamil Nadu	28	10.39N	77.03E
Polur	Tamil Nadu	21	12.31N	79.10E
Ponnani	Kerala	28	10.47N	75.58E
Ponneri	Tamil Nadu	21	13.20N	80.15E
Poonch	Jammu & Kashmir	22	33.46N	74.06E
Popocategeti, Mt	Mexico	86	19.00N	98.30W
Porahat	Jharkhand	17	22.36N	85.28E
Porbandar	Gujarat	23	21.37N	69.49E
Porompat	Manipur	25	24.48N	93.57E
Poronaysk	Russia	81	49.20N	143.00E
Port Blair	Andaman & Nicobar Is	13	11.41N	92.43E
Port Elizabeth	South Africa	83	35.58S	25.37E
Port Elizabeth	South Africa	85	33.58S	25.36E
Port Jackson	N.S.W., Australia	95	33.50S	151.15E
Port Louis	Mauritius	83	20.10S	57.31E
Port Moresby	Papua New Guinea	95	9.28S	147.13E
Port Nolloth	South Africa	85	29.16S	16.52E
Port of Spain	Trinidad & Tobago	91	10.40N	61.31W
Port Okha	Gujarat	23	22.15 N	69.10E
Port Philip	Victoria, Australia	95	38.30S	144.40E
Port Radium	Canada	87	66.40N	118.00W
Port Said	Egypt	83	31.15N	32.18E
Port Sudan	Sudan	83	19.38N	37.08E
Port Swettenham	Malaysia	72	3.02N	101.24E
Port Villa	Vanuatu	95	17.45S	168.18E
Port-au-Prince	Haiti	87	18.40N	72.20W
Portland	Maine, USA	89	43.40N	70.15W
Portland	Oregon, USA	89	45.30N	122.40W
Portland Bill	England	79	50.31N	2.27W
Porto (Oporto)	Portugal	77	41.08 N	8.37W
Porto Alegre	Brazil	93	30.01S	51.11W
Porto Alegre	Brazil	93	30.03S	51.10W
Porto Grande	Brazil	93	0.43N	51.23W
Porto Novo	Benin	83	6.23 N	2.42E
Porto Velho	Brazil	93	8.45S	63.54W
Porto-Novo	Benin	87	6.30N	02.36E
Portree	Scotland	79	57.24N	6.11W

Names	Country/Region	P. No.	Lat.	Long.
Portrush	N. Ireland	79	55.13N	6.40W
Portsmouth	England	79	50.47N	1.05W
PORTUGAL	W. Europe	77	40.00N	13.00W
Potosi	Bolivia	91	19.38S	65.48W
Potsdam	Germany	80	52.24N	13.04E
Poznan	Poland	80	52.25N	16.50E
Prague	Czech Republic	80	50.05N	14.25E
Praia	Cape Verde Is	83	14.55N	23.31W
Pratapgarh	Uttar Pradesh	24	25.34S	81.59E
Pratapgarh	Rajasthan	23	24.03N	74.78E
Prenees, Mts	France-Spain	80	43.00N	1.00E
Presidente Prudente	Brazil	93	22.09S	51.24W
Preston	England	79	53.46N	2.40W
Pretoria	South Africa	83	25.45S	28.12E
Prezemysi	Poland	80	49.47N	22.45E
Prieska	South Africa	85	29.41S	22.44E
Prince Charles, Mts	Antarctica	99	72.00S	67.00E
Prince of Wales, C.	Alaska, USA	89	65.35N	168.00W
Pristina	Kosovo	77	42.40N	21.10E
Proddatur	Andhra Pradesh	20	14.45N	78.35E
Propria	Brazil	93	10.15S	36.51W
Providence	Rhode I., USA	89	41.50N	71.27W
Pucallpa	Peru	93	8.25S	74.30W
Pucara	Bolivia	91	15.03S	70.25W
Puducherry, Union Territory	South India	13	11.56N	79.53E
Pudukkottai	Tamil Nadu	28	10.23N	78.52E
Puebla	Mexico	89	19.02N	98.10W
Pueblo	Colorado, USA	89	38.20N	104.00W
Puerto Maldonado	Peru	93	12.37S	69.11W
Puerto Montt	Chile	91	41.30S	73.30W
Puerto Rico	West Indies	87	18.15N	66.20W
Pugal	Rajasthan	23	28.31N	72.51E
Pulacayo	Bolivia	91	20.25S	66.41W
Pulicat, L.	Tamil Nadu	21	13.25N	80.21E
Pulivendla	Andhra Pradesh	20	14.26N	78.16E
Pulwama	Jammu & Kashmir	22	33.51N	74.56E
Punch	Jammu & Kashmir	22	33.46N	74.09E
Pune	Maharashtra	27	18.31N	73.55E
Punganuru	Andhra Pradesh	17	13.25N	78.37E
Punjab, State	India	12	30.40N	75.50E
Puno	Peru	93	15.53S	70.03W
Puri	Odisha	26	19.48N	85.52E
Purnia	Bihar	24	25.49N	87.31E
Puruliya	W. Bengal	25	23.20N	86.25E
Puttalum	Sri Lanka	17	8.02N	79.50E
Puttaparthi	Andhra Pradesh	27	14.12N	77.45E
Puttur	Karnataka	28	12.45N	75.10E
Pyay	Myanmar	73	18.47N	95.20E
Pyinmana	Myanmar	73	19.44N	96.12E
Pyongyang	North Korea	71	39.00N	125.30E
Q				
QATAR	Asia	67	25.30N	51.10E
Qingdao	China	70	36.05N	120.24E
Qiqihar	China	70	47.13N	123.58E
Quaidabad	Pakistan	14	32.19N	71.59E
Quebec, and Prov.	Canada	87	46.48N	71.15W
Queen Charlotte, Is.	Canada	86	53.00N	132.00W
Queen Elizabeth, Is.	Canada	86	80.00N	90.00W
Queensland, State	Australia	95	26.00S	147.00E
Quelimane	Mozambique	85	17.53S	36.51E
Quetta	Pakistan	75	30.12N	67.00E
Quillacollo	Bolivia	91	17.26S	66.16W
Quillagua	Chile	93	21.40S	69.30W
Quito	Ecuador	91	0.10S	78.35W
R				
Rabat	Morocco	83	34.02N	6.50W
Rabigh	Saudi Arabia	74	22.50N	39.05E
Radhanpur	Gujarat	23	23.50N	71.38E
Rae Bareli	Uttar Pradesh	24	26.14N	81.16E
Rahuri	Maharashtra	20	19.23N	74.42E
Raichur	Karnataka	28	16.12N	77.21E
Raiganj	West Bengal	25	25.37N	88.12E
Raigarh	Chhattisgarh	26	21.54N	83.26E
Rainier, Mt	USA	89	46.50N	121.50W
Raipur	Bangladesh	18	23.00N	90.50E
Raipur	Chhattisgarh	26	21.15N	81.41E
Raisen	Madhya Pradesh	26	23.15N	77.50E
Raj Nandgaon	Chhattisgarh	26	21.05N	81.05E
Rajahmundry	Andhra Pradesh	27	17.00N	81.48E
Rajapalaiyam	Tamil Nadu	21	9.27N	77.36E
Rajapur	Maharashtra	20	16.39N	73.33E
Rajasmand	Rajasthan	23	25.03N	73.59E
Rajasthan, State	India	12	27.00N	74.00E
Rajgarh	Rajasthan	19	28.39N	75.26E
Rajgarh	Madhya Pradesh	26	24.00N	76.47E
Rajim	Chhattisgarh	26	20.59N	81.55E
Rajkot	Gujarat	23	22.18N	70.56E
Rajmahal	Jharkhand	24	25.03N	87.53E
Rajmahal Hills	Jharkhand	11	25.00N	87.00E
Rajnandgaon	Chhattisgarh	26	21.06N	81.02E
Rajouri	Jammu & Kashmir	22	33.24N	74.20E
Rajpipla	Gujarat	23	21.55N	73.26E
Rajsamand	Rajasthan	23	25.04N	73.53E
Rajshahi	Bangladesh	18	24.22N	88.39E
Rajur	Maharashtra	20	20.08N	78.50E
Rajura	Maharashtra	20	19.45N	79.26E
Raleigh	N. Carolina, USA	89	35.47N	78.39E
Ramagiri-Udayagiri	Odisha	17	19.04N	83.55E
Ramanagaram	Karnataka	28	12.54N	77.12E

Names	Country/Region	P. No.	Lat.	Long.
Ramanathapuram	Tamil Nadu	28	9.22N	78.52E
Ramban	Jammu & Kashmir	22	33.15N	75.15E
Ramdurg	Karnataka	20	15.58N	75.22E
Rameshwaram	Tamil Nadu	28	9.17N	79.22E
Ramgarh	Rajasthan	19	28.10N	75.00E
Ramgarh	Jharkhand	24	23.38N	85.34E
Ramkola	Chhattisgarh	17	23.40N	83.08E
Ramnagar	Madhya Pradesh	17	24.11N	81.12E
Rampur	Odisha	17	21.05N	84.22E
Rampur	Uttar Pradesh	24	28.48N	79.05E
Ramree, I.	Myanmar	73	18.51N	93.28E
Ramtek	Maharashtra	20	21.24N	79.20E
Ranaghat	W. Bengal	18	23.11N	88.37E
Ranchi	Jharkhand	24	23.23N	85.23E
Rangamati	Bangladesh	18	23.38N	92.15E
Rangpur	Bangladesh	18	25.42N	89.18E
Rania	Haryana	14	29.28N	74.54E
Ranibennur	Karnataka	20	14.33N	74.41E
Raniganj	W. Bengal	18	25.52N	87.52E
Ranikhet	Uttarakhand	24	29.40N	79.33E
Rann of Kachchh	Gujarat	10	24.05N	70.38E
Ranpur	Odisha	17	20.04N	85.23E
Rapur	Andhra Pradesh	20	14.12N	79.36E
Raqqa	Syria	74	36.00N	38.55E
Ratangarh	Rajasthan	23	28.05N	74.39E
Ratanpur	Chhattisgarh	17	22.17N	82.11E
Ratlam	Madhya Pradesh	26	23.31N	75.07E
Ratnagiri	Maharashtra	27	17.08N	73.19E
Ratnapura	Sri Lanka	69	6.42N	80.24E
Raurkela	Odisha	26	22.25N	85.00E
Ravenna	Italy	80	44.24N	12.11E
Ravi, R.	Pakistan	14	31.00N	72.30E
Rawalpindi	Pakistan	75	33.37N	73.06E
Rawatsar	Rajasthan	19	29.16N	74.26E
Rayachoti	Andhra Pradesh	20	14.04N	78.50E
Rayadrug	Andhra Pradesh	19	14.42N	76.53E
Rayagada	Odisha	26	19.09N	83.27E
Razam	Andhra Pradesh	20	18.28N	83.48E
Razmak	Pakistan	14	32.40N	69.56E
Reading	England	79	51.28N	1.00W
Reasi	Jammu & Kashmir	22	33.05N	74.50E
Recife (Pernambuco)	Brazil	93	8.09S	34.47W
Reckong Peo	Himachal Pradesh	22	31.30N	78.15E
Red Sea	Africa, etc.	82	20.00N	39.00E
Red, R.	USA	89	34.00N	96.00W
Regensburg	Germany	80	49.01N	12.07E
Regina	Canada	89	50.28N	104.36W
Rehli	Madhya Pradesh	16	23.38N	79.05E
Reims	France	80	49.15N	4.02E
Rekapalle	Andhra Pradesh	20	17.34N	81.20E
Rekong Peo	Himachal Pradesh	22	31.32N	78.16E
Rennes	France	80	48.07N	1.40W
Reno	Nevada, USA	89	39.30N	119.50W
Repalle	Andhra Pradesh	20	16.02N	80.53E
Reunion	Indian Ocean	98	21.00S	56.00E
Revilla Gigedo, Is	Mexico	86	19.25N	110.30W
Rewa	Madhya Pradesh	26	24.31N	81.19E
Rewari	Haryana	22	28.12N	76.40E
Reykjavik	Iceland	77	64.00N	21.30W
Rhine, R.	W. Europe	76	51.50N	7.00E
Rhodes, I.	Aegean Sea	76	36.30N	28.20E
Rhodope, Mts	Bulgaria	76	41.30N	24.30E
Rhone, R.	France	80	43.35N	4.39E
Ribeirao Preto	Brazil	93	21.09S	47.48W
Riberalta	Brazil	93	21.09S	47.48W
Richmond	Virginia, USA	89	37.34N	77.24W
Riga	Latvia	77	56.57N	24.09E
Rio Branco	Brazil	93	9.59S	67.49W
Rio de Janeiro	Brazil	93	22.53S	43.17W
Rio Grande	Argentina	91	53.45S	67.46W
Rio Grande do Sul	Brazil	93	32.03S	52.10W
Rio Verde	Mexico	86	21.58N	100.00W
Riyadh	Saudi Arabia	67	24.39N	46.41E
Road Town	Virgin Is	86	18.26N	64.38W
Roanne	France	80	46.02N	4.04E
Robertsganj	Uttar Pradesh	24	24.42N	83.04E
Robertsonpet	Karnataka	21	12.58N	78.16E
Rochester	New York, USA	89	43.09N	77.36W
Rockhampton	Queensland, Aust.	95	23.45S	150.30E
Rocky, Mts	N. America	86	45.00N	110.00W
Rohilkhand Plain	Uttar Pradesh	16	28.30N	79.00E
Rohtak	Haryana	22	28.54N	76.38E
Roing	Arunachal Pradesh	25	28.08N	95.51E
ROMANIA	E. Europe	77	46.00N	25.00E
Rome	Italy	67	41.55N	12.28E
Rondonopolis	Brazil	93	16.29S	54.38W
Roorkee	Uttarakhand	14	29.52N	77.53E
Roosevelt, I.	Antarctica	99	79.30S	162.00W
Rosario	Argentina	91	32.55S	60.42W
Rosario	Brazil	93	2.58S	44.16W
Roscommon	Rep. of Ireland	79	53.38N	8.10W
Roseau	Dominica	87	15.20N	61.24W
Ross Sea	Antarctica	99	74.00S	178.00E
Rostock	Germany	80	54.05N	12.08E
Rotterdam	Netherlands	80	51.56N	4.30E
Rouen	France	80	49.30N	1.00E
Rudolf, L.	Kenya	82	4.00N	35.40E
Rudraprayag	Uttarakhand	24	30.18N	79.03E
Rudrapur	Uttarakhand	24	29.02N	79.28E
Ruhea	Bangladesh	18	26.10N	88.25E
Rupnagar	Punjab	22	30.58N	76.32E
Russel	New Zealand	95	35.17S	174.10E
RUSSIAN				

Names	Country/Region	P. No.	Lat.	Long.
FEDERATION	Asia	81	62.00N	105.00E
Ruwenzori, Mt	Uganda	82	0.42N	30.25E
RWANDA	Cent. Africa	83	2.00S	30.00E
Ryukyu, Arch.	Japan	72	26.00N	128.00E
S				
Sabah (N. Borneo)	E. Malaysia	72	6.00N	117.00E
Sable, C.	USA	89	25.07N	81.07W
Sacramento	California, USA	89	38.30N	121.30W
Sadaseopet	Andhra Pradesh	20	17.40N	77.58E
Sagar	Karnataka	26	16.37N	76.51E
Sagar	Madhrya Pradesh	26	23.50N	78.50E
Sagar, I.	W. Bengal	18	21.40N	88.10E
Sagauli	Bihar	17	26.47N	84.48E
Sahara Desert	Africa	82	20.00N	5.00E
Saharanpur	Uttar Pradesh	24	29.58N	77.23E
Saharsa	Bihar	24	25.55N	86.35E
Sahibganj	Jharkhand	24	25.13N	87.40E
Sahibzada Ajit Singh Nagar	Punjab	22	30.41N	76.43E
Sahiwal	Pakistan	14	31.58N	72.22E
Sahpur	Pakistan	14	32.16N	72.31E
Sahyadriparvat, Ra.	Maharashtra	20	20.30N	76.00E
Saidpur	Uttar Pradesh	17	25.32N	83.16E
Saidpur	Bangladesh	18	25.48N	89.00E
Saiha	Mizoram	25	22.27N	92.58E
Saipan	Northern Marianas	93	15.12N	145.45E
Sakhalin	Russia	81	50.00N	143.00E
Sakoli	Maharashtra	20	21.05N	80.01E
Sakti	Chhattisgarh	17	22.01N	83.00E
Salem	Tamil Nadu	28	11.39N	78.12E
Salem	Oregon, USA	89	44.57N	123.03W
Salima	Malawi	83	13.45S	34.23E
Salisbury	England	79	51.04N	1.48W
Salt Lake City	Utah, USA	89	40.34N	111.55W
Salta	Argentina	91	24.45S	65.25W
Salur	Andhra Pradesh	20	18.31N	83.15E
Salvador (Bahia)	Brazil	93	13.00S	38.24W
Salvador	Central America	87	13.00N	88.00W
Salween, R.	Myanmar	73	18.00N	97.30E
Salzburg	Austria	80	47.47N	13.02E
Samalkot	Andhra Pradesh	20	17.03N	82.13E
Samar, I.	Philippines	72	12.00N	125.00E
Samara (Kuypyshev)	Russia	77	53.10N	50.10E
Samarkand	Uzbekistan	74	39.40N	67.05E
Samastipur	Bihar	24	25.55N	85.50E
Samba	Jammu & Kashmir	22	32.33N	75.07E
Sambalpur	Odisha	26	21.28N	84.01E
Sambhal	Uttar Pradesh	16	28.35N	78.37E
Sambhar Salt, L.	Rajasthan	19	26.54N	75.13E
SAMOA	Oceania	95	14.00S	172.00W
Samsun	Turkey	74	41.15N	36.20E
Samthar	Uttar Pradesh	16	25.51N	78.49E
San Antonio	Texas,USA	89	29.22N	98.30W
San Blas	Mexico	87	21.32N	105.17W
San Diego	California,USA	89	32.41N	117.08W
San Francisco	California,USA	89	38.48N	122.25W
San Jose	Costa Rica	87	9.58N	84.02W
San Juan	Puerto Rico	87	18.29N	66.08W
San Luis Potosi	Mexico	87	22.10N	100.56W
SAN MARINO	Europe	77	43.58N	12.30E
San Miguel de Tucuman	Argentina	91	26.50S	65.10W
San Pedro	Argentina	91	24.12S	64.55W
San Salvador	El Salvador	87	13.40N	89.10W
San Sebastian	Spain	80	43.21N	1.59W
San'a	Yemen	67	15.22N	44.12E
Sanandaj	Iran	74	35.16N	46.58E
Sanchor	Rajasthan	23	24.36N	71.54E
Sandoway	Myanmar	73	18.28N	94.27E
Sangamner	Maharashtra	27	19.35N	74.16E
Sanganer	Rajasthan	23	26.49N	75.49E
Sangareddi	Andhra Pradesh	27	17.38N	78.05E
Sangareddi	Andhra Pradesh	27	17.35N	78.02E
Sangareddi	Andhra Pradesh	27	17.35N	78.03E
Sangli	Maharashtra	27	16.52N	74.36E
Sangrur	Punjab	14	30.23N	75.83E
Santa Ana	Mexico	89	30.33N	111.07W
Santa Cruz	USA	89	36.58N	122.03W
Santa Fe	New Mexico, USA	89	35.40N	105.55W
Santa Fe	Argentina	91	31.35S	60.41W
Santa Maria	USA	89	34.56N	120.25W
Santa Maria	Brazil	93	29.45S	53.40W
Santander	Spain	77	43.30N	3.50W
Santarem	Portugal	77	39.14N	8.40W
Santiago	Chile	91	33.24S	70.45W
Santo Andre	Brazil	93	23.39S	46.29W
Santo Domingo	Dominican Rep.	91	18.30N	69.59W
Santos	Brazil	93	23.56S	46.22W
Sao Borja	Brazil	93	28.35S	56.01W
Sao Jose	Brazil	93	27.35S	48.40W
Sao Luis	Brazil	93	2.34S	44.16W
Sao Paulo	Brazil	93	23.33S	46.39W
São Tomé	São Tomé and Príncipe	83	0.20N	6.41E
SÃO TOMÉ AND PRÍNCIPE	Gulf of Guinea/Africa	83	0.20N	6.44E
Sao Vicente	Brazil	93	23.57S	46.23W
Sapaul	Bihar	24	26.06N	86.35E
Saraikela	Jharkhand	24	22.42N	85.57E
Sarajevo	Bosnia-Herzegovina	77	43.50N	18.26E
Saran	Bihar	24	25.47N	84.43E
Sarangarh	Chhattisgarh	17	21.36N	83.07E
Sarawak, State	E. Malaysia	72	2.35N	113.30E
Sardarshahr	Rajasthan	19	28.27N	74.32E

Names	Country/Region	P. No.	Lat.	Long.
Sardinia, I.	Italy	76	40.00N	9.00E
Sargodha	Pakistan	75	32.01N	72.41E
Sari	Iran	74	36.33N	53.06E
Sarila	Uttar Pradesh	17	25.46N	79.43E
Sasabo	Japan	71	33.09N	129.44E
Sasaram	Bihar	24	24.57N	84.03E
Saskatchewan, R.	Canada	86	53.25N	104.00W
Saskatoon	Canada	87	52.09N	106.40W
Satara	Maharashtra	27	17.42N	74.02E
Satluj, R.	Punjab	14	31.00N	75.00E
Satna	Madhya Pradesh	26	24.34N	80.55E
Satpura, Ra.	Central India	10	21.59N	74.52E
Satpura, Ra.	Madhya Pradesh	16	21.40N	75.00E
Sattenapalle	Andhra Pradesh	20	16.24N	80.11E
Sattur	Tamil Nadu	21	9.21N	77.58E
Satyamangalam	Tamil Nadu	21	11.30N	77.17E
SAUDI ARABIA	W. Asia	67	25.00N	40.00E
Savannah	Georgia, USA	89	32.06N	81.05W
Savantvadi	Maharashtra	20	15.54N	73.52E
Savanur	Karnataka	20	14.58N	75.19E
Sawai Madhopur	Rajasthan	23	25.58N	76.30E
Saynshand	Mongolia	70	44.50N	110.20E
Scarborough	England	79	54.17N	0.24W
Scilly, Is	England	79	50.00N	6.00W
Scotland	Great Britain	79	56.00N	4.00W
Scutari (Uskudar)	Turkey	74	49.01N	29.02E
Seattle	Washington, USA	89	47.36N	122.21W
Secunderabad	Andhra Pradesh	27	17.27N	78.33E
Sehore	Madhya Pradesh	26	23.12N	77.00E
Seine, R.	France	80	49.30N	1.00E
Semipalatinsk	Kazakhstan	81	50.28N	80.13E
Senapati	Manipur	25	25.15N	94.07E
SENEGAL	West Africa	83	14.00N	15.00W
Senegal, R.	West Africa	82	16.10N	16.25W
Sengottai	Tamil Nadu	21	8.59N	77.18E
Senhor do Bonfim	Brazil	93	10.28S	40.11W
Seoni	Madhya Pradesh	26	22.06N	79.35E
Seoul	South Korea	67	37.31N	127.06E
Seppa	Arunachal Pradesh	'25	27.20N	92.56E
Serampore	W. Bengal	18	22.45N	88.23E
SERBIA	Europe	77	43.30N	20.00E
Serchhip	Mizoram	25	23.18N	92.53E
Serenje	Zambia	85	13.12S	30.15E
Serowe	Botswana	85	22.24S	26.42E
Serra	Brazil	93	20.06S	40.16W
Seshachalam Hills	Andhra Pradesh	20	14.10N	78.30E
Sevastopol	Ukraine	77	44.37N	33.35E
Severn, R.	England-Wales	79	51.40N	2.40W
Seville (Sevilla)	Spain	77	37.25N	5.58W
SEYCHELLES	Indian Ocean/Africa	83	4.00S	55.00E
Shahabad	Uttar Pradesh	17	27.30N	80.05E
Shahabad	Rajasthan	19	25.10N	77.20E
Shahabad	Andhra Pradesh	20	17.10N	78.11E
Shahdol	Madhya Pradesh	26	23.00N	81.30E
Shahjahanpur	Uttar Pradesh	24	27.54N	79.57E
Shahpura	Madhya Pradesh	17	23.10N	80.45E
Shajapur	Madhya Pradesh	26	23.26N	76.18E
Shanghai	China	70	31.15N	121.29E
Shannon, R.	Rep. of Ireland	79	53.50N	8.00W
Sharjah	UAE	74	25.20N	55.24E
Sheffield	England	79	53.22N	1.30W
Shegaon	Maharastra	20	20.48N	76.46E
Shekhpura	Bihar	24	25.07N	85.53E
Shenyang (Mukden)	China	70	41.48N	123.25E
Sheohar	Bihar	24	26.31N	85.18E
Sheopur	Madya Pradesh	26	25.39N	76.41E
Shetland, Is.	Scotland	79	60.30N	1.00W
Shevaroy Hills	Tamil Nadu	21	12.00N	78.30E
Shijiazhuang	China	70	38.00N	114.30E
Shikoku, I.	Japan	71	33.40N	133.30E
Shiliguri	W. Bengal	25	26.42N	88.25E
Shilka	Russia	81	52.00N	115.52E
Shillong	Meghalaya	25	25.34N	91.56E
Shimla	Himachal Pradesh	13	31.06N	77.13E
Shimoga	Karnataka	28	14.00N	75.17E
Shimonoseki	Japan	71	33.40N	131.00E
Shindand	Afghanistan	75	33.18N	62.15E
Shinghar	Pakistan	14	31.45N	69.49E
Shiraz	Iran	74	29.38N	52.31E
Shivamogga	Iran	74	13.56N	75.38E
Shivpuri	Madhya Pradesh	26	25.40N	77.44E
Shiwalik, Ra.	India	10	30.00N	77.30E
Shkoder (Scutari)	Albania	80	42.03N	19.31E
Shravasti	Uttar Pradesh	24	27.24N	82.07E
Shrewsbury	England	79	52.44N	2.45W
Shrigonda	Maharashtra	20	18.41N	74.44E
Shrirangapattana	Karnataka	28	12.26N	76.43E
Shupiyan	Jammu & Kashmir	22	33.43N	74.50E
Sialkot	Pakistan	75	32.31N	74.36E
Sibi	Pakistan	14	29.30N	67.55E
Sicily, I.	Italy	76	37.35N	14.10E
Sidhauli	Uttar Pradesh	17	27.18N	80.50E
Sidhi	Madhya Pradesh	26	24.25N	81.54E
Sidhout	Andhra Pradesh	20	14.28N	79.01E
Sidi-Bel-Abbes	Algeria	83	35.13N	0.01W
Sidipett	Andhra Pradesh	20	18.07N	78.50E
Sidra, Gulf of	Libya	83	31.30N	18.30E
SIERRA LEONE	W. Africa	83	9.00N	12.00W
Sihora	Madhya Pradesh	17	23.29N	80.09E
Sikandra	Uttar Pradesh	16	27.13N	77.58E
Sikar	Rajasthan	23	27.36N	75.15E
Sikkim, State	India	13	27.30N	88.30E
Sil Garhi	Nepal	15	29.12N	81.06E
Silchar (Cachar)	Assam	25	24.47N	92.48E
Silvassa	Dadra & Nagar Haveli	12	20.13N	73.03E
Simdega	Jharkhand	24	22.35N	84.32E
Sindgi	Karnataka	20	16.58N	76.13E
Sindhnur	Karnataka	20	15.45N	76.43E
Sindkheda	Maharashtra	20	21.18N	74.50E
SINGAPORE	S. E. Asia	67	1.17N	103.51E
Singareni Collieries	Andhra Pradesh	20	17.27N	80.20E
Singrauli	Madhya Pradesh	17	24.78N	82.83E
Sinop	Turkey	74	42.01N	35.11E
Sinuiju N.	Korea	71	39.59N	124.30E
Sioux City	Iowa, USA	89	42.32N	96.25W
Sioux Falls	S. Dakota, USA	89	43.35N	96.40W
Sirajganj	Bangladesh	18	24.27N	89.47E
Sirohi	Rajasthan	23	24.53N	72.54E
Sironcha	Maharastra	20	18.51N	80.01E
Sironj	Madhya Pradesh	16	24.06N	77.44E
Sirpur	Andhra Pradesh	20	19.32N	79.45E
Sirsa	Haryana	22	29.32N	75.07E
Sirsi	Karnataka	20	14.36N	74.54E
Sirur	Maharastra	20	18.50N	74.23E
Sitamarhi	Bihar	24	26.35N	85.32E
Sitapur	Uttar Pradesh	24	27.32N	80.43E
Sitka	Alaska, USA	89	57.04N	135.10W
Sitpur	Pakistan	14	29.11N	70.51E
Siuri	West Bengal	25	23.54N	87.34E
Sivaganga	Tamil Nadu	28	9.51N	79.32E
Sivas	Turkey	74	39.43N	36.58E
Sivasagar	Assam	25	26.59N	94.41E
Sivasamudram, I.	Karnataka	21	12.16N	77.13E
Siwan	Bihar	24	26.12N	84.13E
Siwana	Rajasthan	23	25.36N	72.27E
Skagway	Alaska, USA	89	59.30N	135.20W
Skegness	England	79	53.09N	0.21E
Skopje	Macedonia	77	41.59N	21.27E
Skye, I. of	Scotland	79	57.20N	6.20W
Slave, Great L.	Canada	86	62.00N	114.00W
Sligo	Rep. of Ireland	79	54.16N	8.30W
SLOVAKIA	Europe	77	49.00N	20.00E
SLOVENIA	S. Europe	77	46.00N	15.00E
Slvudyanka	Russia	81	51.40N	103.30E
Smolensk	Russia	77	54.45N	32.01E
Smyrna (Izmir)	Turkey	74	38.24N	27.06E
Snowdon, Mt	Wales	79	53.04N	4.10W
Sobral	Brazil	93	3.45S	40.20W
Sobraon	Punjab	14	31.07N	74.54E
Socotra, I.	Indian Ocean	98	12.30N	50.00E
Sofala	Mozambique	85	20.00S	34.00E
Sofia	Bulgaria	77	42.40 N	23.20E
Sogamoso	Colombia	93	5.43N	72.56W
Sohagpur	Madhya Pradesh	16	22.42N	78.17E
Sohan, R.	Pakistan	14	33.10N	72.05E
Sohawal	Madhya Pradesh	17	24.35N	80.50E
Sohela	Odisha	17	21.18N	83.26E
Sokoto	Nigeria	83	13.02N	5.16E
Solan	Himachal Pradesh	22	30.55N	77.09E
Solapur	Maharastra	27	17.40N	75.56E
SOLOMON IS.	Pacific Ocean	97	8.00S	158.00E
Solway Firth	England-Scotland	79	54.52N	2.30W
SOMALIA	E. Africa	83	5.00N	45.00E
Somnath (Patan)	Gujarat	23	21.04N	70.26E
Son, R.	India	17	25.11N	84.51E
Sonakhan	Chhattisgarh	17	21.36N	82.36E
Sonepur	Odisha	26	20.51N	83.59E
Sonhat	Chhattisgarh	17	23.29N	82.30E
Sonipat	Haryana	22	28.59N	77.04E
Sonpur	Bihar	24	25.42E	85.13E
Sopron	Hungary	80	47.41N	16.36E
Sopur	Jammu & Kashmir	14	34.19N	74.30E
Soron	Uttar Pradesh	16	27.52N	78.48E
Sosnowiec	Poland	80	50.07N	19.30E
SOUTH AFRICA	Africa	83	25.00S	25.00E
South America, Continent	**World**	**100**		
South Georgia, I.	Antarctica	99	54.15S	38.00W
SOUTH KOREA	Asia	67	36.00N	127.00E
South Orkney, Is.	Antarctica	99	60.30S	45.00W
South Shetland, Is.	Antarctica	99	63.00N	62.00W
South Snieids	England	79	55.00N	1.27W
SOUTH SUDAN	E. Africa	83	07.00N	30.00E
Southern Ocean	**World**	**101**		
Soutnampton	England	79	50.54N	1.24W
SPAIN	S.W. Europe	77	40.00N	5.00W
Spencer, Gulf	S. Australia	94	34.00S	137.00E
Spey, R.	Scotland	79	57.38N	3.07W
Spezia	Italy	80	44.06N	9.50E
Spokane	Washington, USA	89	47.39N	117.26W
Springbok	South Africa	85	29.44S	17.56E
Springfield	Louisiana, USA	89	39.58N	89.40W
Sri Jayawardenapura	Sri Lanka	67	6.54N	75.54E
SRI LANKA	S. Asia	67	8.00N	81.00E
Sriharikota, I.	Andhra Pradesh	21	13.45N	80.20E
Srikakulam	Andhra Pradesh	27	18.18N	83.54E
Srikakulam	Andhra Pradesh	27	18.17N	83.57E
Srikalahasti	Andhra Pradesh	27	13.45N	79.44E
Srinagar	Jammu & Kashmir	22	34.06N	74.51E
Srirangam	Tamil Nadu	28	10.52N	78.44E
Srivilliputtur	Tamil Nadu	28	9.31N	77.40E
Srungavarapukota	Andhra Pradesh	20	18.06N	83.11E
St Brieuc	France	80	48.31N	2.46W
St Charles, C.	Labrador, Canada	86	52.11N	55.38W
St Etienne	France	80	45.25N	4.25E
St Gallen	Switzerland	80	47.10N	2.15E
St George's Channel	Wales-Ireland	79	52.00N	6.00W
St George's	Grenada	87	12.05N	61.48W
St Helena	Atlantic Ocean	98	15.58S	5.42W
St John	Canada	87	45.14N	66.04W
St Johns	Newfoundland, Canada	87	47.33N	52.40W
St John's	Antigua & Barbuda	91	17.06N	61.51E
St Kilda, I.	Scotland	79	57.49N	8.34W
ST KITTS & NEVIS	West Indies	87	17.20N	62.40W
St Lawrence, Gulf of	Canada	86	48.30N	62.00W
St Lawrence, R.	Canada	86	47.00N	70.00W
St Louis	Senegal	83	16.01N	16.30W
ST LUCIA	West Indies	87	14.00N	60.50W
St Luis	Missouri, USA	89	38.39N	90.13W
St Malo	France	80	48.39N	2.01W
St Nazaire	France	80	47.17N	2.12W
St Paul	Minnesota, USA	89	44.59N	93.08W
St Petersburg (Leningrad)	Russia	77	59.57N	30.20E
ST VINCENT & GRENADINES	West Indies	87	13.00N	61.10W
St. Andrews	Scotland	79	56.21N	2.48W
Stanley Falls	Congo Dem. Rep.	82	0.00N	25.20E
Stavanger	Norway	77	58.58N	5.46E
Stavropol	Russia	77	45.02N	41.58E
Stettin (Szczecin)	Poland	80	53.25N	14.34E
Stewart I.	New Zealand	95	47.00S	168.00E
Stirling	Scotland	79	56.09N	3.54W
Stockholm	Sweden	77	59.20N	18.00E
Stoke-upon-Trent	England	79	53.00N	2.10W
Stonehaven	Scotland	79	56.58N	2.15W
Stornoway	Scotland	79	58.14N	6.23W
Stralsund	Germany	80	54.18N	13.06E
Stranraer	Scotland	79	54.54N	5.00W
Strasbourg	France	80	48.35N	7.50E
Stromboli	Italy	80	38.47N	15.03E
Stuttgart	Germany	77	48.47N	9.11E
Suakin	Sudan	83	19.08N	37.17E
Subarnapur	Odisha	26	20.51N	83.54E
Subarnarekha, R.	Jharkhand	17	22.10N	87.00E
Subotica	Serbia	80	46.05N	19.40E
Sucre	Bolivia	91	19.02S	65.17W
SUDAN	E. Africa	83	11.00N	30.00E
Sudbury	Ontario, Canada	89	46.30N	80.56W
Suez	Egypt	83	30.00N	32.30E
Sui	Pakistan	75	28.38N	69.11E
Sujangarh	Rajasthan	19	27.42N	74.31E
Sujanpur	Punjab	14	31.50N	76.33E
Sukhumi	Georgia	74	43.00N	41.00E
Sukkur	Pakistan	75	27.42N	68.55E
Sula Is.	Indondesia	72	1.50S	125.00E
Sulaiman, Ra.	Pakistan	10	30.00N	70.00E
Sulaimaniya	Iraq	74	35.35N	45.20E
Sultanpur	Punjab	14	31.58N	77.07E
Sultanpur	Uttar Pradesh	24	26.16N	82.07E
Sulu Sea	Indonesia	72	8.00N	120.00E
Sumatra, I.	Indonesia	72	0.00N	100.00E
Sumba, I.	Indonesia	72	9.30S	119.40E
Sumbawa	Indonesia	72	8.26S	117.30E
Sunamganj	Bangladesh	18	25.04N	91.26E
Sunda, Is	Indonesia	67	9.00S	110.00E
Sundarbans	India-Bangladesh	11	22.00N	89.00E
Sundargarh	Odisha	26	22.06N	84.00E
Sunderland	England	79	54.56N	1.25W
Sunkam	Chhattisgarh	17	18.22N	81.46E
Supaul	Bihar	24	25.55N	86.25E
Superior, L.	Canada-USA	89	47.30N	88.00W
Surabaya	Java	72	7.18S	112.46E
Surada	Odisha	17	19.45N	84.29E
Surapur	Karnataka	20	16.31N	76.48E
Surat	Gujarat	23	21.10N	72.50E
Surat	Gujarat	23	21.12N	72.52E
Suratgarh	Rajasthan	23	29.19N	73.57E
Surendranagar	Gujarat	23	22.43N	71.43E
Surgana	Maharashtra	20	20.33N	73.20E
Suriapet	Andhra Pradesh	20	17.10N	79.19E
SURINAME	S. America	91	5.00N	55.00W
Suva	Fiji	97	18.07S	178.28E
Suzhou	China	70	31.18N	120.46E
Svalbard (Spitsbergan)	Norway	76	78.0N	17.00E
Sverdlovsk	Russia	81	56.50N	60.39E
Svobodny	Russia	81	51.20N	128.00E
Swabi	Pakistan	14	34.07N	72.33E
Swansea	Wales	79	51.38N	3.55W
SWAZILAND	S. E. Africa	83	26.23S	31.30E
SWEDEN	N. Europe	77	62.00N	15.00E
Swellendam	South Africa	85	34.02S	20.27E
SWITZERLAND	Europe	77	47.00N	8.00E
Sydney	Australia	95	33.52S	151.12E
Sylhet	Bangladesh	18	24.53N	91.55E
Syrdarya, R.	Central Asia	81	45.00N	63.00E
SYRIA	S.W. Asia	67	35.00N	37.00E
Szeged	Hungary	80	46.15N	20.11E
T				
Tabora	Tanzania	83	5.00S	32.50E
Tabriz	Iran	74	38.02N	46.20E
Tabuk	Saudi Arabia	74	28.30N	36.25E
Tacheng	China	70	46.50N	83.01E
Tacna	Peru	93	18.00S	70.15W
Tacoma	Washington DC, USA	89	47.15N	122.30W
Tadatri	Andhra Pradesh	20	14.56N	78.02E
Taganrog	Russia	77	47.12N	38.57E
Tagus, R.	Spain-Portugal	76	39.00N	7.00W
Taimir, Penn.	Russia	81	76.00N	103.00E
Tainan	Taiwan	70	23.00N	120.11E
Taipei	Taiwan	70	25.02N	121.30E
Taitung	Taiwan	70	22.43N	121.04E
TAIWAN	E. Asia	67	24.00N	121.00E
Taiyuan	China	70	37.52N	112.28E
TAJIKISTAN	Asia	67	35.30N	70.00E
Takht-i-Sulaiman, Mt	Pakistan	75	31.30N	70.02E
Takla Makan	China	70	39.40N	85.00E
Takoradi	Ghana	83	4.55N	1.45W
Talagang	Pakistan	14	32.56N	72.28E
Talaimannar	Sri Lanka	21	9.10N	79.40E
Talcher	Odisha	26	20.57N	85.16E
Talguppa	Karnataka	20	14.10N	74.52E
Tallahassee	Florida, USA	89	30.26N	84.18W
Tallinn	Estonia	77	59.24N	24.45E
Taloda	Maharashtra	20	21.34N	74.19E
Tamatave	Madagascar	85	18.00S	49.00E
Tamenglong	Manipur	25	24.53N	93.30E
Tamil Nadu, State	India	13	11.00N	78.00E
Tamluk	W. Bengal	25	22.18N	87.58E
Tampa	Florida, USA	89	27.59N	82.29W
Tampico	Mexico	89	22.16N	97.50W
Tamsag Bulag	Mongolia	70	47.15N	117.05E
Tana, L.	Ethiopia	82	12.00N	37.15E
Tanakpur	Uttarakhand	24	29.10N	80.18E
Tanda	Punjab	14	31.40N	75.41E
Tanda	Uttar Pradesh	17	26.33N	82.42E
Tandur	Andhra Pradesh	20	171.17N	77.30E
Tangail	Bangladesh	18	24.14N	89.56E
Tanganyika, L.	Cent. Africa	82	7.00S	30.00E
Tangier	Morocco	83	35.49N	5.52W
Tangshan	China	71	39.34N	118.13E
Tanimbar, Is.	Indonesia	72	8.00S	131.00E
Tank	Pakistan	14	32.14N	70.25E
Tantpur	Rajasthan	19	26.51N	77.32E
Tanuku	Andhra Pradesh	20	16.45N	81.44E
TANZANIA	E. Africa	83	4.00S	34.00E
Taolanaro	Madagascar	85	25.02S	46.58E
Tapajos, R.	S. America	90	4.30S	56.10W
Tapi, R.	Gujarat	19	21.20N	74.30E
Tarangambadi	Tamil Nadu	21	11.01N	79.54E
Tarapoto	Peru	93	6.31S	76.23W
Tarapur	Maharashtra	20	19.52N	72.42E
Tarawa	Kiribati	97	01.28N	173.02E
Tarija	Bolivia	91	21.33S	65.02W
Tarikere	Karnataka	20	13.42N	75.51E
Tarn Taran Sahib	Punjab	22	31.27N	74.55E
Tashkent	Uzbekistan	67	41.30N	69.20E
Tashkurghan	Afghanistan	75	36.44N	67.41E
Tasmania, I.	Australia	94	42.00S	146.30E
Taunton	England	79	51.02N	3.05W
Taupo, L.	New Zealand	95	38.45S	176.00E
Tavoy	Myanmar	73	14.07N	98.18E
Tawang	Arunachal Pradesh	25	27.35N	91.59E
Taxila	Pakistan	75	33.40N	72.50E
Tay, R. and firth	Scotland	79	56.27N	3.30W
Tayma	Saudi Arabia	74	27.39N	38.28E
Tbilisi	Georgia	67	41.42N	44.46E
Tefe	Brazil	93	3.24S	64.45W
Tegucigalpa	Honduras	87	14.05N	87.12W
Tehran	Iran	67	35.41N	51.25E
Tehri	Uttarakhand	24	30.20N	78.53E
Tehuantepec	Mexico	86	16.00N	95.00W
Tekari	Bihar	17	24.57N	84.53E
Tenali	Andhra Pradesh	20	16.15N	80.35E
Tenasserim	Myanmar	73	12.06N	99.03E
Teni	Tamil Nadu	28	9.55N	77.23E
Tenkasi	Tamil Nadu	28	8.58N	77.21E
Tennessee, R.	USA	86	35.10N	86.00W
Teofilo Otoni	Brazil	93	17.52S	41.31W
Teplice	Czech Republic	80	50.38N	13.49E
Terai Swamp	India-Nepal	11	29.00N	80.00E
Teresina	Brazil	93	5.09S	42.46W
Termez	Uzbekistan	74	37.14N	67.15E
Tete	Mozambique	85	16.10S	33.35E
Tetyukhe Pristan	Russia	81	44.45N	135.40E
Tezpur	Assam	25	26.36N	92.49E
Tezu	Arunachal Pradesh	25	27.55N	96.11E
Tha Kurgaon	Bangladesh	18	26.02N	88.34E
THAILAND	S. E. Asia	67	12.00N	102.00E
Thakurgaon	Bangladesh	18	26.02N	88.34E
Thal	Pakistan	14	33.24N	70.36E
Thalasseri	Kerala	28	11.45N	75.32E
Thames, R.	England	79	51.30N	0.30E
Thane	Maharashtra	27	19.12N	73.03E
Thanesar	Haryana	14	29.58N	76.56E
Thanjavur	Tamil Nadu	28	10.47N	79.10E
Thard	Gujarat	16	24.23N	71.37E
The Hague	The Netherlands	77	52.06N	4.20E
Theni	Tamil Nadu	28	10.04N	77.45E
Thessaloniki	Greece	77	40.38N	22.59E
Thimphu	Bhutan	67	27.32N	89.53E
Thiruvananthapuram	Kerala	13	8.29N	76.59E
Thiruvarur	Tamil Nadu	28	10.46N	79.37E
Thoothukkudi	Tamil Nadu	28	08.48N	78.08E
Thoubal	Manipur	25	24.38N	93.58E
Thrissur	Kerala	28	10.30N	76.15E
Thunder, B.	USA	89	45.00N	83.20E
Thursday, I.	Queensland, Aust.	94	10.40 S	142.20E
Thurso	Scotland	79	58.37N	3.33W
Thurston, I.	Antarctica	90	73.00 S	100.00W

Names	Country/Region	P. No.	Lat.	Long.
Tianjin	China	70	39.04N	117.15E
Tibesti, Mts	Niger-Chad, Africa	82	21.00N	15.00E
Tibet	China	70	30.00N	88.00E
Tieling	China	70	42.25N	123.51E
Tien Shan, Mts	China	70	43.00N	85.00E
Tierra del Fuego	S. America	91	54.00 S	69.00W
Tigiria	Odisha	17	20.28N	84.34E
Tigris, R.	Iraq	74	35.20N	43.31E
Tikamgarh	Madhya Pradesh	26	24.45N	78.53E
Tilaiya	Bihar	17	24.20N	85.31E
Tilpara	W. Bengal	18	23.58N	87.32E
Timbuktu	Mali	83	16.45N	2.55W
Timmins	Ontario, Canada	89	43.28N	81.19W
Timor Leste	Asia	67	8.50S	126.00E
Timor Sea	Indonesia	72	10.00S	125.00E
Tindivanam	Tamil Nadu	28	12.14N	79.42E
Tinsukia	Assam	25	27.27N	95.21E
Tipperary	Rep. of Ireland	79	52.28N	8.10W
Tirana	Albania	77	41.20N	19.49E
Tirchengodu	Tamil Nadu	21	11.23N	77.56E
Tiruchchendur	Tamil Nadu	28	8.30N	78.11E
Tiruchchirappalli	Tamil Nadu	28	10.50N	78.46E
Tirukkoyilur	Tamil Nadu	21	11.58N	79.15E
Tirumangalam	Tamil Nadu	21	9.49N	79.01E
Tirunelveli	Tamil Nadu	28	8.44N	77.44E
Tirupati	Andhra Pradesh	27	13.40N	79.20E
Tiruppur	Tamil Nadu	21	11.05N	77.20E
Tiruvallur	Tamil Nadu	28	13.08N	79.54E
Tiruvallur	Tamil Nadu	28	13.09N	79.57E
Tiruvannamalai	Tamil Nadu	28	12.15N	79.07E
Titalyah	Bangladesh	18	26.31N	88.20E
Titicaca, L.	Peru-Bolivia	93	15.30S	69.30W
Toamasina	Madagascar	85	18.10S	49.23E
Tocopilla	Chile	93	22.05S	70.10W
Toda Rai Singh	Rajasthan	19	26.00N	75.42E
Toggourt	Algeria	83	33.09N	6.02E
TOGO	W. Africa	83	8.00N	1.00E
Tokelau, Is.	Pacific Ocean	97	9.00S	171.45W
Tokyo	Japan	67	35.40N	138.45E
Toledo	Ohio, USA	89	41.37N	83.33W
Toliara	Madagascar	85	23.22S	43.39E
Tombua	Angola	85	15.49S	11.53E
Tomsk	Russia	81	56.30N	85.12E
Tondi	Tamil Nadu	21	9.45N	79.04E
TONGA	Pacific Ocean	97	20.00 S	172.00W
Tongking, Gulf of	Vietnam-China	72	20.00N	108.00E
Tonk	Rajasthan	19	26.31N	75.50E
Topeka	Kansas, USA	89	39.01N	95.42W
Torbay	England	79	50.26N	3.30W
Tori Fathpur	Madhya Pradesh	26	25.28N	79.08E
Toronto	Ontario, Canada	89	43.39N	79.20W
Toros Daglari (Taurus, Mts)	Turkey	74	37.00N	33.00E
Torres, Str.	Queensland, Aust.	94	10.30S	142.00E
Torun	Poland	80	53.01N	18.37E
Tottori	Japan	71	35.30N	134.15E
Toulon	France	80	43.08N	5.56E
Toulouse	France	80	43.36N	1.26E
Tours	France	80	47.24N	0.42E
Townsville	Queensland, Aust.	95	19.10S	146.58 E
Trabzon	Turkey	74	41.00N	39.44E
Tralee	Rep. of Ireland	79	52.16N	9.43W
Transvaal	S. Africa	83	25.00S	29.00E
Tres Lagoas	Brazil	93	20.46S	51.43W
Trier	Germany	80	49.46N	6.39E
Trieste	Italy	80	45.35N	13.45E
Trincomalee	Sri Lanka	21	8.33N	81.15E
TRINIDAD & TOBAGO	West Indies	87	10.20N	61.20W
Tripoli	Libya	83	33.45N	13.15E
Tripura, State	India	13	23.45N	91.30E
Tromso	Norway	77	69.50N	18.32E
Trondhem	Norway	77	63.26N	10.24E
Troyes	France	80	48.18N	4.04E
Tshane	Botswana	85	24.05S	21.54E
Tsumeb	Namibia	85	19.13S	17.42E
Tsushima, I.	Japan	71	34.20N	129.20E
Tsushima, Str.	Japan	71	34.00N	129.25E
Tuensang	Nagaland	25	26.15N	94.47E
Tula	Russia	77	54.21N	37.39E
Tulijapur	Maharashtra	20	18.02N	76.10E
Tulsa	Oklahoma, USA	89	36.10N	96.00W
Tumkur	Karnataka	28	13.20N	77.08E
Tumlong	Sikkim	16	27.28N	88.40E
Tumsar	Maharashtra	20	21.23N	79.45E
Tunduru	Tanzania	85	11.08S	27.21E
Tungabhadra, R.	Karnataka-Andhra Pradesh	20	15.58N	77.40E
Tuni	Andhra Pradesh	27	17.21N	82.35E
Tunis	Tunisia	83	36.49N	10.10E
TUNISIA	N. Africa	83	33.00N	10.00E
Tupiza	Bolivia	91	21.27S	65.45W
Tura	Meghalaya	25	25.30N	90.16E
Turaiyur	Tamil Nadu	21	11.09N	78.38E
Turin	Italy	80	45.04N	7.41E
TURKEY	W. Asia	67	40.00N	30.00E
TURKMENISTAN	Asia	67	37.00N	60.00E
Turks & Caicos	West Indies	87	21.20N	71.20W
Turku	Finland	77	60.26N	22.18E
Turpan	China	70	42.52N	89.12E
Tuscon	Arizona, USA	89	32.12N	111.00W
Tuticorin	Tamil Nadu	28	8.48N	78.11E
TUVALU	Pacific Ocean	97	8.00S	178.00E
Tver (Kalinin)	Russia	77	56.50N	36.00E
Tweed, R.	Scotland-England	79	55.45N	2.05W
U				
Ubangi, R.	Africa	83	5.05N	19.30E
Uberaba	Brazil	93	19.47S	47.57W
Uberlandia	Brazil	93	18.57S	48.17W
Uch	Pakistan	14	29.13N	71.09E
Udagamandalam	Tamil Nadu	28	11.24N	76.44E
Udaipur	Rajasthan	23	24.35N	73.47E
Udaipur	Tripura	25	23.31N	91.31E
Udalguri	Assam	25	26.44N	92.07E
Udamalpet	Tamil Nadu	21	10.36N	77.17E
Udayagiri	Andhra Pradesh	20	14.52N	79.19E
Udgir	Maharashtra	20	18.25N	77.10E
Udhampur	Jammu & Kashmir	22	32.55N	75.09E
Udine	Italy	80	46.03N	13.14E
Udiyarpalaiyam	Tamil Nadu	21	11.11N	79.20E
Udlegorsk	Russia	81	49.10N	142.05E
Udupi	Karnataka	28	13.20N	74.45E
Ufa	Russia	77	54.45N	56.00E
UGANDA	E. Africa	83	1.00N	32.30E
Uitenhage	South Africa	85	33.46S	25.25E
Ujiji	Tanzania	83	74.56S	29.40E
Ujjain	Madhya Pradesh	26	23.09N	75.43E
Ukhrul	Manipur	25	25.06N	94.24E
UKRAINE	Europe	77	49.00N	33.00E
Ulan Bator	Mongolia	70	47.59N	106.52E
Ulan Ude	Russia	81	52.03N	107.36E
Uliastay (Jibhalanta)	Mongolia	70	47.46N	96.48E
Umaria	Madhya Pradesh	26	23.30N	80.53E
Umea	Sweden	77	63.45N	20.20E
Umrer	Maharashtra	20	20.18N	79.21E
Umtata	South Africa	85	31.35S	28.47E
Umuarama	Brazil	93	23.35S	42.57W
Una	Himachal Pradesh	22	31.32N	76.18E
Unchahra (Nagod)	Madhya Pradesh	17	24.33N	80.37E
Ungvar (Uzhgorod)	Ukraine	77	48.40N	22.18E
UNITED ARAB EMIRATES	W. Asia	67	24.30N	54.00E
UK	Europe	77	51.30N	0.07W
USA	N. America	87	37.00N	96.00W
Unnao	Uttar Pradesh	24	26.48N	80.43E
Upernavik	Greenland	99	72.45N	56.00W
Upington	South Africa	85	28.28S	21.14E
Uppsala	Sweden	77	59.50N	17.45E
Ural, Mts	Russia	81	60.00N	60.00E
Ural, R.	Kazakhstan	81	49.00N	52.00E
Uralsk	Kazakhstan	81	51.12N	51.23E
Uranium City	Canada	87	59.32N	108.49W
Uruguaiana	Brazil	93	29.45S	57.05W
URUGUAY	South America	91	34.53S	56.10W
Uruguay, R.	South America	91	32.00 S	58.00W
Urumqi	China	70	43.49N	87.39E
Ushant (Quessant), I.	France	80	48.30N	5.00W
Uska	Turkey	74	41.03N	29.02E
Ussuriysk	Russia	81	43.40N	131.50E
Ust Kamenogorsk	Kazakhstan	81	50.00N	82.20E
Uthasnagar	Maharashtra	20	19.20N	73.10E
Utm	Germany	80	48.24N	10.00E
Utraula	Uttar Pradesh	17	27.19N	82.28E
Utrecht	Netherlands	80	52.06N	5.06E
Uttangarai	Tamil Nadu	21	12.16N	78.35E
Uttar Pradesh, State	India	13	27.40N	80.00E
Uttarakhand, State	India	13	30.00N	79.00E
Uttarkashi	Uttarakhand	24	30.45N	78.27E
Uvs Nuur	Mongolia	70	50.20N	92.30E
Uyuni	Bolivia	91	20.28S	66.47W
UZBEKISTAN	Asia	67	40.00N	65.00E
V				
Vaal, R.	S. Africa	82	29.40S	23.38E
Vadodara	Gujarat	23	22.18N	73.12E
Vadodara	Gujarat	23	22.00N	73.16E
Vaduz	Liechtenstien	80	47.14N	9.52E
Vaiaku	Tuvalu	97	08.31S	179.12E
Vaijapur	Maharashtra	20	19.59N	74.48E
Vaikam	Kerala	21	9.45N	76.27E
Vaishnodevi	Jammu & Kashmir	22	33.56N	75.00E
Valdai Hills	Russia	81	58.00N	34.00E
Valdivia	Chile	91	39.54S	73.14W
Valence	France	80	44.56N	4.54E
Valencia	Spain	77	39.29N	0.24W
Valladolid	Spain	77	41.39N	4.44W
Valletta	Malta	77	35.54N	14.31E
Valletta Melta	Spain	77	33.54N	14.31E
Valparaiso	Chile	91	33.02S	71.40W
Valsad	Gujarat	23	20.36N	72.59E
Van, L.	Turkey	74	38.30N	43.00E
Vancouver, I.	Canada	87	50.00N	126.00W
Vandavasi	Tamil Nadu	21	12.30N	79.30E
Vaniam, L.	Sweden	77	59.00N	15.00E
Vanivilasa Sagara	Karnataka	28	13.50N	76.25E
VANUATU	Pacific Ocean	97	15.00S	168.00E
Varanasi	Uttar Pradesh	24	25.20N	83.00E
Varazdin	Croatia	80	46.19N	16.20E
Varna	Bulgaria	77	43.13N	27.55E
Varuna, R.	Uttar Pradesh	17	25.25N	83.00E
Varzea Grande	Brazil	93	6.32S	42.05W
Vayalpad	Andhra Pradesh	21	13.48N	78.40E
Vellore	Tamil Nadu	21	12.55N	79.11E
Vemalwada	Andhra Pradesh	20	18.30N	78.56E
Vempalle	Andhra Pradesh	20	14.22N	78.30E
VENEZUELA	South America	91	5.00N	65.00W
Vengurla	Maharashtra	20	15.52N	73.40E
Venice	Italy	80	45.26N	12.20E
Veniyambadi	Tamil Nadu	21	12.41N	78.39E
Venkatagiri	Andhra Pradesh	20	13.57N	79.37E
Venkatapuram	Andhra Pradesh	20	18.17N	80.36E
Veracruz	Mexico	89	19.10N	96.10W
Veraval	Gujarat	23	20.54N	70.22E
Veraval	Gujarat	23	20.53N	70.26E
Verde, C.	Senegal	83	14.45N	17.32W
Vereeniging	South Africa	85	26.41S	27.56E
Verkhoyansk	Russia	81	67.50N	133.50E
Vermont	USA	89	43.40N	72.50W
Vesuvius, Mt	Italy	76	40.50N	14.25E
Vichy	France	83	46.07N	3.25E
Vicksburg	Mississippi, USA	89	32.17N	90.50W
Victoria	Seychelles	83	04.37S	55.27E
Victoria Falls	Zambia	82	17.59S	25.51E
Victoria Land	Antarctica	99	75.00S	160.00E
Victoria West	South Africa	85	31.24S	23.07E
Victoria	Vancouver I., Canada	87	48.25N	123.21W
Victoria, I.	Canada	87	71.00N	112.00W
Victoria, L.	Cent. Africa	82	1.00S	33.00E
Victoria, Mt	Myanmar	73	21.17N	93.53E
Victoria, State	Australia	95	38.00S	145.00E
Vidisha	Madhya Pradesh	26	23.32N	77.51E
Vienna	Austria	77	48.12N	16.22E
Vientiane	Laos	67	17.59N	102.38E
VIETNAM	Asia	67	19.00N	106.00E
Vigia	Brazil	93	0.50S	48.07W
Vigo	Spain	77	42.14N	8.40W
Vijayadurg	Maharashtra	20	16.26N	73.26E
Vijayawada	Andhra Pradesh	27	16.31N	80.39E
Vila Velha	Brazil	93	20.23S	40.18W
Vilhena	Brazil	93	12.40S	60.08W
Villa Cisneros	West Sahara	83	24.00N	16.00W
Villa	Vanuato	95	17.45S	168.18E
Villach	Austria	80	46.36N	13.50E
Vilnius	Lithuania	77	54.40N	25.30E
Viluppuram	Tamil Nadu	28	11.57N	79.32E
Vindhya, Ra.	Madhya Pradesh	26	22.30N	76.00E
Vinh	Vietnam	72	18.43N	105.41E
Vinson Massif	Antarctica	99	78.00S	85.00W
Vinukonda	Andhra Pradesh	26	16.04N	79.47E
Viramgam	Gujarat	23	23.08S	72.07E
Virgin Is. (UK)	West Indies	87	18.30N	64.30W
Virgin Is. (USA)	West Indies	87	18.20N	65.00W
Virudunagar	Tamil Nadu	28	9.35N	77.57E
Visavadar	Gujarat	23	21.22N	70.52E
Viseu Port	Portugal	93	40.40N	7.55W
Vishakhapatnam	Andhra Pradesh	27	17.42N	83.20E
Vistula, R.	Poland	80	54.00N	20.00E
Vitebsk	Belarus	77	55.11N	30.11E
Vitoria da Conquista	Brazil	93	14.53S	40.52W
Vitoria	Spain	80	42.53N	2.39W
Vitoria	Brazil	93	20.20S	40.18W
Vizianagaram	Andhra Pradesh	27	18.07N	83.25E
Vizianagram	Andhra Pradesh	27	18.07N	83.27E
Vladivostok	Russia	81	43.11N	131.53E
Volgograd (Stalingrad)	Russia	81	48.47N	44.25E
Vologda	Russia	77	59.14N	39.43E
Voronezh	Russia	81	51.40N	39.10E
Vosges, Mts	France	80	48.10N	6.40E
Vredenburg	South Africa	85	32.55S	17.59E
Vriddhachalam	Tamil Nadu	21	11.32N	79.24E
Vrindavan	Uttar Pradesh	16	27.33N	77.44E
Vyara	Gujarat	19	21.12N	73.04E
Vyatka, R.	Russia	77	58.35N	49.35E
Vypin, I.	Kerala	21	10.07N	76.17E
W				
Wadi Halfa	Sudan	83	21.53N	31.18E
Wadi	Karnataka	20	17.00N	76.57E
Wai	Maharashtra	20	17.57N	73.56E
Wakayama	Japan	71	34.15N	135.15E
Wakkanal	Japan	71	45.26N	141.35E
Wales	Great Britain	79	53.00N	3.00W
Wallis & futuna, Is	Pacific Ocean	97	13.18S	176.10W
Waltair	Andhra Pradesh	27	17.44N	83.23E
Walvis Bay	Namibia	85	22.59S	14.31E
Walvis, B.	S. W. Africa	82	22.30S	14.00E
Wana	Pakistan	14	32.15N	69.36E
Wankaner	Gujarat	23	22.33N	71.00E
Warangal	Andhra Pradesh	27	18.00N	79.35E
Warangal	Andhra Pradesh	27	17.58N	79.40E
Wardha	Maharashtra	27	20.45N	78.39E
Warora	Maharashtra	20	20.14N	79.02E
Warsaw	Poland	80	52.13N	21.02E
Wash	The England	79	53.00N	0.200E
Washim	Maharashtra	20	20.05N	77.10E
Washington DC	USA	89	38.55N	77.04W
Waterford	Rep. of Ireland	79	52.15N	7.07W
Wazirabad	Pakistan	14	32.15N	74.10E
Wedell Sea	Antarctica	99	72.30N	40.00W
Weifang	China	70	36.52N	119.07E
Wellington	New Zealand	95	41.16S	174.47E
Wenzhou	China	70	28.00N	120.38E
West Bengal, State	India	13	23.00N	87.00E
West Indies	Central America	87	20.00N	75.00W
Western Sahara	W. Africa	83	25.00N	12.00W
Westport	Rep. of Ireland	79	53.48N	9.33W
Wexford	Rep. of Ireland	79	52.20N	6.28W
Weymouth	England	79	50.36N	2.25W
Whitehourse	Yukon, Canada	87	60.42N	134.55W
Whitney, Mt	USA	89	36.36N	118.24W
Wichita Falls	Texas, USA	89	33.51N	98.25W
Wichita	Kansas, USA	89	37.40N	97.20W
Wick	Scotland	79	58.28N	3.07W
Wicklow, Mts of	Rep. of Ireland	79	52.58N	6.05W
Wiener Neustadt	Austria	80	47.49N	16.16E
Wight, Isle of	England	79	50.40N	1.30W
Wikes Land	Antarctica	99	69.00S	120.00E
Williamnagar	Meghalaya	25	25.30N	90.38E
Wilmington	N. Carolina, USA	89	34.18N	77.59W
Windhoek	Namibia	85	22.34S	17.06E
Windhoek	Namibia	85	22.34S	17.06E
Windsor	Ontario, Canada	89	42.25N	83.00W
Winnipeg, L.	Canada	86	52.00N	97.00W
Wittenberg	Germany	80	51.52N	12.38E
Wokha	Nagaland	25	26.01N	94.13E
Wolverhampton	England	79	52.36N	2.05W
Wonsan	North Korea	71	39.11N	127.34E
Woods, L. of the	Ontario, Canada	89	49.00N	94.00W
Worcester	England	79	52.12N	2.10W
Worcester	USA	89	42.16N	71.48W
Wrangel, I.	Russia	81	71.00N	179.00E
Wrath, C.	Scotland	79	58.38N	5.00W
Wuhan	China	70	30.35N	114.20E
Wuhu	China	70	31.20N	118.30E
Wular, L.	Jammu & Kashmir	14	34.20N	74.27E
Wuxi	China	70	31.31N	120.18E
Wuzburg	Germany	80	49.48N	9.56E
X				
Xian	China	70	34.12N	108.59E
Xining	China	70	36.35N	101.40E
Xique-Xique	Brazil	93	10.46S	42.38W
Xun Jiang. R.	China	70	23.27N	111.25E
Y				
Yabolonovyy, R.	Russia	81	58.00N	114.00E
Yadgir	Karnataka	28	16.46N	77.08E
Yakutsk	Russia	81	62.05N	129.40E
Yamethin	Myanmar	73	20.27N	96.09E
Yamoussoukro	Cote d' Ivoire	83	6.48N	5.15W
Yamuna, R.	Uttar Pradesh	17	25.30N	81.10E
Yamunanagar	Haryana	22	30.07N	77.17E
Yanam	Puducherry	28	16.45N	82.16E
Yangon	Myanmar	67	16.45N	96.13E
Yangtze, R.	China	70	31.00N	117.44E
Yantai (Che-foo)	China	70	37.31N	121.22E
Yaounde	Cameroon	83	3.51N	11.39E
Yaren	Nauru	97	0.32S	166.55E
Yarmouth, Great	England	79	52.36N	1.40E
Yavatmal	Maharashtra	20	20.23N	78.11E
Yelandur	Karnataka	21	12.05N	77.00E
Yellandu	Andhra Pradesh	27	17.37N	80.22E
Yellow Sea	China	70	35.00N	123.00E
Yellowknife	Canada	86	63.30N	114.29W
Yellowstone, R.	USA	89	45.48N	110.00W
YEMEN	S.W. Asia	67	16.00N	48.00E
Yemmiganur	Andhra Pradesh	20	15.46N	77.31E
Yenisei, R.	Russia	66	72.00N	87.00E
Yeola	Maharashtra	20	20.04N	74.31E
Yercaud	Tamil Nadu	21	11.48N	78.13E
Yerevan	Armenia	81	40.16N	44.35E
Yernagudem	Andhra Pradesh	20	16.59N	81.33E
Yingkiong	Arunachal Pradesh	25	28.30N	94.46E
Yokohama	Japan	71	35.29N	139.28E
Yol	Himachal Pradesh	14	32.11N	76.23E
York	England	79	53.57N	1.05W
Yukon Terr.	Canada	87	63.00N	135.00W
Yukon, R.	Alaska, USA	89	65.00N	155.00W
Yupia	Arunachal Pradesh	25	27.09N	93.43E
Yurimaguas	Peru	93	5.54S	76.07W
Yushu	China	70	32.59N	96.59E
Z				
Zacatecas	Mexico	89	22.49N	102.34W
Zafarwal	Pakistan	14	32.22N	64.54E
Zagreb	Croatia	80	45.50N	16.00E
Zahedan	Iran	74	29.34N	60.58E
Zambezi	Zambia	85	16.00S	23.03E
Zambezi, R.	S. Africa	82	18.00S	35.00E
ZAMBIA	Cen. Africa	83	17.30S	24.00E
Zangla	Jammu & Kashmir	14	33.37N	77.00E
Zanzibar, I.	Tanzania	83	5.00S	38.30E
Zaragoza	Spain	77	41.35N	0.53W
Zaskar	Jammu & Kashmir	14	33.00N	77.00E
Zaskar, Mts	Jammu and Kashmir	11	33.30N	76.50E
Zavitinsk	Russia	81	50.10N	129.20E
Zhangjiakou	China	70	40.49N	114.51E
Zhengzhou	China	70	34.47N	113.46E
Zhob, R.	Pakistan	75	31.00N	68.50E
Zibo	China	70	36.47N	118.06E
ZIMBABWE	S. E. Africa	83	19.00N	30.00E
Ziro	Arunachal Pradesh	25	27.37N	93.54E
Zomba	Malawi	83	15.22S	35.22E
Zunheboto	Nagaland	25	25.52N	94.29E
Zurich	Switzerland	80	47.26N	8.22E
Zvishavane	Zimbabwe	85	20.20S	30.02E
Zwickau	Germany	80	50.43N	12.29E